ANATOMY
OF A
START-UP

WHY SOME NEW BUSINESSES SUCCEED AND OTHERS FAIL

27 REAL-LIFE CASE STUDIES

Introduction by Randy and Debbi Fields, Mrs. Fields Cookies

Foreword by George Gendron, Editor-in-Chief, *Inc.* Magazine

Edited by Elizabeth K. Longsworth

For the start-ups
High Meadow Business Solutions
and
Cutting Edge, Inc.

May they flourish.

ANATOMY OF A START-UP
Why Some New Businesses Succeed and Others Fail: 27 Real-Life Case Studies

Design: Susan Yousem/ARTWORKS
Typography: Sue Dahl Design

Portions of this book were originally published in *Inc.* magazine. For information about purchasing back issues, please call 617-248-8426.

This publication is intended to provide authoritative information with regard to the subject matter covered. It is sold with the understanding that the publisher is not responsible for the success or failure of the businesses profiled herein or of any other business. The opinions recorded in this book are the sole responsibility of the individuals who rendered them.

Library of Congress Catalog Number: 91-72605

ISBN 0-9626146-8-8 (hardcover)
ISBN 0-9626146-6-1 (paperback)

First edition.

Acknowledgments

Special thanks go to the individuals whose stories are told in the following company profiles—their willingness to risk occasionally embarrassing exposure enables us to learn from their experiences—and to the business experts whose analyses are so generously shared.

As the project editor of this book, I am indebted to many people for researching, writing, editing, fact checking, designing, and typesetting these pages. It was a pleasure and a privilege working with this talented group and their outstanding material. Much of the research, a significant portion of the writing, and a substantial amount of the tender loving care that went into the Anatomy of a Start-Up series was administered by Leslie Brokaw, staff writer for *Inc.* I am grateful to her and to Michael S. Hopkins, executive editor of *Inc.*, editor of the series, and the source of the idea for this book, for their unstinting help and advice.

Sincere thanks go to George Gendron, *Inc.*'s editor-in-chief, for his role in shaping this book with his insightful ideas and comments, and for his eloquent foreword, and to Randy and Debbi Fields for their illuminating introduction. Director of Subsidiary Publishing Jan Spiro, designer Susan Yousem, typographer Sue Dahl, product manager Mary Ellen Mullaney, copy editors Jeanne M. Zimmermann and Ingrid Schorr, and indexer Ed Coleman deserve special mention for their dedicated hard work. Jeffrey L. Seglin, Sara P. Noble, Robert LaPointe, Kathy Apruzzese, Laura McFadden, Zelma Cordero, Elyse M. Friedman, Michael P. Cronin, Sara Baer-Sinnott, Ken Silvia, Christopher Caggiano, Deborah Herzog, and Vera Gibbons provided invaluable help; I am grateful to them and to the many photographers who granted permission to reprint their work.

To the editorial staff of *Inc.* magazine, a special thanks for their continuing pursuit of excellence. In the following pages they have shown us, in a most articulate and evocative manner, the wide range of issues that face start-up businesses.

Finally, for their day-to-day encouragement and moral support throughout this project, thank you to Jan, George, Leslie, and Michael, and to Annie Longsworth, Jigger Herman, Pam and Buddy Duncan, Tom Willis, and Kimberly French.

—*Elizabeth K. Longsworth*

Foreword

Every 30 seconds of every day, someone somewhere in the United States starts a new business. Every 30 seconds someone stakes their money, their labor, their good name on the unshakable belief that they can make or provide something bigger, better, faster, or cheaper than the next guy.

Many entrepreneurs perceive the contours of their newly discovered opportunity dimly at first, and set out intending to give it direction and clarity as they go. Others sketch the shape of things to come on whatever scrap of paper is available at the moment of epiphany. Rod Canion, the founder of Compaq Computer, favored a napkin, since immortalized in a television commercial. Bernie Goldhirsh, the founder of *Inc.* magazine, chose a plain white #10 envelope as his medium.

A growing segment of the start-up population these days, though, takes pains to write a business plan in order to raise capital, convince the first skeptical employees to sign on, or simply to provide a roadmap for themselves. We at *Inc.* are fascinated by these documents, describing as they do some niche, some barely perceptible opening in the marketplace, overlooked—or so its author would have us believe—by the collective resources of corporate America. Our love affair with that quintessential American document, the business plan, is no surprise. We publish one in the magazine each month, and have for several years now. We call it Anatomy of a Start-Up.

Each month we scout the start-up landscape for the most compelling business plans we can find: those that tell us something new about the world in which we do business or about the start-up process itself. One of *Inc.*'s writers takes the material and works it into publishable form—including a summary of the business-plan narrative, a biography of the founder, detailed financial projections and all. Then (and here's the fun part), we locate the toughest, most seasoned, most skeptical experts—investors, industry analysts, even potential competitors—send them our write-up, and let them play venture capitalist. Will the new venture succeed? What are the hidden pitfalls that have been overlooked? How could the plan be changed to increase its chances of survival?

All this provides for some engaging business detection each month. But as time went by, we—and by *we*, I mean *Inc.* readers and staffers alike—found ourselves wondering, So what's happened to these fledgling businesses? How often have the experts been right, after all? Which types of experts provided the most valuable feedback? And, most important, what can we learn from the Anatomy series about why some new businesses succeed while others quickly perish?

We assigned staff writer Leslie Brokaw the task of answering these questions. (Leslie was an obvious choice since she and executive editor Michael S. Hopkins had developed the Anatomy series in the first place.) She came back with her report, "The Truth about Start-Ups," and the accompanying "Scorecard," which appear near the end of this book in The Results. Leslie also captured some provocative responses from founders about what they'd do differently if they had to do it over again, included in the section "If I Knew Then What I Know Now. . ."

It struck us as we reviewed this material that the real truth about start-ups may be that they are as much art as science. That experts will most always dismiss the new, the novel, the unorthodox. That if the process of economic creation is to continue (and it will), entrepreneurs will continue to dismiss the naysaying of the experts. That the process of building something from nothing can be so unpredictable, so chaotic, so downright messy, even members of a *successful* start-up team will disagree about why their company prospered in the first place.

Which prompted the idea for the introduction to this book. We had talked with Debbi and Randy Fields, cofounders of Mrs. Fields Cookies, often enough over the years to know that this wife-and-husband team offered up divergent accounts of their own success. Fortunately, they were in total agreement when it came to answering a list of questions we put to each of them. Hence, the "his" and "her" introduction to the book.

Finally, a modest suggestion about how to get the most out of this book. Read the business plans first. Take a cue from our founders, and forget about the experts—for the moment, at least. Draw up your own list of questions. Will this business make it? Where are the weaknesses in the plan? Is the company adequately capitalized? Have the founders done their homework when it comes to market research? Does the founder have the requisite skills to lead the company? Then consult the experts. When you find yourself agreeing with them a bit too readily, remind yourself that it was the "experts" who predicted there was no future for a manufacturer of IBM clones and that no one would advertise in, not to mention *read*, a magazine for and about small growing companies. Then, and only then, turn to the back of the book and discover what happens when even the best-laid plans meet the market.

—*George Gendron, Editor-in-Chief,* Inc. *Magazine*

TABLE OF CONTENTS

THE COMPANIES *The real story behind each start-up (or: who, what, when, where, and how much), and critical analysis from leading business experts on its chances for success:*

Introduction

BY RANDY AND DEBBI FIELDS, MRS. FIELDS COOKIES

*Starting a business is something to
which people have an intense personal reaction.
It is surprising that people involved in
the same start-up often have very different
experiences of that process.*

Witness Randy and Debbi Fields, the husband-and-wife team from Park City, Utah, who launched Mrs. Fields Inc. in 1977 year as a single store and grew it by 1991 into a baked-goods empire with more than 470 stores and $123 million in sales.

If *Inc.* had been running Anatomy of a Start-Up articles in '77, we would have wanted to profile the then-start-up cookie company. With a CEO who had more will than business experience, and an unusual growth strategy of supporting communications with internally-developed technology, Mrs. Fields Inc. was an interesting company from the beginning. Though we missed them in the start-up phase, we feel that there is still much to learn from these two entrepreneurs, whose distinct but complementary priorities, responsibilities, and styles show how important a diversity of skills is to any successful enterprise, whether it's a start-up or a grown business.

To introduce this collection of Anatomy of a Start-Up profiles, we asked Debbi and Randy to respond separately to the same basic questions about their experiences, without discussing their answers with each other. We were not surprised that when they looked back, they often recalled different problems and achievements—which goes to show that even cofounders can experience their start-up differently. Their responses are consistent with their roles: When asked about mistakes, chairman Randy says he wishes the company had never gone public. President and CEO Debbi, on the other hand, regrets not learning sooner how to delegate.

Most of all, in this introduction to *Anatomy of a Start-Up* we wanted to capture the flavor of how the Fieldses feel and talk about their company. Their enthusiasm for entrepreneurial business is infectious, and their flair for it is…well…obvious.

—*Elizabeth K. Longsworth*

ON THE EARLY DAYS:

Randy Fields, Chairman, Mrs. Fields Inc.: When she launched Mrs. Fields, Debbi had a very limited objective, which was to have a cookie store so she could earn a modest living and enjoy herself. We didn't really have any growth objectives at all. Did we foresee having an empire? No way. Remember the apocryphal but true story about Debbi having to go out on the street and pass samples around?

It was almost a year before we did anything else, because Debbi just didn't feel like she could control the quality of the business from multiple locations. There was a whole series of checkpoints. We knew it had potential beyond just one store, then two years later we were worried about whether it had potential beyond the Bay Area; maybe it was just a Bay Area phenomenon. We had concerns back in the early '80s. Would it work outside the U.S.? There's always been concern about the applicability of this thing.

Debbi Fields, President and CEO, Mrs. Fields Inc.: When I launched Mrs. Fields, the planning went literally one day at a time. I didn't have a business plan, I didn't have an annual operating plan, I didn't think in terms of $250,000 annual sales, I thought in terms of today. When I opened up the store, all that mattered was will these cookies sell? That was my number-one objective.

My very first day, my goal was to do $50. I made $75. I realized how exciting it was to set goals. Once I had a week in place, I'd want to beat the week, and once I had a month in place, I'd want to beat the month. But I didn't start out by saying, OK, this is what I'm going to do. I built the product, I focused on the customer, and all that mattered was that my customers loved the product and were happy.

I took all of those weekly goals and broke them down into hourly targets. Rather than trying to do $5,000 for the week, which to me sounded incredibly difficult, I said to the folks that I worked with, That's $50 right now this hour—can we do it? And we did it. It tied to the $5,000 goal, it tied to the $20,000 monthly goal, it tied to the $250,000 annual goal, but right now, let's do $50. Hourly increments are very manageable—it's amazing. If I walk in and say, OK, you guys, I need for you to do $20,000 this month, people's eyes kind of glaze over and they think, How am I ever going to get there? But if I say, OK, you guys, I need to have an extra $20 this hour, who's going to do it, let's race—we can do it.

And it's fun! You don't need to have anybody tell you you're doing a great job, because when your goal was $50 and you do $70, you feel great. It's like running in a race and coming in first, but it's still a team effort.

Breaking the business down into hourly goals tied it to production: How many of these fresh, warm cookies do we need to bake to make the goal for the hour? It aided us in our inventory management, and our freshness.

It also tied into staffing: How many people do we need to be able to deliver this goal? And it tied into cross-training. If there were only two people in the store, I would change off with another young lady, and she would go to the front for an hour, and all she would do was sell, and make customers feel good. I would be in the back doing all the production for her—all the mixing, all the baking, all the dropping—and I'd keep her in supply. Her goal was to make $75 and to beat my previous hour, then we would change off, and I'd go to the front, and she'd support me. Everybody had to do everything in the store. We all supported each other, so it allowed me to get everything done, and everybody trained, but in the form of spirit and competition.

Competition keeps people really involved in the heart of the business. When you say, Hey, you guys, we're behind, it's raining outside, nobody's here, what are we going to do? Then we are creative—we go outside and sample in the rain with umbrellas, and that's when we get outrageous. Sometimes the impossible happens because you're willing to challenge it.

The system technology that we built the whole business on is based on hour-by-hour management. We tried to take that experience of the fun, the games, the production, the planning, the cross-training, and the people, and put it in a program, which is called Mrs. Fields Hour-By-Hour Management. Everybody keeps score of their hourly goals, companywide.

ON LAYING THE FOUNDATION FOR GROWTH:

Randy: Our technology has been a very significant part of our growth, because it has let us grow the business and maintain store-level controls. It's intrinsic. It's woven all the way through the fabric. The objective was to get Debbi as close to the stores as possible, and to get the store people as close to the customer as possible. The conventional approach to that is layers and layers of people. Debbi doesn't come through layers and layers of people. The more people between her and the customer, presumably the more difficult and problematic the business becomes. So the objective is always to use technology innovatively so that we need fewer people who have more of a customer focus. The only answer to that, really, was a technological answer, which we had to develop.

ON EXPERIENCE:

Debbi: I had no experience, zero, zilch. I just had an idea and I had a recipe. I didn't have the vision, I didn't have a dream. I really wanted to make fresh, warm cookies, and I wanted to make people smile. That was all that I had in terms of a business idea. I've always said we're in the feel-good business. That was my message. People would roll their eyes and say, Oh, gee.

People viewed me as a very young, inexperienced individual, with no proper business background, let alone with a proper college education. And then there was the fact that I was a woman in business—not to say that that was a difficulty, but it was a novel idea, to be a woman in business, 14 years ago.

ON ADVICE FROM EXPERTS:

Randy: We went to experts when we launched Mrs. Fields, and all the experts said, "Is that stupid? They're opening right next door to a bakery, and the bakery sells cookies for 9¢, and they're going to sell them for 25¢. The lady has no business experience." Nobody said it was a good idea. I was in the investment business, so I had a whole staff of Harvard and Stanford M.B.A.s whose business it is to analyze businesses. And they all said it was the stupidest thing they'd ever heard, but Debbi went ahead. All I did was write the check and tell her it was stupid.

There are two issues the experts we spoke with failed to understand. One, as Debbi had observed, the world was beginning a shift to quality. Historically the world had been focused on price. Debbi was saying, 'I know that a 9¢ cookie doesn't taste very good. Mine tastes great. People will pay a quarter for it.' People looking at the market didn't understand the demand side of it, they only understood the supply side.

But the other issue, the real issue, is Debbi's determination. Debbi has been the most significant factor in Mrs. Fields's growth. The unswerving, driving vision of a committed individual is an irresistible force.

Debbi: If *Inc.* had done an Anatomy of a Start-Up on us, the experts probably would have said what Randy said then: Stupid idea, it won't work, it'll fail, you can't build a business on one product. But that's OK; I've always been a believer that the greatest failure is not to try. If you already understand what you're going to lose by thinking about the worst possible scenario, then your challenge is to beat that worst-case scenario.

ON PARTNERSHIP:

Randy: It often occurs to us that it's got to be hard for our close group of people here to figure out who you go to with what. If what you have is a problem with computers or finance, you come to me. Otherwise, you go to Debbi. So we have pretty distinct roles, and we're both gadflies to each other about the decisions we're making. There are some pieces of the business that she handles that I don't even know about, and there are certainly some pieces that I handle that she doesn't know about. But those are what I call the low-level, administrative, mundane kinds of things. Anything that's strategic, or important, we at least share what we're doing with the other person so they can express an opinion. We do not do the same thing, and that's what's important.

The two hardest things for an entrepreneur are to find people who can competently handle the functional areas of the business, and to find people that you trust. If you start out with a partner that you trust, who handles a significant part of the business, then you have a leg up.

Debbi has two key business strengths that are unique and that I admire because I don't have them. One is that she has incredible leadership. She is charismatically gifted as a leader. She has the capacity to somehow transmit a vision across the phone lines and across the world to people so they have the same vision that she does. I don't know how she does it, but it's remarkable. Her other characteristic is she has a mass taste. She knows what people will like to eat.

My role was to make sure there was always enough money to grow, and the computer and control systems, to make sure the thing didn't fly apart from centrifugal force. Because we had to invent and develop our own technologies and our financing arrangements, neither of them were what you'd call easily replicable.

Debbi and I have not disagreed very much. She and I are usually ultimately of one mind. That's not to say that we don't argue about stuff. I'm not being coy—I would tell you if I could think of anything we've ever argued about. She has a better memory for things like that.

Debbi: Philosophically, Randy and I don't disagree. That is a real plus. If we do disagree philosophically, we have already agreed that I'll win. If we get stuck, we'll go with my views, my gut, my intuition about what to do, and what is right. I always know that I can decide, that I'm the absolute individual for this decision, and that's why we always talk about decisions. I know I'm going to win, but I don't want to win and be stupid.

Randy is very numbers oriented. He's a wizard with numbers. And he's a real systems guy. He likes things to be nailed down, and he likes organized, systematic approaches to how things should be run.

On the other hand, I'm very spontaneous. I'm very sensitive, very emotional. I do all the product development, I handle all of the marketing, I handle the training and the development segments, I handle the store operations in terms of all the standards and complying to them. We have clearly divided our areas of responsibility, and that's really worked for us. If couples are going to work together, it's critical that there be experts on both sides of the table, but you shouldn't have two experts on one subject.

One of the benefits of separate responsibilities is that I will listen to Randy. It doesn't mean that I will agree with him or that I will do what he says. Because if I have a strong conviction, I'll do what I want to do. For example, in 1989 I was working on this new cookie. I was in the kitchen just pouring in macadamia nuts, and macadamia nuts are incredibly expensive. Randy walks in with his calculator, which is typical, and he said, "There is no way that you can put all those macadamia nuts in our cookies. There's just no way. We'll never make any money, blah, blah, blah." And I said, "Randy, get out of the kitchen." I never changed the recipe. My view is I'm going to build the best cookie in the whole world, and it's going to have as many macadamia nuts as I can fit into the dough, and I don't really care about the expense, because I don't build on a cost-of-goods model. I build the cookie and then whatever it costs, it costs, which is really unconventional wisdom. Randy was taught you need a cost of goods of X, so you build a product for Y and doesn't it taste good for Z. I don't approach business that way. You build the best product in the world, and you love it, and if you can't sell it for what you need to get it for, then remove it, but don't make it less.

ON BUILDING A TEAM:

Randy: The best role in the world is what I call the role of conciliarity. What I want is somebody who gives me advice. It doesn't mean that I do it. I have to own the decision. What I'm interested in is seeing different points of view. Both Debbi and I have very strong personalities. As a result, people mistakenly assume that we don't want to hear how it really is. The key is to find people who are strong enough to march into our offices and tell us that we're both stupid. I have a whole bunch of people who think I'm stupid, and not just at the board level. I want them at the operating level, because Debbi and I come up with 52 new ideas a day. I want people around me all day long who can go, "Stupid, stupid, stupid."

Debbi: It's really OK for people who are going into their own business to not be masters of everything, even though when you're in a start-up environment you have to learn how to do it all. Everybody has a responsibility to understand all aspects of their business. They do not have to be an expert; they just have to understand it.

Their responsibility is to say, OK if I'm going to make a contribution in this company, I have got to be a specialist. I have got to be great at something that is unique and wonderful and absolutely my thing, because I'm going to grow it and build it and love it and nurture it and develop it. They also need to be able to openly say, You know what? I'm awful with numbers. I want somebody who knows numbers better than I will ever know numbers. And that's the key.

I had accountants and people who had never really dealt with customers. But my view was, if there was ever a problem in a store, the people who work in the corporate office still need to be able to work in our cookie stores. And even though they may not be experts, we train everybody in our corporate offices to work in a cookie store. The reason is, quite simply, they may not be any good at standing at the front of the counter selling cookies, but if push comes to shove and we need to do it, they can do it. Their strength may be that they love computers and what they want to do is sit at a desk and play with the software and develop the software, but if they have to they will go sell the cookies.

We've had situations even here in Park City where we had a serious snowstorm and we had three people in one of our stores who couldn't make it to work, so for the next 48 hours, it was covered by all Park City [corporate] personnel.

The mistake that people make is that they say, I have to be great at product development, and I have to be great at store operations, and I have to do all of the accounting and be excellent at that. That's where problems start occurring.

ON QUALITY:

Randy: The goal, in the end, is to create a happy customer, but we certainly don't do that all of the time. If you ask Debbi what she's unhappiest about, she'll probably tell you she's unhappiest about our customer service. I'm unhappiest with my understanding of middle management and how to better direct and to improve their accountability and responsibility. We're down to the people issues—those are more difficult—and I'm afraid that's process oriented. It never gets any better. You're always in the business of doing it.

Debbi: I learned as a consumer. People would make claims on television—they would say the world's finest, the world's greatest—and it would bother me, because I would go out and buy it, to find out what the world's greatest was like, and I would be disappointed. So that was always one of the little buzz things in the back of my mind: I will never tell customers I'm the best. The customers need to make that decision. I think Mrs. Fields cookies are great, but that's Debbi's opinion. I really believe that it's the responsibility of the consumer to make decisions about the product.

I always shopped at very small mom-and-pop stores, because they cared about me as an individual, and that meant so much to me. I didn't want to be number 45, I wanted to be Debbi. I always sought out those places that knew me as Debbi, and remembered me, and said hi to me, because I felt that I mattered to them in some small way. I may not have, but it made me think I did. So I said, When I go into business, the things that I want are absolute quality, for the customers to be totally satisfied—that's why I put a guarantee on my products—and to keep it real personalized.

I love our product, and I love our people, whether it's the customers, or the people inside our business. That's all I really care about. Everything else I'm learning to do, but if you don't have a product, and you don't have the people, you have no business.

I'm fanatical. Quality and service drive me crazy. They have to be perfect. I'm known for shutting down stores. I don't care what it costs, we will fix it.

We monitor all of our customer comments, good or bad, and I tell everybody that Debbi Fields will reach nirvana in the category of customer service when I'm like the Maytag service man—when I sit at my desk and all I get are customer compliments.

ON CHANGING ROLES:

Randy: One of the things I miss about the early days is the ease with which things could be done. I think both Debbi and I miss those days. Now part of the stress and strain is the sheer number of people.

As we've grown, Debbi and I have had to continue to move up to different levels. Debbi started out as the store manager, so she had to go from a manager to a district manager, from a district manager to a regional director, and a vice-president of operations, and finally, to a president and CEO. All I had to do was find a management team that I could put in place below me to ultimately do my own succession planning. It's probably been easier for me than for Debbi.

Debbi: I do much more planning now, and much more testing. I'm very spontaneous, and it's hard to take a very spontaneous person and move them into a process of, OK, where are we today, and how is that going to impact us for tomorrow? Where are we going to go in a year, or the next three years? Five years is really hard, I think, to look out to. At least I'm able to say I can get to three comfortably. Randy can get to five, but I'm not there yet. My main role today is that I feel like I am the coach. I am the teacher. Instead of telling people what to do and how to do it, and doing it myself, I write the rules of why we've always done it this way before, and what our philosophies and our objectives are. And what we're trying to achieve, short term and long term.

ON FINANCING A START-UP:

Debbi: I started with $50,000. That sounded like everything. . . . I think my parents' home was worth $13,000 at the time. I really felt like that was more than enough. We had secondhand equipment, and Randy painted the floor.

I'm a strong believer in being very conservative in a start-up. I am from the land of you don't need a nice office unless that's what your business is about. If you have to sell a service, and people are going to judge you by your office, then of course, have a nice office. But if an office doesn't help you make the sale, then you can sit on the floor. You can use secondhand furniture. Who cares if there's a carpet? You have to apply all of your financial resources to making the business grow. Either the customer has to benefit, or the product has to benefit. Or the service has to be the very best. You have to apply it to the things that grow your business. Nothing else is important.

The thing that scares me with some start-up companies is when I go and visit them, and they have a great idea that they haven't yet implemented, but they have the most magnificent office building, and the nicest furniture I have ever seen, all high design. It makes me nervous, and the reason is they don't have their priorities right. If you're going to open a retail store, put it all in the retail store. Don't put it in an office.

Randy: Debbi and I run a very, very tight ship, very tight budget—we cannot stand waste. I've seen a lot of companies harmed by having a lot of money and having people spend it as if you can spend your way to prosperity instead of thrift your way to prosperity. It's cultural. I think people are either money spenders or money savers. And I'm fascinated when I meet people who say, "Oh, you know, it's in the budget." What does "in the budget" mean? Does "in the budget" mean it's OK if you don't need to do it, just throw it away?

The amount of money a start-up needs depends, of course, on what they're trying to do and what the start-up requirements are in their industry. But I'm fascinated by watching $10-, $20-, and $30-million start-ups. When you visit there are great offices, and lots of overhead, and lots of secretaries. . . and lots of this and lots of that. . . and no business, but they say, "It's coming, don't worry!"

We started Mrs. Fields with $50,000, and we've had to refinance several times as we grew. We were very reliant in the beginning on bank credit, which we could not do today. It's much harder to start a company now.

ON THEIR MISTAKES:

Randy: Everybody, certainly Debbi and Randy, always makes their own mistakes. The truth is, it is very hard to learn from other people's experience. It's like telling a kid not to touch something that's hot. That's why all of us have touched something hot.

Our biggest mistake was probably going public and then later, significantly changing our strategy from being a cookie-only business to having an expanded range of products. This had a very significant financial impact on the business. If I could go back and undo something, I wouldn't have gone public. Because the change in strategy *was* the right thing to do. But it's real hard to explain that to public shareholders, who have a different kind of interest than we do.

Debbi: I would recommend that anyone starting a business read everything they can about people who have done it successfully and unsuccessfully. But don't let that be your limitation.

Everything we've learned has been on-the-job training. I see that as a huge advantage because many times we've been willing to go out there and challenge the system because we didn't know any better. But conversely, sometimes by not knowing any better, we've made lots of mistakes. It's important for people who are thinking about going into business to understand that mistakes are also part of the learning process. You just have to make a commitment to learn from them and be smart about them, but it's something that happens in business. It's very disappointing and very depressing when those things occur, but you've got to always find a way to win.

My biggest mistake is that I didn't delegate soon enough, fast enough, and really focus a world-class team until the past three or four years. I'm an entrepreneur. I want to do it all. I want to go in and bake the cookies. I want to do all the things that I did at my very first store today! It's really hard for me to let go. I thought I was the only person who could do it. But the truth is, I'm not the only person who can do it. I have wonderful people. I didn't spend enough time teaching and training people along the way at higher levels. I could teach everybody how to mix cookies, that was just a natural thing. But I didn't teach my philosophies on how you would go about marketing—instead I would do the marketing. And it took me a very long time to learn that—I'm still learning it. I have to bite my tongue every now and then, and say, No, no, no, I'm trying to teach.

Now when it comes to marketing, I write out my views and my values associated with marketing, and then I just hand it over to the marketing department, and say, Work around the things I believe in. At Mrs. Fields I don't want marketing to be glitzy, I want it always to be honest, I want it always to be something that I would say myself. So I just give everybody those kinds of parameters, and then let them be as creative as they can be, and step outside the dots, as long as they don't go against our values, as an organization. But learning that has taken time.

ON WHAT MAKES MRS. FIELDS INC. DIFFERENT:

Debbi: There's a lot of difference between us and our competitors in the product. We have a larger variety of cookies, and if our cookies aren't sold within two hours of being baked, they become cookie orphans and go to charity. We don't change our standards on a store even if it's losing us money. We have some stores that, unfortunately, are not successful. They do not do enough volume for what we need for the product and for the customers. The average Mrs. Fields store has to do at least $300 a day. That's how much product we have to have out, and mix, and bake, just to maintain all of our standards. But we don't change our standards just because the store isn't successful. And that's really important. And I'm not saying our competitors do, but I will tell you, we *don't* run it on the basis of, If this isn't working how do we skimp and scrape?

Randy: The three biggest differences between us and our competitors are quality, our control systems, and Debbi's focus on service. From a business strategy perspective, our technology has been a very important part. The technology empowers the people by freeing their time to spend more time on the quality of the product and the service to the customer, which is the driver.

ON ENTREPRENEURIAL SPIRIT:

Randy: I think the entrepreneurial spirit is learned. My guess is the average entrepreneur was interested in money at a very young age, sold things, got jobs, saved money. I used to take vegetables out of my mother's refrigerator, put them in my silly little red wagon, and go door-to-door in my neighborhood selling my mother's vegetables.

ON ROLE MODELS:

Debbi: My mom is an incredibly hard worker. She raised all the girls, then went to work afterwards. My father was a welder and he absolutely loved his job. He may not have made a lot of money, but he was the best welder and he was happy. He was proud of what he did and what he contributed.

He didn't care about money. He would say to me, True wealth, Debbi, is found in family, never money. And he would always say he was a wealthy man, because he had a wonderful family, and terrific people that he worked with, and friends. And I admired him for that.

The other thing he always said was, You have to work hard. You've got to really love what you do. And those were the things that really guided me.

ON MANAGEMENT:

Randy: Management and parenting are identical. I've never been able to figure out the difference between the two. So the question you would ask is, What would happen to my children if I never supervised them? What would they grow up to be? What kind of people would they become? And what will they become if I act as a good parent to them? And the difference between those is the value-added of parenting. Well, the same is true in management. What would happen to those subordinates and to the business, and what difference does it make if I'm there? Now, that's a long way of saying that the real role of management is to get people to do what they wouldn't do without you there. It's not to be a friend. It's to make a difference in the actions and successes of the people you work with.

Debbi: One thing that's really helped me is to tell people what I'm afraid of. Instead of trying to say, No, no, let me control this, I'll just say, OK, here are the rules. You can do this project as long as you do not go over budget, as long as you do not go over the time frame. This is what I'm afraid could go wrong. And I've found that when you tell people that up front, it makes it so much easier to win. Then I don't have to worry, because I've stated my case. It makes it much more of a team approach.

ON STARTING ANOTHER BUSINESS:

Randy: I'm currently launching another company, my computer company. We sell the same computer software that we developed for Mrs. Fields. It's kind of up and running now. We're beginning to sell. We've sold to Burger King, and Sterling Optical, and a couple of other companies.

Debbi: If I were going to start another business it would probably be associated with a health facility and working with the public. I see all these people who go to health spas, and they go on these diets and get really skinny, and then they gain it all back. I'm not a spa-goer—I hate spas—but I do go to places where everybody's on these self-improvement courses. The biggest problem is [people] pay the fee and then there's no follow-up. I would absolutely follow up on every single person. We all go through these highs and lows, and we all need a conscience to call us and say, How are you doing today? Did you exercise this morning? We're going to pick you up and take you around the block. I hate to exercise. It's hard for me. I would probably start a business where I'd take care of those kinds of folks. I would be doing it more for me than for my customers, because I know what it's like.

ON THE FUTURE:

Debbi: I'm not happy yet, because I see so much more that I can do. There's lots to celebrate, but you have to understand my view: Good enough never is. That philosophy runs through the bones of Mrs. Fields. I could never look back and say, Let me tell you what I did. It's not relevant. I want to talk about what I need to do today, and what I need to earn today to get ready for tomorrow. I feel I owe my customers more—they should have better service, and I should work to improve my quality. The stores should be more beautiful, and I should have better training programs. Those are the things that drive me to keep coming in every day and saying, I can do a better job.

THE COMPANIES

The following 27 companies were profiled while they were start-ups. They span a broad spectrum of industries and together face a dizzying array of challenges. Will they survive? At the end of each profile, leading business experts offer their opinions of each business's chances for success.

DRIVE-IN MOVIES

The launch of a hits-only, drive-through video chain

BY TOM RICHMAN

The question wasn't whether Todd W. LeRoy and Michael L. Atkinson were going to launch a business venture together. Late afternoons, when they were both working at Shearson Lehman Brothers Inc., they'd brainstorm over start-up possibilities. Atkinson had already created several restaurant concepts. Maybe their joint venture should have something to do with food.

Hmm . . . food . . . dinner . . dinner and a movie. Gourmet frozen dinners sold in video stores? Messy, but video stores . . . hmmm. A video store . . . a *convenient* video store . . . a chain of drive-through video stores. Of course. That's it. Put them in strip-center parking lots close to commuter routes in suburban locations. Stock them with new releases. People drive up, order some tapes off the menu board, take them home. No hassles. Minimal overhead. Keep it simple. And yeah, franchise them for fast growth and minimal operational headaches.

Cofounders Michael L. Atkinson, left, and Todd W. LeRoy, of Video's 1st in Albany, N.Y.

EXECUTIVE SUMMARY

THE COMPANY:
Associated Video Hut Inc., d/b/a Video's 1st; Albany, N.Y.

CONCEPT:
To franchise a national chain of drive-through video rental kiosks, specializing in hit movies

PROJECTIONS:
100 franchises to be contracted by year-end, 5,000 by mid-1990; each franchised kiosk to earn $33,807 on $139,317 annual sales

HURDLES:
Sustaining above-market rental price; providing customers with promised convenience in a business with severely bunched peak-hour traffic; providing franchisees enough marketing and operations support to earn their loyalty—and continued royalty payments

They got the idea in March 1986, incorporated in May, opened two pilot stores last summer, and sold their first franchise to a Rochester, N.Y., investor group in August. Now LeRoy, 34, and Atkinson, 33, are betting that the company, called Video's 1st, will become the hottest franchise in the country. In fact, they figure it had better become the hottest, because if it doesn't, someone faster is going to adopt the idea—there's no way to protect it—and steal the market out from under them. The greatest challenge they see isn't making the Video's 1st concept work, but using the 12- to 18-month head start they think they have to establish a national market strength before a better-heeled competitor can. There were some dozen franchises open, or about to open, at the end of 1987. LeRoy and Atkinson's objective almost boggles the mind: to move from scratch to having sold 100 franchises for the kiosk-type video rental stores by the end of this year and 5,000 by mid-1990.

Here's why they think they'll make it.

Estimates vary, but in 1986 Americans spent at least $3 billion renting movies to watch on their home videocassette recorders. Last year they spent $1 billion more, bringing the video industry's revenues close to if not slightly more than the take at movie-theater box offices. This year, rental revenues will grow again. As the percentage of VCR-equipped homes increases from about half of those with TVs now to a projected 90% by 1995, one of the studies LeRoy and Atkinson like to cite predicts that the videocassette business will reach $15 billion annually.

Already it's hard to find a strip center, a mall, or a downtown retail district where someone hasn't planted a video store. Most rentals take place at these untold thousands of independent mom-and-pop and franchised outlets. But price competition here has put pressure on profit margins, and with a video store on every block, analysts wonder if the market isn't saturated.

In his research binder, Atkinson has filed a trade association survey reporting that the average video store in 1986 covered 2,089 square feet and stocked 3,478 tapes. But those tapes included 2,417 different titles, meaning that, on average, stores carried fewer than 2 copies of each title. And that, in turn, means that if just one or two other people in your neighborhood want to watch the same tape you hanker to see on the same night, you don't see it. Yet the average store rents just 12% of its titles every day. Some 88% of the inventory sits on the shelves. Brian Woods, Video's 1st's executive vice-president for marketing, likens an unrented tape to the proverbial empty airplane seat. Both represent a sale lost forever.

In an effort to boost margins, industry innovators have come up with two responses to retail saturation: the rack jobber and the superstore.

Rack jobbers maintain bare-bones inventories of tapes at convenience stores, gas stations, and other such places where potential customers are likely to be found anyway. Their emphasis is on convenience.

Superstores, on the other hand, are emporiums; they carry gadgets along with every title a videophile could imagine, in quantity.

These two retail formats appear to be the fastest-growing parts of the video-rental industry. They are, industry observers suggest, the direction in which the market is moving.

What's wrong with this picture, LeRoy and Atkinson think, is that conventional video stores pay a lot of overhead to house a lot of tapes that don't get rented very often. Then they also note that near-

FINANCIALS

VIDEO'S 1ST PRO FORMA OPERATING STATEMENT
(per kiosk[1])

	Monthly Average ($)	Yearly Total ($)
REVENUES		
Tape rental fees		
(116 rentals per day @ $2.95)	$10,260	$123,117
Used tape sales (55 tapes per month @ $20)	1,100	13,200
Popcorn	150	1,800
Other	100	1,200
TOTAL REVENUES	**11,610**	**139,317**
COST OF SALES		
Prerecorded tapes (55 tapes per month @ $60)	3,300	39,600
Popcorn	93	1,116
Other	50	600
TOTAL COST OF SALES	**3,443**	**41,316**
GROSS PROFIT	**8,167**	**98,001**
OPERATING EXPENSES		
Rent	500	6,000
Payroll (12 hours per day, seven days per week)	1,950	23,400
Payroll taxes	234	2,808
General (insurance, supplies, utilities, & miscellaneous)	505	6,055
Royalty payment (7% gross receipts)	813	9,752
Local advertising (2% gross receipts)	232	2,786
Corporate advertising (1% gross receipts)	116	1,393
Note payable, principal, & interest		
($45,000 note @ 12%, five-year term)	1,000	12,000
TOTAL OPERATING EXPENSES	**5,350**	**64,194**
NET INCOME BEFORE TAXES	**2,817**	**33,807**

[1] Depreciation and amortization not included

ly 80% of the people who go to a video store to rent a movie go there looking for new releases, one or more of the 30 or so most popular titles that have only recently been released on video.

As for rack jobbers, Atkinson suggests that convenience store and gas station employees aren't attitudinally equipped to perform the two-way transaction that a video rental involves—checking the tape out, then checking it back in. Employee turnover rates in these outlets are too high, he says, to permit proper training.

Superstores, he thinks, are a great idea—but expensive to build. And, he says, nationwide there are probably only 150 or so remaining markets in the country capable of supporting one of these rental monsters.

So, he and LeRoy reasoned, why not a small, inexpensive video store that carries *just* the current hot titles and in enough depth—say, 10 to 25 copies each—to assure almost every customer of getting the hit movie he or she wants? Or if not that hit, certainly another one. But in any case, not a dog. And why not put these 300 to 750 tapes in a Fotomat-type kiosk for which rent and utilities cost practically nothing? And why not expand this concept quickly? After all, LeRoy points out, the cost to erect one of these units is not very high, a lot less than it would be for a full-service, full-size retail rental store.

Why not?

"We keep asking people to shoot holes in the concept," says Atkinson, "and they can't do it."

By starting out as franchisors with little or no operating experience, Atkinson and LeRoy are, as a practical matter, launching two new businesses. If one fails, so will the other.

First, there's the retail business—the kiosks—to be run by the franchisors. If they stumble, the two entrepreneurs have nothing to sell, and their revenues from franchise sales and royalties will dry up quickly.

On the other hand, while the kiosk concept might be a smash, if the franchisor organization is undercapitalized, poorly organized, or badly run, the business still fails—for lack of support to the retailer.

Here's what they propose to do on the retail side.

At $2.95, Video's 1st's rental price is high compared with the industry average of less than $2. Atkinson and LeRoy say studies show that people will pay more for convenience (double drive-through windows, short waits) and for selection (getting the new releases). Price, the founders insist, is not a critical issue.

If that's true, the Albany-based duo will be more alchemists than entrepreneurs, changing plastic tape to gold. Each kiosk's projected return is nothing short of astounding.

Currently, Video's 1st expects to hand over a turnkey kiosk, complete with training, initial inventory, grand opening, and adequate working capital, to a buyer on his or her site for a total cost to the franchisee of $87,727 or less.

The financial *pro formas* that Atkinson posits (see box on page 6) promise remarkable margins for franchisees. The figures represent an

COMPETITIVE ANALYSIS

	Industry average performance for video retailer	Video's 1st performance assumptions
Store size	2,089 square feet[1]	48 square feet
Tapes stocked	3,478[1]	300
Individual titles stocked	2,417[1]	30
Tapes rented daily	185[2]	120
Percent of stock rented daily	5.3%[2]	40%
Rental price	$1.80[2]	$2.95
Wholesale tape cost (new releases)	$50[2]	$60
Resale price of used tapes	$16[2]	$20
Full-time employees	3[1]	1
Part-time employees	4[1]	4

[1] Video Software Dealers Association
[2] The Fairfield Group Inc.

average month and the annual total, both for the *second* year of a kiosk's operation, when it is in top gear. According to his figures, if roughly 40% of the minimum 300-tape inventory rents daily at $2.95 per day, a prefabricated 48-square-foot kiosk should earn $33,807, or almost 24% before taxes, on annual revenues of $139,317. With about only 50 tapes, or 17% of the inventory, rented per day, a kiosk still breaks even under Atkinson's assumptions. The figures don't account for taxes or depreciation, and they assume that the franchisee has to service $45,000 in debt used to finance the start-up. They also assume the kiosk will sell its used tapes for $20 each, or about one-third their cost new. With the margins Atkinson's rosy scenario predicts, a franchisee's annual pretax return on assets will reach 40% or more.

Furthermore, a franchisee's risk is minimized, Atkinson and LeRoy argue, by the portability of the kiosk. If the first location turns out to be poor, the franchisee can pick up the box and move it someplace better.

Executing a sound retail idea, however, is just half the battle. The business will either fail to take off or stall out in the climb unless several things work well on the franchisor's side.

The franchisor must be well capitalized. Its franchise documents— the agreement it makes with franchisees—must be sound. It has to be able to sell franchises, and it has to be able to support what it sells, which means staffing up at headquarters, but not so quickly that overhead outruns cash.

Inadequate capital, franchise veterans say, trips up most would-be franchisors, and there is more than one way to fall here.

Just getting started requires some money. Except for three pilot stores in Albany, the company's home base, Associated Video Hut Inc. (the name given to the corporate umbrella), won't operate kiosks itself. The founders chose not to divide their energies between operations on the one hand and building a franchise organization on the other. But with no operations, there are no revenues. They've only just begun signing franchise contracts, and it will be some months before they can count on regular royalty payments. LeRoy and Atkinson knew they'd need capital to carry them over that gap.

First they raised $465,000 in early 1987 with a private equity placement, giving up just short of 20% of the company's stock. Calling on their Wall Street backgrounds, Atkinson and LeRoy sold the issue themselves, saving the underwriting fee. This money, they figured, would be all they'd need. Franchise sales, which began in August, would generate enough cash to carry the company for some time, they thought, and they priced their franchise product accordingly.

Altogether, Atkinson figured, each franchise sale would bring $18,500 into the company, even before royalties began to flow. Upon signing a contract, a new franchisee hands over a onetime franchise fee of $18,500 (it was $13,500 before January 1, 1988). When the kiosk is actually delivered from the independent manufacturer to the new franchisee, Associated Video Hut realizes another $5,000 in cash from a markup over the kiosk's cost. Total cash in: $23,500.

Out of the revenues, subtract a sales commission of approximately $3,885. That's the only direct cost, as Atkinson calculates it, in selling a new franchise. So, he figures that he has $19,615 left to cover overhead and indirect expenses—plenty, he and LeRoy thought, until they looked at the payment schedule.

Getting the contract signed probably takes 60 days. They don't get their $18,500 until then. The franchisee has 90 days to find a site and Associated Video Hut has 60 more days to approve it—both of which must happen before the kiosk gets purchased and the franchisor pockets the other $5,000. So it turns out that getting the whole $23,500 could take as long as nine months from initial contact to final setup. The company could find itself that far behind on cash. "That was our one mistake," Atkinson says, "and we recognized it right away." They are currently selling, again through their own efforts, $1 million in five-year, 12 3/4% debentures to cover the shortfall.

When kiosks come on-stream, franchisees will pay a weekly royalty of 7% of gross revenues—toward the high side—plus corporate and national advertising fees that come to another 1%. But Atkinson doesn't expect to begin seeing substantial cash from franchise operations much before the end of this year.

Actual cash flow for the nascent company is as unpredictable in the near term as are the number of franchise sales. One large deal—such as one recently negotiated with a Burger King franchisor who wants to combine drive-through burgers with drive-through movies—pushes the numbers around dramatically. But by ensuring that every direct cost of a franchise sale is balanced by an equal or larger payment from the franchisee, Atkinson believes that he'll avoid selling the company poor—a common error among new franchisors.

As businessmen, LeRoy and Atkinson profess to believe their own projections, but they can't completely shake a personal incredulity. "We keep asking ourselves," says LeRoy, "what are we missing? It's too simple." Atkinson's tendency is to complicate plans—to make the stores larger, to carry more products. The kiosks will sell microwave popcorn, blank videotapes, and possibly VCR head cleaners. But LeRoy keeps leading them back to the basics to work out the bugs. For weeks they engaged in role-playing. They'd get friends or their wives into the office around a conference table and go through simulated rental procedures over and over again. Could they handle peak-hour Friday and Saturday traffic? Cutting average transaction times to as little as two minutes would help, and so would offering plenty of the hottest titles. "People don't mind waiting in their cars," Atkinson claims, "if they know that at the end of the line they're going to get what they want." Keeping franchisees loyal to the system would be another challenge. To meet it the founders devised a program that would provide ad slicks, movie listings for insertion in local papers, four-color newsletters that franchisees could distribute to patrons, and three new radio spots every quarter.

For every issue the role-playing and questioning raised, the partners found a comfortable answer—and the concept, they say, still felt right.

Initially, LeRoy and Atkinson thought it would be logical to develop their franchises by geographical regions, beginning with the Northeast, then the Midwest. But they changed their strategy to pursue an immediate national selling campaign when it became clear that there was no advantage—no economies of scale, for instance—in growing progressively from one area to the next contiguous one.

In marketing franchises, they're not ignoring the individual who might want to buy a single kiosk, but they want to concentrate on potential buyers interested in 3 or more units. Their first sale was 15 units to an investor group in Rochester. They're also thinking that existing mom-and-pop operations interested in expansion may be good sales targets. After all, LeRoy says, someone who is already in the business can open three or four Video's 1st kiosks for the price of a single new conventional store.

There's nothing in the Video's 1st concept—as even the two founders admit—that other people haven't thought of before. LeRoy and Atkinson have lost track of the number of people who have told them they already had the idea for doing drive-through video rentals. "Sure," says Atkinson, "other people think of things. The difference is that Todd and I do them."

WHAT THE EXPERTS SAY

"If you told me you'd make a good profit at a competitive price and a better one at a higher price, OK. But when competitive pricing would knock out your total profit margin, that's troubling."

—*Bill Lanphear*

ANALYSTS

IRA MAYER AND PAUL SWEETING
Editors of "Video Marketing Newsletter," published in Los Angeles

When people ask us about going into video retail, we tell them, I'm afraid, that the time is past. The industry has peaked. There is already a lot of shakeout. Video-rental income will be essentially flat for the next two or three years, and the number of retail video stores has stabilized. There is less and less of an aftermarket for used tapes, which Video's 1st is counting on being able to sell.

Obviously, Video's 1st thinks differently, but if we were advising investors, we'd say no way—steer real clear. The time is over for this sort of thing.

The idea that customers aren't sensitive to price—that they care more about convenience and about getting exactly the tape they want—has always been a nice theory, but history doesn't substantiate it. The pricing of rentals responds to local competition. And it's a cutthroat market. One dollar is not uncommon, compared with Video's 1st $2.95. It sounds nice that people would pay a premium for convenience or mystique, but people have tried it, and it hasn't worked.

They should give up on the idea of being national. Try to grow market by market instead. Go into a market that isn't oversaturated with existing video retailers and blanket it with kiosks, then concentrate advertising and promotional efforts in that market. Get the most bang for the buck. Don't spread yourself too thin for the sake of national ambition.

Look, it's not just that the concept is flawed. It's also the fact that the market isn't ripe anymore—it's mature. We think the window has closed for video retailing.

COMPETITOR

TROY COOPER
Executive vice-president of National Video Inc., a Portland, Ore.-based chain of 580 franchised video stores

I think the concept has some validity, but implementation is going to be much more difficult than they think. They haven't discovered something by magic that no one else has seen. It's a strategy we've thought hard about. But there are problems.

One is that they really underestimated their reinvestment in video-cassettes each month. They expect to do 116 rentals per day, or 3,480 per month. On a minimum inventory of 300 cassettes, which is what the *pro forma* assumes, that's an average of $11^1/2$ rentals per cassette per month. Now this turn rate *is* possible. In our experience, the turn on new releases can be pretty high for the first 30 days—maybe as high as 20 rentals for a particular cassette. But it drops dramatically, to about 8 rentals, over the next 30 days, as the title loses its gleam. And in the third month the turn falls to the norm of 2 or 3 rentals per cassette per month.

Therefore, to average 10 or 11 turns a month over the life of a title, you can't keep it more than 90 days. After that the average drops, and Video's 1st wouldn't meet its revenue needs. So, they have to renew their entire inventory every three months (actually, they'd have to keep inventory fresh by bringing in a third of the total, 100 new tapes, each month while dumping the 100 oldest ones). The problem is those 100 tapes would cost—studios are increasing their prices, not decreasing them—anywhere from $65 to $70 wholesale. That means they would have to reinvest $6,500 to $7,000 a month to keep their inventory fresh—more than twice what they've figured. In fact, it puts them in a negative cash flow. If they really do buy 55 tapes a month, as they say, then they'll have to keep each one for almost six months before the 300-tape inventory is renewed, and that won't work. They wouldn't be carrying the hits, as they claim.

The second problem is that video traffic comes in bunches: 70% of your business takes place on Friday, Saturday, and Sunday, and even that 70% is generally crammed into a few peak hours during each of those days. Now if you have long lines of cars during these peak periods, you're going to discourage people from even lining up. When I go to a McDonald's, for instance, and see six or seven cars in front of me, I just keep going. And I think that's what's going to happen. In a regular store, you might combat the traffic from that peak rush by opening three or four terminals. Also, inside a store customers can browse until they see the line lessen a little—there are things for them to do. And they don't see the line until they get into the store in the first place. The difference in Video's 1st's case is that their customers are going to see the line before they ever turn into the parking lot.

Those are the two biggest weaknesses of the concept: The first means that expenses will be much greater than what they're anticipating, and the second means revenues may be less than what they're anticipating because they can't generate enough rentals during Video's 1st's peak periods.

Will they make it? My gut feeling is no.

But I'll certainly watch them, and watch with interest. And if they *do* make it, then the threat is exactly what they mentioned in the beginning: Anybody can reproduce it. I don't think 12 to 18 months lead time is anything. There will be lots of other people jumping in with the same concept.

FINANCIER

BILL LANPHEAR

Partner in The Early Stages Co., a San Francisco venture capital firm specializing in consumer products and retailing

Would this work as a prospective venture capital investment? Absolutely not. There are two reasons: the inexperience of the founders in their field, and the unlikelihood of building value for shareholders. These are low-volume outlets. It takes more than 7 of them to make a million dollars of sales for the system—nearly 400 of these to make $50 million. That starts to get into lots of problems in terms of controlling that big a network. And of course, even those numbers won't yield much to the *franchisor*, who gets only a small cut of the system's take.

Also, look at their pricing: It's high end. Their projections show that they can totally wipe out profitability if the retail price drops by a third. They're supposing that convenience and multiple copies of the current movies will cause people to shop there instead of getting the movie through some more difficult process at a lower price—a risky supposition. They could fall to break-even by a drop in volume *or* by not being able to maintain their price level, or any combination of those things. Whatever the average price now is—say $2 or $1.99—it isn't stable. It might drop by a dollar. They probably now have, and will continue to have, competitors who are not primarily in the business of renting tapes, and who'll undercut. I'm worried about a concept that depends for all its profitability on a pricing differential. If you said to me that it makes a good profit at a competitive price and a better one at a higher price, so that if they had to be competitive it wouldn't put them out of business, OK. But when it knocks out the total profit margin, that's troubling.

Here's what I would recommend to them:

(1) Invest in providing excellent franchise operating benefits—tape-resale programs, buying programs, signage, marketing tools, kiosk design—so these stores rise above others in the market and we implement better.

(2) Don't defer your own rewards too long; maybe you can make a nice living for a while. Think in terms of getting your rewards in the next two years because the business may not be something you can sell for millions of dollars down the road.

Will you find them in the telephone directory two years from now? I'd say there's a reasonable chance of that. My crystal ball says they'll be around for two and a half years, then I get nervous.

CONSULTANT

ARTHUR GRUEN

Cofounder of Wilkofsky Gruen Associates Inc., a New York City firm specializing in the entertainment industry

In a very competitive market, they're proposing to carve out a nice little niche for themselves. I think their prices are fine, because people *will* pay a reasonable premium for convenience. Their concept makes perfect sense, at least for them as franchisor.

What's not clear, however is what they're going to do for potential franchisees that an individual entrepreneur, acting on his own, couldn't do for himself. Anyone can put up a kiosk and stock it with tapes, just like anyone can cook a hamburger. But having the McDonald's name on your hamburger stand makes it a more valuable asset. What does Associated Video Hut propose to do to add value to the Video's 1st name—which is the main thing they can do for franchisees? If they don't build an identification in the public's mind between product and logo, then they've got nothing to sell.

BARRY ROSENBLATT

President and CEO of Video Library Inc., a chain of 42 company-owned video stores, all in San Diego

I think that in order to do the revenues they need, the lines will be too long. We do 15% of *weekly* rentals in four hours on Saturday afternoon. Using their numbers, they'd be handling during that peak period about 30 to 35 customers per hour. Can you take care of that much business, through a window, without creating massive lines that will turn your customer off? When I think of how long it will take to do a transaction, and when I think about how customers would have to line up to *return* the movies, too, I just can't see it. No one can take care of people that fast.

And there sure *are* reasons to grow from one area into another instead of going national immediately: You've got to handle these things, you've got to take care of them. Franchisees need to be serviced very, very well, or they won't survive—or, even if they do survive, they'll stop paying you royalties, because they'll think you don't deserve them.

ROOMS WITH A VIEW

The "bed-and-breakfast" concept goes urban

BY ROBERT A. MAMIS

I f innkeeping is a cottage industry designed to keep retired folk off the streets, it comes as no surprise that many practitioners earn less than $1,000 a year. But the payoff need not be as puny as it sounds. Such statistics are skewed by humble enterprises called homestays—up-country households that simply rent a room down the hall for a few extra dollars—and by larger operations that involve tax deals, in which case the idea is *not* to showcase the bottom line.

Mom, Pop, and shelters aside, there's something fiscally compelling to the fact that in some inns a long-gone aunt's overstuffed bedroom fetches upward of $325 a night, while the sleek bedroom The Hyatt Regency just built doesn't. Decent profit can be made here, else why has the number of inns increased sharply in the past decade—especially in such cosmopolitan areas as San Francisco, which now lists more

Cofounders Charles and Ann Hillestad preparing for guests at the Queen Anne Inn

than 100? And why would the encroachment of alternatives with atmosphere have spurred hotels to put in personalized "club" floors?

For Charles and Ann Hillestad, a far-from-retired couple in their forties, the 10-room bed-and-breakfast they just launched in Denver may not speed financial independence, but at least it seems they have a crack at it down the road. And starting an inn resolved two ancillary problems: providing a change for Ann, who had been working at the same salaried job for 11 years (Charles elected to remain gainfully employed as an attorney), and getting rid of a neighborhood eyesore.

The eyesore—a ramshackle Victorian that cost them $150,000 in early 1986—has been metamorphosed into the gracious Queen Anne Inn, which opened in January 1987. Queen Anne Inn Ltd. is expected to be profitable within three years, by which time, the plan goes, its occupancy rate will have reached 80%. Maybe so, but the occupancy rate of hotels in downturning Denver is not even 50%, which means that to enjoy a modest income, the Hillestads' three-story hostelry will have to stay nearly twice as full as its higher-rising competitors.

There would be no such contest had not the Hillestads been determined to possess the unreconstructed hulk that sat a few feet from their own modernized home, deflating values on what was otherwise a reviving residential street a cobblestone's throw from the commercial center of the city. After maneuvering their recalcitrant neighbor into selling (see box, "Here Comes the Neighborhood," page 23) essentially the Hillestads' choices were: (1) to raze all 6,000 square feet and enjoy instant appreciation of the house next door (too little return on investment); (2) repair it and resell it as a single home (who needs 10 bedrooms?); (3) turn it into condos (too costly). Or they could (4) convert it into an inn, serve a free breakfast, meet some interesting folks, and have some fun.

Sure enough, within two years, they were having so much fun that even the guests themselves were envious. "A bed-and-breakfast looks so simple, I could do it; I love company and I like to cook," observers often remarked. To which Charles Hillestad, the B and B's de facto chief executive officer, would remark back: "It *is* fun, but a way to escape the rat race it isn't." By then, he had learned enough the hard way to teach a course on inn-starting at Colorado Free University. "This is a tough business," he disabuses dreamers. "It's terribly hour-intensive and you can burn out quickly. Zoning, location, construction, financing, contracts are complicated issues. Undercapitalization is death."

Still, if an inn is well financed, well constructed, well zoned, well situated, et al, it can ensure long-term security for its owners; a particularly noteworthy inn may even bring them a measure of prominence, as

THE COMPANY:
Queen Anne Inn
Ltd., Denver

THE CONCEPT:
An upmarket bed-
and-breakfast inn,
historically authen-
tic, for business
travelers and
tourists in the city.
Significant tax bene-
fits from renovation
investment

PROJECTIONS:
Third-year revenues
of $248,200 at
80% occupancy,
with all potential
profits intentionally
drained into man-
agement salary

HURDLES:
Achieving 80%
occupancy in a
market currently
averaging less than
50%; pleasing both
business and vaca-
tion customers;
surviving long hours
despite small
financial reward

the Queen Anne already has. And the outgo-
ing Hillestads enjoy having company drop in
unexpectedly. "Our guests tend to be educated, monied, adventuresome, well traveled,
articulate, and polite," boasts Ann. "And we
don't have to bolt everything down." Then
there are hidden benefits, such as tax write-
offs for stays at swank establishments to
research how others do it. And, Hillestad
estimates, his own experience as a real estate
lawyer is advertised by the Queen Anne's
just being there. "Running an inn is not
something you're going to make a fortune
at," he acknowledges. "On the other hand,
you're not out there lifting crates."

The Hillestads' concept is to place their
entry into the topmost stratum of full-
fledged bed-and-breakfasts, as measured by
elegance and sophistication. Fastidiously
redone but not materially altered (its intri-
cately carved banisters, for example, have
been stripped and restored), the structure is
clearly more enchanting now than when
originally built, in 1879. In its high-ceilinged
parlor, sherry is available in the afternoon
and a cold (for reasons to be described
shortly) breakfast served in the morning.
Each of the TV- and telephone-free bedrooms has its own private, modern bath and
its own distinctive homelike decor. "We
want it to feel as if we actually live there,"
explain the Hillestads, who actually don't.

In one bedroom, a 360-degree trompe l'oeil of aspen trees make
occupants feel as if they're camping in the wilds—at $84 a night.
Another sports a sunken tub in the middle of the floor. Yet another, a
mirrored Murphy bed. It was such recherché touches that inspired *Bridal
Guide* magazine to name the Queen Anne one of the country's 10 best
wedding-night hotels. "We're selling illusion and escapism," recognize
its hosts, who deliver breakfast in bed, arrange for horse-drawn car-
riages, and lavish champagne on celebrating couples. So far, about a
third of the inn's customers have been urban romantics—locals kindling
or rekindling togetherness. Not casting their lot entirely with hearts and

flowers, however, the Hillestads have put a phone jack and writing desk in every room for businesspeople who have work to do.

And businesspeople are the direction toward which significant growth lies. "We will be able to increase business traffic with no effort on our part at all," Hillestad predicts—a notion sparked when some traveling accountants took lodging there three days a week for several months running. The CPA troupe reported having enjoyed the homey accommodations, even if, like all guests, they weren't allowed to smoke, keep children, or entertain pets. Another indication that the occupancy rate may escape rapidly from its loss-inducing average of 35% in the last quarter of 1987 comes from the number of unsolicited repeat guests and referrals, which in 1987 constituted about one-third of bookings. That number can redouble indefinitely, the Hillestads foresee, because "the rooms are so varied that people come back to try a different one of ours, rather than go to the competition."

At 60% occupancy, there would still be an operating loss, the Hillestads understand, but at least the cash flow would be such that "our lenders would be happy." At 80%, the inn is supposed to show a relatively good profit. Despite the inn industry's growth, there are few hard facts to go on, mainly because innkeepers keep their books very private and very informal. Some of Hillestad's projections were extrapolated from a 1983 study of California inns conducted by an assistant professor of hotel management. "The wise bed-and-breakfast investor will prefer a 6- to 10-room property located in a city," the survey concluded. "This, in conjunction with room rates of at least $50 per night, should result in a healthy occupancy." One odd pattern was noted: the costlier the rooms, the *higher* their occupancy. Sheer priciness, apparently, is perceived to endorse a level of chic worth paying up for.

As new kid on the block, the Queen Anne couldn't risk being so presumptuous. To arrive at a price schedule, "basically what I did is

THE FOUNDERS

Charles Hillestad
cofounder and CEO

Age: 42

Still working full-time as lawyer with McGuire, Cornwell & Blakey, specializing in property law and historic preservation . . . has been practicing law in Denver since 1972 . . . J.D., University of Michigan Law School, B.A., University of Oregon

Ann Hillestad
cofounder and
general manager

Age: 41

Worked 11 years with The Nature Conservancy, a Virginia-based environmental nonprofit corporation . . . served as an administrative assistant there . . . has lived in Denver since 1969

FINANCIALS

QUEEN ANNE INN OPERATING STATEMENT

	Actual Calendar year 1987	Projected Calendar year 1989
SALES		
Room income (average $85/room)	$86,136	$248,200
Occupancy rate	28%	80%
COST OF SALES		
Food (breakfasts)	(4,673)	
Non–real estate taxes	(7,216)	
Room supplies, cleaning, & flowers	(5,382)	
Referrals & fees	(1,249)	
Repairs	(1,970)	
Telephone	(2,692)	
Miscellaneous	(2,507)	
TOTAL COST OF SALES	**(25,689)**	**(81,760)**
Cost per room let	25.21	28.00
GROSS PROFIT	**60,447**	**166,440**
GENERAL EXPENSES		
Hourly wages & related	(13,811)	
Management wages		
Ann (2,500 hours)	0*	
Charles (500 hours)	0	
Utilities	(3,495)	
Insurance	(4,000)	
Advertising & promotions	(12,800)	
Principal & interest payments	(32,155)	
Miscellaneous	(2,443)	
Total general expenses	(68,704)	(100,000)*
NET INCOME BEFORE DEPRECIATION	**(8,257)**	**66,440**
Depreciation	(22,774)	(22,774)
Building (19,930/year)		
Furniture (2,844/year)		
NET INCOME (LOSS)	**(31,031)**	**43,666***

* Note: Income above break-even will go to Ann Hillestad as salary.

20

QUEEN ANNE INN: TABLE OF CAPITAL SOURCES AND USES

SOURCES

Cash invested by Hillestads	30,000
Cash invested by silent partner	50,000
Bank construction loan	200,000
Bank mortgage loan	250,000*
City of Denver loan	70,000
Note from Hillestads	100,000
Note from seller of real estate	15,000
TOTAL SOURCES	**715,000**

USES

Acquire real estate	150,000
Real estate closing fees & broker commission	10,000
Construction	255,000
Pay off construction loan	200,000*
Acquire furnishings, linens, etc.	50,000
Working capital	50,000
TOTAL USES	**715,000**

*Note: Mortgage loan was used to pay off construction loan. Bank debt stands at $250,000. Queen Anne Inn owes $100,000 to Hillestads personally (though this obligation currently is not being serviced). Total long-term debt: $435,000 ($335,000 is being serviced).

take a look at the most expensive hotels in downtown Denver," says Hillestad. "Even if I'm better than those hotels, no one is going to believe it, so our price structure was set lower than theirs." Downtown singles range from a midweek high of $128 to $310 at The Hyatt Regency to a median of $95 to $135 at The Burnsley to a low of $59 to $81 at Holiday Inn. A single at the Queen Anne goes for $54 to $89; a double is a flat $10 more. "We're about the same as Holiday Inn," Hillestad points out, "but look what you get—an 1879 mansion, sherry, breakfast, music, lights on a rheostat, and a refrigerator stocked with free soda."

Close to downtown in a registered historic district, the inn's strongest marketing advantage is location, location, location. That's turf from which competing B and Bs can be held at bay. Three others that have now opened in Denver are farther out of town. "We got in at a time when real estate was depressed," Hillestad says. "Our acquisition of the property and even of the furniture allowed us to come up with good pricing. Others won't be able to do that; their basis will be higher than ours if they want an inn of similar quality."

If Denver's commercial hotels up their prices, the sophisticated Queen Anne will up its own, Hillestad promises. But at the higher prices, will romantics swallow granola and yogurt as all that sophisticated? Not to worry; in a couple of years the city intends to build a convention center only seven blocks away, "and that's just fine with us," say the Hillestads. At about that time, they will consider acquiring nearby properties and forging the resultant compound into a conference facility of their own.

Even now there are revenue enhancers. A business group or wedding party can hire the entire premises at $650 a day, or the downstairs function rooms at $85 an hour. Zoning allows a small retail adjunct— thus a gift shop. So what if space is sorely limited, muses Hillestad; "I can think of a way around that: sell paintings on the walls."

However promising the premise, it came as a jolt to its author that more than five dozen regional lenders and virtually every municipal regulatory agency didn't stand up and cheer. Armed with an outside business appraisal that claimed the property would be worth $452,000 when fully rehabilitated—more than twice as much in equity than the loan he sought—Hillestad began shopping for the presumedly worriless financier. But bank after bank turned him down: There was no precedent for so ambitious a bed-and-breakfast in Denver, they explained, and Hillestad had no track record in hotel management. Soon he was cold-calling the *Yellow Pages*. "I made enough money as an attorney to pay off the loan if not a single person ever walked through the door," recalls the still-incredulous Hillestad. "My credit rating was perfect. I showed that I could bring in a bed-and-breakfast for lower prices per room than a motel, that my labor was much less intensive than a hotel. Some agreed to loan me the money if I would do an office building or an apartment house—which would have sat vacant for two years in this economy."

At last he happened on a bank that was itself a start-up. Its sympathetic officers agreed to spot him $200,000 for construction—but not a dollar more. All told, Hillestad figured he needed a good $370,000— $150,000 to pay for the house, $10,000 for closing and broker fees, and maybe $210,000 for construction. What with his own $30,000, plus a $70,000 redevelopment loan from the city of Denver and the $200,000 from the bank, the total still fell $70,000 short.

To bridge the gap, Hillestad was forced to take on a partner. Luckily, the 1986 Tax Reform Act turned such rehab projects as the Queen Anne into outstanding shelters, inasmuch as the only remaining investment tax credit applies to restoring a certified historic structure or

How the house was bought

After years of unsuccessfully trying to get its owner to fix up the unsightly relic next door, the Hillestads decided their only hope of aesthetic—not to mention property-value—salvation was buying it themselves. But the owner refused to sell—at least to them. The "irascible so-and-so didn't like us," says Charles Hillestad. "He was opposed to everything."

So he set up a corporation using a sister-in-law's address in Arizona and called it Country Inns, Colorado Division Inc. Then he contracted with a local broker to represent the corporation's interest. "Don't tell any lies," he instructed the broker, "but don't volunteer anything, either." Duly impressed by the corporate name, the neighbor not only agreed to sell without inquiring as to the corporation's stockholders—all of them Hillestad, as it happened—but agreed to carry a $15,000 note to seal the deal. No sooner did Country Inns purchase the property than it resold it (at the obligatory small profit) to Queen Anne Inn Ltd., its present owner. "The $150,000 was probably a bit more than it was worth," says Hillestad, who paid a mere $12,500 for his own house next door back in 1975. "But I wanted him out. I went to the neighbors and said, `You have a choice. I know you don't want commercial intrusion; but the choice is Ma and Pa Kettle, or me.'"

a building in a historic district. Dangling that as a lure, Hillestad found an investor who was willing to put in $50,000 in return for being able to tap the inn's operating losses and tax credits. He went ahead and purchased the property for $160,000, fees included. The partnership (see box, "Financials," page 21) put in $145,000, and the seller—an accommodating guy after all—agreed to carry a three-year note for $15,000. That left $205,000 for construction—just enough to go ahead.

To gain the best mutual tax advantage, the outside investor was allotted 70% and our man only 30% interest in the inn. But that imbalance is destined to disappear when Hillestad exercises the option he holds to buy out the co-owner in five years for about $5,000. The passive partner will have had no complaints: reaping some $50,000 in ITCs that can be subtracted directly from federal taxes dollar for dollar, plus a major share of operating losses, he will have earned around 20% annually, after taxes. Nor does Hillestad have complaints: "I took in $50,000 in cash, gave away some ITCs I couldn't use, and I get rid of him in five years. It works out slickly all the way around." Aggressive accounting is sure to keep it that way, pumping negative figures through as needed. "Even if we started rolling in the dough," Hillestad calculates, "Ann could siphon it off in salary." Ann's 1987 wages as 84-hours-a-week general manager: $0.

Flush with capital, Hillestad assumed the officials at City Hall would roll out red carpets, for not only were the Hillestads turning a dilapidated firetrap into an inner-city showpiece, but they were also creating new jobs and would bring in tourist dollars. Instead, City Hall strewed the path with carpet tacks.

Because being held to the same criteria as a full-blown hotel would have required more acreage and rebuilding, Hillestad had to plead for zoning and building concessions. Unless each potential code violation could be identified and resolved early on—the proposed inn had some 30 of them—"you could go through your construction loan and in the end be faced with the prospect of forking over a huge sum of additional money to take care of whatever the building department says was needed for it to issue a certificate of occupancy," Hillestad says. At that stage, he would have been an automatic foreclosure, because the short-term construction loan would be due and no long-term lender would take over the financing without said certificate.

So much for bed; now for breakfast. The next den of bureaucracy proposed that since a bed-and-breakfast inn charged for rooms, by its own definition it was also charging for food. In which case *cooking* that food would necessitate a seven-foot steel sink with three washbasins, along with plastic kitchen walls. Not to be outdone, the division of wastewater management weighed in with demands for a 300-gallon grease trap. "You've got to have all that if you're going to serve even coffee," it insisted. "I'll serve coffee in paper cups," retorted Hillestad. "Well, how are you going to wash the pot?" "Look," he conceded, "the stuff you want me to put in is hideously ugly, and I won't do it. So I'll serve a breakfast in which nothing is cooked."

Six months behind schedule, approval was granted—including the OK to pour coffee in china cups. Although construction costs rose some $50,000 over budget, they could have been under by just as much had not the Hillestads decided to make hay while the sun shone through the studs. In one expensive but hidden improvement, interior as well as exterior walls were stuffed with insulation because "we never liked staying in places where you could hear the people in the next room." As a bonus, 1987's heat and air-conditioning costs quietly added up to a paltry $3,500. Furnishings, linens, and similar accoutrements took another $50,000. In all, opening the Queen Anne's doors required $100,000 more than Hillestad's budgeted $370,000. Which meant that some debt restructuring was in order.

The partnership retired its six-month $200,000 construction loan with a mortgage loan of $250,000 on the newly renovated property. Amortized over 30 years, the mortgage floats at market rates and is due in five years, at which time Hillestad hopes to roll it over for an even larger amount. The $50,000 difference between the mortgage and construction loans made up part of the budget shortfall. To cover the rest, as well as provide working capital to handle operating losses, a line of credit on the Hillestads' homestead next door has been tapped for $100,000 and reloaned to the partnership. The unsecured three-year note from the seller for $15,000 at 10% remains outstanding, but it is a debt of Country Inns, Colorado Division Inc., not of the partnership (see box, "Financials," page 21).

One significant expense not budgeted for was attorney's fees. For nursing business affairs that far, the cost of an attorney would have been about $30,000. It wasn't needed, of course, since Hillestad hired himself for free. And he was worth every hypothetical penny, for no sooner had the inn opened than an inspector stopped by for a serious look. "If we hadn't gone through the process," Hillestad suspects, "we would have been shut down and left with half a million dollars in expenses and nothing coming in."

On March 1, 1987, in a ceremony attended by the mayor himself, all 10 beds-with-cold-breakfasts of the Queen Anne Inn were offered unto commerce.

The inn's maiden year inspired no fewer than 40 stories in regional and national publications. The articles contributed to raising occupancy rates from 7% in the first quarter to 35% by December 31—and spared Hillestad unexpected trouble. "I initially thought we would just go out there and advertise," he admits. "It came as a shock that one-sixth of a page in *Sunset* alone cost $9,000." Given a first-year budget of $8,200 for the combination of advertising *and* phones, the big blitz launch was out. In all of '87, Queen Anne Inn bought only four one-sixth-page ads in a regional weekly handout, nine radio spots on local FM, and one small display ad each in an Aspen and a Vail weekly newspaper. At that, $12,800 was spent on advertising, most going toward a supply of brochures.

During 1987, 1,019 rooms were rented at an average gross of $85 each. However, the gross gets squeezed by commissions paid to reservation services, an important marketing component of the industry that charges as much as one-fifth of the amount received, plus annual fees. Queen Anne's pricing has a 10% commission built in, claims Hillestad. Local taxes eat up 11.8% more, credit-card companies take another 3% or 4%. And paid full-time help is to be added to free up Ann.

In 1987 the books of Queen Anne Inn Ltd. painted one-year-old Queen Anne's portrait in deep tones of red—as expected. Anyone in the inn business will admit it requires a good three years, maybe more, to ramp up to speed. Which means that not only do you need enough capital to open the doors, but enough cushion to absorb a string of operating losses until cash flow breaks into the black. Meanwhile, we should all have the partner's tax advantage.

"Even in an optimistic scenario, the result of all this risk, effort, and invested money is that they bought Ann a chance to earn $6 an hour. Great."

— *Thomas Scannapieco*

DEVELOPER

THOMAS SCANNAPIECO
President of Historical Developers of Pennsylvania (#56 on the 1987 Inc. *500), expert in historic rehabilitation*

I'm afraid the tax planning is seriously flawed. Look at the preexisting agreement whereby a person who makes a $50,000 investment agrees to sell his interest five years later for about $5,000. I think the IRS could totally disallow an option like that, wiping out the ITCs *and* the operating losses taken by the partner, because the deal could be classified as an investment made only for tax benefit.

Even if he does achieve 80% occupancy—a pretty optimistic goal—some of the numbers don't add up. He shows a $43,666 third-year net profit that goes to Ann as salary; at an 84-hour week that's $10 an hour. With 50-hour weeks, it's $17 an hour. But that's not the whole story. If his intention is to pay the "profit" to his wife then he also has to pay payroll taxes, and that cuts the payout by about 20%, or $8,700. But even before *that*, you have to take into account the $100,000 letter of credit that Hillestad seems to have dismissed.

Maybe in his mind he considers that an equity investment, but if it's an equity investment, then before I started counting the money that my wife's earning I would look at the opportunity cost. He could have earned over $10,000 a year passively just by putting that amount of money in an account. And if he borrowed the money as he said he did, then before he computes her salary, he'd better look at the interest cost on $100,000. So now you take that $43,666 "profit" and reduce that by the interest on the letter of credit—which is another, say, $10,000 at 10%—and *then* you reduce the net further by payroll taxes. The bottom line is that, even in an optimistic scenario of 80% occupancy, the result of all this risk, effort, and invested money is that he bought Ann the chance to earn $6 an hour. Great.

The chance that this property is going to appreciate so that they'll recognize a significant capital gain when they sell it is much less than if it were an economic property. If it were an apartment building, a reasonable person would buy it in 10 years at an appreciated value. In this scenario, a reasonable person would not. It's not a business. And his whole tone realizes that—it's apologetic.

The first step Hillestad needs to take is to say that he's going to make this a profitable business. He's got to give up on his apology that this is only intended to be a hobby. He's got to get rid of that attitude. And then he's got to put in some very hard work to come up with a business plan that's credible and that solves some of his problems. I'm sure that this *could* become a business.

OPERATOR

JACK HIRST
Founder of 1811 House, an inn in Manchester Village, Vt.

They need to raise their prices. It's true that the costlier the room, the higher the occupancy. At $54 to $89, as opposed to $128 to $310 at The Hyatt Regency, I think the Queen Anne is way low. He's tried to slightly underprice Holiday Inn, and that's a mistake.

People want something other than a Holiday Inn. They want atmosphere and ambience, and they're willing to pay for it. Eighty-percent occupancy is a wow figure, no doubt about that, but it's reachable. I think he could easily do better occupancy than the hotels.

He should get himself into the inn-listing books, which are free, and that would fill him on the weekends. He should save the $12,000 he spent on advertising because you can't effectively sell rooms that way. And to fill rooms during the week, he should pound the pavements trying to make prearrangements with local businesses, providing a discount for visitors they lodged with him.

With enough publicity he could do very well.

OBSERVER

SARAH SONKE
Director of the American Bed-and-Breakfast Association, Crofton, Md.

There are almost 4,000 commercial inn properties of this type operating in the United States. Only 5, that we're aware of, have an occupancy rate of 80%. The average occupancy for a successful inn in a metropolitan area is 60%, which would not be profitable for the Queen Anne.

I simply can't be convinced that occupancy will reach 80% in the third year. When I checked with members [of the American Bed-and-Breakfast Association running similar inns] they all immediately scoffed at the figure—one said occupancy wouldn't get that high unless the Olympics and the Pope both came to town at the same time.

The inn should decide on its image: Is it catering to romantic getaways or business clients? Occupancy during weekdays will tend to be business travelers, who need special services in order not to disrupt their schedules. The idea that "we will be able to increase business traffic with no effort on our part at all" is simply naïve.

It might be wise to look at where the profit is and hit that first, and then maybe diversify a little bit later.

I don't think this is going to work—but if it's going to have a chance, somebody needs to work on marketing.

OPERATOR

CARL A. GLASSMAN

Cofounder with his wife, Nadine, of The Wedgwood Inn of New Hope, New Hope, Pa.; also teaches at the Hotel and Restaurant Institute of Bucks County College, in Newtown, Pa.

In innkeeping there are three ways to make money. One, the tax-shelter nature of the business. Two, the operating profits if it is successful. Three, the capital gains: If you buy in a strong tourist-related or corporate-related market, the property will appreciate—probably faster than it would as a residential property. The Queen Anne is not apt to make it in the last two.

An inn isn't mature until it's in its fifth year. It's highly unrealistic to jump from 28% to 80% in less than three years, because you're tied to building your own client base. It takes two years or more just to get listed in the travel books. And even though the inn is essentially downtown, it's really out of the mainstream; travel agents have never heard of it, there are no big signs, no one drives by. They're projecting to be 30 points above the average for Denver. And Denver is 10 points below the national hotel average, so the math doesn't make it. They also don't have the advertising budget capable of producing those numbers. They've been relying on chance. Right now they're cute and cuddly, but when they come into adolescence they won't get as much press.

Less than 5% of business travelers are interested in this type of lodging. If the company put them on the road, they want to take advantage of it. Most want to stay in a $150 Hyatt and have all the amenities right there so they can bill them to their room and it goes right to the corporate account.

In the end, you have to conclude they'll never make it big unless they expand. Eight to 12 rooms is good at an initial stage. Then there is a step to 14 to 18 rooms. Then to more than 24, when you become a small luxury hotel—that's when you get some economies of scale. That's where the money is, and the support staff to free *you* up.

But the cash flow from the operation won't enable the business to expand. They'll need an injection of new capital. They may have to borrow it. But then I'm not sure they'll be able to retire, say, a $400,000 loan out of cash flow. It may come down to their own faith in the business and their willingness to lend personal monies at low interest to the corporation, which they can then set up to be paid back in 10 years or so.

If the inn doesn't do as well as anticipated, they could sell their house next door and move into the inn. In an owner-occupied inn, even if you net only $10,000, it's highly disposable income. Food, heat, light, electricity, shelter, maybe 90% of your car is written off. So the money you do draw out you can use for luxury items.

One more thing: Visitors don't come to inns for the museum effect. They come as much to see the innkeeper as they do the inn. I didn't get a feeling that Charles was there at all; and Ann has to be careful not to burn out at this rate. The day-to-day operations of an inn aren't intellectually stimulating, quite frankly. They have their rewards, but after five years, how many times can you tell someone how you got into innkeeping and what cloth you used to cover that chair?

ANALYST

BARBARA NOTARIUS

Editor of Bed & Breakfast News; *seminar organizer, Croton-on-Hudson, N.Y.*

I don't think they're going to reach 80% occupancy. They're building a reputation as this wonderful, romantic, touristy place, but remember, there's very little tourism directly related to Denver. What people do is fly into Denver, rent a car, and leave.

If they really do appeal to the wedding crowd and the people who want to get away for a romantic escape, they're going to fill up on the weekends. But in order to bring yourself up to 80% occupancy, you've got to produce weekday business. Putting a telephone jack and a desk in a room is not enough to attract the kind of business clientele that they're pushing for, because they're looking for an upscale market. And unfortunately a place that doesn't have a commercial kitchen or a liquor license is not going to appeal to the broad segment of the business market. I think the lack of a kitchen is going to present real problems in terms of growth.

It's more important for him to raise their revenues right now, because he can do that more easily than he can raise his occupancy rates. To kill himself for 80% occupancy, when he could raise his room rate by $5, get 70% occupancy, and still do as well, is unwise.

To me, this is an extremely risky venture. If I were Hillestad, I would want to get tied into the airlines; I'd commit, say, four or five rooms every single day of the week to an airline, and have a kind of package in which people fly into Denver as a stopping-off place—on their way to a ski area, on their way to the Air Force Academy, on their way to the hiking in the national parks—and get a night at the inn as a cooperative venture. That would be a way to get those rooms filled.

He's set a big, big job for his wife. I think people make a mistake when they don't consider their time worth something. You can keep up the enthusiasm for only so long without seeing some real money come in.

THE MONEY GAME

*Can Blackstone Bank succeed
by focusing on markets other lenders ignore?*

BY JOSEPH P. KAHN

In 1986, Roxbury, a predominantly black district of Boston, attempted an unusual ploy. The community proposed to secede from the city proper and reincorporate itself under the name Mandela (after South African dissidents Nelson and Winnie Mandela). As a piece of political strategy, the referendum fizzled; it was soundly defeated at the polls. As a symbol of community frustration, however, the movement was significant. In many of Greater Boston's poorer, more ethnically insulated neighborhoods, people heard the news about their region's booming economy and wondered why the gravy train was passing them by.

Their concerns had merit. To a large extent, Boston's heavily Brahmin banking establishment shunned them, major developers ignored (or exploited) them, and politicians dutifully counted their votes—only to vanish with their tax dollars after election time. Need operating capital to feed a growing business, or a pipeline into federal funding? Good luck.

Blackstone Bank & Trust Co. cofounders Ann Hartman and Daniel Dart

THE COMPANY:
Blackstone Bank & Trust Co., Boston

CONCEPT:
Create a small, low-cost community bank, offering high rates to depositors and personal service to borrowers

PROJECTIONS:
Assets of $115 million by June 1990, with return on equity of 21%; income per share of $0.21

HURDLES:
Maintaining a stable deposit base while soliciting price-sensitive, mobile deposits; keeping loan quality high and contact with borrowers frequent as the funds that need to be loaned grow rapidly

Around Roxbury, leaders knew, the celebrated Massachusetts Miracle often meant nothing more than getting someone at the State House to return your phone calls.

While Roxbury considered its political fate, Daniel Dart and Ann Hartman had a different dilemma on their hands. Approval of their application to charter a new bank to be called Blackstone Bank & Trust Co., filed in September 1986, was being mysteriously delayed, to the point at which they began to fear the worst. Their plan—to create a community bank making loans in Roxbury and in Boston's South End, to make it a low-cost provider of basic financial services, and to attract depositors from all over the country by offering top-end rates on deposit accounts—seemed reasonable on paper. Both officers, though young, had a wealth of big-bank experience. Both had strong ties to the area and were intimately acquainted with Boston Redevelopment Authority projections of job growth, population growth (Roxbury up 10%, the South End up 20% by 1990), and investment in the two communities (a new subway station, the Copley Place retail development, a $275-million expansion of Boston's Prudential Center).

Well on their way to raising the minimum $4 million in start-up capital required by state banking regulators, Hartman and Dart were convinced that while most of Boston appeared "overbanked," their target neighborhoods did not; only three branch offices existed in the South End, six in Roxbury—with no bank headquartered in either community. On the lending side especially, this competitive vacuum suggested the kind of value added to the community that regulators look for when considering new charter applications. So what was the problem?

The problem, as it often is in Massachusetts, turned out to be political. Word leaked to Blackstone's founders that one of the charter's signatories, facing a tough reelection fight, wanted to see which way the Mandela referendum went before approving the proposal. Only after the referendum was defeated—actually, on the same *day*—did Dart and

Ann O'D. Hartman, 37, senior vice-president and chief lending officer

Daniel J. Dart, 32, president and chief executive officer

Ann Hartman graduated from Smith College in 1973 and immediately joined Bank of Boston as a management trainee. Ten years later, having served as a loan officer for, among others, Bill Rodgers's running-clothes company, she was elected a vice-president in commercial lending. Her interest in small-business customers convinced her that a new era in banking signaled a new career opportunity for herself. "There's an aura about starting a bank," Hartman admits. "People would hear what Dan and I were doing and faint away. Most had no idea how banks work—nor any desire to learn."

Dan Dart did. At State Street Bank, Dart had risen to the position of vice-president of marketing of the mutual-funds services division when he hit the proverbial wall. Eager to develop an insurance strategy at the bank, he instead was spending most of his time troubleshooting for unhappy mutual-fund customers. The more displeased clients he saw, the more turnover he had to deal with among bank personnel. At the same time, Dart recognized that the distribution system for mutual funds (primarily phones and mail) made sense for the low-overhead, high-yield banking profile suggested by industry deregulation. A call to the Massachusetts State Banking Commission in November 1985 gleaned the necessary information on how to start a bank of his own. Dart was encouraged to get in touch with another young banker who understood the local market: Ann Hartman.

"We found we shared similar backgrounds, philosophies, and ideals," explains Dart. "The more we talked, the more we realized what a good fit this could be."

Hartman learn that their application had been approved. Eight months later, in July '87, Blackstone Bank & Trust opened for business.

"These neighborhoods had a horrible reputation," concedes Hartman, 37. "Not only did bankers not think them `tame' enough [to invest in], but people literally feared for their safety down here. We don't look at it that way. From our perspective, this area is pretty mainstream."

Community banking, she adds, is as much a state of mind as it is a function of resources or geography. "You need to know the territory and who the local players are," she avers, "but you also need to know how your customers want to be treated. We don't offer the lowest loan rates—in fact, we charge a premium for our [lending] services. But we don't take six weeks to make a decision, either. Or turn down a loan for no apparent reason. Borrowers come to us because they know they can always get Ann or Dan on the phone. Not everybody needs that kind of service. But a lot of people seem to want it."

FINANCIALS

BLACKSTONE BANK & TRUST CO. OPERATING STATEMENT

	June 1988 (actual)	June 1990 (projected)
REVENUES		
Interest & fees from loans	$344,000	$1,121,681
Interest on investment securities & federal funds	82,000	108,100
Noninterest income (miscellaneous fees, appraisals, reports)	16,000	25,000
TOTAL REVENUES	**442,000**	**1,254,781**
COST OF REVENUES		
Interest paid on deposits	224,000	698,625
Provision for loan losses	58,000	30,000
TOTAL COST OF REVENUES	**282,000**	**728,625**
GROSS PROFIT	**160,000**	**526,156**
OPERATING EXPENSES		
Salaries & employee benefits	52,000	90,000
Rent & utilities	8,100	16,200
Office services	13,800	27,600
Furniture & computers	12,100	24,200
Marketing & PR	10,000	20,000
Miscellaneous	20,000	40,000
TOTAL OPERATING EXPENSES	**116,000**	**218,000**
NET PRETAX INCOME	**44,000**	**308,156**
Provision for taxes	0	104,773
NET INCOME	**44,000**	**203,383**
Income per share	0.10	0.21

Speaking as someone who never balances his checkbook or shops around for the best CD rates (journalists tend to be notoriously bad money managers, perhaps because we have so little to practice with), I address the question of how a bank makes money with some trepidation. The logical answer seems simple: by dealing with customers like me. Actually, according to Dan Dart, the real explanation is not much more complicated than that.

"We rent money for a fee," says Dart, 32. "Or, to put it another way, think of our deposits as finished-goods inventory. We mark that inventory up and sell it at retail, principally in the form of commercial loans. The difference is, we don't actually own our deposits, nor do we give away our loans on a permanent basis. What we're really in is the money-renting business."

All banks make their profits off the spread between what they pay to depositors in interest rates and what they earn from borrowers (or other investments) on "rented" money. At most banks, these constituencies are primarily one and the same. Not at Blackstone, where the deposits are mostly national and the investments largely local. Most banks have traditionally pursued growth through bricks-and-mortar expansion: more branches, more customers, more products, more volume. Again, not Blackstone. To Dart and Hartman, these concepts are at best unwieldy, at worst obsolete.

"A lot of banks are driven by a market-share mentality," points out Hartman, "and that's fine if it works for them. Here we're more driven by an earnings-per-share philosophy. Our belief is that a bank can stay small and still turn a respectable profit—if it knows how to keep costs down and make use of technology. I tell customers that the picture of banks they carried in their heads doesn't exist anymore."

You can pretty much tell that just by strolling through Blackstone's two-floor, 3,700-square-foot headquarters. Downstairs is a main office housing four account executives and the vice-president of retail banking, who smile frequently and greet customers by name (there are no tellers and no automatic teller machines, or ATMs). The account execs will cash a check if you insist, but they wouldn't know a velvet rope if one crawled through the lobby and bit them on the ankle. Upstairs, where the executive offices, computer room, and mortgage banking department are squeezed together, sits an old Mosler safe tucked inside a nondescript closet. Take a gander, folks, at Blackstone's main vault. It looks like something Butch Cassidy would drag outside and ask Sundance to stick on his horse.

A decade ago, Blackstone could not have operated this way. Or at least not for very long. Today, thanks to such innovations as shared ATM networks and financial data-processing services, coupled with fundamental changes in banking's regulatory climate, it's a different ball game. Perhaps the biggest change was the passage by Congress, in 1981, of the Garn-St. Germaine Act. This legislation effectively deregulated the industry by phasing out interest ceilings on deposits over a six-year period. Like other industries before it— trucking, airlines, the phone company—banking deregulation in turn created niche opportunities that cost-cutters have rushed to fill.

The late 1980s have seen the industry shaken up by deregulation. At one end has come a wave of mergers and acquisitions rolling above a sea of red ink, as hundreds of thrift institutions have tottered and failed—some due to outright fraud, many more from the pressure caused by conversion to stock ownership. Banks thus infused with large amounts of new capital have been forced to lend that money out, and quickly; in cases in which commercial-lending expertise has proved less than stellar, fast-growth banks have seen their loan portfolios become riddled with bad debt.

At the other end, meanwhile, new players have been arriving on the scene. Some bill themselves as "boutique banks": specialty banks offering limited product lines, often to a preferred clientele (oil-and-gas companies, agribusiness concerns, wealthy individuals with leather-bound portfolios, and so forth). A subset of this group are the so-called *de novos*—mostly full-service banks targeting narrow geographical areas ill-served by larger lending institutions.

As a low-cost provider, Blackstone is not precisely any of the above. With low minimum deposits and a distinct antielitist bias, it is definitely no boutique. And although it does target a narrow community of borrowers, Blackstone's low-overhead strategy dictates severe restrictions on the product line it offers to depositors. No IRAs or Keogh plans or credit cards. No discount-brokerage or financial-planning services. Not even an on-site ATM, although the bank does belong to a New England-based network with some 20,000 outlets. "Our products are plain vanilla," says Dart. "Money-market accounts, NOW accounts, CDs—that's it. We call full-service banks `brokerage houses,' because what attracts their customer base is really investments. We're not looking for investors, just savers. And if a customer needs to transact business with a teller, he wouldn't be happy here."

On the lending side, Blackstone has a similarly stripped-down look. Specializing in commercial loans to small businesses—they include developers, an equipment-leasing company, restaurants, and professional offices—the bank decided to eliminate both consumer lending ("lots of competition on rates there") and asset-based lending ("too complicated, too labor intensive"). Adjustable-rate mortgages are held in-house as attractive investments. Long-term, fixed-rate residential loans, which often pose a higher risk due to interest-rate fluctuations, are routinely packaged and sold into the secondary-mortgage market (Fannie Mae and Freddie Mac). Nothing extraordinary there. So why would borrowers come to Blackstone when they could save a point-plus elsewhere? For one thing, many are unhappy with the service they've been getting at other banks. For another, at Blackstone they don't have to deal with committees or trainees.

"Dan and I are on the loan committee," says Hartman, who after 12 years with the Bank of Boston, managing a $300-million portfolio, relishes the idea of bringing big-bank services to small-business customers. "When we opened, practically everyone I saw had some horror story to tell about dealing with one of the big banks in town. And to borrowers, cost [of a loan] is only one consideration. What's the turnaround time? Can I get a straight answer next week, or am I going to get strung along? In terms of my market, how knowledgeable is this banker? Dan and I don't delegate these decisions. When one of us approves an application, it's approved, period."

Clearly somebody is happy banking with Blackstone. In a year of operation, the institution grew from $4 million in deposits to $46 million, with an average climb now of $5 million a month. Last April, when its loan portfolio reached the $25-million mark, Blackstone started breaking even; by June, it was turning a tidy profit. Growth is an issue for any business, and banks are no exception. But banks cannot grow simply by generating deposits. They must lend that money out, and profitable lending is a function of knowledge, experience, research—and philosophy. In many ways, Blackstone's approach is a conservative one. The bank solicits deposits only after the corresponding loan commitments have been written. In other words, it doesn't shovel in the money and then figure out what to do with it later. When deposits threaten to outpace loans, the bank adjusts the balance by lowering CD rates.

"One California bank I know of grew from $10 million to $800 million in the space of 18 months," notes Dart. "When the regulators finally stepped in, 98% of its loans turned out to be nonpaying, and the bank president turned out to be a former dentist. It cost the FDIC more than $1 billion to clean up the whole mess. Bigger is *not* better."

And periodontists do not sound loan officers make.

Ever wonder who the most discriminating depositors are? Yuppies with oodles of disposable income? Computer hacks with access to this minute's market rates? Guess again.

"Florida retirees," says Dart. "They sit on the beach reading all the literature on which banks are offering the highest yields. Then they move their money about accordingly. If you can reach them with your numbers, the post office and telephone do the rest."

Ordinarily, reaching them would be a problem. By law, Blackstone is limited to advertising only in New England. Nevertheless, it currently has depositors in 48 states. How does it pull this off? Free publicity.

Week after week, Blackstone's rates on money-market accounts place the bank high up the list of average yields posted by *The Wall Street Journal* and the newsletter "100 Highest Yields." Both have national circulations. Voilà: coast-to-coast depositors.

By advertising with direct-response coupons in *The Boston Globe* (which has distribution in Florida), Blackstone also reaches those nimble-fingered retirees. It was a *Globe* ad, in fact, developed by the Boston firm of Witham, Childs & Siskind, that truly put Blackstone over the top. "No branches, tellers, velvet ropes, marble lobby or toaster ovens," boasted the headline, "just the best rate in the State." Not only did the campaign win praise from the trade industry (*AdWeek* mentioned it in a piece on the bank last February, and *Bank Marketing* named it January's Bank Ad of the Month), but it also drew an astonishing response from customers. In one week, $4 million in new deposits came in, quadrupling the expected $1-million windfall.

Marketing to its other customer base, borrowers, is more a one-on-one proposition."The community knows we're here," says Hartman, who has pulled in a number of former Bank of Boston loan customers herself. "When Dan and I were out selling stock, we spoke to a lot of groups and met other people socially. Our best marketing tool is basically word of mouth—customers referring other customers. We probably get two or three refugees from big banks in here every week."

Keeping overhead down has its risks. By locating outside Boston's financial district loop, Blackstone pays a certain price in terms of lost prestige and visibility. In Dart and Hartman's view, they more than make up for that by paying a modest $21 a square foot for office space, versus up to $40 per square foot downtown (they hold a five-year lease on their current site). Blackstone's monthly operating costs, including rent, insurance, computer time, salaries, benefits, and the like, comes to about $100,000. It incurs no costs from branch banks. By way of contrast, New England's two leading lending institutions—the Bank of New England and BayBanks—have 486 and 222 branches, respectively. Big nut, big difference in profitability.

Given Massachusetts's tight labor market, another concern of Blackstone's founders was attracting qualified help. They started with 10 employees and have added 3 more—with room for an additional 13 as the need arises. The hiring problem was solved through a combination of job flexibility and competitive compensation. Blackstone pays half again as much as a starting teller's salary for its account executives, puts its small staff of loan originators on commission, and provides equity kickers for key management people (5 bank officers in all). The bank has no chief financial officer and no secretaries—if Dart wants to send out a

COMPETITIVE ANALYSIS

	Blackstone 6/88	Blackstone 6/90 (projected)	Industry average[1]
SIZE			
Total assets	$44.5 mil.	$115.0 mil.	$83.3 mil.
Total deposits	$34.1 mil.	$103.5 mil.	$74 mil.
Employees (full-time equivalent)	13	18	52
PROFITABILITY			
Return on average assets	NA[2]	2.57%	0.86%
Return on average equity	NA[2]	21%	10.54%
Interest-rate spread	3.62%	3.76%	3.86%

[1]Averages for all U.S. commercial banks in the $50-million to $150-million asset range.
[2]Not available.
Source: Veribanc Inc., Wakefield, Mass.

letter, he types it himself. Three employees are working mothers, one of whom does bank work on a part-time basis.

Blackstone started looking for capital in the summer of 1986, a go-go season for bank stocks. Hartman and Dart initially offered 400,000 shares of common stock at $10 per share, with the stated policy that dividends would be forsaken for retained earnings. According to Dart, lending institutions were going public at "outrageous multiples" that summer, creating the impression among potential investors that they could make a quick killing trading in new-bank issues. Because they understood that equity turnover often resulted in management turnover, the founders set forth a strategy that would minimize their own risk of being tossed into the street.

"Our personal goal was to be able to manage the bank over the long haul," Dart explains. "It was really nonspeculative in nature. We wanted to sell the stock ourselves, but we also wanted a diversified group of [investors] who shared similar investment goals, who were willing to let the bank grow with us. We probably could have found three or four investors who wanted to kick in $1 million each, but instead we deliberately went after a much broader base."

Over a six-month period, Dart and Hartman succeeded in lining up 90 buyers, at an average investment of about $50,000 apiece. Some were friends, some movers and shakers in local communities. No investor was allowed to purchase more than 15% of Blackstone's equity. At the same time, written into the bank's bylaws were several anti-takeover provisions. One specified that any move to unseat a director (board terms are staggered over three years) would require a two-thirds vote of the board. Another, termed a "poison pill" provision, allows the bank to issue preferred stock to current shareholders. A third states that in the event 10% or more of the bank's outstanding stock is sold, that block of shares cannot be voted.

Advised by their attorneys that such restrictions could make it difficult to market their offering, Dart and Hartman stuck to their guns. Yes, they'd invested personal savings jointly to the tune of about 15% of Blackstone's equity. No, they were not looking to cash out soon. Or, for that matter, to feel pressured by one or two investors to take the money and run.

"The problem with taking it and running," explains Hartman, "is what do we do next? Start another bank? Retire? Even on my worst days, that has no appeal."

The capital needs of lending institutions do not, of course, remain static for very long. By federal law, banks must maintain a 6% capital-to-assets ratio (the ratio of thrifts is only 3%). Otherwise, the regulators fear, a bank can weaken its capital base to the point that a rash of non-performing loans could wipe it out. That's especially true in today's shaky banking climate, where the vagaries of local economies (the Texas oil industry, to cite one dramatic example) can shred a portfolio.

As Blackstone approaches $60 million in assets, therefore, another round of capital will soon be called for. Three options are currently being contemplated: issuing more common stock; creating a class of preferred stock; and floating subordinated debt, convertible to common stock. Whichever route they take, the founders know that they will draw the regulators' close scrutiny. Already they've been audited twice in the past year.

"If one bank fails because its capital-to-assets ratio falls too low," notes Hartman, citing the example of one Texas bank used as a personal piggybank by an unscrupulous developer ("You supply the dirt," went its slogan, "and we'll supply the green"), "the regulators come into yours next and set the ratio at, say, 10%. They can't hold you to that legally, but they can make life tough if you don't comply. Taking out the systemic abuses on the next guy may seem unfair, but that's the way the game is played."

Which is not to say that community banking is a no-risk proposition for Blackstone. At $5 million in growth per month, the danger of burnout is real. Macroeconomic issues aside, bad loans could result from management's inability to scrutinize each application thoroughly enough. And then there is the question of whether Dart and Hartman can maintain their personalized approach to customer service without working 14-hour days—never mind bankers' hours.

"The two main asset-management issues are interest-rate risk and credit risk," explains Dart. "Credit risk—borrowers being unable to meet loan obligations—is a fact of life with small-business customers, because growth companies don't always manage their finances well. Interest-rate risk arises when what you pay depositors exceeds what you make off investments. Because we're not burdened with a lot of long-term, fixed-rate investments, we believe that risk is minimal."

Dart concedes that New England's move toward interstate banking could open up the playing field soon. As more banks are bought up and consolidated, he figures, more small-business customers will fall through the cracks. And that will open up further opportunities for low-cost/high-service providers like Blackstone.

"We're operating in a $3-*trillion* industry," he points out. "To get hung up on market share would be dumb. All we're looking for is a solid reputation in our community and a profitable niche in our marketplace."

Plus a nice chunk of those Florida retirees.

"It's a tough thing to perpetually chase money with high interest rates, but they're doing it. If someone else's rates go higher, some portion of those deposits will shift."

—Kendrick Bellows Jr.

OPERATOR

CARL J. SCHMITT

Founder, chairman, CEO, University National Bank & Trust Co., a small, eight-year-old bank in Palo Alto, Calif. Former head of California State Banking Department

What Hartman and Dart are doing is the Schwab approach—raising deposits not on the quality of service, not on building loyalty, but on brokered deposits: nonloyal, price-sensitive, broad-based accounts. And they even say they're going to regulate how much business they get merely by adjusting their interest rates to turn the spigot off and on.

That's OK, as long as they know that when rates start moving away from them, they'll have to chase the deposits with price—and when that happens, they'd better have a variable loan portfolio. Because if they're having to chase deposits on price, then costs are going to be moving up based upon the credit market. For example, when prime is at 21%, the six-month T-bill might be at 18%—and you might be paying 18% to your CD customers. If you had taken your deposit base in former months and put it into fixed-rate mortgages at 10%, you'd be 8% underwater—a gross negative spread.

That's the classic problem of many banks: They get into a position of lending long and covering short. Much of our industry has passed off the rate risk and ignored it, based on doing variable-rate mortgages. That's fine, but those mortgage rates are not as variable as the deposit side is; typically the variable-rate mortgage has an annual cap of 2%, and we have seen periods in which the deposit interest rates have run up more than 2%—which means you can still get your spread squeezed.

If the deposit side of banking is science, then the lending side is art. There's no reason Blackstone's strategy can't work. You *can* get a little higher price by providing service on the loan side, there's no question about that.

Is Blackstone a riskier bank because it's going into traditionally redlined areas? Absolutely not. The risk is in the quality of the lenders. If they're good lenders and good loan officers, and they know how to structure and read the community, it will probably be less risky than many major Boston banks that have got large portfolios in South America, in tankers, and in the oil patch. It's that simple.

I like their concept, but it will be three to seven years before we'll know how well they'll do, because we'll need to see how well they'll manage their loan portfolio. That's the Achilles' heel, and the main question mark.

OPERATOR

KENDRICK BELLOWS JR.
Founder and chairman, The Burlington Bank & Trust Co., a community bank in Burlington, Vt., due to open shortly; formerly CEO of Bank of Vermont

It's a tough thing to perpetually chase money with high rates, but they're doing it.

On paper they've got what appears to be pretty hot money— money that, because it's been wooed in at a high rate, could leave. If someone else's rates go higher, some portion of those deposits will shift. They may be hedging against that by running at a somewhat lower than average loan-to-deposit ratio (average in my terms would be something around 90%). They're more like 70% to 75%—though it's hard to say for sure, given that they're in a growing business. On the surface that appears to manifest some concern with what we call liquidity—the possibility that some segment of those hot funds could be withdrawn. They would be wise to keep that loan-to-deposit ratio lower than average.

One of my concerns for them is that, as they grow, they'll lose that close contact with customers, which is one of the harbingers of loan difficulties. They've really got to project their personalities and their experience. If you're paying attention, you don't get surprised very often. The bigger banks tend to build layers, and those layers are like walls between customer and decision maker. I think that's more often the cause of loan payment difficulties

than is the underlying character of borrowers. The same borrower will be a better borrower at a small bank than at a big bank; the difference is contact with the decision maker, and the advice and counsel of the banker/manager.

I don't see much risk in competition from larger banks. I think larger banks will regard Blackstone as sort of a gnat for a long time to come, and gnats don't do much to elephants.

Their numbers suggest that they're growing faster in asset terms than in profitability terms. That's not unusual, but they're 18 months ahead of their asset forecasts and just about on target for profitability, which suggests that their margins aren't quite what they hoped they'd be.

I think they've got a good chance of making it. Time will tell. They may need some capital. They're running around 8% on capital-to-assets, which in the big picture is OK. But they may get some regulatory pressure to raise additional capital, in part because of their dependence on high-rate purchased money and in part because of the nature of the loans they're making—questions about loan quality.

ANALYST

HASSELL MCCLELLAN
Professor, Boston College School of Management; teaches strategic management of financial institutions

The big issues will be how quickly Blackstone wants to grow, and how it will ensure that it's managing that growth. It's amazing to see repeatedly how banks can't resist the temptation to get big—which adds to costs. With Blackstone I don't think it's a question of how big is too big as much as ensuring that as it grows, a gap does not develop between the size of its loan portfolio and its deposit base. As the bank grows, the founders will have to bring on additional staff who'll have to be almost their clones: entrepreneurial, very smart, and extremely hardworking.

I think Blackstone is well positioned, but it does face the risk that big banks will decide they can make money loaning to Roxbury businesses. And if those banks throw a lot of money at the area, it will be very costly for Blackstone to compete. If the big banks compete with lower prices, Blackstone may find itself under some price pressure—unless it can, in fact, really build a loyal borrower base and maintain the notion that clients can always get better service from Blackstone.

It's shown a considerable measure of success already—its growth rate has been extremely good for a start-up bank. In the future? I think it'll be successful. Blackstone should resist the temptation to get a lot bigger.

JAMES K. BOYER

Chairman, National Penn Bancshares Inc., Boyertown, Pa. After 18 years in the banking industry, he now runs a holding company with investments in six start-up banks

I'd be a little concerned about their target market. Hospitals and professional offices are fine. But restaurants have about the highest mortality rate of any business I know. If I were in Hartman and Dart's shoes, I'd cultivate the professional community even more—particularly accountants, who present excellent loan opportunities.

This is a high-risk field for investors. Regulators tend to give management skills at least one-third weight in evaluating new banks. The faster the growth, the more the regulators keep tabs on you. In terms of management skills, however, these people seem very experienced. If they can handle the loan volume, generate good-quality loans, turn the deposit spigot on the way they seem to, then they should be able to sustain growth.

Future financing could be a problem. I question the option arrangements. Antitakeover clauses are all right—we have them here—but if they protect management and prevent you from taking action if management doesn't do the job, then as an investor I'd be less interested. You can always sell your stock, of course, but this market is very thin.

I do like the fact that Dart and Hartman have a large personal stake in the business. Whenever we invest, the fundamental question is, Are the founders asking investors to put money into something they believe in? Clearly, that's the case here.

I don't see how they can sustain this growth curve without some risk. If they asked me, I'd rather see slower growth, not faster. But I'm quibbling. Quite honestly, this plan has a lot of pizzazz.

GOOD VIBRATIONS

*A new recording studio
stakes its pitch on service, but
will its customers care?*

BY BRUCE G. POSNER

John Deane

Somehow I had expected to be dazzled by the activity at Sanctuary Recording Inc. For days, I had been tuning in the latest sounds, looking forward to seeing how recording artists—straight out of *People* magazine—put their ideas on tape. During the taxi ride from my hotel in midtown Manhattan down to Lower Broadway, I was envisioning rooms full of exotic equipment—electronic gizmos that could produce the effects of 60-piece orchestras. Turns out I was a little early.

From the sound of power drills echoing down the 100-foot hall, it was clear that the opening of New York City's newest recording studio had been put off. In many ways, it was still a construction site. The electricians were running cables through walls. The finish carpentry was yet to be completed. Aside from the newly installed gray carpeting on most of the floors, the space was empty. Not a keyboard to be found. Not even a chair. But in a matter of weeks, Tom Silverman insisted, it would all come together. Sanctuary, located on the ninth floor of an old garment warehouse, would soon throb with activity. And what used to be 6,000

Tom Silverman, founder and owner, Sanctuary Recording Inc., in New York City

square feet of open loft area, he told me in mid-April, would have a whole new identity.

For about two years, Silverman, 34, had been working day and night toward that moment—pinning down details, studying the marketplace. There were dozens of other recording studios within a 10-minute cab ride—and hundreds of them within a half hour. But in spite of all the competition, Silverman was amazingly confident. While most studios put their resources into the latest equipment, Sanctuary, he explained, was going to offer something different. His model wasn't another drab studio with "battery acid for coffee," but a service-minded hotel, maybe even an inn.

Silverman had already spent more than $380,000 on the construction—much of it behind the walls in extensive sound-proofing and electrical work. And in May, he needed to begin generating income. A few weeks before that target, there were already signs that word of Sanctuary was beginning to spread. The studio's full-time manager, Howard Kessler, had recently booked 80 hours of time in the studio's most expensive room for The Washington Squares, a folk-rock group recording a new album. It's not the kind of group that Silverman expects the studio to draw—he anticipates more business from dance-music, R&B, and pop types—but he's not picky. He's happy to cater to anyone who will pay.

When musicians use a recording studio, they pay an hourly rate for the privilege of using a room and some of the owner's equipment. If they need other equipment, clients either bring their own or rent it. Depending on what they're working on, they'll spend from two hours to several months doing and redoing their work. Oftentimes, they end up working all night putting down a few tracks, breaking only for meals or a few hours of sleep. But despite all the time and energy that goes into recording, mixing, and editing sound, most studios don't do much of anything to make the lives of their clients less frazzled. Among other things, most studios are seedy or sterile, with crummy bathrooms, no showers, and nowhere to take a nap.

Sanctuary is aimed specifically at professional musicians and engineers who are tired of the drudgery of such a studio life. Sure, it's going to have a lot of snazzy equipment ($700,000 worth). But at least half of the thinking, it seems, has gone into making it—in Silverman's words—"very un-studiolike." It has a full kitchen, a private bath with shower, a guest room, four private lounges, and a full-time staff of at least four people who'll be on hand 24 hours a day. To give it some style, Sanctuary will be furnished with sofas and whimsical artifacts from the 1950s that Silverman has been collecting from all over

THE COMPANY:
Sanctuary Recording Inc., New York City

CONCEPT:
Midpriced recording and music production studio emphasizing service and comfort

PROJECTIONS:
Third-year pretax profits of $890,660 on revenues of $1,764,740 (net margin: 51%). Profitable from third month of operation

HURDLES:
Convincing artists that comfort can help them perform better, that it's worthwhile to forgo some state-of-the-art equipment for ambience; achieving positive cash flow quickly enough so that thin capitalization won't hurt

the country. And despite its investment in comfort and image, Sanctuary will charge the same kinds of rates as its midpriced competitors.

Silverman didn't pull his idea out of the blue. Among other things, he is the founder of an independent record company in New York City called Tommy Boy Music Inc. (now half owned by Warner Bros. Records), which has specialized in dance and rap music since its inception. Over the past decade, Silverman has spent many a long night behind control panels of studios all over the city. (He likes the business so much that he built a studio in his uptown apartment.) But none of the studios he used—none of the midpriced ones, anyhow—provided the overall service he was looking for. He'd book time in them, paying an average of $75 for a studio hour in the Times Square area, but he wasn't happy. And neither, he sensed, were a lot of other people.

Silverman says he got serious about building his own commercial studio only a year or so ago, when his studio at home was being converted into a baby's room. But listening to him talk, it seems he's been thinking about it for years. "I knew what all the scams were," he says. In fact, the section of his business plan called "The Competition" reads like the memoirs of a disgruntled record producer who's had his fill of studio experience:

Competitor 1: Small studios, relatively claustrophobic. Dirty old bathrooms. "Two-elevator building, with one usually out of service . . . In the sleazy Times Square area." Booked 80% of time.

Competitor 2: "One elevator which, when not broken down, features the nauseating smell of dead rats . . . Its look could be best described as `fraternity house.' Near Times Square." Booked 80%.

Competitor 3: "Features an even lower grade of the `fraternity house' style . . . One small bathroom on premises. Also near Times Square." Around 60% booked.

Competitor 4: "Clean and sparse but no discernible style . . . No

Tom Silverman, 34, founder and owner
Age: 34
Chairman and founder, Tommy Boy Music Inc., which since 1980 has become one of the top 10 independent record companies in the United States and is half owned by Warner Bros. Records . . . partner in New Music Seminar, a music-industry convention . . . owner and publisher, *Dance Music Report,* a trade publication, since 1978 . . . B.A., Colby College, Waterville, Maine

Howard Kessler, general manager
Age: 28
At Sanctuary since January . . . studio manager of Eastern Artists Recording Studio, East Orange, N.J., 1986 to '88 . . . assistant to music director, radio station WXRK, New York City, 1985 . . . manager, Mr. G's nightclub, Fairmont, W. Va., 1981 to '82 . . . B.A., Salem College, Salem, W. Va.

real lounge areas . . . On the fourth floor of a one-elevator building. Lower Broadway." Booked 60%.

It would have been one thing, says Silverman, if these studios were cheap. But they were all charging around $125 an hour (mostly without a sound engineer) and the elevators were still breaking down. Initially, Silverman considered building a small studio around the corner from his record company on First Avenue between East 90th and 91st, filling it with his own equipment.

But when his plan fell through, he began thinking about doing something in a lower-rent area of the city—and on a much bigger scale. Instead of one or two income-generating rooms, he considered four or five. The loft on Broadway had many selling points—12-foot ceilings, four elevators, natural light—and the neighborhood, known as NoHo, was coming up fast. So last August, Silverman signed a 10-year lease at $11 a square foot and began pulling his ideas together.

MARKETING: Like a new hotel or restaurant, the challenge for a new recording studio is getting people to try it. But you won't see a lot of advertising for Sanctuary in *Recording Engineer/Producer* or *Mix* magazines. Nor, says Kessler, will there be a grand opening of any kind. (Sanctuary's promotion budget: $1,542 a month.) He and Silverman believe that in the recording business, word of mouth is everything. And the best way to get people talking, they say—next to being the site of a few big hits—is to show them what you have and how you can meet their needs.

SANCTUARY RECORDING INC. PROJECTED OPERATING STATEMENT
(monthly)

	Year one	Year three
Utilization rate	51%	72%
REVENUES		
Rentals: studios A & B (average $95/hour)	$58,529	$83,568
Rentals: editing rooms (average $55/hour)	30,012	48,382
Other rooms	10,241	23,192
Equipment rentals & tape sales	5,329	7,314
Discount	19,557	15,394
GROSS REVENUES	**84,554**	**147,062**
EXPENSES		
Manager's salary & bonus	3,422	5,766
Other payroll	14,576	16,546
Rent	4,465	5,308
Payroll & rent taxes	3,067	3,446
Utilities & telephone	3,415	3,265
Supplies, contingencies, & decorating	3,091	3,320
Promotion	1,542	1,500
Maintenance	500	1,000
Legal & accounting fees	1,750	1,000
Bad debt (5% prediscount revenues)	5,206	7,757
Miscellaneous	2,058	3,855
TOTAL EXPENSES	**43,092**	**52,763**
NET OPERATING INCOME	**41,462**	**94,299**
Depreciation/amortization	12,917	13,217
Interest & principal	16,384	6,360
NET PRETAX PROFIT	**12,161**	**74,222**

Since February, Silverman and Kessler have been meeting privately with record producers and engineers and walking them through the newly renovated space. ("Years ago," Silverman says, "the best contacts were the record companies. But now the engineers and producers make most of the decisions about where the work is done.") They spend part of the time going over the four-page list of equipment. But they're quick to point out that they'll gladly rent anything customers want.

Sanctuary is spending hundreds of thousands of dollars on hardware. That may be less than many of its competitors are spending, Silverman explains, and the company won't go after "all the latest gee-gaws." ("I want to maintain cash flow," he says.) But he's confident that the things it will have will make technical types drool. Among them: a Synclavier synthesizer, an API console board with moving fader automation, and a Studer 24-track tape recorder. In contrast to the more ephemeral gear many studios are purchasing, he says, "a lot of our stuff is classic—it gets better with age."

Although Silverman and Kessler think Sanctuary's equipment list will be a lure, they're wagering that some of their best selling points will come under the heading of "feel and vibes." Sanctuary's studio A, for example, the highest-priced studio, has a spacious control room (30 feet by 22 feet) and a south-facing window. It has an adjoining guest room, and down the hall is the private bath. Having a place to rest or to grab a hot shower, argues Silverman, can make the difference between a so-so recording session and a truly great one. "A producer might be able to work 20% longer without fatigue."

But you don't have to spend $120 an hour to have pleasant sur-roundings, either. Each of the other sound or editing rooms (ranging from $55 to $70 an hour) is attached to its own lounge and close to the four elevators. To keep work areas totally private, there are combination keypad locks outside of every door. Everything Sanctuary does, Kessler says—from the quality of coffee to the fresh fruit and flowers to the atti-tude of employees—will be geared to making clients feel welcome. "If somebody wants 10 pounds of beluga caviar," he says, "it will be here."

Silverman and Kessler plan to spend the early months pitching Sanctuary to engineers and producers they know—primarily people who specialize in dance music. They're offering 20% discounts during the first year to selected customers who pay cash. Some business—maybe 10%—could come from Tommy Boy Music's own rap and dance-music groups, Silverman says, although they won't get better rates than other clients. At some point, Silverman may do a mailing to advertising agencies and jingle houses in hopes of diversifying the clientele; because ad agencies book shorter periods, they'll pay substantially higher rates.

This month, during the New Music Seminar, a music-industry con-vention with which Silverman has been associated for many years, Sanctuary will become a lot more visible. For several nights, Silverman says, "we'll be holding technical classes in the studios." The hope, of course, is that this exposure will lead to future business.

According to the company plan, the business will start out slow, with utilization of 20% during May. But by the end of the first year, Silverman thinks the facilities will be booked an average of 50% of the

C O M P E T I T I V E   A N A L Y S I S

	Sanctuary, annual projection 1989	Sanctuary, annual projection 1991	Industry average* 1987
Age of company (years)	1	3	13
Revenues (in $ thousands)	1,015	1,765	418
Net profit margins	14%	51%	NA
Employees	6	18	10
Control rooms	2	2	1
Room utilization rate	51%	72%	NA
Prices ($/hour)	$30 to $120	$30 to $120	$96 to $160

*For New York City studios
Source: *Pro Sound News*

time. If they are, Sanctuary will have revenues of about $1 million—and profits of $146,000.

OPERATIONS: Sanctuary was designed for maximum flexibility. The six studios and editing rooms can be rented out at the same time to different clients. Or they can be used in conjunction with one another, since they are all wired together. While Silverman thinks the flexibility is important, the key to Sanctuary's success, he says, will be the extent to which it runs differently from other studios.

The main ingredient in making the business work, Silverman expects, will be a staff of service-minded people. He's confident that Kessler, who ran a successful studio in New Jersey, has the ability to run the business on a day-to-day basis and to find and motivate good people. Kessler will initially be paid $30,000 per year, plus 8% of aftertax profits.

Unlike a lot of studios, Sanctuary has chosen to operate without staff engineers (although it will have assistant engineers working around the clock). The main reason, Silverman says, is to give clients the freedom to use the people they want—and to save on overhead. Good engineers, he says, earn $600 to $700 a week on staff whether they're busy or not. Free-lancers, on the other hand, can make two or three times that rate on their own. As a service to clients, Sanctuary will maintain a book of free-lance engineers and make referrals at no extra charge. Silverman hopes the system will become a spin-off benefit by encouraging free-lancers to channel work to Sanctuary.

In other areas, Sanctuary will be extremely well staffed. Kessler says he'll have six full-time employees right off the bat to provide basic coverage 24 hours a day, seven days a week; as things get busier, he'll add more. He has already hired three assistant engineers, who have agreed to work 60-hour weeks at $300. (During slow periods, he wants them to learn how to operate and maintain equipment.) He has also hired six receptionists at $7.50 an hour, and a maintenance technician ($650 a week) who will be at Sanctuary Monday through Friday and will be available all other times, reachable by beeper.

Over and above the paid staff, Kessler is planning to make use of unpaid interns. To keep the facility clean and operating smoothly, he expects to pay a cleaning crew $200 a week and a part-time bookkeeper $160 a week.

Recognizing that employee turnover is one of the industry's big problems, Sanctuary is hoping to generate some loyalty by offering free health insurance after three months on the job. But turnover notwithstanding, Kessler says, Sanctuary's one inflexible requirement of staffers is a positive attitude. People who aren't interested in making things pleasant for clients will be replaced.

FINANCE: About a year ago, when Silverman first approached his Chemical Bank lending officer about a $400,000 loan, the response was promising. His record company and other ventures were making money, and he had 12 separate accounts with the bank. Overall, he expected the space renovations at Sanctuary to cost about $250,000, and the remainder of the money would be earmarked for recording equipment, furnishings, and working capital to cover two months of negative cash flow. He was also planning to contribute nearly $500,000 worth of equipment he already owned.

Before Christmas, the bank extended him a loan for $100,000 at one and a half points over prime, and Silverman was expecting to get approval for the other $300,000 within a matter of weeks. But in mid-May, he was still waiting. Silverman thinks last October's Wall Street crash spooked the bank's credit people; he now has "major-league doubts" about whether Chemical will provide any more money.

Fortunately, he was able to tap other sources to keep things moving. Last January he arranged to borrow $100,000 from his father at 10% on a short-term basis. (He plans to repay half of it in August and the other half next January.) And he pulled together another $90,000 of his own from savings.

After spending about $325,000, Silverman was about $225,000 to $250,000 shy of the amount he needed to open Sanctuary. The reason: The construction costs exceeded the original estimates by $150,000. He has pitched the plan to another New York City bank—and he had also discussed selling 20% of Sanctuary to an industry contact from Miami for $300,000. The second bank offered to lend him $95,000 for two years at one point over prime, Silverman says. The amount was too low, and the bank wanted him to shift some of his other accounts, which he was not eager to do. The potential investor is no longer in the picture.

To minimize his financing needs, Silverman has moved about $50,000 of the new equipment he intended to buy to phase two of his business plan. To cover the resulting equipment shortfall, he has contracted with a leasing company for a five-year lease. He is paying a fixed rate of 12% on $103,000, which he and his wife have personally guaranteed.

Silverman reckons he has spent 60 or 70 hours huddled in front of his computer, fine-tuning his plan. Having been involved in other businesses—and being so familiar with other studios—he thinks he has a huge advantage over his competitors. So he's confident that Sanctuary will be a winner. By the third year, his projections show, the company will generate aftertax profits of $511,197 on revenues of $1,764,740. And that is if it's booked only 72% of the time. At higher utilization rates, which he says are entirely possible, profits would be even greater.

But even Silverman concedes that there are at least two areas in which Sanctuary could be on shaky ground. The first has to do with how his costs will be affected by technology—or, to be more specific, by his clients' demand for it. And the other has to do with whether or not he can execute the service idea he's bet his success on.

For the past few years, new sound equipment has been sweeping through recording studios in New York and elsewhere like wildfire. Every few months, industry people say, there's a hot new toy. And it's hard not to buy it. Many of Sanctuary's direct competitors, for instance, have recently gone way into debt to buy state-of-the art SSL (Solid State Logic) boards, which cost up to $300,000. Despite all the publicity, Silverman doesn't think he needs to have one in order to be competitive. "We're trying to see through the fad stage," he says. Whether prospective customers will buy this philosophy remains to be seen.

The execution question is more straightforward, if also more difficult to resolve. "The key word around here is going to be service," Silverman says. "We're not in the recording-studio business, we're in the hospitality business." But it's not certain whether Sanctuary can deliver what it says it will. No matter how important service is to the people in charge, getting employees to care about it is something else.

And finally there's a more fundamental question, the answer to which Silverman and Kessler take for granted. Will customers really *care* about the comforts they think are so important? Or is the niche too narrow? True, the hottest studios in New York—including the place where Springsteen and Madonna record—may not offer fruit baskets as standard policy, Kessler observes. But he and Silverman think that in the future clients will expect more.

"Once people try us," Kessler says, "they won't want to work anywhere else. We're going to put fun back into the recording studio."

> *"How's he going to manage both businesses? If he ends up spending 15 hours a day with this new venture, Tommy Boy Records will suffer—and Sanctuary needs for Tommy Boy to stay healthy."*
>
> — *Cornell Richardson*

FINANCIER

CORNELL RICHARDSON

Chief executive officer of C.N.R. Enterprises Inc., in New York City, formerly bank lending officer specializing in the entertainment industry

Silverman is wise to try building on his industry experience. The transition from record making to a studio makes sense. It's not like he's going from making shoes to making women's apparel.

My main concern when I put my banker hat on is that he doesn't seem to have projected for the unexpected. His construction costs, for example, have run way over budget. The cost overruns forced him to seek additional short-term financing. But my sense is that short-term solutions won't work. He should be looking for long-term financing.

One area in which I think he's especially exposed is receivables. In my experience, 9 out of 10 people in this type of business don't understand the cash-conversion cycle. He can't just do his billing and expect to see a check in a couple of days. His numbers seem good, but to me they look like a best-case scenario. Why? Because even an established record company can drag you out for 30 to 60 days. I'm not sure that he can afford that. All he needs is one major company dragging him out for 90 days and he can be blown out of the water. Two or three bad receivables a month can wipe out his entire net profit for the year.

I worry, too, how realistic Silverman's been about his own time commitments. I know he's going to have a good manager, but does he realize that Sanctuary is going to take a lot of time from his other venture anyway? Does he have the depth of management, at either Tommy Boy Records or Sanctuary, to back up his own divided attention? Before I loaned him any money, I'd want to know how he planned to manage both businesses. If he ends up spending 15 hours a day with this new venture, Tommy Boy will suffer—and Sanctuary needs for Tommy Boy to stay healthy.

POTENTIAL CUSTOMER

PHILIPPE SAISSE

A 31-year-old New York City producer and musician

I don't doubt that Silverman's concept will have appeal for some people in the music industry. The prices seem very attractive—around half of what we pay sometimes—and he has a solid reputation for doing things right.

Personally, however, I have questions about whether it's the kind of place I'd want to work. Why? Because many of the things he's doing to make the place comfortable aren't high on my list—and he's downplaying things that are important. When you're producing a record and you have your budget and your reputation on the line, you can't afford to take chances. I like to work in places that have 24-hour maintenance people, because there's about an 80% chance that something will go wrong. Things tend to break down around 3:00 a.m. Even if you can prove to me that it will only take 10 minutes to rouse an engineer with a beeper and get him in, it gives me confidence if the guy's there in the shop. Having somebody on the spot is worth a lot more to me than having fruits, flowers, and a shower. For that matter, so is having an SSL console.

As far as the environment Silverman is trying to create, my feeling is that when I go into a recording studio, I go to work. I sense that's the way a lot of people operate in New York. There's a lot of financial pressure in this business and, to be honest, I've never been in a situation where, after working for 14 hours, I wished there was a shower. My feeling is, Let me out of here! At 4:00 a.m., I'll take a shower at home. I've been in this business a long time, and I can't remember ever thinking, I wish the vibes were better.

If I *were* looking for a relaxed place to work, I'm not sure this would be the place. I'd be inclined to go out of town—to upstate New York or to the Caribbean. For Barbra Streisand, it's probably important to be as comfortable as possible. But for the music we do— and the hard-edged music that's being produced in New York City— pressure is important. You don't want bed-and-breakfast hosts, you want people who are totally geared to making sure that you have all the equipment you need and that everything works.

POTENTIAL CUSTOMER

CAROL COOPER
Partner in Done Properly Productions, a New York City production company that specializes in music remixing and production

It seems Sanctuary is going to be very much in line with the way younger talent makes music today. Most established studios don't recognize that dance music and other electronic music made now is recorded much differently from other music. A lot of the younger producers in New York making hit records don't even read music. They rely heavily on polyphonic keyboards, drum machines, sequencers, and other things that are linked through computers. Most of the work is done in the control room, and Silverman understands this and compensates for it.

Editing, for instance, has become an increasingly important part of making records. There's no reason to do editing in a regular studio and pay all that money. Usually, we're doing recording in one place and editing someplace else. I like the way they're going to have two separate editing rooms with lower rates. As for their choice of equipment, it doesn't bother me that they're not investing in the latest stuff. It's better that they have things that are proven—things that sound good.

OPERATOR

CRAIG HUBLER

General manager of Sunset Sound Recorders Inc., in Los Angeles

I have a lot of reservations about what Silverman is trying to do and how he's going about it.

He's right to put emphasis on service and staffing. And he's right to keep promotion expenses to a minimum. The best salespeople are your customers—this industry is very close-knit.

His philosophy of equipment—having less than the state of the art—is fine if he can sell it to customers. But it's risky. A lot of people are becoming used to seeing SSL consoles when they walk into a studio. So other stuff, no matter how good it is, can be a turnoff.

Overall, I think Silverman is biting off more than he can chew. Rather than starting out with one room and adding on if and when he's successful, he's trying to create a five-room studio business from the ground up. It's great if he can book his rooms 12 hours a day, seven days a week, but I think it's unlikely—at least in the first few months. This is a very competitive and volatile business, and he's heavily financed. This is a cash-flow business, not a bottom-line business, and his thin capitalization will hurt.

My feeling is that Sanctuary's projections are insanely profitable for a new studio in a competitive market.

POTENTIAL CUSTOMER

JOE MARDIN

Independent producer/arranger for such artists as Chaka Khan, New Man, and Aretha Franklin

It's a gamble to open a place in New York that tries to be so different. Everyone has preset ideas about going in and working a certain way, and not many are thinking, Oh, I have a kitchen? I have a bath? A lot of people don't care about those things. Some people will, but I think they'll be at the upper end of the market, artists who plan to spend long periods of time in the studio.

Dance musicians are different. Most of them really want to get in and out of the studio quickly. That's just the way they work, the way they save money. The idea—it's reflected in the music—is to work quickly, make it happen without a lot of contemplation.

I'd make one particular recommendation: Tom Silverman probably has a lot of friends and prospective clients he could line up. He's got a good reputation. His record company, Tommy Boy, had one of the handful of million-selling singles last year. Despite all that, Silverman says he's not going to give the label special treatment. I don't see why he shouldn't. A Tommy Boy affiliation would be a strong selling point, make the place real. The connection would have commercial value. If a few hits come out of the place, and it picks up the Tommy Boy mystique, I think people will be attracted to working there.

CHEAP COUNSEL

*Does every citizen need a lawyer on
private retainer? The founder of Landmark
Legal Plans Inc. thinks so*

BY JOSHUA HYATT

Patricia Barry Levy

As soon as you hear about him, you're going to think Christopher P. Nolan works at your company.

That's because someone *like* him probably does. He's one of your top people, but also your harshest critic. Even as he's pocketing commission checks—in Nolan's case, $2,465.57 one day, $29.40 the next, and $371.68 the day after that—he's thinking that your marketing approach is lousy and your financial acumen worse. As founder, you always fear what he's thinking: *What do I need this guy for?* You just hope it's an impulse he'll never act on.

After all, it took even Nolan himself a few years to make the leap.

Christopher Nolan, founder of Landmark Legal Plans Inc., in Denver

EXECUTIVE SUMMARY

THE COMPANY:
Landmark Legal Plans Inc., Denver

CONCEPT:
Legal plans for businesses and individuals offering specified legal services and a discount retainer for an annual fee

PROJECTIONS:
Pretax net of $58,700 in 1989. In 1993, sales of $47.8 million, with more than $11 million in profits (about 24% pretax net)

HURDLES:
Questionable demand; getting insurance brokers to sell plans; delivering customer volume to lawyers quickly enough to keep them interested in providing services

He first started considering it back in 1985, when he was a salesman at Pre-Paid Legal Services Inc., in Ada, Okla. The company, which by 1987 ranked 92d on the *Inc.* 100 list of the fastest-growing public companies, specialized in selling legal plans, a nascent concept that sounded great: For a relatively small yearly fee, the average person could keep a lawyer on retainer. The problem, Nolan thought, was the way that the plans were marketed.

Like most companies in the field, Pre-Paid used multilevel marketing to sell the plans. Via tent shows, it recruited part-time salespeople to buy the policies and then sell their friends on the idea of joining up. The part-timers would receive a cut of every sale their recruits made.

Multilevel marketing got the product on the street—and sold it—very fast. But Nolan believed the strategy was better suited for selling a tangible item than a service like legal plans. The problem, as he saw it, was this: The sales force had every interest in selling a plan but none whatsoever in servicing it. Understandably, most customers had questions about the unfamiliar plans. Unable to find answers, they checked the "no" box when it came time to renew.

Many fine prospects, Nolan observed, simply wouldn't buy anything sold through multilevel marketing. "Is this like Amway?" he'd hear as the door was closing. Small-business owners were the worst. "Their fear was that once you sold them a plan, you'd try to recruit them to sell the product," says Nolan.

Nolan didn't think the attorneys were getting a good deal either. Most plans paid them less than $2 per plan per month—not enough, Nolan felt, to keep them motivated. *You really should start a company of your own,* some of them urged.

No way, he thought; surely there's another company that sees the same opportunity. In search of it, Nolan jumped to a competitor, where he encountered what in his view were the same problems. Unprofessional salespeople. Underpaid lawyers. Unfocused marketing.

Christopher Nolan, 37, chairman and CEO

Sometime in 1983, as Christopher Nolan was giving a seminar on real estate, a man emerged from the crowd and asked him, "How much are you spending on an attorney?" Too much, replied Nolan—who, as a real estate investor, was plunking down as much as $6,000 a month for a lawyer to handle contractor's agreements, mortgages, and so on. That's when the man told him about pre-paid legal plans. Nolan bought one. He found it actually cut his legal bills in half. "I became intrigued," he says.

Once Nolan becomes intrigued, he generally follows up. Not long after graduating from Northern Michigan University in 1973, Nolan entered the securities industry, where he helped wealthy clients pad their portfolios with tax shelters. What intrigued him then, he says, was that most of them had made money, and buckets of it, in real estate.

Off he went to a real estate seminar given by Albert J. Lowry, a then-popular (now bankrupt) lecturer on the subject. Not only did Nolan take the plunge into real estate—he claims he made about $160,000 gross his first year—but he eventually accepted Lowry's invitation to tour nearly 160 cities, telling 1.5 million people about how Lowry's system had worked for him.

But Nolan, now 37, claims none of his previous jobs fully prepared him for the challenge of starting Landmark Legal Plans Inc. Well, maybe one. As a kid, he led groups of people on fishing and hunting trips through the wilderness of northern Ontario. "It was great for honing people skills," he says. "You can drop me in the middle of anywhere, and I'll do just fine. So Landmark doesn't scare me all that much."

"I became even more convinced that it was a great idea," he says, "and that nobody was doing it right."

Chances are that the Christopher Nolan at your company will criticize and carp but stick around to enjoy those regular commission checks. Not so *this* Christopher Nolan.

"I am sure I can do better," says the 37-year-old founder of Landmark Legal Plans Inc., based in Denver. "I'm betting everything I have on it."

Let's suppose your business is bickering with a supplier over whether that company fulfilled the terms of its contract last month, or you're not sure how to comply with a new piece of legislation. And what are your rights if your spouse is a louse or your car a lemon?

If you're well heeled, you probably already have an attentive lawyer to handle such matters. But for most people, contacting an attorney—and, more to the point, paying one—is as appealing as spending a night in jail. Those people will even pay up front to make sure they have an affordable lawyer lined up.

FINANCIALS

LANDMARK LEGAL PLANS INC. PROJECTED ANNUAL OPERATING STATEMENT

	Fiscal year 1989 (and % of sales)		Fiscal year 1993 (and % of sales)	
SALES				
Business plans	$702,600	(40%)	$19,131,400	(40%)
Individual plans	1,053,800	(60%)	28,697,200	(60%)
TOTAL SALES	**1,756,400**		**47,828,600**	
COST OF SALES				
IMS commissions (brokers)	737,600	(42%)	15,010,800	(31.4%)
Access attorneys	316,200	(18%)	10,588,800	(22.1%)
NIA commission (administration)	210,800	(12%)	4,782,900	(10%)
TOTAL COST OF SALES	**1,264,600**	**(72%)**	**30,382,500**	**(63.5%)**
GROSS PROFIT	**491,800**	**(28%)**	**17,446,100**	**(36.5%)**
OPERATING EXPENSES				
Corporate salaries/bonuses	210,800	(12%)	3,947,200	(8.3%)
Printing & advertising	53,200	(3%)	837,900	(1.8%)
Seminars & training	16,900	(1%)	267,000	(0.6%)
Legal fees	20,300	(1.2%)	75,600	(0.2%)
Miscellaneous marketing	14,500	(0.8%)	23,700	(0.05%)
Telephone	7,500	(0.4%)	114,000	(0.2%)
Postage	10,500	(0.6%)	166,300	(0.3%)
Rent	22,200	(1.3%)	123,200	(0.3%)
Equipment	44,700	(2.5%)	250,200	(0.5%)
Supplies	5,300	(0.3%)	83,200	(0.2%)
Miscellaneous	27,200	(1.5%)	142,900	(0.3%)
TOTAL OPERATING EXPENSES	**433,100**	**(24.7%)**	**6,031,200**	**(12.6%)**
NET INCOME BEFORE TAXES	**58,700**	**(3.3%)**	**11,414,900**	**(23.9%)**

At least that's the presumption behind legal plans. For a yearly fee, consumers receive certain legal services. Usually these include half-hour phone consultations, letters and calls to third parties (suppliers, landlords, and so on), the review of such documents as leases and contracts, and the writing of wills. For all of these, consumers call on their "access attorney," whose number is printed on a wallet-size card.

For more specialized legal matters, such as bankruptcy, the access attorney turns to a list of "referral attorneys." Typically, plans offer these lawyers at about 25% less than their usual hourly rates. Some plans include a roster of legal matters, such as deeds and misdemeanors, with maximum-fee caps. For the most sophisticated work, such as a merger, Landmark offers specialist firms at a 10% to 25% discount.

Since 1977, when a Supreme Court ruling paved the way for such plans, marketers—which now include such heavyweights as Amway and Montgomery Ward—have been seeking a balance between a plan that consumers are eager to buy and one that lawyers are willing to service. At the rates they've been used to getting, access attorneys aren't very eager to provide many free services. At the same time, plan marketers need to lure consumers. Hence there have been plans that, for instance, boast of covering such potentially expensive transgressions as vehicular homicide. Read the fine print, though, and you'll see that alcohol- or drug-related charges aren't covered—which excludes, by one lawyer's reckoning, around 90% of all those cases. "Some plans verge on being illusory," notes David Baker, an industry consultant.

Getting lawyers to back legal plans isn't easy. After all, the plans require attorneys to turn their traditionally lucrative approach, based on high margins and low volume, right on its head. When he decided to launch Landmark Legal Plans, Nolan knew that a plan couldn't succeed unless the lawyers had a stake in it. So last spring, he met with 30 attorneys from eight different law firms. What do you like about legal plans? he asked. What would it take to get you to service one? Well, they said, we'd like to see a plan handled by professional marketers so we don't have to spend half our time briefing customers on what they just bought. Furthermore, they said, if you're going to ask us to slash our margins, you'd better deliver us volumes of clients; so far, the marketers are the only ones who seem to be making money.

Not anymore, Nolan vowed, I'm going to make it worth your while.

Landmark now offers two plans—one for individuals, one for businesses with revenues under $4 million—that enable attorneys to earn roughly 50% more than competing plans, Nolan claims. True, Nolan is calling on attorneys to provide more free services, but he's carefully chosen areas that will add up to only about 15% more work, he says. Whereas most plans offer free will preparation, for instance, Landmark offers two free wills and any number of children's trusts. And the plan offers fee caps in 15 areas, at least 5 more than most.

Nolan is hoping to lure customers from his competitors, which haven't done badly in opening up the market. Pre-Paid started by selling about 5,000 plans in 1977 and is up to some 300,000 a decade later. Nationwide Legal Services Inc. has grown from sales of $56,000 in 1983 to more than $1 million last year. Landmark's individual plan is about 30% more expensive than Pre-Paid's; Landmark's business plan is priced just a bit higher than Nationwide's, which is similar in content. Nolan insists that customers are "more interested in service than in price. If they call an attorney, they want to talk to an attorney *today*."

Most potential customers, he contends, still haven't been exposed to the legal plan concept. Only 42 million people now own one, and Nolan believes that the market for individual plans is as large as 155 million, about 70% of the U.S. population. Less than 1% of small businesses, he claims, have a legal plan. "Around 75% of the market is wide open," he says. Some companies have bitten off pieces of the market through direct mail (Montgomery Ward) and multilevel marketing (Pre-Paid, Nationwide), but "nobody has really figured out how to sell it to the mass market," Nolan says.

Nolan knows firsthand that the demand exists. He claims that at Pre-Paid, he could fill a ballroom with 200 people, tell them about the plan, and expect 10% to leave with one. At Nationwide, with what he judges a slightly better product, he could usually count on 50%.

Shortly after going out on his own in May 1987, Nolan got hold of information about five West German companies that sell legal plans. Aside from examining usage rates, renewal levels, and profit margins, he was heartened to discover that 80% of all West Germans subscribe to plans. "It's just a matter of educating people here," he says. "There's no reason to think it wouldn't happen here like it did there."

Three of the five companies, he adds with a smile, now post annual revenues of *more than $1 billion.*

The legal plan concept sounds an awful lot like insurance: Pay up front for services you might need later. But Nolan, borrowing from his European counterparts, is operating strictly as a middleman. That should, he says, enable him to grow faster. As an insurer, Landmark would have to wrestle with capitalization and licensing requirements that vary from state to state. But Landmark does not pay out claims, nor does it depend on actuaries to set its fees. The company receives an annual amount up front—say, $195 for most individual plans and $570 for a business plan—and wrings its profit margin from that fee. (A company that buys individual plans for its employees can obtain a group discount that sinks as low as $110 apiece.)

A Landmark fee makes more stops than a cable car as it chugs its way toward the bottom line. To keep his start-up costs down and enable Landmark to expand fast, Nolan has signed deals with two national companies, each of which will skim percentages off the top of each fee:

Insurance Marketing Services Inc. (IMS) will sell Landmark's plans through its network of some 1,700 insurance agents, and National Insurance Administrators Corp. (NIA) is handling all the paperwork and record keeping, as well as maintaining a toll-free number to answer brokers' or clients' queries. "This way," Nolan says, "we can concentrate on the marketing side."

Marketing is especially important because renewals are key to improving Landmark's profitability. For its efforts, IMS takes away 42% of each new plan, 2% for itself. As with any insurance product, the rest will be split among various combinations of general agents, distributors, and producing sellers—depending on exactly who was involved in the sale. When a plan is renewed, though, the IMS percentage drops to 24%.

Likewise, NIA's straight percentage slips from 12% to 10% in the second year. Only the access attorneys, who have a direct effect on whether consumers like the plan enough to renew, receive the incentive of a bigger percentage the second and third years. In the first year, access attorneys receive 18% of each fee; in the second year, 20%; and in the third, 30%. For the third year and thereafter, the attorneys are contractually locked in to receiving $5 per month for every individual legal plan and $14 for each business plan they service.

If he can raise working capital, Nolan plans to open branch offices that will serve both as marketing headquarters and as training centers for lawyers and brokers. Outside of Colorado, his first branch will be in Phoenix. Using that as a model—"I know it won't hold for cities like Chicago and L.A.," he notes—he expects most branches to break even at the end of the first year. Branch managers will be virtually the only salaried employees in each office; the rest, as many as eight district managers, will receive a commission out of revenues. "I'm trying to lock down as many costs as possible," says Nolan.

Landmark's profit on each plan sold should be a slender 3% during the first year, climb to about 15% the second year, and hit 24% by the fifth year, depending on the renewal rate. According to projections, the company will break even in its first year. "As long as we keep selling contracts, we'll keep making money," Nolan says.

To succeed, Nolan must reach three different markets: the lawyers who will service the plan, the insurance brokers who will sell it, and the consumers who will buy it.

Most legal plan marketing strategies have employed multilevel marketers following the same general dictum: Where there's no will, there's a way. Lured by the prospect of a cheap will, consumers join up, get the document, then depart.

The lawyers, who have generally worked at bargain-basement rates, haven't had much incentive to convince customers to stay. Their goal is to see as many people as possible in the hopes that one of their customers (or a customer's friend or relative) will be struck by a heavy object and initiate a lucrative personal-injury suit.

Because legal plans are so low cost (read: low commission), direct selling is simply too expensive. Still, no other plan has caught on with insurance brokers before. But, says IMS president Ron Roesener, "this one is much simpler. It's very understandable for the brokers." Nolan is counting on the IMS insurance brokers to bring in at least two-thirds of Landmark's sales.

With beefed-up services and the credibility of the broker behind it, Nolan believes Landmark can attract a different class of consumers than do the multilevel marketers or the direct mailers. The brokers' slick marketing presentations will aim squarely at the middle-class and upper-middle-class clientele Nolan is seeking—litigious enough to need a plan, wealthy enough to afford one. Some people, he figures, will snap up a Landmark plan because, say, they have just run over a cat; unlike an insurer, Landmark covers those preexisting conditions for which a lawyer hasn't already been hired. Even the higher price, he says, will serve as a competitive advantage. "People figure, 'What kind of lawyer am I going to get for 100 bucks?' " Nolan says. "In lawyers, people want quality."

Eventually, Nolan also plans to sell through financial planners and business consultants. An experienced speaker, he hopes next spring to start leading seminars on issues that will attract entrepreneurs. He expects more than 60% of Landmark's customers to consist of companies buying group business plans for their employees through the same agent that sells them group health plans. "It's cheaper than a raise," notes Nolan, "and the perceived value is very high."

To encourage plan holders to renew, Landmark will churn out newsletters and other literature to remind them to use their plans. But what Nolan is really counting on to keep plan holders coming back are the attorneys. His approach to motivating them is about as subtle as a gavel to the cranium. "Let's face it," he says, "money does talk." For each individual plan they service, the access attorneys will receive $3 per month the first year, $4 the second year, and $5 the third year. The scale for business plans runs from $6 to $10 to $14. That doesn't sound like much, Nolan concedes, except when the volume is turned up.

The idea is for the plan to be profitable whether or not that big personal-injury case happens to limp in. Richard Hughes, a senior partner at the law firm that serves as one of Landmark's access firms in Denver, contends that "three dollars per month per plan can be profitable by itself. You just have to be efficient." Hughes estimates, for instance, that it takes his firm only about 30 minutes to execute a will, often by mail. Besides, he adds, the firm saves the marketing costs of bringing in new clients.

Nolan hopes the incentive pay will prompt access attorneys, 50% of whom will also be servicing other plans, to "honor my plan first." By contract, access firms must answer all calls within 24 hours. They are also required to send out welcoming letters to each new plan member.

As for referral attorneys, Nolan contends that $68 an hour enables most to make a profit of $10 or more an hour. He arrived at that figure after discovering that big insurance companies pay attorneys $65 an hour for volume business. To qualify with Landmark, referral attorneys must own at least $300,000 in malpractice insurance, show areas of expertise, be in good standing with the local bar, and have been practicing law for at least five years.

In June 1987 Nolan sold his house in suburban Michigan, raising about $25,000 to put into the business. He knew that wouldn't cover the legal and accounting expenses, so he accepted a lucrative consulting contract—$10,000 a month for six months—in Dallas. Nolan put aside what he could to live on, originally thinking he might launch the company in the Lone Star State. Upon further study, he decided to head for Colorado, where the regulations concerning legal plans are as thin as the mountain air.

Between December 1987 and March '88, he ran through most of the money he had saved. He had to draw up contracts with access and referral attorneys and with insurance brokers, at a cost of about $20,000. Accounting fees for the *pro forma* ran to more than $3,000. Printing brochures and letterhead stationery cost another $12,000. He saved money by working from what he called "the executive dining room"— his house. Last January, when Nolan began thinking about hiring, he decided he would have to move to improve his credibility. The problem became apparent when he interviewed Randolph Orr, now vice-president of marketing. Orr plopped down on Nolan's couch and said, "I just want to know: Exactly what kind of scam are you running here?" In March Nolan began occupying space in the Colorado Club Building, which offered him a no-rent deal as long as he agreed to rent offices once Landmark was up and running.

By then, Nolan was exhausted, and so were his funds. Looking for more, Nolan has made the rounds of venture capitalists but says "they want too much of the company." What he'd really like is somebody who will put in $250,000 without demanding a controlling interest.

Nolan estimates that Landmark will need about $300,000 to keep both the Arizona and Colorado offices running for the next year. But that also assumes that the offices will bring in *no* sales all year; in truth, Nolan expects to see about $30,000 a month from each office by the end of the fall.

If that happens, then he can spend the $300,000 just the way he wants: opening as many as four more branch offices this year. The start-up costs of each office will run to only about $25,000, most of that for a computer with a modem and a terminal. Nolan plans to lease the furniture and space. Once an office is set up, it will cost about $17,000 a month to operate a branch.

Nolan is also hoping to raise at least $3 million by December through a public offering of less than 30% of Landmark's stock. With that cushion, he would be able to speed his growth, opening more than eight branches a year after this year.

But Nolan isn't counting on that. "This company could finance its own growth," he says. "If I can't raise the money, we'll just grow slower. It's tough."

Christopher Nolan isn't just introducing a new product in a proven market; he's trying to build a market where, as Hughes puts it, "there has been a lot of crawling, stumbling, and falling."

Ultimately, it may turn out that consumers are dubious about the guidance they get from attorneys whose profits depend on dispensing wisdom fast. Companies, having watched group health premiums rise an average of 40% last year, may not be in the mood to add legal plans as a benefit for their employees.

But assuming there is the strong market Nolan sees, Landmark is most vulnerable in its distribution system: the insurance brokers. "I'm betting very, very heavily on brokerage community acceptance," Nolan admits. "I am putting all my eggs in one basket." There are several potential holes in that basket.

One is that the brokers might not push the plans because they require too much explanation. New insurance-type products, as opposed to marketing twists on familiar products, take forever to catch on. Brokers might decide they'd rather spend the time selling a higher-commission product like group health insurance.

If the brokers don't push fast enough, the lawyers' interest may wane. "Where are all those clients?" has been the parting shot of many a legal plan lawyer.

Finally, there is the one risk that any small company in a new industry must anticipate. Most big insurance companies have avoided writing legal plans because it is hard to assess the risk. Watching Landmark may give them some ideas. Big ideas.

By that time Nolan hopes that Landmark will be the perfect acquisition target, though it's hard to imagine him returning to work for somebody else. He does not, after all, speak fondly of his former employers.

"I was as big a sucker as anyone else," he says. "But those companies didn't know how to do it. There's big demand for this product, and I've got the formula that works."

"Prepaid legal services is an industry that hasn't succeeded in this country; there's a lot of missionary work to be done. And whenever I hear talk of missionaries, I remember that missionaries do good work but don't usually get wealthy."

—E. Bulkeley Griswold

MARKETER

KATE KINKADE

President, Time Financial Services, a Reseda, Calif., insurance brokerage firm; managing editor of California Broker *magazine*

Nolan's certainly right in that he's created a plan less complicated for the broker and buyer, which seems to offer more benefits than other plans. I would recommend the plan to my clients over other plans I've seen, absolutely.

His problem, though, is depending on the broker as a means of marketing. He plans on getting a substantial number of his clients from group sales, but I don't think the market's there. Employers aren't ready to put money into it. They have to provide medical and life insurance because everyone else does, but there's no pressure to offer a group legal plan. And with recent increases of up to 40% for the medical plans, they've been cutting back on benefits, not adding new ones. Brokers are already struggling to put together reasonable packages of basic insurance for their clients. Convincing those clients to do anything else now is tremendously difficult.

Nolan also shouldn't depend on the brokers to sell the individual plans. If I sell one of those plans, I'll only make $40—and it's hard to make me do that for $40. Having brokers sell the business plans, however, is reasonable. For the broker it's more profitable—$120 to $150—and it's a good service for the client. I can see marketing that plan.

I would recommend that he sell the individual plans directly, with advertising and direct mail. I know it's expensive, but brokers just won't be eager to market it.

Will he succeed? Not with the current marketing plan. If he can figure out a way to get the company off the ground with a smaller number of customers and then grow slowly, he might get somewhere. But with the money he's thinking of putting into it and the number of people he needs to sign up, I think he could go bankrupt.

FINANCIER

E. BULKELEY GRISWOLD

President, MarketCorp Venture Associates, a Westport, Conn., venture capital firm specializing in consumer products and services

I would not invest in this as it's presently constituted, and as it stands now, I don't think it will succeed. I've just read too many plans from individuals who have observed an industry but not run a company or been accountable for profits and losses. They see a need, but a lot of it is still supposition and hasn't been tested properly. Prepaid legal services is an industry that hasn't succeeded in this country; there's a lot of missionary work to be done. And whenever I hear talk of missionaries and development of a business and proving a need, I remember that missionaries do good work but don't usually get wealthy.

I think Nolan is running into the market too fast. He's got to test his thesis: how he'll market his plan and service it, and what kind of renewals he'll get. He's got to withdraw from three or four of the markets he's talking about, take one particular area, run a fairly decent test, and do some focus-group work with the consumers and with attorneys' groups to see exactly what they are willing to do and how appealing his fees are.

The money he says he needs now is far too little. It's probably more like half a million to a million dollars to take a market and test it. When he says venture capitalists want too much of the company, it's the classic story of the guy who's sold his house and is betting the ranch, is now in search of that next chunk of dollars, but is very unwilling to consider giving up control. And that potentially can lead to failure. He can't let the fear of losing control get in the way of doing it right.

He also talks about raising $3 million with an equity offering—but if you think having an IPO in your second year of business is a godsend, then you haven't done it before. All of a sudden you're trying to satisfy shareholders instead of really building the fundamental strengths of the business. You could

end up getting too much equity too fast during the period you ought to be doing testing. And if you have a good public offering and the stock price goes to inordinately high levels and you do not perform, there will be disappointment—and those shareholders tend to sell that stock pretty quickly. Then there are all the attendant costs of an IPO and the amount of time it takes to do it. For all those reasons, it's better to forestall that kind of financial arrangement until you've proven the concept, built the team, and have some strength under your belt.

COMPETITOR

HARLAND STONECIPHER
Founder and CEO of Pre-Paid Legal Services Inc., a legal service company he started in 1972. In 1987 the company was #92 on the Inc. 100

There are a couple of problems here. The biggest fallacy of Nolan's plan is its marketing. I don't think anybody's had more experience trying to work with insurance brokers than I have, and it's been one of the most disappointing things I've ever tried. It did not work.

Despite the fact that we've signed up literally thousands of brokers across the country, that we pay higher commissions than Landmark, and that we advance those commissions, the amount of prepaid legal services sold for us by brokers wouldn't pay our light bill. These people are used to selling life insurance and health insurance, which is a totally different ball game. With legal plans, there has to be some education about the product before the sale—you have to introduce the consumer to the product and convince him there is a need for it before he'll buy it—and most insurance brokers for some reason can't do that, or won't.

Second is the middleman strategy. It's a great theory—I wish I could do it—to farm everything out. That's what he's doing, saying he's going to get somebody to do his marketing and pay him a percentage. And get somebody to do his administrative work and pay him a percentage. And get people to do the legal work and pay them some percentage. Then he's going to be left with 28% for doing nothing? If I could get that kind of work, I'd be doing it.

He says he's not going to increase the workload of his attorneys by more than 15%. Now you talk about a product that's illusory! If you're going to increase their workload only by 15%, then you're talking about selling services that people aren't going to use. There are many legal services that people legitimately need and use. If you're selling an illusion, sooner or later somebody's going to catch you.

ANALYST

DAVID BAKER
Consultant in the legal plan industry for five years; previously administrator of The Ohio Legal Services Fund, which covered about 6,000 workers in Columbus

Nolan's comment about looking for $250,000 at this stage and wanting

to get it without losing equity control is somewhat revealing. I think it wouldn't be a good deal for an investor. In my mind, that money should be spent on market research, regulatory analysis, and some detailed planning, instead of running out and trying to get the product on the streets.

Nolan needs to analyze the regulatory impact on his plan. In a large number of states, they won't allow him to operate this closed-panel approach—where he is referring customers to individual law firms—on a for-profit basis. The disciplinary rules that govern the bar in many states simply won't permit for-profit legal plans. A majority of states will require underwriting on Nolan's plan by a licensed insurer.

Maybe he'll be able to turn decent profits in the limited number of states he's able to operate in without regulation. But in the long run, he might well need to get an underwriter. Without any regulatory problems, he's probably got only five or six states to sell in. What happens after that? It's really an oversight.

He's sharp, he's aggressive, and I like some of his analysis. He's going up to $5 a head, and that's sure as hell going to stimulate the attorneys. At $5 a month, it's a gold mine; it's a gold mine at $2 a month. He should have attorneys jumping up and down, rolling out the red carpet when any plan holder walks into the office.

HOLLYWOOD SHUFFLE

Filmstar Inc. is out to free Hollywood producers from the studios' stranglehold. But will producers take the risk?

BY TOM RICHMAN

Darryl Estrine

Getting into the movie business is easy. Really. All you need is a lot of money. If you have that, then you can find a script, producer, director, and some stars; make the movie; and advertise and promote it. If lots of people like your movie, you make a bundle. If nobody likes it, you lose your shirt.

You might make the bundle, but the odds are better you'll lose your shirt.

Harlan Kleiman, a veteran of the theater and television businesses, wanted to get into the movies, but a couple of things about the conventional strategy troubled him. First, he did not have a lot of money—some, but even a well-rewarded corporate executive like Kleiman can't finance a movie out of his take-home pay. Also, the prospect of losing a bundle didn't appeal to him much. So over several years he sought an alternative strategy for entering the business, one that did not take a lot

---

Harlan Kleiman, founder of Filmstar Inc., in Los Angeles

EXECUTIVE SUMMARY

THE COMPANY:
Filmstar Inc.,
Los Angeles

CONCEPT:
One-stop supermarket of financial and marketing services for independent film producers, which would provide them an alternative to turning their movies over to studios

PROJECTIONS:
Expected May 31, 1989, year-end loss of $961,000 on revenues of $3 million; projected 1990 profit of $520,000 on revenues of $9.7 million

HURDLES:
Getting the capital required to (1) acquire the operating subsidiaries the concept calls for and (2) back the loans and letters of credit it must extend in order to attract independent producers, especially those making the A movies sought in foreign markets

of money and that improved the odds of keeping his clothes. Eventually, he worked out his concept and launched his company, Filmstar Inc. Now he has to execute the plan.

Which doesn't mean Kleiman has donned a beret to shoot pictures—though at one time he wanted to. That he now does *not* makes him a bit of a maverick in an already-idiosyncratic industry. To appreciate how Kleiman is different, you have to know what is normal, if *normal* is a word that applies anywhere in the fantasy business of Hollywood.

Producers are close to normal. These hardworking people actually make movies. They pull together the story, the actors, the director, and the technical crew. They're responsible for all the arrangements—for equipment, locations, transportation, and so on, everything including lunch. They get the film shot and then edited. In theory, producers also own the movies they make, but in actuality, they usually do not own them for long. That's where studios come in.

Studios solve problems for producers, beginning with the biggest one: money. Producers usually do not have money; studios do. So to finance their movies, producers often try to sell the project to a studio. If it buys the producer's proposal, the studio owns all the distribution rights to the movie. In effect, the producer has become an employee of the studio while producing the film. He or she gets a negotiated fee and—if the picture is a hit—maybe profit participation. Studios solve other problems, too. They provide producers with everything from accounting and payroll services to advertising and promotion services—even lunch. They just bill all of that, along with a healthy chunk of their overhead, to the producer's film. The charges quickly accumulate. Typically, a studio-made film must generate in sales more than four times its negative cost—the cost to film the movie before distribution prints are made and before advertising charges—before it breaks even and before the producer who originated the whole thing sees a nickel of profit.

That's what Kleiman faced when he decided he wanted to make movies a few years ago. No tenderfoot in the entertainment industry, Kleiman had specialized in pay TV and home video. He had been head of programming for Home Box Office and senior vice-president of the cable division of Warner Communications Inc. Years earlier he had cofounded the Long Wharf Theatre in New Haven and lectured on theater at Harvard, Yale, and New York Universities. Now armed with a script, he went to a studio. The people there told him the deal, and he didn't like it. "The odds," he says between courses at a Hollywood sushi restaurant where he is well known, "were with the house. `OK,' I said, `I'll be an independent producer.' But then I learned that there is no such thing. An independent producer is just dependent on more people."

What he means is that every service a studio provides a producer can also be found outside a studio. Producers can hire an independent payroll service or an independent accounting service; they can hire writers, film editors, and publicists. They can raise their own money, too, by preselling the distribution rights to their movies to theatrical distributors, video distributors, and cable- and broadcast-TV outlets. Then they can do the same thing in the foreign markets. They are, it is true, independent of the studio, but you

THE FOUNDER

Harlan Kleiman
chairman and CEO

Age: 49

Source of idea:
Attempted to produce a movie in Hollywood and was disgusted by the terms the studios tried to exact

Personal funds invested: $650,000

Equity held:
Nearly 30%

Other businesses started: Long Wharf Theatre, regional professional theater in New Haven; Caravatt-Kleiman Inc., video software; Leslie Kleiman Inc., pay-TV video production

Typical workweek:
65 hours

Outside board of directors: Yes

What I lose sleep over: Running a publicly traded company

can see the problem with this independence. "How was I going to make a movie," Kleiman recalls asking himself, "if I had to do all this other stuff?" Kleiman could not understand how he was supposed to be a full-time artist and a full-time businessman at the same time. "So I said to myself, If I'm an intelligent producer with this problem, there must be others with the same problem."

Where there is a problem, every entrepreneur knows, there is an opportunity. Kleiman talked to independent producers. It wasn't fair, they told him, that studios grabbed practically all the profits from a film

FINANCIALS

FILMSTAR INC. PROJECTED SALES AND PROFITS
(in $ thousands)

	Fiscal Year 1989 (5/31/89)	Projected FY 1990	Projected FY 1991
Revenues[1]	$2,976	$9,703	$17,186
Net income (loss)	(961)	520	1,545
Cash, year end	581	2,680[2]	1,356

[1] In 1989, 82% from distribution services; in 1990, 95% from distribution services; remainder from payroll services
[2] Assumes $5-million private debt offering, FY 1990

just for fronting the money. Sure, it was their money, but there are two kinds of equity, and the studio system took no account of the sweat that producers invested in their films. What if he could devise a plan that would allow producers to retain more of the upside potential and not burden them with all the managerial minutiae that filmmaking entails? They would like that, they said. So, rather than make movies himself, Kleiman decided he would see if he could devise a better way of helping producers make movies.

Here was his idea: He would put together a one-stop service super-market for indies. They could come to this company and arrange for whatever they needed: financing, distribution, payroll, marketing, mer-chandising, and so on. They could buy single services or all of them— whatever the situation demanded. But this company would be different from a studio in two fundamental ways.

First, it would be cheaper to use than a studio. Studios are vertical-ly integrated movie manufacturers with everything under one figurative roof. Their overhead costs are inevitably high because of hard-to-detect inefficiencies, cross-subsidies, and the price of corporate management. Instead, Kleiman imagined a synergistic collection of profitable, autonomous businesses that he could acquire and operate under a hold-ing-company umbrella, each business providing one of the services that producers were looking for. The Filmstar synergy, he says, will come from one subsidiary company feeding business to another.

Second, studios take risks that Filmstar would not. Studios finance movies. They can claim most of the profit when a film does well, but they take the bath when a film flops. Kleiman's companies would not invest their own money in a producer's idea. They would, for the most part, operate on a fee-for-service basis. That means that Filmstar's income from a picture would be largely insensitive to the film's box-office, TV, or home-video sales.

Of course, Kleiman would rather be associated with profitable films than with losers. Filmstar's biggest challenge as a foreign distributor, for example, is to acquire the rights to films that will make lots of money for the overseas subdistributors that are Filmstar's customers. But under Kleiman's plan, one or two overbudget disasters would not bring his business to its knees as they might if he were relying on box-office sales to recoup his expenses.

The idea seemed appealing. Where most people with a similar idea had gone wrong in the past, Kleiman says, was in not being able to resist the camera's lure—that is, getting into the filmmaking business themselves. Making movies is seductive and sexy and can be terribly profitable. However, it is awfully risky, especially for a start-up with no inventory of films to provide continuing revenues. Also, when a company like Filmstar makes its own films, it becomes a competitor to the independent producers who are the market for the services it offers. Eschewing its own productions may mean that Filmstar will never pocket huge profits from an *E.T.*-like success, but its standard fees will keep rolling in. Each portfolio company would have its own market, its own management, and its own *projectable* income. That—projectable income—is what Kleiman keeps stressing as the characteristic distinguishing Filmstar from other industry start-ups.

Furthermore, Filmstar wasn't just a plan to make money. Kleiman hoped it might change Hollywood, allowing some producers to make films they could not make under the studio-dominated system. He points out that the so-called 20-80 rule is applicable in the movie business: Even though studios make only 20% of the pictures, they pocket 80% of the industry's revenues. "This was a way for me to be part of the system while having an opportunity to build something that might affect the system," he says.

Kleiman spent most of 1986 and '87 and some $600,000 of his own money trying to figure out how to raise more cash and turn his concept into a business. Without adequate capital, he couldn't acquire a going concern, and without a going concern, he couldn't raise capital—until he hit on the notion of making Filmstar's first business the business of sales. Specifically, Kleiman thought he could raise money to capitalize a company that specialized in foreign distribution of U.S. films. Why that?

To start, being a foreign distributor would require relatively little capital. Filmstar would just be the sales representative between the film producer and the foreign subdistributors who actually place films in movie houses. Foreign sales of U.S.-made films were growing faster than domestic sales. In fact, the eight major overseas markets together— Japan, Germany, France, the United Kingdom, Italy, Spain, Scandinavia, and Australia/New Zealand—were nearly as big as the U.S. market. In 1988, for instance, the film industry generated $8.6 billion in domestic sales—about 30% of that from box office, 40% from home-video sales, 10% from pay TV, and the rest from broadcast TV and other sources. Sales to those same outlets overseas came to $7.1 billion. For 1989 foreign sales will probably fall just short of $9 billion, better than a 25% increase over last year.

Foreign distribution, Kleiman thought, would be cheap to get into and could be lucrative if done well. This could launch his company. The business plan he prepared to attract investors stressed the foreign-distribution business and barely mentioned the larger concept—blue sky, the lawyers feared—at all.

Other people bought his idea. A group of friends invested $900,000, which, at his own insistence, Kleiman tucked into escrow until Filmstar could raise public equity as well.

What Kleiman had not figured on was the effect of Black Monday on his progress. The Wall Street underwriter that was to take Filmstar public went under a few days after the crash and before the offering. Kleiman found another underwriter, off-off-Wall Street, and despite the dismal market conditions, went ahead with his company's initial public offering. By February 1988 he and the underwriter had managed to sell units of stock and warrants worth $1.3 million, not the $5 million he had originally wanted. However, added to what was in escrow, that came to $2.2 million, enough to get him started.

If it's done right, foreign distribution *can* be a cash-positive business almost from day one. You get money before you deliver the product, and you do not have to pay your supplier until well after the product is delivered. Also, there is little risk that you cannot control—if, again, it's done right. Foreign-distribution deals can take countless forms, but here is how a typical one might work.

A producer brings a film to Filmstar for foreign distribution. (Domestic rights have probably already been sold to one of the major studios, which control most domestic distribution.) Filmstar's vice-president of worldwide sales, Sudy Coy, a 16-year veteran in the business, looks at the movie and, based on her knowledge of the foreign markets, estimates the minimum guarantee she thinks she can get for the movie from the international subdistributors she'll license to. Then Filmstar

PRODUCER'S CHOICE

Why movies make money (or don't)

An independent producer can get a movie financed in one of two ways: (1) sell the movie to a studio, which pays the producer a flat fee, typically 5% of the negative cost and a percentage of the profits, and assumes liability for all costs; or (2) use services such as those offered by Filmstar to make and market the movie, retaining ownership, eventual profits, and also liability for losses, if any. Here's how a ledger might look for making the same film under each scenario.

1. Actual cost of making film (payroll, equipment, location expenses, meals, and so on) before interest and charges, expected to be lower with Filmstar

2. Independent producer borrows from commercial bank; studio film is financed internally with imputed interest assigned

3. Unsecured loan from commercial bank for independent producer, estimated rate 5% over prime; 2% over prime imputed for studio loan

4. Guild fees, residuals paid to artists

5. Film's share of box-office receipts

6. Studio typically charges 15% to distribute independently produced films for which the producer provides for print and advertising costs, 35% for in-house films

7. Negotiated distribution fee: 7.5% to 10% net rental income

8. Studios manufacture and sell videocassettes, paying straight 20% royalty to producer; assumes video sales of $18 million

9. Does not include payments for production-related services covered in negative-cost line item, so does not represent total of Filmstar revenues on project

10. Producer's only income is the predetermined flat fee, which was part of the film's negative cost

COSTS (in $ thousands)	Filmstar	Studio
Negative cost[1]	$8,000	$10,000
Prints and advertising	4,000	4,000
Finance charges[2]		
Two-year production loan at 11%	1,760	2,200
3% bank-commitment fee	240	—
One-year loan for prints & advertising[3]	560	440
15% commitment fee	600	—
SUBTOTAL	**15,160**	**16,640**
15% studio overhead charge	—	2,496
Miscellaneous[4]	1,200	1,200
TOTAL COST BEFORE DISTRIBUTION	**16,360**	**20,336**
SALES (minus cost of sales)		
Domestic theater film rental[5]	15,000	15,000
(Studio distribution fee)[6]	(2,250)	(5,250)
(Filmstar fee)[7]	(1,275)	—
Video		
Producer's royalty[8]	—	3,600
Sale of video rights	4,400	—
(Filmstar 10% sales fee)	(440)	—
Pay TV, cable (minus distribution fee)	2,400	2,400
Foreign distribution	—	11,200
Presale of rights	3,200	—
(Filmstar 25% sales fee)	(800)	—
(40% studio distribution fee)	—	(4,480)
(Dubbing, subtitles, etc.)	—	(2,400)
NET SALES	**20,235**	**20,070**
SUMMARY		
Total picture sales	25,000	32,200
(Studio distribution fees)	(2,250)	(12,130)
(Filmstar commissions)[9]	(2,515)	—
Total picture cost before distribution	(16,360)	(20,336)
NET PROFIT (LOSS)	**3,875**	**(266)**
Net to producer	3,875	500[10]

will propose a deal to a producer. It might, for instance, offer to split the foreign income 75-25, keeping the smaller share for itself. And it will usually offer to guarantee the producer some minimum payment—usually 60% of the minimum guarantee Coy expects to command from the foreign subdistributors. If she estimates a $1-million guaranteed minimum, Filmstar will offer to guarantee the producer $600,000. If Coy's estimate is right and she actually gets a $1-million guaranteed minimum in the foreign market, the producer will end up with $750,000—minus Filmstar's out-of-pocket selling expenses for that film and commissions. In her smoke-husky voice, Coy will tell you that her record for being on the money is very good. If it stays that way, these deals hold hardly any other risk for Filmstar.

If the film does better than everyone expects, Filmstar and the foreign subdistributor will split the overage, with Filmstar's share declining as the gross rises. Filmstar in turn passes this revenue back to the producer after taking out its sales fee—25% in this case.

The nice thing is that Filmstar has not put a single dollar at risk in the deal. The subdistributor could be buying a pig in a poke. The kicker is that the payouts are often structured so that Filmstar gets its cash from the subdistributor months before its payouts to the producer are due.

In the 12 months ending last May 31, its first full year in the business, Kleiman's foreign-distribution arm handled rights for 11 films—7 completed and 4 in preproduction. That makes Filmstar a significant but not major player in an industry that produced more than 500 feature films in 1988.

The company is building its relationships with foreign subdistributors and with producers—the suppliers of films. The subdistributors, Coy says, will do business with anyone who can supply them with a continuous flow of the pictures their audiences want to see. Right now the taste of fans overseas as well as here is running to high-budget productions—so-called A films as opposed to cheaper B and cheapest C movies—in the action-adventure genre. That means, she and Kleiman both acknowledge, that Filmstar has to hustle to continue upgrading the movies it can procure for foreign distribution.

Here, again, is where Kleiman's synergistic concept comes in. Theoretically, the company's foreign-distribution arm will gain an advantage in attracting makers of quality films, because Filmstar will also offer producers services such as:

Financing. Whatever else they might need, producers always need money. Filmstar plans to be able to help producers raise it in several ways. For instance, it might issue a producer a letter of credit, which the producer could use as loan collateral in exchange for future distribution rights. Filmstar could make loans directly to producers—both pay-or-play and bridge loans. The first helps producers get a commitment from their talent, who will not sign without a promise of pay whether or not they are "played." The loan lets a producer make that promise and get on with fund-raising. Bridge loans help producers finish films when other cash has run out. With either type of loan, Filmstar will negotiate not only repayment but future rights and, if it can, some equity in the picture. It still won't be taking much of a risk, though. Any loans or letters of credit will be backed by distribution rights to the film. Filmstar could also act as a producer's agent or broker, arranging for a bank or other lender to discount the producer's receivables (presold distribution rights, for instance) for production financing.

Payroll. A Filmstar subsidiary can handle a production's payroll accounting and disbursements—such as employee paychecks, workers' compensation insurance, and tax withholding.

Marketing, advertising, and media buying. One or more subsidiary companies could provide the creative as well as production services required to market and promote a producer's film.

Product licensing. Want to buy a Batman T-shirt or an E.T. doll?

Product merchandising. Actors do not drink Coke on camera because they necessarily prefer it to Pepsi. Coca-Cola has paid for that tacit endorsement.

Production services. Someone has to run the budget and manage the staff while a movie is being made. A Filmstar company, for a fee, could do that.

Financial management. With all the money producers are going to make working with Filmstar, they are going to need help managing their personal finances. Another Filmstar company could do that.

Filmstar *could* do most of these things, but so far it does not. The company lacks the capital required to acquire the operating subsidiaries and provide financial services to independent producers.

So far, Filmstar has acquired a small payroll company that services television awards specials and is expanding into television series and films. It has issued one letter of credit to the producer of *Bethune*, which stars Donald Sutherland as a Canadian doctor working in Mao's China.

The trial partnership Filmstar had with a company to provide film marketing services didn't work out—a personality conflict, Filmstar's Peter Kares says.

Kares, 46, is the president of the company and owned Producers Funding Corp., which Filmstar acquired in early 1988. But the company's arrangement with an East Coast merchant bank for production loans to producers that Filmstar brought to the bank didn't pan out. Kares's role now is to scout out the films whose foreign-distribution rights Filmstar would like to acquire and to strike deals with these producers.

Kleiman has hired 31-year-old Robert Wolpert, a product of Harvard Business School whose last activity was training for triathlons, to help him structure his holding company and act as its chief of operations. "My personal interest," Wolpert says, "is making the acquisitions work." However, managing acquisitions is not an acute issue just now with only a single portfolio company showing on the organization chart. As yet, Kleiman and Wolpert have not articulated how the organization will be structured and managed when there are more.

Kleiman spends most of his time these days in meetings, on the phone, and booking flights—all in a search of companies to acquire and for new capital to help him acquire them. Though he has a preferred order of acquisitions in mind, he recognizes the necessity of responding to opportunities as they arise, he says. He'll take them in the order in which he can get them—assuming he can afford them. He would also like to expand the distribution business to television and video.

Filmstar has to raise more capital if Kleiman's ambitions are not to be frustrated. Its only significant equity infusion was the $2.2 million that came in the original private placement and IPO. There are some warrants outstanding, but they are not likely to be exercised unless the price of Filmstar's stock picks up. It has traded at slightly less than $2 a share, more than $2 off its post-IPO high of 4 1/8. With an investor loan of $350,000, the company bought a certificate of deposit that it used to collateralize part of the bank letter of credit it gave to the producer of *Bethune*. It sold part of the rights to pay for the rest. Recently, an investor group signed a letter of intent to drop $1.25 million into the company.

Currently, Kleiman is circulating a business plan in hopes of finding an underwriter to help him sell several million dollars in debt or convertible debt. Debt at this point would be preferable to equity, Kleiman says, in order to minimize equity dilution. The largest chunk of the money, if he can get it, will back the financing arm of the business. The ability to issue bankable paper to producers will make Filmstar a stronger player in the competition to acquire foreign rights to the big-budget, potential blockbusters that overseas moviegoers increasingly prefer.

The company's batting average to date isn't bad, apparent testimony to Kares's eye and Coy's sense of what the market will pay. "Every film we have acquired to date," Kleiman claims, "has been or will be profitable." Nonetheless, Filmstar's May 31 year-end audited financials show a heavy loss. While the company has written contracts worth, it says, $9.5 million, its auditors won't permit the company to claim these revenues until they are received. Sales for 1989 were $3 million with a loss of $961,000.

Almost everyone who moves to Hollywood gets star struck. Who *doesn't* want to be in the movies, given the chance?

Not he, Kleiman insists, in his fifth-floor Wilshire Boulevard office in West L.A., a few blocks short of Beverly Hills. Filmstar will not make movies. "I want a business that's very simple. I want one level of business we can control and predict and one level with upside potential that we don't have to put a lot of money into. I'm not afraid to deal with the mundane and make it exciting. I get thrilled with the opportunity to drive just a part of this industry."

"What's keeping it from being hugely successful is money. I don't know whether I'd lend to it now, given how undercapitalized it is."

–Carol Wakefield

FINANCIER

CAROL WAKEFIELD

Vice-president of entertainment division, Tokai Bank, Los Angeles; frequent lender to film projects

The one-stop shopping idea has merit. Most of the independents I deal with don't know how to put the whole project together and get their film done. They need somebody in the early stages who can do it for them—so a company like Filmstar should have a lot of business.

What's keeping it from being hugely successful is money. It's at the point in its corporate life when an equity investment might be more appropriate than debt financing. I don't know whether I'd lend to it now, given how undercapitalized it is. I'd never lend to it unsecured.

Maybe Filmstar should try a public offering again or bring in an investor with big bucks. Some kind of subordinated debt offering might be interesting, but it's not ripe for bank financing.

OBSERVER

PAUL KAGAN

President, Paul Kagan Associates, Carmel, Calif., which publishes "Motion Picture Investor" and 29 other media-industry newsletters

Conceptually, it's the right idea at the right time. The movie business probably has more need for a company like this than most because the creative people—the producers, writers, directors, and actors—don't have financial expertise.

Filmstar has to pick the right films. It has to finance them carefully; it can't overextend its credit resources. It also must watch its corporate overhead. And it must be sure it gets into the right distribution networks and theaters.

Filmstar has to focus on wooing the best of the independent producers. If it does that, it can create a much-needed niche business.

RETAIL BROKER

DAVID ALMQUIST

Associate vice-president, Prudential-Bache Securities Inc., Laguna Hills, Calif., specializing in investment opportunities

This concept is overdue in Hollywood. Put yourself in an independent producer's shoes. Would you go to work and sell your soul to a studio, knowing that really you had a very limited upside? I don't think I would.

So Filmstar may open a new segment, though it'll take time for producers to become aware of the possibility of getting paid what they're worth. It makes sense from an incentive standpoint; we'll probably see lots of little companies jumping in and operating similarly.

Any good company is sometimes too aggressive and can run short of capital. But I think these are capable, experienced people who are going to know when to stop and say, "We've got to regroup and get additional capital; we can't stretch ourselves too thin."

Harlan is smart to try to maintain as much equity in the company as possible. But I certainly wouldn't see it as a negative if he came out with a debt offering.

For Filmstar, credibility is the foremost issue. Producers want to be associated with credible names. Filmstar needs to establish credibility.

COMPETITOR

RICKI AMES
Vice-president of international sales, Enoki Films USA Inc., a worldwide distributor and producer of children's programming and feature films

Until independent producers have the necessary clout or money, Filmstar could be valuable to them—*if* it gets its act together and offers one-stop service. But its concept has to be complete.

The only things it is offering are payroll and foreign distribution. And foreign distribution is not something that independent producers want to give up if they don't have to. Most are also distributors, and foreign distribution is the way you make your money. We'd rather distribute on our own than pay Filmstar a percentage to do it.

HEAD OF THE CLASS

*Will parents pay more for day care
if the centers are positioned as schools?*

BY STEPHEN D. SOLOMON

N othing in business is quite so powerful as a demographic wave read correctly. The wave Joseph Scandone wants to ride—the entrance of mothers into the labor force—is still far from cresting. About 56% of all women with children under age six were working in 1988, up from 25% in 1965. Liz Claiborne read it right. So did Kinder-Care. Reebok, too.

And now so has Joe Scandone—or so he thinks.

Almost two years ago Scandone started Carousel Systems Inc., a day-care company based in the Philadelphia suburb of King of Prussia, Pa. He plans to build a network to compete with industry leaders Kinder-Care Learning Centers Inc. and La Petite Academy Inc., which run 1,253 and 700 child-care centers, respectively. An old idea, perhaps, but Scandone feels he has a new twist, a second play on the demographic wave that the established companies have ignored.

Joseph Scandone, founder of Carousel Systems Inc.

SERVICES

When Kinder-Care started in 1969, says Scandone, it "developed a product for the emerging working woman who, until then, left her kids with somebody she knew. The mother was a low-level service worker who just needed a place to drop her kids off. Kinder-Care and the other companies that followed delivered safe, secure, sometimes loving care with a hot lunch."

But a good number of today's working mothers, says Scandone, are different, and the existing chains don't serve their needs. They hold high-paying managerial or professional jobs, want less baby-sitting and more emphasis on education, and are willing to pay a premium for it. Though the established chains have responded with educational curricula, Scandone calls these changes little more than window dressing. "We found that parents are looking for nursery-school quality," he says.

Scandone saw that there was plenty of room to maneuver within the industry. Day care remains essentially a mom-and-pop business ringing up annual sales of about $15 billion. Although the national chains grew 200% during the 1980s, they still accounted for only 5% of all child-care centers operating nationwide. Last year only nine chains had as many as 24 centers. The rest were much smaller operations, many of them nonprofit or run in a provider's home.

Scandone's response is a second-generation child-care company. "We're taking a nursery-school program and fitting it between day-care hours," he says. For Carousel, whose units will operate under the name Goddard School for Early Childhood Education, the major departure from traditional child care will be the hiring of teachers certified in elementary education or early-childhood development. Goddard Centers will be licensed by the state not only as child-care centers but also as educational facilities, an unusual status in the industry.

Scandone will charge 10% to 15% more than the national chains, or up to $1,000 more per year in big-city markets. He is targeting affluent parents who might otherwise choose independent centers or a Kinder-Care. "We'll take the cream from the national chains," he predicts.

The other big departure from the norm is that the Goddard Centers will be owned not by a faraway corporate parent, but by franchisees. Parents will be greeted at the door by an owner whose livelihood depends on their satisfaction, not by a manager dispatched from company headquarters. "Parents will feel, touch, and see that Goddard schools are different," promises Scandone.

A long driveway leads to the front door of a stone Cape Cod–style house in Malvern, Pa. It is, like many houses in this affluent Philadelphia suburb, set on a wooded lot blanketed now by snow. A discreet sign outside carries the Goddard name.

EXECUTIVE SUMMARY

THE COMPANY:
Carousel Systems Inc., King of Prussia, Pa.; franchisor, Goddard School for Early Childhood Education

CONCEPT:
Create a national chain of franchised day-care centers targeting upper-income parents who want more formal education for their children

PROJECTIONS:
Franchisor operating profits of $170,000 this year and, in 1993, profits of $2.65 million on $11.75 million in royalty and franchise fees from 240 centers; franchisee gross profits of $113,000 on revenues of $530,000 (21% margin)

HURDLES:
Meeting high-margin projections at each center; maintaining quality while aggressively expanding; differentiating Goddard enough to support premium pricing

Inside the front door is a brown horse that once rode on a carnival carousel. Nearby are the children's cubbyhole mailboxes, filled with handwritten notes from teachers to parents explaining that day's lessons. Kids in one room are singing Christmas carols as their parents listen; in another, a teacher named Jennifer is preparing a midmorning snack. "Whoever is quiet will get their snack first," she announces, and a hush falls over the assembled.

This is the first of Joe Scandone's two child-care centers, and the model on which the franchised centers will be based. Each week, every class in the center focuses on the same subject—in March, for instance, they'll learn about weather one week, pets another, dinosaurs a third. Each teacher formulates his or her own lesson plan appropriate for the age group, designed to advance four important developmental skills: cognitive, physical, social, and emotional.

Scandone's purchase of the center in 1986 was no attempt to pursue a lifelong passion for child care. He was simply looking for a business to run. He had spent 12 years at the General Accounting Office reviewing a variety of federal initiatives such as Head Start, the early-education program. Then he served for 6 years at General Electric Co.

In 1986 Scandone quit G.E. and began analyzing various business opportunities. The demographic changes that gave rise to the child-care business intrigued him, as did the fragmented nature of the industry. Might there be room for another national chain? By the time he had opened two centers two years later, he had become excited about building a national company. But he didn't know how to do it.

For advice, Scandone sought out Tony Martino, for whom he had worked more than 20 years earlier, when he was a high-school student. Martino had distinguished himself by building three major franchise businesses. In the 1960s he had grown AAMCO into a network of more than 500 transmission-repair shops, with sales of some $100 million. Martino had sold AAMCO and founded MAACO Enterprises, now a chain of 450 shops that specialize in painting and collision work. And he did it a third time in the 1980s, growing SPARKS into a string of auto tune-up centers before selling it.

Martino liked the child-care idea so much that he offered to help Scandone franchise the business. It is, after all, one of the fastest ways to build a national company. And speed mattered. Scandone felt certain that if he did not move quickly, competitors—perhaps the big chains themselves—would vault past him. So Scandone and Martino started the company in 1988, the latter providing virtually all of the $250,000 capitalization and taking a majority of the stock.

F ranchising does pose some difficult challenges, though. It has never worked in the child-care industry. Kinder-Care had tried franchising when the company started in the late 1960s but had given up and switched to company-owned centers. Other day-care franchisors had shut down or followed Kinder-Care's route.

All these operations had one problem in common—the inability to control the quality of service delivered by the franchisees. It is difficult enough to control a franchised MAACO shop, where the procedures are relatively amenable to lists in an operations manual. But dealing with kids means a wild card every minute, more than a match for anyone who would distill a day's activities into a neat routine.

Scandone and Martino, however, argue that franchising is the biggest *advantage* they have for delivering quality child care. They dismiss the failed attempts by saying that, until now, nobody brought to child-care franchising the kind of track record they do. More than that, though, they believe local ownership will make the difference. "Quality control might be a big problem," says Martino, "but it won't be one-tenth of what you'd experience from a company-owned location. Quality is inherent in the fact that the owner is there. An owner will always do a better job than a manager.

"Remember that a manager is on a career path, and you rarely find one who says, This is the top, I've arrived. We turn over managers all the time at the MAACO shops. But the owner will be there a long time. His view is longer." If an owner allows quality to slip, Martino promises he will move quickly to revoke the franchise.

Quality control, the founders point out, will be a primary responsibility of the local operations manager, who will work with 10 or so franchisees and visit their facilities once or twice a month. Having a large

THE FOUNDER

Joseph Scandone
president and CEO

Age: 41

Family status: Married, two daughters, 16 and 18

Workweek: 50 to 60 hours

Board of directors: None

Other businesses started: Two child-care centers in the suburbs of Philadelphia

Last job: Manager of human-resources operations, General Electric Information Services Co., a division of G.E.

College degree: B.S. with major in accounting from Philadelphia College of Textiles & Science; executive degree from Wharton School at University of Pennsylvania

Loses sleep over: The inconsistencies of local officials in approving child-care centers, which cause facility-opening delays beyond Scandone's control

Role model: Lee Iaccoca; "He's very customer oriented."

Vacations: Stays at houses he owns in Ocean City, N.J., and West Palm Beach, Fla.

staff of teachers will be another quality check, since they are likely to be sensitive to any shortcuts a franchisee takes in the educational and developmental program. Those teachers also will be, Scandone hopes, Goddard's most persuasive selling point.

Even if Scandone has correctly perceived that parents want more education from child care in the 1990s, he still must effectively market his idea. Because he's franchising, he must worry about two groups of customers. One is made up of prospective franchisees. What will he offer them that is worth a substantial franchise fee and royalty? But perhaps the most important group of customers is the parents themselves. Will they see a clear difference in quality in the new centers?

As any working person knows, good child care is expensive. The cost varies with the age of the child—typically it's highest for infants—and by region of the country. What costs $330 a month for a toddler in Boulder, Colo., can cost $730 in Boston. By pricing his service 10% to 15% higher than his competitors, Scandone is aiming for an upper-middle-class customer in a major metropolitan area who can afford to spend an extra $500 to $1,000 per child each year. For the most part, that means families with incomes above $50,000.

Scandone says they're an underserved part of the market. When he analyzes a potential site, he uses census data to analyze the demographics within a five-mile radius, looking at such variables as family income, the number of working mothers, and the number of children under age six. Then he counts the spaces available in local child-care centers; usually, he says, there is plenty of room for another provider.

It's unclear, though, how many of these affluent parents he'll be able to corral. Less than one family in four earns $50,000 or more, and many of these are overburdened already by mortgage and credit-card debt. Others have more than one child, which would multiply the cost of switching to a more expensive provider like Carousel.

Scandone, then, faces a difficult marketing challenge—reaching potential customers with a message that Carousel is clearly different. He is confident he can do this by using the usual media—radio, newspapers, and the *Yellow Pages*—to drive home the theme of education and childhood development. If the ads and word of mouth bring in parents for a look, he says, a tour of the facility will sell it to them.

"What we're charging extra for is visible and identifiable," says Scandone. "By seeing the number of teachers we have in the schools, they'll know what distinguishes us." Customers, he says, were not difficult to recruit in his own two centers. "I haven't met any price resistance, and my own schools are 12% to 15% higher than the competition."

If the franchisees can indeed attract customers, Scandone's projections demonstrate that the higher fees will bring them some huge margins. Each center should reach break-even in its first year, he says. By the end of its second year (see box, "Financials," page 92), it should be enjoying gross margins of about 21% by filling 80% of its seats. That would be two to three times the margins of the industry as a whole and of its two leaders, Kinder-Care and La Petite Academy.

If that sounds optimistic, Scandone points out that his own two child-care centers see gross margins in the high 20s. Reaching those lofty heights requires the kind of leveraging that represents the heart of his concept. Salaries in the child-care industry are dismally low. By offering 15% more in total compensation than his competitors—but still only about $15,000 a year—he says he can attract certified teachers and thereby position his service as an educational and developmental center. The $30,000 in resulting payroll expense should bring in up to $70,000 in additional tuition revenues, Scandone figures—actually more, he adds, because the emphasis on education will also enable franchisees to fill a higher proportion of their licensed spaces.

Another key to profitability will be the efficiency of each franchised

FINANCIALS

GODDARD SCHOOL FOR EARLY CHILDHOOD EDUCATION
FRANCHISEE PROJECTED ANNUAL OPERATING STATEMENT

REVENUES

Tuition: infants (15 @ $6,240/year)	$93,600
Tuition: toddlers (15 @ $5,640/year)	84,600
Tuition: preschoolers (68 @ $4,500/year)	306,000
Tuition: part-time differential	
(25% premium over full-time)	42,368
Registration fees	3,430
TOTAL GROSS REVENUES	**529,998**

OPERATING EXPENSES

Franchise royalty (7% gross revenues)	37,100
Taxes & payroll expenses (for director,	
5.578 teachers, & 7.971 aides;	
franchisee/operator receives no salary)	213,523*
Rent	91,000
Advertising & *Yellow Pages* listing	22,400
Phone, utilities, & building maintenance	20,400
Insurance & professional fees	9,508
Supplies, snacks, contingencies,	
& miscellaneous	23,495
TOTAL OPERATING EXPENSES	**417,426**

GROSS PROFIT
(before taxes and interest expenses)   **112,572**

*Salaries will vary depending on city of operation

Carousel Systems (franchisor) Projected Profit & Loss

REVENUES
(in $ millions)

	11.75
1.65	
1990	1993

NET PROFIT
(in $ millions)

	2.65
.17	
1990	1993

 # OF CENTERS

	240
15	
1990	1993

center. This doesn't mean saving money by making a smart buy on red crayons and construction paper; it means running full classes for as much of each day as possible. Most states set teacher/student ratios—say, one adult for every 8 preschoolers. So centers that routinely get a multiple of 8 toddlers are very efficient; those that bring in 18 kids require a third adult to look after only 2 children—and profitability suffers.

Juggling children to fill each class to capacity is one of the toughest parts of the business, but Scandone thinks franchisees have more incentive to do it well than managers in a national chain. "It goes right into their pocket," he says.

Scandone encourages franchisees to fill open slots with part-timers and after-school children up to the age of 10. Since these kids bring in a premium of about 25% per hour over the tuition of full-time kids, filling one spot with two half-timers can deliver 125% of the expected revenues for that space. Skillful scheduling of after-school children, he says, should produce extra revenues of $42,000 a year, or about a third of gross profit.

The ideal franchisee, says Scandone, is someone with business acumen who has no prior experience in the industry. Scandone wants franchisees to follow his system to the letter, and he fears that experienced child-care providers would be difficult to control and eventually would graft too many of their own ideas onto his model, producing a hybrid that compromises the image he wants to project. So among the first people to sign franchise agreements were an engineer, an insurance executive, a computer company vice-president, a real estate developer, and a supermarket retail manager. "What I'm looking for," says Scandone, "is someone who's worked in a corporate environment and supervised people."

The initial investment for a 122-child center is about $140,000, of which $25,000 is a franchise fee paid to Carousel. The royalty is 8% of gross revenues, discounted to 7% if payment is timely.

The fee and royalty seem relatively steep for the child-care business. Profit margins are very thin, an average of less than 5% on an aftertax basis. Unless the Goddard centers are far more profitable than the average, the royalty could drain the bottom line of each franchisee. To sell the franchises, then, Scandone must show that Carousel's support will make the centers much more successful than they would be on their own.

In Scandone's system, the franchise owner runs the business end of the operation and delegates responsibility over the educational program to the center director, a certified teacher. Most child-care centers combine these responsibilities in one job. The teaching program itself, detailed in an operations manual, was designed by one of Scandone's staff, Suzanne duPont, and consultant Fran Ritter, director of the child life department at The Children's Hospital of Philadelphia.

Aside from the curriculum, Scandone points to services that he says more than justify the fees and royalties. Carousel helps franchisees secure financing and assists them in identifying a promising site for a center. It provides support in recruiting, advertising, and public relations. For instance, last fall the company helped one franchisee place a children's playhouse and information desk in a local mall as a way of spreading the word among parents.

Carousel puts new franchise owners through two weeks of intensive training in all phases of the business. Once centers are open, Carousel will have operations people in the field to provide ongoing support.

Bud Gosnell, a 51-year-old engineer who in January became the first franchisee to open, says he couldn't have started without Carousel's help. "I'd have had to design the facility, get a curriculum, start from scratch," he says. "I don't have the savvy for that. They're already in the business, and that gives me a shortcut. They'll teach me how to run it."

Like other franchisees, Gosnell had heard about Carousel through a newspaper advertisement. In the future, a Carousel salesperson will work with interested people, guiding them through the process of approvals and signings. Scandone figures an average salesperson, after a six-month break-in period, will handle about 15 franchise sales a year, which he says will continue to be generated by ads and word of mouth. The marketing tool that will clinch the sale, he says, will be a tour of one of the Goddard centers, where thoughts about *pro forma* projections will dissolve into pleasant images of running a business for kids.

Successful sales and openings could produce attractive returns for Carousel. Scandone's *pro forma* projects profitability this year, Carousel's second full year of operations. It won't be until 1993 that the royalty fees will begin to produce significantly more revenues than the franchise fees; Scandone predicts operating profit of $2.7 million on revenues of $11.8 million that year. Scandone has a big incentive for moving the revenues up quickly; under his agreement with cofounder Tony Martino, he receives a bonus each year that is 12.5% of the royalty fees.

On the expense side, Scandone enjoys a major advantage from his association with Martino. He runs Carousel from the MAACO headquarters and receives its franchising support services—probably of higher quality than he could get on the outside—essentially at cost. This subcontracting also enables him to run a very lean shop; even now, Carousel's payroll includes only three people other than Scandone.

He also plans to hold down expenses by carefully directing the company's growth. Instead of opening centers wherever potential owners show interest, he'll grow the company in geographical clusters of about 10 centers each. That way, he says, he can deliver a high level of support with only one operations person in the field assigned to each cluster.

The first cluster will be in the Philadelphia area, the second in suburban Washington, D.C. Two centers opened in January, and Scandone expects to have 15 operating by the end of this year—65 by the end of 1991. Then he expects the pace to quicken even more, with 240 units in operation in 1993.

That's the kind of pace that only Kinder-Care and La Petite

Academy have been able to sustain until now. It certainly places into sharper relief the central questions about Scandone's business. Can he maintain a high standard of quality in a franchised operation that is growing quickly? Can he differentiate Carousel from its competition? Will parents be willing to pay an extra $500 or more for his service?

"I'm not the first guy to deliver quality and charge more for it," he says. "If the perceived quality is there, people will pay for it."

"Child care is as far from a commodity business as you can get. It's very difficult to maintain quality, especially when you're franchising, especially with people who've never done it before."

—Michael J. Connelly

OBSERVER

DICK RICHARDS
President, Childcare Center Brokerage & Development, St. Louis, which develops and brokers centers for the nation's largest day-care chains; former director of real estate for Kinder-Care

I agree that small centers can operate at greater margins than national chains, as long as the operators are qualified. But it's really presumptuous to think franchisees can attend a two-week training program and then be qualified to operate a child-care center. They should be brought into existing operations as interns, be given a longer orientation period, and be evaluated themselves by Carousel. If I were Scandone, putting together a high-end operation, I'd want to be convinced that the people I put out there know the industry inside and out. If you're selling this as the crème de la crème, you'll need to market it on the qualifications of the staff. And informed parents care less about the appearance of the place than they do about the philosophies and values of the operators.

If I were Scandone, I'd set more realistic objectives: 5 centers this year, 10 next year, maybe 10 more after that, once my management was in place. There's a danger in trying to be the next Kinder-Care—inadequate management leads to inadequate care, and parents pick up on it

real fast, leaving you with empty centers. If they grow more conservatively, they can be successful. It'll be interesting to watch, because of their franchising experience.

FINANCIER

MICHAEL J. CONNELLY
President, Lepercq Capital Management, New York City, managers of a $32-million venture fund that has invested in child-care centers

It's true that this will continue to be a fast-growing business, there aren't any dominant players, and the market they're going after is the most attractive one—the higher end, people who are looking for something other than custodial care. But their notion that they can do the rollout as quickly as they're planning and be able to make the margins they're projecting as consistently as they say just isn't realistic, even if they can do it with a few centers.

I feel confident saying no company in the history of the child-care industry has done what these guys are projecting. They expect franchisees to reach break-even in 12 months—in practice it usually takes 18 to 36 months, and that's for centers that don't have to take 7% off the top just to pay a franchise royalty.

Then there's quality control. Scandone is going to take people who have no experience in early-childhood education and turn them into owners of early-childhood-education businesses. He's going to try to do it at the highest end of the market, with the most sophisticated clientele. One of the requirements of a developmentally appropriate curriculum for early childhood is flexibility. The criticism, for example, that's leveled at Kinder-Care by the educational community is not that it is custodial. The criticism is that they've McDonaldized the curriculum, so that if it's the third Tuesday in March, three-year-olds all over the country learn the letter C. That's perceived by the educational community as being an inappropriate way to develop the cognitive skills of three-year-olds.

This is not a commodity business; child care is as far from a commodity business as you can get. And it's very difficult to maintain quality, especially when you're franchising with people who've never done it before. Scandone says that he'll pull a franchisee if someone is not providing the level of quality that he insists on; well, how's he going to know? How's he going to measure it? If you do a bad job on transmissions, people's cars break down and they have to get towed in, and it's an expense—but it's just money. You do a bad job on child care, you're risking a whole lot more than money. I don't believe the sophisticated market he's going after will be comfortable leaving its children in the care of people with so little experience. I just don't think it'll work.

COMPETITOR

ROGER BROWN
Chief executive officer, Bright Horizons Children's Centers, Cambridge, Mass., which developed and operates 26 worksite child-care centers on the East Coast

I don't know that franchising is going to work at the high end; it would be much more appropriate as a low-end strategy. Part of the reason involves teachers—if you were a teacher, where would you rather work, a place that allows you to create your own curriculum or a place that hands you a manual and says, "This week we're doing rabbits"? Hiring the best people is going to be difficult in this context.

If you want to do the high end, you ought to hire teachers who have a good background and give them autonomy. See, what they're touting is the fact that the entrepreneur-franchisee has financial autonomy in running the center, and that that's going to lead to better results than a company-managed center could get. But if you want to be on the high end educationally, you need to have that same autonomy in the educational program.

OBSERVER

ROGER NEUGEBAUER
Publisher and editor, Child Care Information Exchange, *Redmond, Wash., an industry trade publication*

The Carousel people present Kinder-Care as their main competition, and that's misleading. Their real competitors are the small chains with three to six centers that can be found in every community in the country. They run quality centers and charge a higher fee. They're after the same market Carousel is. Much of the growth in the past five years has been in this area, and now all the big chains are going after it, too.

There's nothing about franchising that prohibits it from working in child care, except the amount of the royalty. Average day-care profit margins are in the range of 5% to 6%. Even the yuppie centers are not dramatically above that. If you tell franchisees that the first 7% to 8% goes to the franchisor, that's not very encouraging. No chain over the past 10 years has been able to maintain profit levels above 15% for more than a few years; how is Carousel going to do it? Companies we've surveyed in the 8% to 10% profit range are already charging 15% more than their competitors, just as Carousel plans, so that premium alone isn't enough.

NOT FOR PROFIT

This is one nonprofit facing a very businesslike question: Can it get beyond the stage where it's a novelty and find a way to take its concept national?

BY TOM RICHMAN

Frank Siteman

O f all the enterprises that *Inc.* has examined in the Anatomy of a Start-up series, City Year Inc. is singular. Not only is it a nonprofit venture, but it has customers who don't pay, investors who don't measure their returns in cash, and employees who are intended to be the principal beneficiaries of the enterprise. Nonetheless, City Year founders Alan Khazei (rhymes with *daisy*) and Michael Brown insist they are fundamentally entrepreneurs, only of a different sort. "We're interested," says Brown, "in ways of making society work better."

Toward that end Brown and Khazei, while still Harvard undergraduates, began working on a concept for a national youth service corps for

City Year Inc. founders Alan Khazei (left) and Michael Brown

EXECUTIVE SUMMARY

THE COMPANY:
City Year Inc.,
Boston

CONCEPT:
Develop a "franchis-able" model for a privately funded, nonprofit youth ser-vice corps that cre-ates real value for its sponsors, its employees, and the community at large

PROJECTIONS:
A 250-member Boston corps (up from 75 kids this year) requiring a budget of $5 million and generating 480,000 person-hours of community service by 1993; then expansion to other cities

HURDLES:
Attracting continued private-sector funding and intro-ducing some federal government financing without compromising the program's aims

kids from all walks of life. The objective was enhanced citizenship. They reasoned that if you could show young people early in their lives that they could work together on societal problems, the experience would give them a heightened sense of citizenship, which they would be inclined to exercise for the rest of their lives. This was the underlying concept for City Year, launched in 1988 in Boston as a model for a youth service corps that would eventually expand to other cities nationwide. Since City Year was conceived neither as a jobs program nor solely for the poor, it was ineligible for federal funds. Khazei and Brown realized early on that they were going to have to finance it with money they raised on their own. So they had to turn their con-cept into a program they could organize, operate, and sell.

The elements of the City Year program are simple. It recruits a limited number of young people, ages 17 to 22, from varied educational, economic, and ethnic back-grounds; organizes them into teams of 8 to 12; and sends them out to perform physical and human service work in conjunction with schools, agencies, and other nonprofits across the city. The financing for the program comes entirely from private sources—the local busi-ness community, foundations, and philan-thropic institutions. The benefits—in theo-ry—accrue not only to the kids but also to the sponsors and the community. In 1987 Khazei and Brown worked with two colleagues—Neil Silverston, then a recent Harvard Business School graduate, and Jennifer Eplett, who would later enter that institution—to write a plan that explained their concept, strategy, and objectives and contained a projected budget. They pro-posed to operate a nine-week summer pilot program in 1988 to prove the project's feasibility. Then the plan called for full-time operation with 50 kids in 1989–90. If that worked, the plan said, they'd look toward national expansion.

The 1988 summer pilot, like the first full-year program Khazei and

Brown envisioned, would consist of five teams of 10 kids, with each team supervised by a salaried young adult. The teams, like the City Year corps overall, would contain a deliberately diversified group: about half male, half female; half city residents, half suburban; half white, half minority; half poor and working class, some middle class, and some upper class. They'd wear uniforms—T-shirts with the sponsors' names on them—and all 50 would work out together as a corps every morning before splitting up and heading off to team projects. Those would include park-cleaning and shelter-painting chores, but they would also get the kids involved with people—homeless people, people with AIDS, students, the elderly in public housing projects, and so on. All Brown and Khazei needed to start was $200,000, 50 kids, a staff, and some projects.

Although federal tax dollars weren't available to City Year, private-sector funding also made sense philosophically for a couple of reasons. One was that Brown and Khazei saw themselves providing to the public sector what other entrepreneurs contributed to the private: innovation. "Without political pressures," Khazei says, "we've been able to design a program the way we think it should be. I have the feeling that we'll have a major impact on public-service-program design. After all, you can't reform the computer industry from within IBM. That's why we needed Apple." If the City Year concept works in the long run, Khazei and Brown expect that government money will come in—just as corporations eventually buy into successful small-business innovations.

Another reason that private-sector funding fit Brown and Khazei's plan was their assumption that corporations, like individuals, have civic responsibilities. "In the 1990s," says Brown, "there's a growing perception that doing good is going to be part of doing well." City Year, he

FINANCIALS

CITY YEAR INC. PROJECTED OPERATING STATEMENT
(in $ thousands)

	Fiscal 1989 (actual)*	Fiscal 1990 (estimated)	Fiscal 1991 (projected)
Support and revenues			
Corporations & foundations	$719	$886	$1,200
Individuals & events	16	100	300
Interest income	10	20	23
In-kind support	196	116	65
TOTAL SUPPORT & REVENUES	**$941**	**$1,122**	**$1,588**
Expenses			
Field operations	$50	$396	$601
Training	10	15	19
Education	13	54	62
Recruiting/youth development	—	30	91
Evaluation	—	13	14
Project development	—	22	31
Scholarships	—	197	387
Fund-raising	34	59	82
Management/general & administrative	119	144	207
In-kind expenses	101	85	60
TOTAL EXPENSES	**$327**	**$1,015**	**$1,554**
Support & revenues less expenses	614	107	34
Fund balance, beginning of period	29	643	750
Fund balance, end of period	643	750	784

*A development year spent raising funds, with no program in operation.

and Khazei reasoned, would give companies an opportunity to do good in a new way.

City Year's major donors, without exception, say the concept was what first attracted them to the program. "This was definitely entrepreneurial, the first time it had ever been done," says Kay Kilpatrick, contributions secretary at General Cinema Corp., in Chestnut Hill, Mass., whose $100,000 contribution to City Year in 1989 made it a team sponsor. "We bought into the excitement generated by Michael and Alan about the idea that you could get kids of different backgrounds to function together."

Indeed, the diversity principle is a key premise of City Year. It differentiates it from other youth service programs and is a major selling point in Khazei and Brown's pitch to potential sponsors.

"We bought into Alan and Michael's vision of what City Year could be," says Susan Flaherty, former director of corporate contributions at New England Telephone, which also came in with $10,000 for the pilot program and $50,000 for the spring semester to be a team sponsor.

Khazei and Brown's vision got the sponsors' attention, but what swung the decision in most cases was the impression that City Year's management could actually pull it off. "They came to us with a very detailed proposal," says Kilpatrick, "that discussed how they would recruit, the hours that would be worked, the amount of the kids' stipends, and so on."

"They had a long-term vision of where things could go," says William W. Bain Jr., chairman and founder of management-consulting firm Bain & Co., "and practical ideas of how to get there. They understood that even lofty goals require planning and work." Also, Bain says, he quickly grew confident that Brown and Khazei would attract other major contributors—that he wouldn't be alone.

There was nothing soft or mushy about their sell, says Jim Ansara, president of Shawmut Design & Construction Co., a Boston contractor and City Year contributor. "They looked at problems from a business perspective." From the beginning, Ansara says, City Year paid a lot of attention to budget and numbers. "With other nonprofit organizations, that's usually the last thing they worry about."

In their pitch to potential corporate donors, Brown, Khazei, and vice-president of development Lonni Tanner don't hesitate to mention self-interest—the publicity, for instance, that comes from having 10 kids doing good works around the city with their sponsors' names on the back of their T-shirts. "Self-interest and the common good—you can't separate them," says Brown.

For the 1988 summer pilot Khazei and Brown raised a little more than the $200,000 they needed, most of it from four corporate team sponsors: Bank of Boston, The Equitable, General Cinema, and Bain & Co. Most of the nearly $1 million they needed during the 1989–90 year also came from sponsors. All four original sponsors returned, along with Reebok International, General Atlantic Partners, and New England Telephone. The $1.5 million budgeted for the current year was, by late summer, mostly pledged or in hand.

Tanner filled the balance of City Year's needs with cash donations from two group sponsors, one a collection of Boston-area law firms and another of contractors and developers; from a fund-raising event for the general public called City Year for a Day; and from smaller cash donations from companies and money from foundations.

She also received a variety of in-kind contributions: computers from Apple, muffins from Bethany's, a local sandwich place. Even City Year's 8,600-square-foot South Boston offices are a donation from The Boston Wharf Co.

Apart from raising money to finance their program, Khazei and Brown had another constituency to convince. They had to design and run City Year so that it would appeal to the mix of kids they wanted to attract.

The pair hired a recruiter, Kristen Atwood, who systematically covered the city and suburban schools as well as other places that kids hang out. Within the limits of honesty, Atwood tailored her pitch to each "market." In city schools, she says, the idea of service wasn't well understood. "But if I talked about a jobs program and how the experience can help them, that they understood." On the other hand, she found that suburban kids felt sheltered, unexposed to real issues. "To them," she says, "the idea of service appealed." To all of them, though, she stressed the idea that kids from different backgrounds have a lot to learn from one another. "If you're not comfortable with that," she told them, "then you probably don't belong here." City Year accepted about one out of every three applicants for the first year's program, and the single most important criterion after diversity, Atwood says, was commitment.

"It was a radical-looking group," says Kenny Lopez, 22, a corps member last year. Lopez lives in a poor section of Boston and says he has had 15 jobs in the three years since he left high school. City Year promised to pay him $100 a week with a $5,000 scholarship at the end of the year. Atwood's offer, Lopez says, sounded as good to him as any other until the first day the corps convened. When he saw who showed up, he says, "I'm thinking, This is not going to work."

From the other end of the socioeconomic spectrum, Atwood recruited Jen Murray, 19, from a posh town in bosky New Hampshire. She was just finishing four expensive years at a New England prep school and had no plans. "City Year appealed because 900 million people hadn't done it before, my parents knew nothing about it, and it was *my* choice."

During the 1989–90 year, City Year teams, among other things, did the following: renovated a rock and rose garden in a long-neglected city park and got nearby residents to become patrons of specific benches or bushes to help ensure their future maintenance; designed and operated an afterschool program at a low-income housing project; and cleaned years of accumulated filth out of an elderly-housing project in a tough section of the city and helped residents organize themselves for shopping forays.

"I think they took away [in benefits] as much as they gave," says John Van De Carr, coordinator of volunteers for the Pine Street Inn, a homeless shelter in Boston's South End. In the summer of 1988 team members cleaned, painted, and fixed the shelter—jobs that Van De Carr says would otherwise not have been done. "But in the process," he says, "they learned what it's like to be homeless, mentally ill, alcoholic."

"Whenever we get ready to thank them," says Mel Reicher, former director of the Boston Living Center, a drop-in residence for people with AIDS, "they thanked us. `I never had an opportunity to work with people with AIDS,' they said, `and now I know I can handle it.' "

Lopez says he learned over the nine months that life isn't all about money. "It's about what you can do for yourself and others." He's decided to go to college, he says, and later work in child care. Murray says that for her, City Year "was all about being yourself and finding out what you like, not what others tell you you should like."

Of the 57 kids that Atwood recruited in 1989 (7 were added at midyear), 44 finished out the year. In June 1990, when they graduated from the program and talked about their experiences to an audience of politicians (Massachusetts senator Ted Kennedy, Boston mayor Ray Flynn), corporate executives, the media, parents, and peers, there couldn't have been an unaffected heart in the place.

One Hispanic boy spoke for his team. "I've always been on the outside," he told the several hundred people there. In the fall he'd confided to the kids on his team that he was gay. The reaction at first wasn't pretty. Kids that age aren't tolerant of differences. But in the end he was the one the others picked to represent them at graduation, their biggest day, a measure of their acquired esteem. "I learned this year," he said, beaming, "that without me this wouldn't be a team."

Without exception, City Year sponsors of the first September-to-June program already say they think they got what they paid for. "Some nonprofits don't deliver what they promise," says General Cinema's Kilpatrick, "but City Year did. At the basic level, they delivered a team of kids that did some things that made a difference in some people's lives."

Brown says that the City Year staff has already begun to quantify in dollars some of the returns on supporters' contributions. They can, for instance, put a dollar figure on the value of the labor provided to nonprofit agencies—money that they would otherwise have had to spend on the projects City Year kids did for them. New England Telephone's Flaherty says that this ripple effect, as she calls it, appeals to her. "We give a little money to City Year," she says, "and they give priceless support to other institutions that we're interested in—the Pine Street Inn, for instance, and the Boston Food Bank."

Still at issue, however, are two things: continued corporate support for a program that in a few years will no longer be new and Brown and Khazei's plans for City Year's long-term expansion.

Some current City Year sponsors say their principal interest is start-up funding, not maintenance. Others say they're in it for the long haul. If there's a majority view, it is the same one that Khazei and Brown hold, that some government funding in a private-public partnership eventually will be required.

Legislation sponsored by Senator Kennedy to allow federal funding of programs that, like City Year, aren't need-based was passed by the Senate earlier this year. That could be a blessing or a curse. Khazei and Brown hope the money comes in a form that does not crimp their creative style. Keeping themselves off the federal dole has given them license to do some things with City Year that otherwise they never could have done. It's made administrative life easier, for instance. They've had to create internal accounting and management systems, to be sure, but they've not had to comply with the horrendous paperwork requirements that plague federally funded programs.

Although the Senate passed Kennedy's measure, the House, according to a Senate aide, is more inclined to approve funds that could be spent only on the disadvantaged. Should that happen, City Year would have a difficult choice to make regarding its most important tenet—diversity.

Notwithstanding speculation on that score, the founders' own plans for the expansion of City Year have changed. Originally Brown anticipated that after the summer pilot and a successful first year, he and Khazei would immediately begin spreading City Year franchises—cookie-cutter programs run by people with Boston City Year experience—to other cities. After discussions with sponsors and others, Brown and Khazei believe the better strategy is to help City Year grow in Boston before attempting to expand it. The idea is that taking advantage of economies of scale and increasing the program's influence on a local level will make it easier to expand in the long run.

"With 200 to 300 kids in the corps," says Brown, "you could have a tremendous impact here. Now there are only 400 young people in gangs in Boston, but we know the impact that's having on the agenda of the city. With a City Year corps of 300, we'd be mobilizing at the same level but for good."

"The founders need to begin to articulate what is the *real* value they are giving to their underwriters. It ought to be more than just PR."

– Eugene Wilson

COMPETITOR

ROBERT BURKHARDT

Director, San Francisco Conservation Corps, San Francisco, a multicultural youth leadership work program that was the first of its kind in the United States

City Year has already succeeded in that even if it stopped tomorrow, it has produced some new ideas that have great value in youth service.

One critical issue is City Year's ability to make the transition to more stable funding. It's one thing to attract corporate support with this fire-in-the-belly idea and another thing to expect the same support three or four years from now, when City Year is a more institutionalized program.

I wonder about its expansion plans. When I look around the United States, I don't know how many cities, never mind suburban areas, could support such a program.

The salaries City Year pays its professional staff—$20,000 to $25,000 a year—are also worrisome. No one can raise a family on that. Youthful idealism is good for a couple of years, but eventually you've got to buy a house or even put a new set of tires on the car.

I applaud Khazei and Brown's wisdom in realizing that they have to grow in Boston before they try the McYear approach, but I doubt that they'll have the opportunity to expand before other folks in other cities beat them to it. That's OK. The capital they are accumulating at City Year is social capital, which you can share, not financial capital, which people tend to hoard.

OBSERVER

ROBERT REICH

Professor, John F. Kennedy School of Government, Harvard University, Cambridge, Mass.; has written extensively on national economic policy and public-private partnerships

Not-for-profit enterprises, especially innovative ones such as City Year, defy the normal measures of success. You can't look to the normal for-profit standards. For City Year, success would be creating a precedent, a model for the country. It would mean changing the way that people think about solving public problems.

One of City Year's strengths is that its concept is simple and direct; it's unassailable. One can't take issue with its goals or its means.

One problem, though, is that there are likely to be a few glitches. City Year works with a large number of young people, and eventually something will go wrong. Corporate sponsors hate the thought of their names being associated with scandal or embarrassment. So the real test of long-term corporate support will come after there have been a couple of bloopers. To survive that, the program needs a reservoir of credibility and trust, and that takes several years to build.

I don't see a role for the federal government here. Local programs don't work well under the aegis of federal control. But I can see City Year being adopted by a city-suburban partnership. Lots of towns adopt sister towns in foreign countries. Why can't they adopt an inner-city district five miles away?

POTENTIAL SPONSOR

EUGENE WILSON

President, The ARCO Foundation, Los Angeles; an organization within ARCO charged with the strategic investment of a percentage (1.25%, pretax, in 1989) of the company's earnings in philanthropic causes

Different companies would react differently to City Year depending on how sharply focused they are in their grant-making priorities. For ARCO, City Year would be a good fit. Because it operates in the West and Southwest, ARCO looks very carefully at things like multicultural diversity and interaction, which are two of City Year's main precepts.

Besides being a strategic fit with our goals, I would agree that Khazei and Brown have a hardheaded business plan coupled with a good awareness of what kids need to understand these days.

One of my concerns is that so many of these things depend on the unique energy of the creators. You might want to replicate City Year in Dubuque or Atlanta or somewhere, but the risk is in trying to identify people with the same passion to run it. Quality control may not be the same.

I also have some concerns about the kinds of service the kids would provide. I don't know if City Year has spent enough time choosing the kinds of services that encourage kids to recognize their own leadership capacities, so that there's a lasting societal effect.

City Year's founders have gotten big money from a handful of corporate investors. Whether they'll be able to get government support is not as big an issue as whether they can expect a handful of companies to continue to come in with six figures. City Year needs to figure out what it can do to broaden its base of support—maybe accept smaller donations—so it will be an easier investment for corporations to swallow over a longer period of time.

The founders need to begin to articulate what is the *real* value they are giving to their underwriters. It ought to be more than just PR. How is this thing going to have a long-term effect at the point where corporate and community needs converge? If that can be identified, then they'll have a stronger case to make to their sponsors than just having kids wear T-shirts. I don't think that will last long enough for them to be viable over the long haul.

OBSERVER

ROBERT FRIEDMAN
*Chairman, Corporation for Enter-
prise Development, San Francisco,
a nonprofit consulting organization
that facilitates public-sector
entrepreneurship*

For a nonprofit, the growth of City Year has been meteoric, and it has also developed a remarkably diverse funding base. Had I been asked to assess its chances out of the gate, I would have been hard pressed to predict such success. It's impressive.

City Year's major hurdle, however, is that donors, corporate or otherwise, have a short attention span. The nonprofit marketplace is much more predisposed to funding new projects than to growing existing ones. So I don't think you can count on your old customers. It also seems that $100,000 is a relatively high buy-in.

The diffuse nature of City Year's goals makes it difficult for underwriters to pin down who is benefiting and therefore why they should continue to support it. Right now it's a housing program and a social-service program and a social-fabric-building program and whatever else. Either City Year succeeds in selling itself on its own unconventional terms by getting lots of folks to start thinking in new ways, or it has to start characterizing itself in more traditional funding terms and pitching itself at traditional funding sources. Either way, it depends on being able to show more precisely what the benefits are versus the costs and on being able to move from a start-up strategy to a maintenance or growth strategy—the classic entrepreneurial problem.

City Year's attempt to quantify its value-added is important for feedback on performance and especially as a key to getting continued support. But I'm worried that it doesn't charge a fee for its services. As public and foundation budgets get tighter, there's the tendency [for potential sponsors] to say, If this is such a good service, why isn't someone paying for it?

New Brew

Microbrewery and restaurant become one

BY CURTIS HARTMAN

Andy Goodwin

To walk through the Irish teak doors into Sieben's River North brewery on a Friday night is to think that lightning has struck. It is still shakedown time, but after three months of business the joint is jammed.

The benches and picnic tables in the lower-level beer garden are full, and there is a 15-minute wait for restaurant seats on the platform level several steps above. The 900-gallon copper brew tanks—the working heart and symbol of the concept—are polished and gleaming. Beer aficionados, drawn by the chance to sample five different brews right at the source, sit cheek by jowl with trendies checking out what the *Chicago Sun-Times* has called the city's "most fun" new restaurant. Young single professionals in suits and ties wait with denim-clad couples from the suburbs—and with a solitary grandfather in a fedora, a nostalgia buff who remembers the old Sieben's, Chicago's most famous beer garden, closed more than two decades ago.

Brewpub and restaurant: Sieben's River North Brewery Inc., in Chicago

RESTAURANTS & FOOD

After a 20-year hiatus, brewing has returned to the windy city and been welcomed with open arms. But Sieben's River North is more than a return to the past, regardless of the period advertisements that line the gray walls. It is more than a brewery, too, regardless of the storage cellars hidden downstairs, and it's more than a restaurant, regardless of the exposed beams, lacquered brick, and linen napkins above. Sieben's is a new phenomenon entirely, a "brewpub," a hybrid adaptation of micro-brewing that combines manufacturing *and* retailing. With the brewpub, America's microbreweries have created a niche within a niche, "the most exciting area of brewing in America today," according to Charles Papazian, president of the 10-year-old Association of Brewers. Since 1983, when California became the first of the 23 states that now permit on-premises sales, 32 brewpubs have been built, 9 in the last year alone.

The business plan that spawned Sieben's River North had painted an optimistic picture. As principals of Chicago's first and only brewpub, the corporation's six stockholders would serve a metropolitan market of some 6 million adults. By creating a limited partnership, they expected to raise nearly $1 million in capital, opening virtually debt free. James Krejcie, 33, then president of the corporation and the operation's supposed future general manager, promised gross margins of 44%, $200,000 in pretax profits over the first 12 months of business, and $1.8 million in profits over five years.

The assumptions were wrong. Over the eight months of construction, the original $1-million price tag would double, adding a million dollars in debt. The menu, initially planned as a modest sampling of finger foods, would grow and the margins shrink. Shortly after its September 1987 opening, Sieben's had a competitor, with perhaps two more local brewpubs scheduled to open in 1988.

The income projections were wrong, too. The estimates prepared by the accounting firm of Blackman Kallick Bartelstein predicted the operation wouldn't become profitable until the fourth month. Instead, it was making money within its first 60 days.

When Jim Krejcie sat down to write his business plan in July 1986, he had already put four years into the project. He'd hoped originally to open a restaurant, a high-concept operation like those he'd worked in during his time under innovative Chicago restaurant king Richard Melman, of Lettuce Entertain You Enterprises. But Krejcie, the night manager and co-owner of a liquor store, had shifted his sights after stumbling onto the brewpub idea at a 1982 Colorado microbrewery conference. A brewpub was just another concept, he decided—like a restaurant built around "a big soup kettle"—but a good one.

He began putting together a general partnership and turned for

EXECUTIVE SUMMARY

THE COMPANY:
Sieben's River North Brewery Inc., Chicago

CONCEPT:
Combination microbrewery/restaurant; beer, with 97% gross margins, to be more than half of total sales

PROJECTIONS:
Sales in second fiscal year of $3.7 million, with pretax profits of $590,000 (16%). Considering expansion to other cities

HURDLES:
Sustaining sales when novelty and PR blitz wear off; improving food quality; controlling costs in order to boost net profits and reach acceptable return on investment

brewing expertise to a fellow Chicagoan he had met just before the Colorado conference, Ron Siebel, who as president of J. E. Siebel Sons' Co. is heir to an illustrious brewing tradition. Since 1872 the family firm has served as research chemists and technical consultants to the brewing industry; since 1900 it has run a training school for brewers, the Siebel Institute, the only school of its kind in the western hemisphere; since the mid-1930s it has published the brewing industry's trade journal. Siebel had dreamed of adding a microbrewery to his interests for years but had always been discouraged by the numbers and scale involved, until he too became a brewpub convert. Eventually, his brother Bill Siebel, current president of the Sieben Brewing Co., and Joe Pickett Jr., now vice-president, would join the venture as well.

All of them knew the relevant history. In five years, the number of microbreweries had grown from 7 to 76, including the 37 that opened last year alone. While total annual micro output remains less than Miller and Anheuser-Busch spill, micro beer sales have been rising as fast as 50% a year. Sales of the giant mass-market brands have stayed flat.

Few micros actually managed to turn a profit, though. It's not enough to brew great beer. You have to market and distribute it, and keep the quality high. With neither pasteurization nor added chemicals, micro-brewed beer demands refrigeration to hold its flavor. But few retailers or distributors are willing to bother with such special handling or even to carry a microbrewery's products at all, given the tiny volume involved.

The brewpub is one alternative to regular retail channels. Rather than battle for limited space on distributors' trucks and store shelves, a brewpub need only get people through the front door, a marketing challenge far less daunting. Selling at the source keeps quality control in the hands of the manufacturer. With no kegging or bottling, line costs are low, while the brewer captures the retailer's, the distributor's, and the manufacturer's profit.

The potential margins are heady indeed. At an average price of $2.15 a glass, gross manufacturing margins can exceed 97%.

By the time all the general partners gathered, Krejcie's efforts had provided the project a long head start. Beginning with $10,000 borrowed from his mother, he had assembled most of the key assets, including the brewing equipment, the location, and the Sieben name. Sieben had been closed for 20 years; reviving its logo tied Krejcie to Chicago's oldest beer garden and to a colorful past that included Prohibition raids and gangster shootouts.

The location, 20,000 square feet in an old factory on West Ontario Street, initially seemed a gamble. Although the street had been dubbed Entertainment Alley by the local media, the site was on the fringe, blocks away from the existing nightspots of River North, the latest Chicago neighborhood to be rehabbed and gentrified. By the time Krejcie signed the lease, however, River North had grown hotter still, adding operations like Hard Rock Café and Ed Debevic's, sending the galleries and shops all the way down to the Sieben's site. Area real estate was running at between $15 to $25 a square foot by the time Krejcie signed the lease, but he made the owner of the building the sixth shareholder, then negotiated a seven-year rate of $4 per square foot, plus $3 per barrel produced, and 3% of food sales after $400,000.

Krejcie started circulating his prospectus in August 1986, and by the end of November had raised $800,000 from 35 limited partners. It wasn't the terms that most attracted investors, Krejcie recalls, as much as his enthusiasm for the romance of the project—and perks that included $100 of noncumulative credit each month for free food and beer.

Krejcie found spending money even easier than raising it. Final construction costs ran $1.75 million—$87.50 a square foot. Added to the

KEY PERSONNEL

Laurel Hanson, general manager
Age: 36
Previously restaurant-opening coordinator, training director, and troubleshooter for Levy Organization, Chicago, 1982 to '86 . . . general manager, Cardozo's restaurant, Chicago, 1979 to '82

Bill Siebel, president of general partnership
Age: 42
Also executive vice-president of J. E. Siebel Sons' Co., Chicago

Ron Siebel, founding general partner
Age: 45
Also president, J. E. Siebel Sons', a 116-year-old brewery consulting-and-education company, and operators of Siebel Institute, foremost brewing school in the United States

soft costs of $250,000, preopening costs were double what the partners had planned.

"If I had sat down with the six general partners and said it would cost $2 million, not one of them would have stayed in the project," Krejcie admits. "But I figured once we had a million, it would be easy to get the rest."

Krejcie was right. Sieben's preopening debt included $550,000 in leased restaurant and brewery equipment, with a five-year payback at between 13% to 15% interest, and $500,000 of bank debt at $^{1}/_{2}$% to 1% over prime.

For Ron and Bill Siebel, the beer was the key: two ales, a lager, a stout, and an occasional special, each different in style and design. It took five months at Siebel Institute to formulate and test the products. Out of the institute at the same time came Sieben's brew master, Peter Burrell, a 30-year-old geologist-turned-brewer chosen from among the students.

In April 1987, Krejcie, enmeshed in the construction project, hired Laurel Hanson to steer the operation to its scheduled September opening. Hanson had just launched a consulting career after five years with the Levy Organization, a Chicago-based operation with more than 20 restaurants. She had been director of training, then project coordinator for start-ups, and in the latter position she had opened up some 18 different operations, including a 387-seat house. When Hanson spoke, the partners listened.

Hanson was skeptical of Sieben's menu plans—"too beer-hall oriented," she said, "just a few sandwiches and pretzels and mustard." She decided she would keep the original ham, liverwurst, and salami sandwiches that had been the hallmark of the old Sieben's. But then she expanded the menu from those three items to a three-page extravaganza ranging from chili dogs to roasted marinated breast of chicken, with four salads, three soups, six appetizers, and five desserts. "More than a meal," she labeled it, "good Midwest American food." She'd stress quality and value: bratwurst from specialty markets, a restaurant exclusive on the city's best corned beef, and call brands in the liquor well.

Hanson admits "the idea of the change made the partners nervous and scared," particularly since her new menu would demand a $255,000 kitchen, not the basic $55,000 one planned for in the budget. But consider our target customer, she argued: men and women between 25 and 45, earning in the $25,000-to-$55,000 range. They eat out regularly and demand a broad range of choices. Beer would remain the main profit

FINANCIALS

SIEBEN'S RIVER NORTH OPERATING STATEMENT
(four-week period)

	Actual 11/2/87- 11/29/87	Projected 10/31/88 11/27/88
SALES		
Beer	$138,718	$146,034
Food	112,587	137,469
Liquor	15,870	15,503
Other (emblematics; banquets)	7,191	8,000
TOTAL SALES	**274,366**	**307,006**
COST OF SALES		
Beer	3,968	4,177
Food	55,661	49,489
Liquor	5,737	5,604
Other	1,826	2,032
TOTAL COST OF SALES	**67,192**	**61,302**
GROSS PROFIT	**207,174**	**245,704**
OPERATING EXPENSES		
Payroll & related expenses	83,259	98,989
Building rental & costs (taxes, utilities)	19,991	19,991
Equipment rental	4,500	4,500
Insurance	3,461	3,846
Advertising, promotion, & printing	23,662	12,280
Other	38,738	31,600
TOTAL OPERATING EXPENSES	**173,611**	**171,206**
Depreciation	9,303	9,303
Interest expense (loans & notes)	5,389	5,389
Interest expense (limited partnership debentures)	6,154	6,154
TOTAL EXPENSES	**194,457**	**192,052**
NET INCOME BEFORE TAXES	**12,717**	**53,652**

generator, she agreed, but a broader menu would mean vastly increased volume, even if it pushed food costs up.

Hanson set her prices after conducting three different price/ration feasibility studies, looking first at other operations in River North, then at other high-value restaurants in Chicago, and finally at other brewpubs across the country. She charged less than her neighbors—$4.95 for a chef salad, $12.95 for a sirloin strip steak or the Saturday-night rib special—accepting higher food costs and lower margins. "We sell more beer doing that," she insisted. With the final menu, food sales are expected to generate 45% of total revenues—at 36% cost of goods sold.

Sieben's counted on a public relations splash to announce the launch. While the partners spent $6,000 for advertising in the local newspapers, most of their marketing money went for promotion. An outside agency flooded the press with stories about the return of the brewer's art and tradition to the city of big shoulders, winning free coverage on all the local TV and radio stations and most of the newspapers in town. Before the opening, the streets were flooded with 30,000 copies of the new menu, printed inside a newspaper headlined "Sieben's Saga Spans Centuries" and "The Tradition Continues."

No sooner had it held its grand opening than Sieben's was "discovered." The *Chicago Sun-Times* reported "the herd has been marching to Sieben's in droves." And within two months the place was operating at a profit, with a Saturday-night wait that stretched up to two hours. While critics panned the food (see box "The Beer's Great, But . . . " page 118), the room's 398 seats were turning one and a half times at lunch and three to three and a half times at dinner, with the average check per person running $7 at lunch and $18 at dinner.

On November 1, with construction still unfinished, the general partners asked Jim Krejcie to resign as the president of Sieben's. By late November, the operation was grossing $270,000 for a four-week period, more than double the $120,000 that the business plan had projected. On January 1, Laurel Hanson was named general manager, with a limited partner's share.

Its preopening public relations campaign gave Sieben's a huge push. But the "herd," commentators say, inevitably will move on, discovering the next hot spot. Then the concept will be tested by the staff's ability to execute.

Jim Krejcie, now general partner without portfolio, is critical of the direction the operation has taken. "This is a restaurant business, not manufacturing," he insists. "We should be taking 25% to the bottom line [aftertax income], but our food costs are extremely high because of the cost of the menu and because nobody is watching the buying. I'd like to chop the menu in half; I'd rather be known for the greatest hamburger in town than try to be everything to everybody. The other partners are already talking about the next project, or franchising, but we don't know what we're doing *here* yet."

COMPETITIVE ANALYSIS

Number of microbreweries in United States and Canada		115[1]
Number of "brewpubs" (subset of micro category)		32[1]
One-year growth in number of micros, 1987		65%[1]

	Typical brewpub or restaurant	Sieben's actual:
Size of facility	4,000 square feet[2]	20,000 square feet
Average brewing capacity	10 barrels[2]	30 barrels
Start-up costs	$350,000 to $600,000[2][3]	$2 million
Annual sales (projected)	$700,000 to $1 million[2]	$3.6 million
Beer price per glass	$2.15[1]	$2.25
Cost of sales, beer	3%[2]	3%
Average dinner check per person	$19[4]	$18
Cost of sales, food	35%[4]	49%

Sources: [1] Association of Brewers; [2] *Brewpub Manual*
[3] Brewing Systems Inc.; [4] National Restaurant Association

While Hanson acknowledges that her food costs are too high, she stands behind the menu, expecting to be able to hit 36% once the inevitable jitters and loose ends of the opening are worked out. "We can be very high achievers once we have our controllable expenses down," she predicts. "I'm aiming for a pretax profit of from $45,000 to $60,000 on $270,000 of sales each four weeks—if we did that I would smile all the time."

It will take staff training to make her smile, Hanson says. A few prices may be raised and a few portions shaved, but she expects to improve the numbers primarily by putting tighter controls in the kitchen and educating the entire staff in the art of portion control. She expects staffing levels, down to 130 from the opening 180, to drop a bit more, and hopes to develop a compensation system for management based on performance. Hanson herself earns a percentage of gross margins on top of her salary.

With the PR bonanza played out, Sieben's marketing will shift to a more basic strategy. Its outside agency has been released, and the budget has been cut to 4% of sales, to be spent advertising in the weekend sections of the local papers. Hanson has named an assistant to help create regular table tents announcing promotions on special brews and to develop brochures inviting tour groups to visit.

Ron Siebel, who remains president of his family's business while

THE BEER'S GREAT, BUT...

Our man dines at Sieben's River North

When I went to Sieben's for dinner, pad and pen in hand, I had already spent a day talking with general manager Laurel Hanson. When I sat down, she alerted the kitchen and put the wait staff on notice. It didn't seem to matter, though. The service was inept, the food mediocre.

First, the good news. The beers were great—rich, full flavored, lightly carbonated, and fresh. The lager was smooth and clean, the Amber ale bitter and almost British in style. These were clearly the products of a master brewer. The heavily malted stout, served cold, was as good as you can get this side of Dublin, and would be reason enough to draw me back to Sieben's if I lived in Chicago.

But I'd go for the beer, not for the food. I'd had a terrific bratwurst at lunch, along with a lager-and-cheddar soup that was thick and flavorful. But the dinner was a disaster. Peel-and-eat shrimp were steamed in ale—for about two minutes too long. The fish of the day, a Hawaiian aluha, was overcooked as well. The chicken wings were sweet enough to seem candied, with a burning aftertaste that speaks of too heavy a hand at the spice rack. "A great beer deserves a great steak," the menu promised, but the center-cut sirloin strip the kitchen delivered didn't match the hype. Ordered rare, it arrived well done. So I sent it back—and waited 45 minutes for a piece of meat that was dry and flavorless.

The service wasn't any better. It took my guest and me two hours to order, eat, and pay for our meal. One empty water glass was filled, the other left empty. The staff was friendly but confused. Much of the time we were just ignored.

Unfortunately for Sieben's, I was not the only reviewer to be less than dazzled. The *Chicago Sun-Times* called the operation "a go-for-the-gusto . . . kind of place," serving "good suds-buster stuff that goes well with the different styles of beer." But while its reviewer had kind words for the pork chops and chili, he too complained about soggy fish, mediocre chicken, and tough and stringy vegetables.

"Excellent beer and passable food" was the verdict according to the *Chicago Tribune*, which called the kitchen, charitably, "uneven." The critic slammed the decor, too, saying it has "the allure of a well-thought-out tourist attraction." The *Tribune* also compared Sieben's with Tap & Growler—the first local brewpub to open in competition—and gave its nod to T&G. The competitor, the *Tribune's* critic wrote, takes "the edge" for food and "wins the ambience category hands down." More important, the *Tribune* liked T&G's beers better, if only because T&G offers a wider selection.

After dinner, general manager Hanson was standing by the bar, eager for my verdict. My honesty got the better of my tact.

Hanson was mortified, as was her chef, who came over to apologize. This is his first big restaurant kitchen, the chef explained, he's working an average of 60 hours per week, and he hasn't yet found a competent assistant. He should have been at the stove, he admitted, but he'd been downstairs in the office, working on his costs.

brother Bill heads up Sieben's River North, admits to being surprised by how different the finished brewery is from what he'd expected. "I'd envisioned a basic Sieben's—and worried about how to fill it. But we kept expanding, almost by accident, the more we talked to restaurant people. Now we have two complex businesses here, a brewery and a restaurant, and on a day-to-day basis we have to run it as a restaurant so we can charge for the beer."

It is the beer, Siebel insists, that will keep Sieben's at the top of a market that could soon have four brewpubs. "You're going to find the imitators out there," he says, "but the public is going to be able to tell the difference." Sieben's beer will be available only on site, although Siebel has already gotten calls from restaurants that want to serve his product. In the future he may offer limited amounts of draft beer packaged for take-out.

When Ron Siebel thinks of the future, however, he primarily thinks of expansion. After 116 years serving other brewers, J. E. Siebel Sons' has a son in the brewery business himself, and Sieben's River North is just a start. "We won't do another brewpub here in Chicago," he says, "but as a group we'll look to other markets. I'm not sure yet how that should work—the brewpub concept is valid, but it has to be tied to local people. I doubt you'll see a franchise, but that could be possible, too."

"High-concept places like this tend to be more fad than long-term fashion. If you can't fall back on good food, you've got a problem."

– Nancy Kruse

OPERATOR

PATRICK LYONS
Founder and CEO of That's Entertainment Inc., a Boston-based group of eight restaurants and nightclubs

The herd won't stay forever; if you get six months out of it you're in God's pocket. When that first binge is over, you've got to have a base from which to build your business.

Sieben's seems to have the concept and the product—certainly when it comes to the beer. The key to the venture's success, however, will be management—they'll oversee execution and maintain consistency—and that's where Sieben's seems vulnerable.

The introduction of Hanson and the exit of Krejcie, for instance, is troubling. It seems to have been a committee decision. But was it a committee that came up with this concept? No, it was an individual who championed the project, and that's important. A business like this requires one person with a proprietary interest, someone who believes in the project heart and soul, who'll work 100 hours a week and make sure the salt-and-pepper shakers aren't greasy.

At Sieben's it looks like the proprietary interest of the brewery people, the Siebels, shows through in the quality of the beer. But they've linked their beer wagon up to a food wagon, and if the food doesn't maintain the same quality and standards that the beer does, there'll be problems down the road—I wouldn't want to be on the tail end of those debentures.

But they've got some time to correct their problems; I'm sure they've got a year. Their foundation is good. It'll come down to details.

CONSULTANT

NANCY KRUSE
Principal of Technomic Inc., a Chicago restaurant analysis and consulting firm; a Sieben's customer

They are going to have to come to grips with some fairly serious issues. The first is concept burnout: What is their staying power when the herd moves from their high-concept operation to the next? High-concept places tend to be more in the camp of fad than long-term fashion. For now people will go to see and be seen, to be first inside the trendy spot. But two years from now, or less than that—six months from now—there will be another new high concept on the horizon that will siphon off a lot of their business. That's when they'll be tested.

Then there's the food. I did eat there and was disappointed. The menu was a little too ambitious. And if you can't, in the long run, fall back on good quality at good prices, then you're going to have a problem. That's where the negative reviews may come home to roost. If you don't learn from them, you may be on shaky ground.

Their price points, which are moderate, make sense, and I think they'll pick up a fair amount of business from the casual after-work crowd as opposed to those looking for a particularly special evening out. But their food costs are way high. They should be 36%.

Still, I like the concept, and it's in a good location—an area that is very, very hot. For this kind of operation, a very good spot.

FINANCIER

JAMES BROCK

Operator; founder of Koolau Brewery Inc., Honolulu, and manager of a venture fund

Their problems at this site are to get their returns up and to control their costs. They spent too much money for what they've got. They have to realize that $13,000 a month pretax, which is what they're showing now, is not an adequate return on a $2-million investment; even the projected $54,000 per period in pretax profit is not enough. This is a very high-risk business. At this stage, I would want to see 24% aftertax profit. I think they *can* get there, but whether or not they can build a chain is another question.

I don't think it will be easy to replicate. There *is* going to be at least one chain of brewpubs. Five or six groups are attempting to put one together. However, if anybody can do it, it's probably Ron Siebel, because he has such influence.

He may find that the best way to do it is as a joint venture: he's very

well known in the brewing industry, so he could go into an area and find someone who has the desire and experience to run the restaurant and joint venture it. Use his expertise with the brewing aspect as one of the legs, use the success of Sieben's as the leg to draw capital, and use the local manager to run the operation. I don't think it works as a franchise; a joint venture has more chance of success.

Generally, though, the concept is good. At the River North site alone, I think they'll succeed. I don't think there's much question about that.

OPERATOR

BILL OWENS

Analyst; founder of Buffalo Bill's Brewpub, in Hayward, Calif.; publisher of American Brewer Magazine

The Siebel Institute is a focal point in the industry, one of the two or three places where you can seriously study brewing. So one of the main strengths of this place is that the Siebels are principals and the beer is taken seriously. Their beer margins will be excellent because they sell only their own, not the products of others as well. And if you're producing quality beers, people will come back to you.

If they're making a mistake, it's with food. It should be kept simple. This should be a brewing business with food on its coattails, not a restaurant with the brewery as a gimmick to lure customers. With 49% food costs versus the cost of manufacturing beer at 3%, common sense says emphasize the beers.

Overall, they'll do quite well. In fact, I'd say their projections are off by 25%—too *low*. The Siebels have moved to brewpubs at the right time. Today there are 700 wineries in California and 22 breweries. Within 10 years, there will probably be 1,500 breweries and still only 700 wineries.

COOKIE MONSTERS

R.W. Frookies Inc. is betting its all-natural product can grab shelf space now occupied by such classics as Oreo, Fig Newtons, and Mallomars

BY PAUL B. BROWN

Ken Kerbs

This is just a suggestion, but if you're under 30 you might want to skip ahead to the 11th paragraph. It is there that the story of Richard S. Worth, and his plan for "reinventing" the $4-billion cookie industry, begins in earnest.

At that point we'll show you how his creation, the Frookie, came about; why he thinks a cookie sweetened with fruit juice, not sugar, will forever humble the likes of Nabisco Brands (maker of Oreo Cookies and Fig Newtons), Keebler (E.L. Fudge and Chips Deluxe), and Procter & Gamble (Duncan Hines cookies); and explain how a wealthy suburban kid became a farmer, then a jam maker, then ended up in the cookie business.

But before we can do that, we have to talk a little bit about THE SIXTIES. (When Worth says it, it comes out like that, all capital letters.)

Richard Worth, founder of R.W. Frookies Inc., Englewood Cliffs, N.J.

Back in THE SIXTIES, Worth, scion of the Worth clothing store family, was a psychology major at New York's Hobart College and doing quite well, thank you. He liked school. He graduated near the top of his class, and by the standards of the times (tune in, turn on, drop out; don't trust anyone over 30; etc.) he was almost normal.

Almost. The problem was music. Like most people his age, Worth used the local rock-and-roll station to provide the soundtrack for his life. That was fine. After all, back then radio celebrated youth. And perhaps nothing was more celebrated than Woodstock, the 1969 rock concert that helped define a generation. Almost anywhere you went on the Hobart campus, you could hear the opening lines of THE SONG written to canonize THE EVENT.

I came upon a child of God, he was
walking along the road
And I asked him, "Where you going,"
and this he told me
He said, "I'm going down to Yasgur's farm
I am going to join in a rock 'n' roll band
I am going to camp out on the land
I am going to try to get my soul free."

Now, most psych majors listened to "Woodstock"—and the reference to Yasgur's farm, where the concert took place—and said things like "neat" and "groovy." Then they went back to running rats through mazes. "Woodstock" was a very nice song written by Joni Mitchell, but that's all it was: a song.

Not to Worth, though. To him, "Woodstock" was a rallying cry. I mean, Worth asked at the time, how could you listen to the chorus ("We are stardust/We are golden/ And we got to get ourselves back to the garden") and not understand that we had to return to a simpler life.

If you remember the times, people used to say stuff like that a lot,

Richard S. Worth, CEO

Age: 39

"What if Nabisco responds tomorrow; what happens if we have problems lining up distribution; what if we outstrip capital?" asks Richard Worth, as he anticipates a visitor's questions. "A company should be judged by how it has thought about the 'what ifs.'"

Worth has been thinking about them since college. Having decided there that he wanted to become a farmer, Worth worried he might run out of money while doing so. The solution? He first spent three years working. His résumé boasts that he increased sales by 100% in his four months as a bread salesman in upstate New York. He then started an underground-sprinkler company that quickly became "second in residential sales" in the Boston area.

All that time, Worth saved every cent he could, and it paid off. His eventual move to Canada led to a $10-million jam company. You can see the juxtaposition of struggling young man and successful businessman everywhere you look. While Worth is in the process of building an $800,000 house in Long Island's swank Amagansett, his office has a ragged couch and a gaping hole in the wall.

The ambivalence remains today. Worth refers to his company as a form of "social capitalism," with 35% of the stock being held by "partners in crime"— the bakers, distributors, and professional-service providers who are helping launch Frookies.

After spending some time with Worth, you get the feeling that he is only partly joking.

and some even acted on it. So only a few eyebrows were raised when Rich Worth, from Boston's posh Brookline suburb, the same little Richie Worth who had never even changed a flat tire, told friends he was going to Canada to buy a farm and live off the land.

And so he did. Oh, along the way there were some adventures, like the time a friend left him to look at an abandoned farm, then drove away, not to return for five days. There were the 12-hour days he spent unloading tuna boats to earn money to buy coffee and tea—things he couldn't produce on the farm. And then there was the tree that fell on him before he learned the right way to cut them down. But for seven years, Rich Worth did live off the land. Joni Mitchell, if not Worth's parents, would have been proud.

With that, let's end the flashback and welcome back the under-30 set. (You'll recognize them. They're the ones who think Woodstock is Snoopy's fluffy yellow friend.)

There was Richard Worth, blueberry farmer, living off the land, and things were fine until January 27, 1978, the day Jonas Worth was

FINANCIALS

R.W. FROOKIES INC. PROJECTED OPERATING STATEMENT

	Year one	Year five
Cases sold (@$11.80/case)	80,000	891,000
SALES	**$944,000**	**$10,513,800**
COST OF SALES (@$7.08/case)	**566,400**	**6,308,280**
GROSS PROFIT	**377,600**	**4,205,520**
% gross profit	40%	40%
EXPENSES		
Start-up costs	53,750	0
Advertising & promotion (non-TV)	325,684	792,914
TV advertising	0	800,000
Product demonstration	47,184	262,756
Broker commissions	23,592	62,756
Payroll	53,400	205,800
Administration & miscellaneous	74,220	394,075
Interest expense	(3,990)	(7,011)
TOTAL EXPENSES	**573,840**	**2,711,290**
NET PROFIT BEFORE TAXES	**(196,240)**	**1,494,230**
% net profit	(20.8%)	14.2%

born. As he held his new son, Worth had an amazing insight: Richie Worth was now a grown-up.

"I wasn't going to leave my son a farm that produced $3,500 a year," Worth recalls thinking. "On that day, both Jonas and Sorrell Ridge were born."

But while everyone knew what Jonas would grow up to be— healthy, smart, handsome—nobody knew what Sorrell Ridge would become. Named after the place Worth farmed, it would be a company, of course. But selling what?

Blueberries? Everybody did that. Blueberry pies? Boring. What else can do you with blueberries? Make jam, maybe?

Yeah. Jam.

So Rich and his then-wife, Suzanne, started making jams. But people who "have to get back to the garden" can't make traditional jams filled with sugar, corn sweeteners, citric acid, and sodium citrate. The

Worths created a fruit-only wild blueberry conserve. Fruit-only peach and raspberry followed. Local supermarketers liked them. So did distributors, and within two years Worth was running a $1-million company. Sales quickly hit $2 million, then $3 million. Four years later, after listening to some major companies explain the benefits that would come from national distribution and bulk buying, Worth sold to Allied Old English Inc. for a bunch of cash and 3% of future sales.

He stayed until 1985, but without management control. It just wasn't fun anymore. So while still with Allied Old, Worth started looking for something else to do. He didn't have to look very far. Opportunity could be found in the next supermarket aisle.

During the time he was building up Sorrell Ridge, "all natural" had moved from the counterculture into the mainstream. As Worth meandered through grocery aisles in the summer of 1983, he found all-natural cereals, ice creams, hot dogs—even dog food. In fact, the cookie section was the only place without an alternative to chemical- or preservative-filled products.

"It was," he says, "the classic opportunity, and one made for me. If I could sell all-natural jams, I could sell all-natural cookies." Worth, now 39, has never had a problem with self-confidence.

But while Worth was convinced he could do it, Allied Old wasn't. The company had no interest in an all-natural cookie.

Undaunted, Worth quit to develop one.

It took three years, but after thousands of batches and more than a couple of pounds added to his middle that he's still trying to lose, Worth had an all-natural cookie. One trick: It was sweetened with fruit juice instead of sugar. Hence the name. Fruit juice. Cookie. Frookie. (The official name is R.W. Frookie. The R.W. stands for Rich and Randye—his second wife—Worth.)

The nation's supermarkets did not exactly turn cartwheels when told about it. Here's how Worth's sales calls usually went when he started knocking on doors last August.

Supermarket buyer (often snarling): "We don't need an all-natural cookie."

Worth: "You mean to tell that me that the cookie aisle is different from every other part of your store where you have an all-natural alternative?"

Buyer: "Nobody likes fruit cookies."

Worth: "You're probably right, but this isn't a fruit cookie. It's only sweetened with fruit juice. And I bet you can't even taste the fruit. Frookies come in 'normal' varieties like chocolate chip and oatmeal raisin. There isn't a passion fruit in the bunch."

Buyer: "I've been to the health-food stores. All-natural cookies taste lousy."

Worth: "Eat this."

With that, Worth would shove a Frookie at the buyer, who would have to agree: The cookies are pretty good.

Buyer: "OK, but I don't have room to stock another cookie."

And that brings us to the heart of the marketing problem facing our hero. The supermarket buyer is right. Merely having a better product no longer guarantees you a spot on the aisle. Some background will help explain why.

Every year roughly 8,000 new food products are invented. Some come from people like Worth, but most are created by the big boys. For example, RJR Nabisco Inc., which owns 37% of the cookie aisle, has introduced as many as seven new kinds of cookies in a single month. The nation's resourcefulness when it comes to inventing snacks is endless. Supermarket shelf space, however, is not.

If Worth is going to get space, he will have to find new places within the store where his product can be sold or convince supermarkets to stock his Frookies instead of someone else's cookies. Ideally, he will do both.

Lord knows, Worth is trying. He has designed freestanding displays that can be placed at the end of the cookie aisle, and he offers to stage promotions that boost store traffic—and Frookie awareness. When he got Cincinnati Reds rookie sensation Chris Sabo to appear at a suburban Ohio market, 3,000 people showed up, and both the store and Frookies were on the local TV news.

The intent is to get stores to give Frookies a try. If they do, Worth is prepared to make the most of it. Listen to Kroger's Sam Gingrich, who was the first supermarket executive to decide to carry Frookies.

"The packaging shows he can play with the big boys. The colors [soft purples and greens] are outstanding. They jump out at you. And he has done subtle things. The boxes are printed so that you can stack them either horizontally or vertically." Gingrich is so impressed with Frookie's sales that he is creating permanent Frookie shelves.

Given the extremely competitive nature of the cookie business, Worth will need all the friends like Gingrich he can get. And he is getting them, in part, by selling them one-third of the company cheap.

The idea is simple. Suppliers may treat you well, but partners will treat you even better. Says Worth: "A distributor may handle 500 to 1,000 products, but if he's a shareholder you become one of the products he really devotes his time to."

A quick visit with Bob Schmitt, marketing manager of Shur-Good Biscuit Co., a distributorship, proves he's onto something. If you spend even five minutes with Schmitt, who owns 1.9% of the stock, you could get the impression that Frookies is the only thing his company supplies to supermarkets in Kentucky, Indiana, and Ohio.

Schmitt raves about how Frookies are perfect for people on diets that restrict sugar and cholesterol. He waves gushy letters praising the product, and he is especially proud of the promotions he has designed to entice supermarket executives. If a buyer takes enough cases, he gets a T-shirt that reads "I got `Frooked' by Shur-Good Biscuit Co." (Worth and most of his colleagues like to use some form of the word Frookie as a verb.) If they order more, they can get Frookie watches and other premiums.

Worth is right. Partners are enthusiastic. Says Schmitt: "This is the most incredible product I have ever seen."

Partners are also understanding when it comes to getting paid. Consider Consolidated Biscuit Corp., Worth's baker, whose 5.2% owner-ship makes it one of the two largest shareholders. Consolidated gives Worth months to pay his bills, while Worth requires supermarkets to cut a check within 20 days. So to a large extent, Consolidated is financing Worth's operation.

All this helps explain why cash flow has been positive from the beginning.

Whatever money Frookies saves is going into advertising and pro-motion, all designed to get supermarket shelf space. It has to, because of a decision Worth made early on.

If you are going to market a unique, high-quality food product, you have two choices when it comes to distribution. You can sell through the Pathmarks, Winn-Dixies, and Alpha Betas of this world, or you can market through specialty shops.

In many ways, selling through the smaller stores is easier. The buy-ers are willing to try new things. They'll give you a bit longer to prove yourself, and perhaps most important, you can charge more. Most spe-cialty cookies—and Frookies, thanks to its all-natural ingredients and good-for-you appeal, can easily be placed in that category—sell for $2.99 for a six- to eight-ounce bag. Frookies' six-and-a-half- to seven-ounce boxes retail for $1.79 to $1.99.

"At $2.99, you are asking supermarket shoppers to think about the purchase," says Worth. "We are priced to compete with the likes of Oreo and Fig Newtons. If I went through the gourmet and specialty stores, I'd have a $2-million to $3-million business. Frookies can be a $100-million company."

That's not a ridiculous hope. At $100 million (wholesale), Frookies would represent just 3.33% of the entire cookie market. On average, "healthy alternatives" in any food category rack up 10% of sales.

But to achieve $100 million, Worth must get the product on the shelf, and that takes us full circle. He can't get $100 million in sales unless he has significant shelf space, and he can't get on the shelf unless he can prove Frookies will sell.

The problem is only bound to get worse because of a relatively new phenomenon in the supermarket industry: slotting fees, a practice that forces manufacturers to pay to get retailers to carry their product.

Here is how it works. Before a supermarket will accept a new product, it demands that the manufacturer pay for what the store describes as the cost of stocking the new product and taking an old one off the shelf. The fee can be seen as a form of insurance that protects the supermarket should the new product bomb.

The fees are rapidly becoming the norm. "Slotting allowances have become such an accepted part of doing business that the main concern of retailers and wholesalers involves getting their fair share from manufacturers," begins a recent article in *Supermarket News*.

Worth has firsthand experience. One supermarket chain in Connecticut told him that it would be happy to display Frookies in its 60 stores, if he paid $1,000 per store.

Worth, who raised just $500,000 to start Frookies, doesn't have that kind of money. That means—once again—he has to be resourceful. While slotting fees are spreading faster than kudzu after a rain, they are not yet universal. If he moves quickly, Worth can still get into some stores without them.

Worth's best hope, though, is to create so much demand for Frookies that supermarkets are forced either to waive the slotting fee or reduce it. "If we can get into one chain that doesn't have the fee and do well, we can force its competitor to take us in."

But again, Worth is forced to try to create a big demand without using big dollars. A general rule of thumb in the cookie business is that you must spend $10 million on national advertising to be heard. Worth hasn't spent anything on advertising, instead using promotions and point-of-purchase displays to get customers to try his cookies.

The initial results are encouraging. Customers are responding to the cookie's good taste and all-natural appeal in surprising numbers. In his first three months, Worth sold 70,000 cases of cookies. According to his business plan, that wasn't supposed to happen until the middle of year two. Numbers like those may make it easier for Worth to raise the $5 million he thinks it will take to make Frookies a national company. That money—which will probably come from the sale of additional stock—would go toward funding TV commercials and beefing up distribution. In the best of all possible worlds, that will increase demand and keep Frookies moving out the door.

Continued success raises an interesting question. What happens when the industry's cookie monsters notice that Worth is nibbling on their lunch?

Keebler officials say it takes them less than a year to create a new brand that responds to a competitive threat. And while Worth hopes his cookies can be found in half of all supermarkets by year's end, Keebler and its kith and kin don't have to worry about distribution.

"The giants *are* a problem," says Worth, taking another drag on one of the cigarettes he just can't seem to quit. "But we have a few things in our favor. We have about a nine-month lead time, and we are already working on new products that I would rather not talk about. Second, consumers tend to be loyal to the people who create a category. Third, the large companies have an interesting marketing problem. If they introduce a new, all-natural product, they are going into direct competition with their other less healthy products. And finally, if they do enter, I think they will increase the size of the category, and that can only be good for us."

On the surface, that sounds fine. But it sure would have been more convincing had Worth not popped an antacid right after he said it. Within arm's reach he keeps the largest jar of Tums we have ever seen.

You do have to wonder how much of his bravado is whistling in the dark. Worth's entire line of credit at United Jersey Bank is exactly $1.5 million, and three of his seven employees work for him part-time while they try to develop their own food products.

Yet the orders are coming in to his office in Englewood Cliffs, N.J., at an amazing rate. He has experience with a similar product, and he is contracting out almost everything that could cost him money: baking, packaging, and distribution. Perhaps most important, Frookies do taste good.

"This is a war, and even if I lose, I win," says Worth. "Say the big boys do come in and take over the market. They aren't going to get all of it. I'll be left with a $15-million or $20-million company at worst."

Maybe. But: Can he get distribution? Avoid the slotting fees? Get established before the big boys respond?

Or will the Frookie crumble?

Getting back to the Garden is a wonderful idea. But—as Adam and Eve found out—you still have to deal with snakes.

"Launching a new food product when you're also a new company— such as Frookies—is not quite impossible, but it's extremely difficult."

—*Don Stroben*

CONSULTANT

CATHY ORR

Vice-president and founder of Shelf Watchers Inc., Orange, Calif., which verifies grocery product placement and inventory for manufacturers and brokers

Including the distributor in the profits of the company as a shareholder is interesting; it may help solve some of the basic problems that come up with distributors. But it won't work on a large scale. There are too many distributors. In Los Angeles alone, there are at least four or five that Worth would need. To get national distribution, Worth would have to include each one. I don't think a distributor is going to be too thrilled when he finds out somebody else got a cut and he didn't.

I'm also worried about Worth's marketing funds. If he selected 20 markets in the United States that he really wanted to cover—the minimum for a national product—then according to his year-five financials he'd be spending only $80,000 per market for advertising and promotion, including TV. That's way low. Manufacturers figure on spending $1 million per market to bring out a new product. That's a minimum.

But even with promotion like that, Worth could end up spinning his wheels. The name of the game is to be on the shelf, and shelf presence has to be constantly monitored and supported. Brokers and distributors won't do that, even if they tell you they will. How can they? They have far too many clients and products to look after. Keebler has its own salespeople and merchandising people—they're trying to persuade store personnel to give them your space. And of course, because they're so big, they're getting more distributor/broker attention than Frookies to begin with. As far as store people are concerned, it's "out of sight, out of mind," and since Worth won't have his own people in the field, Frookies will be out of sight.

FINANCIER

DON STROBEN

Managing general partner, Princeton/ Montrose Partners, Montrose, Calif., a $17-million venture fund with positions in consumer food products

I like Worth's experience. He's already had one success, and he stuck with it even after he sold it. So he has some idea of the continuing problems of growth and development. That experience is very meaningful.

If I were Worth, I wouldn't go national. I would pick New England or the MidAtlantic region, stay in that area, and work to develop a very strong local and then regional brand. In absolute dollars, if you could build up a business doing between $5 million and $8 million in sales, you could then sell that business to somebody else who was more able financially to carry on the marketing effort. As people who invest in the field have seen, the grocery trade is now renting space— and that means you have to have financial resources. Launching a new food product when you're also a new company—such as Frookies—is not quite impossible, but it's extremely difficult. There may be a slice of the market for a specialty cookie, but I don't think I would ever finance a cookie company.

You can't fight the big guys if you're an entrepreneur.

CUSTOMER

LEE SALO
Buyer and merchandiser for Raleys Inc., a $1.2-billion supermarket chain with 53 stores in northern California and Nevada

Would I carry it? I don't know. I'd want to have the first introduction from the company and not the distributor, because the distributor doesn't have enough knowledge. There'd have to be advertising in every geographic area where we have a store—radio would be prime, along with coupons in the papers. There'd have to be money budgeted in each quarter for both those things, as well as in-store promotions. We don't like stand-up racks in the aisles—we like to keep the aisles nice and wide for our customers.

I go by gut instinct. And my instincts say that Frookies is the wrong name, although I see its merit in the natural-foods market. I think it's priced too high. It's probably not as good as the products from Na-

ture's Warehouse, another juice-sweetened cookie that we sell at $1.79 for eight ounces, compared with Frookies' $1.99 for six and a half to seven ounces.

FINANCIER

BILL MULLIGAN
General partner, Primus Venture Partners, Cleveland, a $105-million venture fund that has recently invested in consumer food products

The concept itself is intriguing. He's identified and is attempting to capitalize on a growing interest in healthful foods. And I haven't seen much that's been done with that trend in the cookie section. I wouldn't say it's actually a health-oriented product. The package says each Frookie is "the good for you cookie." I would take exception to that. It claims to have "no cholesterol." Well, a lot of cookies have no cholesterol. It delivers no more than 0.63 grams of dietary fiber; that's very, very low. And the calorie content is relatively high—45 calories per cookie—so it's certainly not a diet treat by any means. I don't see it as a health food; I see it as a healthier junk food. That may ultimately force the company to position it a little differently.

I like the packaging, though. I think the name is good. And I think the pricing is very good. Keeping in line with Oreo will enable consumers to look at Frookie as a trade-off, a way to at least avoid some things, like sugar, without stepping up in price.

The way they're financing the

business—selling equity to the people they need to do business—sounds, on one hand, very creative and low cost. But I think it will become very cumbersome. Worth is looking for follow-on financing right now, and I think that these people he's dragging around behind him are going to be an anchor. If we were to walk into this deal and see he had locked up relationships with a baker, professional organizations, and distributors—who are literally the lifeblood here—we'd be concerned.

In the event you have problems in the company and you have to do another round of financing, you suddenly have a number of people with different points of view on what created the problems and how they ought to be treated. Severance becomes tougher. What happens if a distributor in a key marketplace falls flat on his face—yet he's a shareholder? You don't have the same degree of flexibility that you have if he's not a shareholder.

We always find with early-stage companies that things change daily—suppliers change, customers change, methods of distribution change—and for good reason: You become smarter in the business as you go along. Given that, I'd worry about being locked into so many things on day one.

I don't think Frookies is going to make it if Worth intends to sit back and merely be a marketing organization. Instead, he should focus on a few accounts—like Kroger, which he has—and not try to blow out a national program for 20 different supermarkets. Demonstrate the ability to sell in enough quantity to justify your position on the cookie aisle. Confirm that this product is in demand by the customer, that it can capitalize on this growing interest in healthful foods, and that its taste is at least not a barrier. Get that done in a couple of cases, and then you can take that success story and get positioned on the cookie aisle. If Worth makes some of those changes, I think he's got a good shot.

COMPETITOR

JOSEPH SIMRANY
Vice-president of marketing, Sunshine Biscuits Inc., Woodbridge, N.J., third-largest cookie manufacturer in the United States

I'm always amazed. Everyone wants to get into the cookie business—Frito-Lay (Grandma's Cookies) and Procter & Gamble have tried—and everyone is a marketing expert.

In Worth's favor, he makes a decent-tasting cookie, which appears to be made with excellent ingredients. Conceptually, he is going in the right direction. I say that because that is the direction we're going, and we got there first. People are concerned about the things they are giving to their children, so a year ago we eliminated all coconut oil from our products, and we are in the process of eliminating all saturated fats. Frookies may have thought it would have the field to itself, but it doesn't.

THE PERFECT BUSINESS?

BY MICHAEL S. HOPKINS

Ed Kashi

P{.}ut yourself in Rick Cardin's shoes. You've got a Harvard B-school doctorate, you've done a decade of prestigious and lucrative consulting work, and now you want to build a business of your own. What kind? You don't know. All you know is that you want to do it right. So starting from scratch, you systematically devote all your skills, training, and experience to determining what would make the single best start-up concept in the land.

It takes three years.

This is what you come up with.

As any venture capitalist, securities underwriter, or marketing type will tell you, sometimes a company's appeal has less to do with its product than with, well, its *story*. Here's Rick Cardin's.

It's 1981. Cardin, 35, is in Massachusetts, where he's spent most of his life being the kind of guy you wish you could hate: Phi Beta Kappa at Tufts; Harvard M.B.A. with distinction; Harvard doctorate; director at

---

O! Deli Corp. founder, chairman, and CEO Frederick Cardin

THE COMPANY:
O! Deli Corp.,
San Francisco

CONCEPT:
A publicly traded, national chain of franchised sandwich shops selling breakfast and lunch items at fast-food prices "to working people during working hours." Differentiated from competitors by location strategy, menu, and quality of management

PROJECTIONS:
Five hundred units by 1993; 2,000 by 1998. Capital based on the units' sales as they begin operations during the year. Systemwide sales of $112 million in 1993, with franchisor revenues of $9.4 million and pretax profits of $2.8 million

HURDLES:
Preventing the push for fast growth from leading to poor locations, inadequate controls, diminished quality, and diluted image. Sustaining the concept, even if it limits growth

a renowned management-consulting firm.

Except you can't hate him. He's tall, charming, smart, and modest—a disarming combination. And he works hard. While billing—*billing*—as much as 70 hours per week to major international companies for advice on strategic planning and organizational structure, he has also helped grow the consulting firm threefold. He's a success. He's making $175,000 a year.

But he'll tell you, looking back, that by 1981 something had happened to him. After seven years solving other people's problems, and all the overachieving years before that, he'd come to a pair of conclusions. First, it wasn't fun anymore. "To be a successful older consultant, of which there aren't many," he says, "you have to enjoy one specific field and stick to it." Cardin's loves, however, were general—and generalists have no future. Especially when it comes to money.

Which brought him to his second conclusion: If he'd devoted the same seven years of skill and effort to an enterprise of his own, he'd have built a company by now. He'd have a stake, not just a paycheck, however plump. "And making the business grow was what I'd loved most all along," he says. He'd have been more satisfied, happier, possibly even rich. So at year end he quit. Rick Cardin was now an entrepreneur.

One problem, though. He was an entrepreneur who had no idea what business he wanted to build. He knew only that whatever it was—remember his résumé?—he wanted it ambitious. He wanted the perfect start-up. And he was convinced that logic could get him there.

Because he'd had no time to spend it, he'd piled up enough cash to live on for a while. He took a year to travel, read, relax, and think. Then he began his search—conducted with his customary analytical vengeance. For six months he wandered through

THE FOUNDER

Frederick A. Cardin, chairman and CEO

Age: 42

The truth, says consultant-turned-company-builder Rick Cardin, is consultants don't invent new solutions, they find the old ones that fit. "You assume every problem you come across has already been dealt with by someone else, so you go see what they've done."

Which is exactly what Cardin did after deciding that becoming a franchisor was the best way to make a business out of creating and selling businesses. For nearly two years, he networked his way through the industry's elite (in the guise of prospective franchisee) and learned everything he could from at least 75 national franchisors. The research led to The O! Deli Corp.

Did it ever trouble him that the neighborhood deli has so steadfastly resisted franchising? Surely sandwiches would have gone the route of hamburgers, chicken, and pizza unless there were some compelling reasons they couldn't. "I think I know the reasons," Cardin says. "Perceived competition; low gross volume; fewer opportunities for vertical integration; and an unglamorous reputation." He adds: "I think our concept deals with them all."

---

the offices of more business brokers than he could count. What's for sale? he'd ask. What are buyers after? How about pricing? Cash-flow expectations? Typical seller financing? *Tell me what you know.*

If there is an epiphany at the heart of every business, then this is when Cardin had his. In office after office, whether flyblown or plush, he'd find more people looking for companies than there were companies for sale. He'd see letters from would-be buyers stacked two inches high, dwarfing the quarter-inch of businesses being offered. He'd hear brokers telling him: Forget the specifics. The product most in demand is businesses themselves. Period.

That's when Cardin got his idea. His simple, straightforward idea—"so obvious that an idiot could have thought of it," he says today. His business, he decided, would be *the creating and selling of businesses.*

At this point in the story we'll skip some steps—though you can be certain Cardin didn't. He moves to San Francisco. Time passes. There's this woman.

By late 1983 he's concluded that creating and selling businesses means franchising. With companies going for only three to five times cash flow, there wasn't enough return in a straight sale to make starting them worthwhile. As a seller, you needed recurring revenues. You needed royalty checks.

Franchising made sense for buyers, too. "It takes almost the same steps to start a small business as a large one," Cardin remembers thinking.

O! DELI PROJECTED ANNUAL OPERATING STATEMENT
(per unit)

PROJECTED FRANCHISE GROWTH

SALES (operating Monday–Friday,@ $2.33/check) 7:00 a.m.–5:00 p.m.	**$300,000**
COST OF SALES	
Product (35% of sales)	105,000
Labor, including management (20% of sales)	60,000
Labor benefits	12,000
Total cost of sales	177,000
GROSS MARGIN	**123,000**
DIRECT OPERATING EXPENSES	
Advertising	3,000
Utilities, maintenance, supplies, etc.	19,350
Royalties	18,000
TOTAL DIRECT OPERATING EXPENSES	**40,350**
GENERAL & ADMINISTRATIVE	**7,900**
INCOME BEFORE OCCUPANCY/ DEPRECIATION/INTEREST/TAX	**74,750**
Total occupancy costs	24,000
INCOME BEFORE DEPRECIATION/ INTEREST/TAX	**50,750**
Profit before depreciation/interest/tax	**17%**

Units
Annualized systemwide sales* (in $ millions)

1988   1993   1998

*Annualized systemwide sales based on full volume for all stores open at end of fiscal year. For 1988, end of fiscal year is March 31, 1989

"You find or design a product; you negotiate a lease; you find equipment to manufacture that product. Whether for a $10-million factory or a delicatessen, it takes all those steps. And if you do it once, for the first and maybe only time in your life, you're a rank amateur dealing at every step with people who do that step as their lifework." People need help. He could start a company to provide it. "Basically," he realized, "franchising is the consulting business." Except you keep getting paid. This revelation in mind, he spent the next year trying to divine the ideal franchise concept (see box "Cardin's Guide," page 140).

In the end (to skip still more steps), all indicators pointed to the last place Rick Cardin, Ivy League theoretician and globe-girdling *bon vivant*, ever expected to end up: sandwich shops. As the Guide explains, it was the business that best met all criteria—stable, nonfad, recession proof, limited risk, potentially public, pleasant to work in, easy to add value to, and more.

It was late in 1983—when he was stalking every franchise-world notable who'd help—that Cardin met Joseph S. Sanfellipo, whose own résumé read like night to Cardin's day. Then 35 and co-owner of a transmission-repair franchisor that he had expanded in five years from 5 to 100 units, Sanfellipo had founded or cofounded a dozen companies, mostly in franchising, since quitting school and leaving home at age 12. He had been a millionaire at 24, bankrupt at 30, and a millionaire again a few years later, as he pushed Gibraltar Transmission Corp. to a position among the market leaders.

Sanfellipo, a franchising insider, pointed Cardin toward at least two more top players: Neil Frumkin, a longtime franchise real estate guru for many companies, including Pizza Hut Inc., which added 2,000 units under his direction in the late '70s; and Lester Singer, Touche Ross & Co.'s expert on restaurants and franchising. Both men came on as directors.

Sanfellipo himself, at Cardin's pleading ("One thing I've done is surround myself with streetwise guys"), joined the company as president—receiving or buying from Cardin enough stock to become an equal partner. Today the two split about 60% of the company's stock.

At last, in November 1985, they opened their first O! Deli, the company-owned test store, on the corner of Market and Van Ness in San Francisco. They figured O! Deli would be a store that sold sandwiches to working people during working hours—a chain of franchised sandwich shops, each open Monday through Friday, 7:00 a.m. to 5:00 p.m. The delis would serve healthy, high-quality sandwiches, soups, breakfasts, and snacks—at fast-food prices—from locations primarily in office complexes and financial districts. The company would grow to 500 units by 1993, and to 2,000 by 1998.

It would, pledged the characteristically ebullient Sanfellipo, "replace the mom-and-pop deli the way 7-Eleven replaced the corner market and McDonald's replaced the hamburger stand. This is one of the last segments of the food business that hasn't been franchised."

Said Cardin (momentarily immodest): "Ten years from now, we'll be able to do a case study of how to start a business right."

It's a nice story. And, as we'll explain later, it's probably what enabled O! Deli to go public last summer, netting $1.7 million in cash

Or, How to Create Your Own Perfect Franchise

It took almost two years, but eventually Rick Cardin, consultant, delivered to Rick Cardin, client, a four-page, 18-point treatise entitled "Ideal Characteristics of a Franchise Business." Want to invent the perfect fast-growth, born-to-be-big franchise concept? Navigate by these attributes. That's what Cardin did.

Below is just part of the list. "Ideal characteristics" are in boldface, followed by how Cardin thinks O! Deli reflects them.

The ideal franchise would be:
• **A stable, nonfad concept.** "American" sandwiches in a variety of tastes at low prices are "everyday foods," encouraging repeat business—60% of O! Deli customers return three times a week.
• **Recession proof.** People will always eat. Moderate prices always appeal.

People buy franchises in good times (they have money) and bad (they need jobs).
• **A limited risk.** Delis are among the easiest businesses to resell; lots of people feel confident they can run one. An O! Deli is inexpensive enough that there are many potential buyers, including those looking to purchase a job.
• **In a rapidly growing segment of rapidly growing industry.** The percentage of restaurant sales captured by franchises has more than doubled since 1970, to more than 43%. Sandwiches are the fastest-growing category of franchised restaurant sales, in percentage terms, yet they still account for only 2% of the total market.
• **A cash business.** O! Deli has minimal cash needs, inventory requirements, or receivables problems.
• **Potentially number one in a national**

despite never having made any money and not yet fielding more than a handful of units. To paraphrase market maker Michael Underwood at Denver's RAF Financial Inc.: Of a strong team and a sexy tale are attractive investment properties made.

Still, there are a lot of sandwiches to be sold on the way to 2,000 units. And a lot of franchisees to be signed up—and kept happy. If the concept doesn't make sense at the store level, then it won't matter how well Cardin, Sanfellipo, and crew perform their "consulting" role. The mail sacks at O! Deli corporate won't be heavy with royalty checks if franchisees can't find customers.

Not to worry, claims Cardin. Signs of America's hunger for sandwiches are legion, especially among O! Deli's target customers. A U.S. Commerce Department report estimates that franchised sandwich shop sales grew 31% in 1988, to $1.3 billion. Though that rate is more than double the growth of the runner-up among eight restaurant categories, the sandwich category remains in its infancy, accounting for less than

niche. The number-one position is still open for a chain serving a broad line of sandwiches, salads, breakfasts, and desserts at fast-food prices. Rarely has the market-segment leader been overtaken in franchising.

• **An enjoyable place to own, manage, or work.** Food is fun and interesting; everyone has experience with it. O! Deli is a people business largely catering to regulars who enjoy what they buy. O! Deli's hours—7:00 a.m. to 5:00 p.m., Monday–Friday—provide the fun of the restaurant business without its typically exhausting schedule.

• **Competitive with major chains from start.** O! Deli doesn't seek the suburban corner lot most chains want, and it exploits locations unsuitable for many: small, odd spaces; high-rise offices that won't permit cooking but want food service. O! Deli can market effectively without expensive TV or print ads—its customers are nearby working people who can be reached directly through coupons and free promotions.

• **Proud of its product.** O! Deli delivers quality and value in healthful food. Everything about O! Deli says, "We respect our customers."

• **Able to generate publicly traded franchises.** The history of fast-food franchisees taking a modest number of units public provides O! Deli franchisees with the possibility of earning substantial returns on their equity and effort and of funding rapid unit growth.

• **A chance for franchisor to give real value to franchisee.** O! Deli can provide many valuable services to individuals in the food business: enhanced appeal to landlords; expertise in commercial-lease negotiation; equipment and purchasing discounts; equipment-selection advice; operating and administrative systems; and the combined operational lessons of a number of units.

2% of the franchise restaurant market. "With a national trend toward more healthful eating," says the report's author, "lighter fare like sandwiches will be in demand, particularly for lunch. Sandwich shops appear to be one of the prime growth markets for prospective restaurant franchisors."

The healthier-food shift is widely acknowledged—it's why McDonald's sells salads now, and it's why O! Deli sells nothing greasy, deep-fried, or grilled. And the lunch trade is O! Deli's chosen high ground.

Statistics indicate that almost half of all fast-food sandwich-shop traffic comes at lunchtime. Cardin will chase the lunch crowd, and its promise of lucrative repeat business, in two specific ways. First, by offering what he calls a "varied-taste" menu at fast-food prices, and second, by operating where the lunch crowd lives—office complexes and industrial parks.

O! Deli's prices couldn't be higher than customers would be willing to pay every day. Research suggested that a "complete lunch"—

sandwich, drink, dessert—should run between $3.50 and $4. That meant the average sandwich needed to go for about $2.50 or $3—which is low. To keep the prices there, while still using high-quality ingredients and preserving the 35% food and paper cost that protects gross margin, O! Deli serves slightly smaller portions than some sandwich customers have come to expect. (No problem, says Sanfellipo: "At O! Deli you pay only for what you eat," not for New York–deli inspired overflow.)

The taste, too, had to be a potentially everyday choice. Cardin likes to say that most fast-food chains, even such rival sandwich makers as Subway Sandwiches & Salads, Sandwich Chef, and Schlotzsky's Sandwich Shops, are "one-taste" concepts. Who, he asks, wants to eat an oil-and-vinegar splashed hero every day of the week? O! Deli counters with a studiously traditional and nonfad menu, raised on the pillars of turkey, ham, roast beef, and cheese.

What ties together these menu and pricing strategies, and perhaps does the most to differentiate O! Deli from its competitors, is the company's location strategy.

Follow the logic. Because the shops are relatively inexpensive to build and run (little space, no grilling equipment, small staff) they don't need to match hamburger-joint revenues in order to make an adequate return. Because they don't need to generate big sales, and because they're conceived to encourage repeat business, the shops can be content just to serve working people during the workday and to cater to a relatively small market area. And finally, because they can be content to serve people in their workplace, and because the absence of cooking makes the shops attractive to commercial landlords leery of grease and odor, they can locate in office towers, where most other chains can't. The result? They're closer than any competitor to their perfect customer, the only customer they think they need.

I s this enough of a market to generate $300,000 per shop in annual sales? The folks at O! Deli think so. Cardin calls the projection "conservative," though the national average for sandwich-shop revenues is about $260,000. The key is the repeat business. Already, O! Deli claims, 60% of its customers return three times a week.

If location is counted on to lure customers, it is counted on even more to lure franchisees. "For one thing," Sanfellipo says, "it is the perfect franchisor response to the constant franchisee question, `What can you *really* do for me?'" What O! Deli thinks it can do is get sites and achieve lease terms that few shop owners could capture on their own.

The good fit between O! Deli's concept and the standard granite-and-glass office plaza enables the company's management to pitch the shops to landlords as commercial-property amenities—the sort of perk that makes buildings more attractive to tenants. Delivering tenants, of course, is the sort of benefit that makes retailers more attractive to landlords.

"I think we offer building managers a lot of advantages," says Cardin. "Our food is simple but high quality. We have the skills and experience to control the operation, to supervise the quality of the service, and to maintain the value of the site."

Most prime office space in desirable markets is managed by giant firms like Trammell Crow Co. that would prefer not to deal with mom and pop, who too often have "questionable finances and questionable business sense," according to Jeff Johnson, northern California leasing manager for Chicago-based JMB Realty Trust.

Johnson has placed one of the first O! Delis in an Oakland, Calif., building run by JMB, one of the nation's largest commercial-property owners. "Of all the different leases we work on, the ground-level food-service lease can be the most difficult. If [O! Deli] makes it easy, if it comes in with professionalism, a strong concept, and strong resources, I think it's going to be attractive to a lot of building owners."

That would make O! Deli attractive to a lot of potential franchisees as well, but for a location-related reason more subtle than high foot traffic or great lease terms: lifestyle. During his research mission at the feet of America's business brokers, Cardin discovered that people loved to buy delis. Why? "Everybody thinks they can run one, you don't need much capital to pick one up, and everybody thinks they can assess the risk—and know whether a deli will make it or not—on a gut level. It's a business they understand."

The trouble with most delis, though, as with restaurants, is the schedule. The days are long—most delis stay open into the evening— and often include weekends. The hours are legendary for their misery.

But not at O! Deli. The concept and most locations conspire to shut the shops down whenever people aren't in their offices. And Cardin has tried to add other lifestyle sweeteners, too: The concept caters largely to regular customers who enjoy what they're getting, which means they ought to be pleasant to deal with (unlike the customers at a transmission shop); and it requires no specialized employees (increasing personnel flexibility and eliminating any anxious and vulnerable reliance on a few skilled workers). The selling point is simple: O! Deli aims to be fun.

It also, of course, aims to make money. Though the franchise fee of $25,000 is higher than some sandwich shops (Subway charges $7,500 and an 8% royalty, compared with O! Deli's 6%), the total start-up investment of $75,000 to $125,000 is much lower than the price of opening, say, a Burger King, which could run as high as $1 million.

The low entry fee was important to Cardin even before he invented O! Deli. About $100,000, he found, was the price that kept most potential buyers in the game, including those looking to purchase a job. By fitting the concept under that limit, he not only made franchises comparatively easy to sell, but also less risky for franchisees because the units are easier to *re*sell. The small price tag offers other benefits, too. While the standard Burger King produces higher revenues and gross profits, its return on investment doesn't come close to Cardin's projections for O! Deli. Historically, the hamburger chains return about a dollar of sales per year for every dollar invested. An O! Deli franchise that meets the unit forecast of $300,000 in sales can be expected to kick back about $2 in revenues for every dollar put in. A big difference, if Cardin is right.

It's hard to imagine that the office Cardin and Sanfellipo share, a walk-up above their San Francisco pilot store, has changed much in the two and a half years since it opened. Unlike their restaurant decor, their literature, or their board of directors, it looks and feels like the start-up that the company remains: cramped, noisy, and littered, with desktops awash in stained coffee cups and mail.

It's equally hard to imagine that the place will look different two years hence. O! Deli will still be a start-up. When the current fiscal year—its first as a public company—ends on March 31, the two executives expect to have 20 stores operating and annualized systemwide sales of $6 million. They will again have lost money, though they won't predict how much.

They *will* predict when they'll turn the corner: at the 50-store level, which may come as early as year end, fiscal 1990. It will be at least fiscal '91 before O! Deli shows a full-year bottom line that's black.

Getting to positive cash flow will have cost the company about $2 million, twice what Cardin anticipated—a run-up he attributes to increased development and franchise support investment to prepare for swifter-than-expected expansion.

However much the need for it outstripped forecasts, capital was not hard to come by. Cardin has kept away from both venture capital money and bank debt, opting to raise $85,000 by selling 8.5% of the company privately, selling some dividend-paying preferred stock to directors and shareholders for $240,000, taking out a $150,000 Small Business Administration loan, and contributing $150,000 himself.

Last summer, O! Deli collected what will soon be $1.7 million more in cash by going public through a reverse merger with a Denver-registered blind-pool public shell. At root, the deal involved selling 35% of the company to the shell company's investors for the cash. Equally important to Cardin, it enabled O! Deli to become public at enormously reduced cost, both financially and bureaucratically. (O! Deli is traded in the pink sheets.)

Can O! Deli reasonably hope for the kind of rapid future growth its projections call for (500 units by 1993 and 2,000 by '98)? Maybe. Though only 11 stores were operating when *Inc.* went to press in February 1989, O! Deli had agreements for 240 more. Fifty-two of these were sold directly, to single-unit franchisees or in territories (such as the deal with a Massachusetts-based, multiunit Burger King franchisor to build 20 stores in five years). But O! Deli expects quicker growth to come from two other franchise marketing approaches.

The first makes use of joint ventures with "area franchise developers." A New Jersey company, Delimax Corp., has agreed to build 190 O! Delis in New Jersey and Connecticut over 10 years. For these units, Delimax will in effect function as franchisor, performing all the tasks that O! Deli corporate normally does. For taking on that management load, the area-development franchisor gets half the 6% royalties, which are still sent to O! Deli, and half the initial franchise fee for each store. So O! Deli's net is cut 50%, but its management investment drops almost 100%. Similar deals are being discussed with others.

Newer to the company's thinking is the second strategy: re-franchise existing chains that could be effectively repositioned as O! Delis. In some cases, O! Deli may buy a chain outright, then sell locations off individually as franchises—collecting not only the franchise fee, but whatever profit it can make on the rollover of the business. In other cases, a chain might sell its locations directly to O! Deli franchisees, without O! Deli ever holding title. The franchisees get good value on depreciated facilities and equipment. The seller gets improved odds that the buyers, backed by a franchise system, will stay in business long enough to repay the note he usually has to extend. O! Deli is now negotiating with a 12-unit chain on this sort of deal, in which O! Deli has no financial risk.

If some of these plans sound a note of frenzy in what otherwise seems a fastidiously controlled program, Cardin and Sanfellipo are aware of it. Asked to name the stumbling blocks most likely to trip them, each talked about the pressure to grow. Yet ramping up fast is integral to their strategy. Remember Cardin's Guide: Rarely has the leader been overtaken in a franchise market. If that observation is accurate, some would say O! Deli is already too late to the game. The company's biggest competitor, Subway Sandwiches & Salads, has more than 2,900 units, adding more than 1,000 of them in the past year alone.

Subway, Cardin would say, is "one-taste" fare, not exactly O! Deli's style. But that's an awfully fine line to draw.

Expanding too fast, becoming too spread out geographically, and delegating too much management oversight to outside contractors can rapidly give life to age-old franchising woes: loss of control, slippage of quality, deterioration of image. And how fast can O! Deli multiply without straying too far from its carefully honed concept, "selling sandwiches to working people during working hours," and all the site-selection and management-style criteria that strategy entails? Neither of the executives is sure.

They'll just keep trying to move the sandwiches. "If you have enough sales," says Cardin, "you can work out the rest."

"I'm afraid Cardin is in this to grow a business, not to operate restaurants. And that doesn't work, because this is ultimately about running restaurants."

—Ron Shaich

COMPETITOR

RON SHAICH

Co-chairman, Au Bon Pain Co., Boston, a bakery café selling sandwiches and baked goods at 43 company-owned and -operated and 16 franchised units across the country

O! Deli has taken a concept that's very interesting and, unfortunately, positioned the company so the concept won't be allowed to develop. They've guaranteed themselves trouble in three specific ways: by being public; by deciding to franchise and even *sub*franchise; and by pushing for such extraordinarily rapid growth.

The public companies that succeed in this business are mature, stable companies, not ones like O! Deli, which I guarantee will change. The market doesn't deal with change particularly positively, so Cardin and his team have put pressure on themselves from the start.

Another pressure they've brought on themselves comes from franchising. I'm basically negative on franchising, but particularly for them—because it will make altering and controlling their stores more difficult. The food business, no matter how they cut it, is a manufacturing business. It's not about a better concept; it's about 1,000 little details that make the concept work. You succeed or fail depending on how well you can execute at the point of sale—how well your franchisees can execute.

When you franchise you lose control—the control you need to change things. And O! Deli is even going into subfranchising, which doubles the risk. Think of it this way: With subfranchisors, you're three levels removed from the customers buying your food. How much control do you think you have?

It's true that franchising is easy to sell, and they have a wonderful story. The question is whether they can deliver. But there will be bumps along the road, and being franchised will make it more difficult to iron out those bumps.

Their growth expectations won't help, either. The wisest people in the food business say you don't grow a company more than 30% to 40% a year. More than that and you just can't execute. And out of every 100 great concepts, 99 fail because of bad execution.

I'm afraid Cardin is in this to grow a business, not to operate restaurants. And that doesn't work. As an operator, I've seen any number of people try it, and almost all of them fall by the wayside—because this is ultimately a business of running restaurants.

The probability of their meeting their business plan is minimal.

COMPETITOR

FRED DELUCA

President and founder, Subway Sandwiches & Salads, Milford, Conn., a franchised sandwich-shop chain with more than 2,900 units in the United States and Canada

I think the founders have some very good qualities, but I also think they present a particular problem. They don't have the technical operating skills that you need in the sandwich business. Being experienced in franchising or administration or finance isn't the same. They haven't done this stuff, and they won't have the necessary intuitive knowledge about how the business works.

Their location strategy will compound the problem. While it's good strategy to open in downtown offices, we've found those sites the most difficult of all to run. You need more operating expertise to succeed there, not less. Volume is bunched; you may get 75% of your business between 11:30 and 1:30, Monday through Friday. So you've got to be fast and still maintain quality and control. If you don't push enough sales through during those peak times, the location will fail because of too little volume. What we've learned is that if you set up downtown, the operator had better be there running the place, not dividing his time among multiple locations.

O! Deli may also have underestimated how tough it is to get sites in the first place. It's the most difficult aspect of franchising. We now have 1,000 franchises sold to people who need sites.

FINANCIER

BRUCE V. RAUNER
General partner, Golder, Thoma & Cressey, Chicago, a $400-million

private equity fund with positions in several multiunit service chains

Cardin is right that a franchise food-service company can add value in real estate deals. Building managers love a substantial chain that has a reputation and a critical mass. So that could work.

However, I'm worried about the focus on growth. It's incredible how much they come across as being top-line oriented as opposed to bottom-line oriented. They're always talking about the number of stores, the size of the business, being the market leader—and all that stuff is nice, but only after you've got a business that's proven to work.

The focus ought to be on who is in the store making sure that sandwich quality is outstanding and service is quick—not on setting up subfranchisors, selling territories, and having franchisees go public. McDonald's is the best food franchisor there is, and it learned the hard way that you don't want large area franchisees, public or otherwise, who are working beyond the reach of personal control. Burger King and Popeye's Famous Fried Chicken are fighting those battles now. The whole purpose of franchising is to have a partner—the franchisee—who lives and breathes the business, who gives blood, sweat and tears to make it work.

Cardin needs to think of his franchisees as partners, not people it's easy to sell delis to because they think they know delis. People don't know delis. That's the kind of cocktail-party knowledge that gets people in trouble.

The way he went public adds to

my concern about Cardin's eagerness to sell units. Going the backdoor route through a shell on the Denver exchange implies that the company is of poor quality. It's very hard to raise subsequent rounds of financing being public the way he is, because of image. The little pink sheets that slide in and out of shells don't attract quality investors. People think of those companies as promoter driven. A serious underwriter would tell you that O! Deli's real IPO is almost yet to come.

There are reasons why sandwiches haven't made it as a chain; sandwiches are very hard to do on a consistent basis. They're labor intensive and very difficult to automate and standardize.

There are an awful lot of chains around the country trying to do sandwiches, soups, and other healthful foods now. They, too, stay away from fried, smelly, cooking-intensive foods that would keep them out of office buildings and similar locations. But so far none of those chains has been able to grow. And the main reason is that it's damn hard to do any of those foods consistently.

There are pluses and minuses about Cardin himself. He seems very bright and driven, and he seems like a winner. But he hasn't done anything like this before—and the start-up desert is littered with the bleached bones of former consultants. Even the streetwise former transmission guy hasn't done this. He needs some good food people—operations people—on his team.

His chances? It's certainly more probable than not that he fails. Or doesn't have a quality profitable chain two or three years from now.

ANALYST

STEVEN ROCKWELL
Vice-president, Alex. Brown & Sons Inc., Baltimore, the oldest investment banking firm in the country

I think they should move slower—a company is better off running a smaller number of restaurants extremely well, and growing more slowly, than trying to blanket the country as quickly as possible.

I'd also like to see O! Deli operate more stores itself. If it's such a good deal financially, they should put some money into their own units. It would give them more credibility. They'd know the problems a franchisee faces and could learn to serve franchisees better.

A major risk is that their desire to grow very rapidly could force them into some secondary locations. The other major risk is just quality of the operation itself. If they get some poor operators, then sales will not meet projections.

I don't think I'd invest at this point. With 11 units open, it's too early. It's still very risky. Will they succeed? I think it's a 50-50 proposition. Which I would say is higher than with the typical restaurant. In their favor, they do have some capital behind them. If they run into problems early on, they'll have the money to work their way out of them.

EDUCATING OCTAVIA

*Or, a crash course
in the art of starting up*

BY EDWARD O. WELLES

A man and a woman lie on a Caribbean beach under a penetrating sun. They are on seasonal parole from icy Boston to the island of Nevis, where the light and colors are as fresh as the fruits and vegetables the land offers. The woman is an architectural preservationist—with a career in need of some serious restorative work. Her job has become too many drawings, too much consulting, and too few real buildings. She wants to make something she can touch, feel, and hold. Here, on her first trip to the Caribbean, she feels alive, her senses quickened by the colors and the dream-scape of the beach. She remarks on this to her husband—and by the way, she adds, slicing another mango, somebody should start a business packaging all this beautiful produce and importing it to the United States.

Cut to New England, two years later, the winter of 1989.

Octavia Porter Randolph is sitting in her shoebox of an office in a Waltham, Mass., high rise, a full-length parka flung on a nearby chair.

Octavia Porter Randolph, founder of Oualie Ltd., in Waltham, Mass.

A February wind whistles outside, across a landscape of oyster grays and pewter blues. Behind Randolph hangs a wall-sized map, resplendent as a tapestry, of the island of Dominica, where pepper sauce is about to come out of a processing plant and into colorful bottles marked with the name Oualie, which translates, roughly, as beautiful waters—and someday soon, Randolph hopes, as flowing cash.

At the core of Oualie (pronounced oo-walley) Ltd.'s metamorphosis from beachbound vision to up-and-running business lies a story whose title could be "Educating Octavia." Here is a woman for whom the past two years have amounted to a crash course in the art of starting up. In that time, she has made hundreds of cold calls, hung out in grocery stores to watch how merchandise moves, and tapped the talents of people who know more about the food business than she does. She has studied everything from the economy of the Caribbean Basin to the placement of bar codes on soft-drink labels. It is the sum of this effort that has brought Octavia Randolph this far, allowed her to move at least from a sunstruck epiphany on the beach to a cramped office overlooking a snow-swept parking lot.

Oualie has created an initial line of six Caribbean-inspired specialty and snack items, some of which will hit retailers' shelves this September. Each is packaged in vivid, attractive colors. The line includes: a low-sugar carbonated juice made from papaya and passion fruit; two conserves, one made with mango and lime, the other with passion fruit and papaya; chips, cut extra thick, made from fried bananas, not potatoes; a salsa based on fruit, not tomatoes; and a pepper sauce made from Scotch Bonnet peppers, which are native to the Caribbean Basin.

Randolph's intent is to make high-quality snack items and everyday prepared foods. She is not selling another can of chili powder that sits in your kitchen cabinet for as long as you own your house. She claims she is making foods that add accent to daily life, round the clock, through the seasons. You can drink Oualie sparkling fruit juice at breakfast, lunch, or dinner. The chips you can eat anytime, anywhere. They go well, by design, with Oualie salsa. "This is food you rip open the bag and eat," Randolph says. "Retailers love that kind of product."

The U.S. market for gourmet and specialty foods reached $10 billion in 1986 and is expected to grow to $14 billion by 1990. The natural-soda market currently exceeds $100 million and is growing at 4% a year. But Octavia Randolph knew little of this in January 1987 when she returned from Nevis, determined to start a company and change her life.

Her first day of work Randolph called on the Boston chapter of SCORE (Service Corps of Retired Executives), the FDA, USDA, and U.S. Customs. She began studying the Caribbean Basin Initiative, a government program that encouraged U.S. investment in the islands. She subscribed to trade journals to learn how specialty foods were bought, sold, packaged, and processed. She knew where she wanted her line to end up: in high-end specialty food stores in the Boston area. She would start local and build a following, "customer by customer." Randolph made the rounds, noting what was on the shelf and how it looked. She asked a lot of questions and got some free advice. "People in the food business like to talk about food"—a good thing, since Randolph had budgeted zero for market research.

That figure matched her first-year outlay for advertising; packaging, not promo spots, would be crucial. "The food business is a marketing business," she says. "The packaging is so emotional. It's the only statement a little company like Oualie can make to the potential purchaser." In April 1987, after interviewing four design firms, Randolph chose Clifford Selbert Design Inc., in Cambridge, Mass.

"We hit it off," recalls Clifford Selbert. "She was willing to give us a lot of freedom as well as some clear direction. That's rare in a client."

Randolph found the first design too understated. It looked like a wine label—too much white space. Selbert rejoined that the colors she wanted were too dark, too brooding. You didn't want people picking up jars of jam and thinking of voodoo. They agreed to punch up the colors, make them hotter. Several months later they had a bright, eye-catching label—something a curious customer would at least pick up.

Although Randolph felt confident about her design sense, she was egoless enough to know that she needed a lot of help when it came to running a business. In May 1987 she recruited Oualie's only other full-time employee, Deborah Pepin, 31, through a referral resulting from a cold call. Pepin, Oualie's vice-president of sales and distribution, came

Octavia Porter Randolph

Age: 36

Given the origins of her company, it's hard to argue with Octavia Randolph's self-characterization: "There's an element of recklessness or courage—or both—in me." It's an element that's been there a while.

Here's an abridged bio: Randolph dropped out of an all-girl prep school at 17 and headed West in 1969 to breathe the liberating air of San Francisco. From there she stayed on the road less traveled, which led to Mexico where, as she puts it, "I hung out." A year later, resettled in Los Angeles, Randolph landed an office job in an architectural business by day and took drafting courses at night. That paid off with a job in a structural engineering firm. Randolph's interest came to focus on architectural history and preservation, a field in which she worked as a consultant for the next 12 years. Randolph believes it is this experience that those who would doubt her management skills shouldn't overlook. "I've always been very self-directed," she says. "That's why I can do something crazy like turn my back on 12 years of work and start a food company."

from the largest specialty-food importer in the United States, where she had been a sales representative. She brought with her contacts from the more than 200 accounts she serviced and knowledge gained from a decade in the industry.

Pepin advised Randolph to trim Oualie's beverage offerings from two to one—much easier to interest the trade in a single drink. When Randolph said she wanted to market a mustard, Pepin told her to forget it; there are already too many out there. Pepin also suggested they put their conserves in 9-ounce jars as opposed to the standard 15-ounce jars the European competition used. Europeans eat more jam than Americans. The price per ounce would be the same, but Oualie's jar would cost less.

Meanwhile, Randolph enrolled in an entrepreneurship course at Boston University in the spring of 1987. She then angled for acceptance at a business incubator in Waltham, Mass., and in September got in. She knew the center, with eight nascent businesses under one roof, would be a fount of business knowledge. She also counted on getting a lot of free advice from its 10-member advisory board of accountants, lawyers, consultants, and other professionals. One of those people, a business strategist, now sits on Oualie's board.

In August, Randolph approached Odette Bery, the chef and owner of a well-known Boston restaurant. Bery had written a cookbook in 1986 that had caught Randolph's attention. Randolph also knew that Bery, one-quarter Indian, had lived and cooked in Africa and the Caribbean.

She also was classically trained, having attended both the Cordon Bleu cooking school in London and Maxim's Academy in Paris before she turned 20. Randolph wanted Bery to help formulate Oualie's recipes.

Randolph went to the restaurant and for 20 minutes laid out the Oualie spiel, during which Bery—impassive as a statue—listened in total silence. As Randolph finished she thought to herself, "All is lost."

Bery leaned forward, finally speaking. "I think what you're doing is terribly exciting, and I'd like to be involved."

Bery, working as a paid consultant, has since formulated four of Oualie's first six recipes, at a total cost to the company of less than $3,000. She shares Randolph's conviction that Caribbean cuisine is on the cusp of acceptance. Randolph's knowledge of and feeling for food impresses her as well. "Octavia looks for what I call clean flavor. In her conserves the sugar is down to a minimum, and they have an exquisite flavor. She's not looking for quick shelf items. She's looking for quality shelf items."

Getting help in kind was easier than getting it in cash. Randolph figured she'd need somewhere between $300,000 and $500,000 to start the business and get the first six products out the door. She was looking for no more than 10 knowledgeable private investors. "Good investors bring more than money," she says, "they bring wisdom." She was also determined to pay her consultants in dollars, not stock. "You don't want to end up with a million shareholders each owning a fraction of the company. That's a rotten way to create a company. Those people can give you a lot of grief down the road."

Randolph could afford—barely—to keep things so closely held. She had $75,000 of her own money. "I knew with that I could at least get going, write a business plan, produce samples, and say to people, `Here, open your mouth and taste this.'" People then would open their wallets.

Not exactly.

As 1987 turned into 1988—the stock-market crash hardly a dimming memory for would-be investors—the company was stuck in neutral. Randolph, as usual, was moving ahead in high gear. A spate of cold calls led her to a state-of-the-art food processing lab at the University of Massachusetts at Amherst, where she talked scientists into mixing up a large test batch of mango-lime conserves, no charge. Oualie did sales tests of the conserves with 15 retailers comprising its target market in March 1988. "This," Randolph recalls, "was a sanity check, just to make sure we weren't on Mars."

Thirteen of the 15 retailers signed purchase orders on the spot, based on tasting just the one product. Some ordered the entire line. The 15th, Bloomingdale's, was interested but prohibited by company policy

FINANCIALS

OUALIE LTD. PROJECTED OPERATING STATEMENT

	Year one	Year two
SALES		
Salsa	$311,825	$1,269,468
Banana chips	311,825	1,259,802
Jams	173,666	737,614
TOTAL SALES	**797,316**	**3,266,844**
COST OF SALES		
Salsa	204,142	767,031
Banana chips	183,145	681,892
Jams	117,800	442,618
TOTAL COST OF SALES	**505,087**	**1,891,541**
GROSS PROFIT	**292,229**	**1,375,343**
% gross profit	37%	42%
EXPENSES		
Payroll	173,223	276,308
Professional services	20,000	18,250
Advertising	20,400	24,000
Travel & entertainment	12,000	20,200
Miscellaneous (rent, office services, insurance, etc.)	36,579	64,719
Interest	(14,744)	(32,939)
TOTAL EXPENSES	**247,458**	**370,628**
PRETAX INCOME	**44,771**	**1,004,715**
% NET PROFIT	**5.6%**	**30.8%**

from writing a purchase order without finished product. Randolph figured maybe she wasn't on Mars when, during one sales pitch, a buyer ate an entire jar of jam.

Jack Kavanagh has spent the past 38 years in the food industry. He is currently general manager of Roberts & Associates, which, with 261 employees, is New England's third-largest food broker, handling such hefty multinational clients as Motts, Guinness, and Quaker Oats. Roberts is a full-service broker, dealing with both distributors and retailers. When Octavia Randolph and Debra Pepin looked for someone with clout to help them break into the right distribution channels, Kavanagh's name came up.

Kavanagh sees people with new food ideas every week of the year, but when he met Randolph and Pepin in May 1988 he sat up and took notice. "The wheels started turning in my head."

What grabbed him was Oualie's drink, Caribe Crash. Beverages, he knew, had more risk and more opportunity for the entrepreneur than foods. This is because the market for them is so huge, yet so fragmented. A tiny niche could turn into a large gold mine. In industry jargon, beverages have more "velocity" than foods. The chips, the jams, the other fancy foods were nice, but it was the drink that would drive this company out of start-uphood.

The drink also stood alone. This was vital in the era of tight shelf space. Bring a distributor a new line of drinks, and you'll be shown the door. Conversely, one good drink can always be shoehorned into the cooler. Caribe Crash reminded Kavanagh of one such success story: Orangina, a stand-alone drink made by Pernod Ricard.

And Caribe Crash was well positioned. Orangina comes in an 8.45-ounce size. Caribe Crash would be 10 ounces. It was targeted at women, but at that size men would buy it, too. A 10-ounce serving would also leave people thinking, as Randolph puts it, "Gee, if only there were just a little bit more." It would bring people back for another bottle.

Moreover, Kavanagh saw the drink as more than just another upscale gourmet drink. He knew he could sell it to a broader market: convenience-store shoppers. "It used to be that women never went into the c-stores," he says. "They were seen as dirty, high priced, and crime-ridden. But that's changed. For women ages 18 to 35, c-stores have become destinations, not emergency stops." Kavanagh labels this group "cherry pickers." They shop selectively for a few items, including high-quality beverages. Kavanagh also knows that "almost 75% of the shelf space in convenience stores is taken up by groceries, but they account for only 28% of profit and volume. The fastest-growing areas are food service and beverages. The convenience stores could happily get rid of grocery space tomorrow and fill it up with something else."

What Jack Kavanagh saw filling convenience stores that day when he met Octavia Randolph and Deborah Pepin were bottles of Caribe Crash.

Kavanagh's advice may have been sound, but Oualie couldn't follow through on it. Money was again the problem. By January 1989 Randolph found the inflow of investment capital slowing. Having received commitments for $200,000, she decided it was time to launch the company.

But with only $200,000, Randolph and Pepin had to make a hard choice. They decided to produce the four products with the highest margins and the greatest "synergy": the two jams, the chips, and the salsa. Sales from these would hopefully break loose the additional $100,000 in capital Oualie needs to produce the other two products: the pepper sauce and Caribe Crash. The drink had a thinner margin, and Randolph and Kavanagh further reasoned that it made sense to wait on it until the business was better capitalized. It would have been fatal if they had started producing Caribe Crash on a shoestring, run into huge demand, and then not been able to meet it.

Oualie has established relationships with four co-packers who will produce its products under contract agreement. Two co-packers are in New England, two in the Caribbean (Jamaica and Dominica). Of its first four products, three will come from one co-packer in New Hampshire, which will ship directly to retailers during the company's first year of operation, with Oualie picking up the UPS bill. The fourth product, the chips, will be handled through Roberts & Associates, the food broker.

In Oualie's first month of distribution, September 1989, its first four products will go to approximately 70 outlets in the Boston area—high-end specialty grocery stores. By the end of Oualie's first year, Randolph foresees servicing 250 retail accounts with an average monthly order of 25 cases per store. She expects sales for the year to reach nearly $800,000, with a net profit of $45,000.

By the second year, Randolph sees Oualie going through standard distribution channels with Jack Kavanagh's help. Sales, she projects, will climb to about $3.2 million, net earnings to $1 million.

Randolph believes that by starting local and overseeing distribution in the first year, she will establish better rapport with retailers. Oualie will do a lot of in-store demonstrations and tasting of the line, as well as stocking of the shelves, hiring trained professionals on a part-time basis to do much of the work. Specialty retailers welcome this kind of active involvement by manufacturers. It means free promotion, free labor. Going the specialty-store route accomplishes two other aims. First, it allows Oualie to sidestep the slotting fees that food companies pay supermarkets just to put their products on the shelf. Second, selling through the specialty trade gives Oualie more control over quality of presentation, something Randolph is obsessive about.

By limiting availability, Randolph can worry less about the capital needs and quality-control problems she would likely face if demand were to soar. By starting small and staying select, Randolph believes she can build a local and loyal following among Oualie's target audience: educated and working women, ages 25 to 44, with family incomes of $30,000 and up.

But if Randolph is cautious, she is also ambitious. She foresees a tripling of sales from year one to year two—with her juice product still not yet in distribution. She sees Oualie as a national brand, which means getting her products into supermarkets. That's a long shot, considering that each year 8,000 new food items are introduced in the United States, and the average supermarket stocks only 10,000. Is Randolph intimidated by the odds?

"No, not at all," she says. "Our aim is to produce sales figures in the specialty stores that we can then confidently take to the distributors, persuading them to carry the product." The distributors then will approach the supermarkets with the Oualie line, which Randolph asserts will be wanted. Why? "Supermarkets these days are looking even more for products that provide the long dollar." Grocers want higher-margin products like Oualie's.

Jack Kavanagh has an expression to describe many of the hopefuls who want to break into the food business: "Everybody wants to get to heaven, but most people aren't prepared to die to get there." He explains: "An awful lot of people who come in here have wonderful ideas, but I'm also looking for enthusiasm and commitment. That's very, very important. Octavia has shown me a lot."

In May 1988 Randolph heard that the CEO of Ocean Spray Cranberries Inc., Jack Llewellyn, would be speaking at a seminar in Boston. She called his office, saying she would be there and wanted to know if Llewellyn might have a few minutes to speak with her. No, said his secretary, his schedule that day is tight. Thanks very much for your interest. Good-bye.

Randolph attends the lunch. Afterward, as Llewellyn is being whisked out the door to his next appointment, she buttonholes him: "I'm the lady who called your office." Llewellyn replies, "Give me a call." Randolph does—later that same day—and is promised a 15-minute appointment. The meeting extends to 45 minutes, ending with Llewellyn asking, "How can we help you?"

In short order she has an appointment to meet with Ocean Spray's director of purchasing and marketing and a senior purchasing agent. (Ocean Spray buys fruit from 52 countries.) In the midst of that meeting Randolph allows that, gee, she sure wishes she had a way to test-market her fruit drink. Brief, awkward silence. "Well, uh, perhaps we could bring you into an Ocean Spray focus group."

Randolph returns some weeks later with bottles of Caribe Crash. Nineteen women, ages 35 to 54, taste the drink; 17 say they would definitely buy it.

Randolph has no formal relationship with Ocean Spray, yet clearly she has its CEO's ear. Llewellyn has offered to have the company's senior purchasing agent come to Randolph's office one day in the future to help her smooth out any wrinkles relating to her purchasing arrangements. That kind of validation offers hope as Oualie's moment of truth nears. "Keeping up my momentum is going to be a challenge," admits Randolph. "I know there's going to be a wonderful reception for these products. People will taste them and say they're great. But then what?"

She answers her own question by further admitting that good-tasting food and zippy labels won't carry the day. Running the business day to day could get thorny. "Managing the co-packer relationships will be hard. I'm cognizant of how many little ways we could be tripped up." She hopes by year's end to have enough money to hire a full-time operations person.

While Randolph knows there is no turning back, she wouldn't have it any other way. "One of the most remarkable things about these past two years is that I've learned so much about something I didn't know anything about before: business. What continues to astonish me is how helpful people are if you have a vision and you communicate it to them. They are eager to assist you. That's a tremendous and continuing revelation to me, and I hope someday I'll have the chance to give some of that back; to teach someone else some of what I've learned."

"Her plan is really inconsistent with the available financing. The question 'What can I sell?' is a lot different from 'What can I successfully market given our cash resources?' "

—*Skip Cummins*

COMPETITOR

BOB KEIM

Co-owner, Vine Inc., a small Martha's Vineyard, Mass., manufacturer of grape-flavored sparkling water

Oualie is very, very similar to our company. We didn't have any experience in this, and we decided we wanted to do it. I took a year for planning and research, and Randolph has done the same kind of thing.

My problem with her plan—and this doesn't mean she can't pull it off—is that I had a lot of difficulty just learning the beverage business, and she's trying a number of products. That's very ambitious. I think Jack Kavanagh was right to tell her, "Limit your selection." Even though it's all fancy foods, every product is different. The government regulations on food are different from those on beverages. The production and manufacture of these things are completely different.

Something always goes wrong, and if something goes wrong with more than one product, I don't know how she could handle it.

FINANCIER

SKIP CUMMINS

General partner, The Vista Group, New Canaan, Conn., a $335-million venture capital firm with positions in two food companies

I think she's working, but she's not working smart.

Randolph's plan is inconsistent with the available financing. She has to come up with reasonable milestones given the money she's got. The question "What can I sell?" is a lot different from "What can I successfully market given our cash resources?"

I'm concerned she really has no focus. I think she ought to work on at most two products. With one product she ought to go into the distribution outlets she's talking about—specialty shops. I think that's a good strategy. She can do that with a manageable amount of capital, and she can control the amount of time required to support the outlets by controlling the number of shops she's supplying. By doing that she will prove that the dog will eat the dog food. And for the other product, she should do some sort of deal with a corporate partner who can somehow take the time and money to support the soda.

By setting two goals—getting a good deal on the soda for distribution efforts, and proving that she can get distribution with one product in a test market of Boston-area specialty shops—she's now set two reasonable milestones.

I wish she'd worked her buddy network better. Where are the advisers who have a track record of successful performance? Consider the design firm: She didn't choose it because it had successfully designed the package for the Dove Bar or Soho soda. She went by personal chemistry and low rates. And Jack Kavanagh could have been tapped for help with creative financing. Randolph could have said, "Jack, I don't have the money to do soda, but you're interested in it, what companies do you know of that would work as good partners?" He said the soda's the hot product, and she seemed to let it drop.

Also, I think she's making a serious mistake not compensating consultants with stock; it can provide a lot of leverage in a start-up. If I were Randolph, I would set up a pool of stock for five key consultants—in marketing, for instance, and maybe for her chef and Kavanagh—preserving her most precious asset, which is cash. It's hard to say exactly how much of the company she'd have to give away, but a pool of 10% would seem reasonable.

Because I think she will have a very difficult time building a major company in the market that she's chosen, a large venture capital firm like ours would not be interested in investing. However, that doesn't mean that she can't still build a $3-million to $5-million, profitable specialty-food company. I think she should measure success by her ability to get to that point.

OBSERVER

SUSAN FRIEDMAN
Executive editor, The Gourmet Retailer Magazine, *North Miami, Fla.*

Randolph's entering the market at a fine time. At the most recent international fancy-foods show, the Jamaican representation was larger than it's ever been, with 10 manufacturers. There are two Caribbean cookbooks recently published. I think Caribbean cooking is beginning to be well received.

But there's a contradiction that concerns me. She's looking for quality shelf items, but she's also working with an individual with an interest in going broader in the market—like putting the soda into convenience stores.

She has to make up her mind where she wants placement. If she wants to go specialty right now, I think she should avoid discussing the mass aspect, because that could be a real turnoff for the specialty independents. They're competing with the supermarkets, and they want to be able to offer unique product.

I think she has something special. But she *has* to determine if she wants to go specialty or mass market.

WHOLESALE CUSTOMER

ARI WEINZWEIG
Co-owner, Zingerman's Delicatessen, Ann Arbor, Mich.

She deserves a lot of credit—she's done her homework, she accepted that she didn't know everything, and she got help. Randolph was smart not to go with the soft drink first, yet I question whether the product line is focused enough to the outsider. What do two jams, banana chips, and soda have in common? They might not even end up in the same area in a store. I don't come away with the feeling that Oualie has a cohesive line of products.

The question I always ask myself when we sell something is, Why would anyone want to buy it? Right now there are way too many jams on the market. The chips seem more unique; they'd give her a better chance to get attention. I'd consider starting with just the chips.

It seems to me that she also has two different long-term strategies for distributing her line. It's common that producers want to sell to both supermarkets and specialty stores, but they aren't at all related. If I know that in two or three years she wants all these products in supermarkets then I might sell them, but I'm not going to put a lot of energy into it. It's just not worth it for me. She should think more about this. It's very common from the producer's point of view to see the supermarket as a panacea. It isn't. I'm not sure what her priorities are.

THE NEXT BIG THING

Fast and focused, Pizza Now!
is bidding to be the next McDonald's

BY JOSHUA HYATT

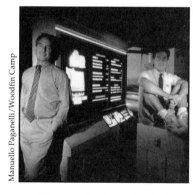

Manuello Paganelli/Woodfin Camp

Philip Goldman taps the steering wheel. Then he checks his watch. "Can you believe how long this is taking?" he asks.

Almost a minute has passed since he leaned out of his car window and ordered a regular 95¢ hamburger. "This is unbelievable," he says, shifting a bit. Just as he finishes speaking, a hand juts out from the booth next to him; behold the awaited delight. "Finally," says Goldman. And to think he wasted nearly 90 seconds waiting—roughly 30 seconds more than he planned.

Goldman's restlessness arises less from a personality quirk than from a zeal for market research. After all, both the hamburger stand from which he now roars away and his own venture, Pizza Now! Inc., seek to exploit a perpetually growing niche: impatient people. Goldman anticipates that both his franchisees and his customers will be fidgety.

Philip Goldman, founder of Pizza Now!, with son Scott, director of operations

EXECUTIVE SUMMARY

THE COMPANY:
Pizza Now! Inc.,
Phoenix

CONCEPT:
Resimplify fast
food, offering
consumers speed
and value with a
franchise chain
of drive-through
pizza restaurants
promising fresh
pizza in three
minutes or less

PROJECTIONS:
Nine company-
owned and 50
franchised units
operating by end
of 1991; estimated
income per fran-
chise unit before
taxes and deprecia-
tion: $75,400 on
sales of $520,000

HURDLES:
Beating competition
from established
chains including
McDonald's, which-
may roll out pizza
later this year;
attracting experi-
enced franchisees
to a low-yield-per-
unit concept

His franchisees, he asserts, could recoup their original investment in four short years. And Pizza Now! plans to lure consumers by transforming pizza into the speediest of fast foods. Goldman claims that his company will make good on the early, now-abandoned, promises of such giants as McDonald's and Burger King.

That fast-food's elders have lost some of their zing is as plain to see as the burger that Goldman clutches. Today's visit to a thriving Rally's Inc. franchise roughly two miles from Pizza Now!'s first and only unit, in Phoenix, supports his belief that McDonald's and its ilk have strayed far enough from their origi-nal recipe to make them vulnerable to low-end competitors. Battling soaring costs, the fast-food giants have tried to leverage expenses by expanding their menus and hours. The result? Increased prices and slowed service, Goldman claims.

Armed with such anecdotal ammuni-tion and with research showing that about 60% of all fast-food consumers whisk their food off premises, a generation of diehard restaurant fundamentalists has sprung up in the past five years. Five-year-old Rally's— with 1990 sales projected at about $60 million and the #5 slot on the *Inc.* 100 ranking of the fastest-growing small public companies—has led the Big Mac attack. Rally's small units offer limited menu items, minimal seating, and two drive-through windows, making them as bare as a 1950s McDonald's and nearly as cheap.

Rally's may be the most formidable proponent of what Goldman terms "the resimplification of fast food," but plenty of others want to crawl through the same window of opportunity. Back in 1988 Goldman had also turned his mind to burgers, after failing with four Cincinnati fast-food chicken outlets. But a six-week national tour convinced him there were already too many players positioning themselves as the back-to-basics alternative to burgers.

Then he consulted Gregg Pancero, a friend and the owner of four Italian restaurant franchises. It's too late for burgers, Pancero agreed, but why isn't anyone trying drive-through pizza?

Goldman was intrigued. Pizza Hut Inc., which had invented a fast six-inch pizza, still did most of its business during dinnertime hours. If Goldman could speed the process up, he could position pizza for the $3.50-and-under lunch crowd that flocked to Rally's and its kind. There ought to be room, he figured: As of 1989 pizza represented one of the fastest-growing segments of the food industry. And off-premise consumption of fast foods had grown 23% since 1985.

Put simply, Pizza Now! offers one of the nation's most popular foods conveyed through two of the most popular means: drive-through, which should comprise the majority of sales, and delivery. "Drive-through is really our niche and our competitive advantage," says Goldman. "But to optimize the return on investment, we have to have delivery."

Goldman's career has been seasoned by both tremendous success (he built up 28 Arby's franchises with $17 million in sales) and abject failure (the now-defunct Marco Pollo chain of chicken outlets "cost me a ton of money"). The 46-year-old intends to stay in touch with the market as he grows. Even so, he ambitiously figures on opening nine company-owned units by the end of next year and selling at least 50 franchises during the same time span. And, yes, he is well aware that McDonald's may roll out pizza nationally later this year, and that Pizza Hut is toying with drive-through service.

"Look, I wasn't about to invest a million dollars of my own without knowing that I had a good shot," he says. "I've learned that the Midas touch is a bunch of bull. But we do have something innovative here. I'm sensitive to what is out there. Our product is more consistently high quality, and it's more accessible. So I don't know what they can do to us.

THE FOUNDER

Philip M. Goldman president and CEO

Age: 46

Family: Single, three sons

Source of idea: Friend in restaurant business

Personal funds invested: $1.7 million

Equity held: 97%

Salary: Zero

Workweek: 70 to 80 hours

Education: Left Clemson College after three years

Outside directors: No

Other businesses started: Kabuki Japanese Steak House, sold in 1975; Marco Pollo International, liquidated in 1986

What I'd do if I weren't doing this: Run a bed-and-breakfast in Santa Fe

"After all," he adds, tossing away the hamburger wrapper, "what is McDonald's doing about Rally's?"

Nary a person alive, Goldman will grant, has ever craved drive-through pizza. "But," he adds, "it's an entrepreneur's job to stay a step ahead." In fact, Goldman's grand marketing strategy requires him to grab a defensible foothold in the market before anyone else.

One way Goldman hopes to lure both consumers and franchisees is by emphasizing the proven quality of the pizza. By using the same sauce and dough Pancero uses, he can point to a track record. "People will say that one pizza is definitely better than another, and you rarely hear that about hamburgers," theorizes Goldman. "I can create a distinguishable difference, flavorwise, and that gives us a hook." (But *has* he? For the results of *Inc.*'s informal taste test, see box, "Time is on His Side," below.)

No such duodenal dialectic will take place, however, unless Goldman can convince consumers to give Pizza Now! a try.

Since opening his Phoenix unit in November, Goldman has been mailing out 5,000 direct-mail pieces a week to homes in his three-mile-radius delivery area.

Pizza Now!'s larger pizzas cost about the same as Domino's, and the $1.59 individual-sized pizzas run about 40¢ cheaper than Pizza Hut's and, for that matter, about the same as a McDonald's Quarter Pounder. Although the local Pizza Hut franchise has been meeting Goldman's prices during special promotions, it still doesn't offer the mini-pizza all day at his price or in three minutes. Nevertheless, Goldman's mailings

TIME IS ON HIS SIDE

We're all for fast, but how does it taste?

It's unfair to compare Pizza Now!'s pie with the kind you get from your local old-country purveyor; as founder Philip Goldman will gladly point out, that version takes at least 20 minutes to make. Goldman's individual pan pizzas usually arrive in less than 60 seconds and set you back only $1.59. That in mind, the slightly stiff dough and somewhat chewy cheese seem like reasonable trade-offs.

The larger pizzas, which aren't as good a deal and take around seven minutes, taste about the same as any big-chain fare—which is, Goldman believes, "perfectly acceptable."

And the competition? Pizza Hut's individual pan pizza tastes almost the same—but can cost 40¢ more. Both Pizza Hut and Pizza Now! deliver satisfaction if you're in a rush, but neither has created a fast-food pizza for all time.

don't hammer away on price or time. Instead, he touts quality, characterizing Pizza Now! as The Fresh Choice and extolling the virtues of its "zesty" tomato sauce and "handmade and freshly baked dough." In doing so, he hopes to earn some pricing flexibility, heading upmarket from his pizza peers.

The design of Pizza Now!'s tiny 600-square-foot structure itself constitutes a marketing tool. Goldman's generous description of the copyrighted shape is "asymmetrical," but the modular structure looks more like a breakfast-cereal prize that the assembler got too frustrated to finish. The eyesore is also an eye-catcher: Some 49% of the customers Goldman has surveyed say they just happened to be driving by when the structure caught their attention (in contrast, about 36% were lured through direct mail).

The unit currently conducts about 1,400 transactions a week, up from its earliest days but far from its peak of more than 2,000. Goldman expected the figure would drop 20% after six weeks or so as a novelty. It dropped more, he says, because renovations to the mall surrounding his unit have cut down on parking—bringing fewer of the harried young families, hurried students, and ravenous businesspeople he hopes to attract.

But as hard as Goldman works at enticing consumers, he seems almost to discourage potential franchisees. Drop him an inquiry, and he shoots back a detailed three-page questionnaire. To gain market penetration swiftly, Goldman intends to target only experienced restaurateurs. Pizza Now!, he stresses, is not for the retired car mechanic.

Given the price tag, even a retired auto executive might have difficulty coughing up the required capital. Pizza Now! may be a cheap undertaking compared with the arched enemy—a McDonald's unit can chomp through about $1.6 million, Goldman claims, before anybody eats—but it still requires an investment of around $325,000, not including the land.

Goldman counters sticker shock by claiming that franchisees can look forward to a speedy payback. By investing $325,000, a franchise can generate sales of $520,000 or so. Because the cost of the facility is so much less than a standard fast-food unit, the net margin before depreciation and taxes rises to a robust 15% (see box, "Financials," page 169). That translates into a four-year payback, probably half the payback period of a major-chain fast-food unit.

Not that Goldman expects franchisees to open just one unit; he wants franchisees to commit to at least five. "Instead of spending $1.6 million to open one giant fast-food restaurant, they can open three Pizza Now! units," says Goldman. "That way, they spread the risk."

But the relatively bare-bones entry fee isn't the only way Goldman minimizes downside risk. The prefabricated modular unit offers two clear advantages. First, it allows the unit to get up and running within 30 days from the time permits are issued, cutting by about one-third any carrying costs. And if the unit should fail, the operator can tow the entire structure to a new location or to a new owner and can probably recoup some 85% of the original investment—including $75,000 in equipment, a $13,000 point-of-sale system, and the $135,000 modular unit itself.

Obviously, each unit's location is crucial to its performance. Goldman plans to retain approval of every site, checking that such factors as the traffic count meet his strict guidelines. When a big hamburger chain locates at a mall, its lease often precludes the developer from flirting with another burger flipper. But few leases mention drive-through pizza. "That creates a lot of opportunity for us," says Goldman.

While Goldman claims that he is counting on industry word of mouth to attract franchisees, he has already approached and signed up two franchisees on opposite ends of California. Both are former colleagues from Arby's and are busily scouting sites.

It is 11:10 a.m., and the five-member Pizza Now! crew is carrying out its duties like a drill team. During a yearlong tryout in Indianapolis in 1988, Goldman spent $175,000 figuring out how to make pizza quickly. He broke the process down into simple, repetitive tasks. "This is how you do it in a small space," he says, pulling a pizza from the oven. "A large space lets you be sloppy."

Working space consists of a stingy 425 square feet. The standard Pizza Now! formation includes one or two cooks stationed at the pizza table, an order taker at each of the two cash registers, and a puller who boxes and cuts the pizzas as they emerge from the conveyer oven. In the next room are a dispatcher and a handful of drivers, practically sitting on four phones and a fax machine.

Ohio restaurateur Gregg Pancero, a minority investor in Pizza Now!, introduced Goldman to conveyer ovens. Unlike traditional deck ovens, where pizza needs frequent shifting to compensate for hot and cold spots, these ovens feature preset and preprogrammed temperatures and times. After receiving an order, the pizza maker builds the pizza and then simply places it on the appropriate conveyer belt.

As a trade-off to provide speedy service, Pizza Now! offers only three kinds of six-inch pizzas within the three-minute pledge: cheese, pepperoni, and a five-item deluxe. The pizzas actually emerge from the oven in about a minute, but, says Goldman, "we're easing consumers

FINANCIALS

PIZZA NOW! FRANCHISEE *PRO FORMA* OPERATING STATEMENT
(freestanding restaurant)*

SALES	**$520,000**
Cost of goods sold	
Food purchases (27%)	140,400
Other	36,400
GROSS PROFIT	**343,200**
Percent gross profit	66%
OPERATING EXPENSES	
Labor & benefits	145,600
Royalty fee (4%)	20,800
Advertising (5%)	26,000
Ground rent	25,000
Utilities	15,000
Delivery expenses	6,500
Miscellaneous	28,900
TOTAL OPERATING EXPENSES	**267,800**
NET PROFIT BEFORE DEPRECIATION & TAX	**75,400**
Percent net profit before depreciation & tax	15%
Depreciation	43,642
NET PROFIT BEFORE TAX	**31,758**
Percent net profit before tax	6%

*The above analysis is based on *Inc.* estimates.

into believing that. If you say `pizza in a minute,' it sounds like it's something other than freshly baked." Custom concoctions, such as a classic anchovy-pineapple combination, require a couple of minutes to build and nearly six to bake.

To preserve freshness, Goldman doesn't bake the pizzas beforehand and freeze them. The dough arrives from Cincinnati every six weeks. Based on anticipated demand, pans of sized and shaped dough are moved from freezer to refrigerator to thaw. From there they are pulled out, sauced, and baked. During slow periods the pizzas are kept in warming ovens for up to 20 minutes—"a more controlled atmosphere than heat lamps."

To achieve crucial efficiency, Pizza Now! relies on tailored software. Among other capabilities, it keeps a tab of what is sold each hour; the operator decides how many and what kind of individual pizzas will be needed between noon and 1:00 p.m. this Monday based on demand during the same time last week. Goldman discards about 20 six-inch pizzas a day, roughly 5% of production.

Because the facility is so cheap, Goldman expects operators to spend more lavishly on food such as fresh mushrooms. Goldman admits that, at 27%, his food costs—the silent killer of many an eatery—are higher than he would like. As more units open up, he expects to shave a couple of percentage points, though it's unlikely he'll match the 23% range he says the giants generally achieve.

No matter how you deliver it—through a window or by truck—pizza's margins, like the product itself, hold up handsomely. On average, pizza provides a pretax margin of about 25%. Delivering a pizza cuts into that margin a bit, but the difference is not all that significant because most drive-through customers buy individual pizzas, which cost $1.59. The minimum delivery order, on the other hand, is $5. So, says Goldman, the gross profit may be higher with delivery, but "you can generate a lot more dollars faster with drive-through." Goldman wants Pizza Now! units to maintain a three-to-two ratio of drive-through/carry-out to delivery. "It's not just that we want to maximize efficiency," he says. "Drive-through is our competitive edge. And that's easy to communicate."

Leftovers are even more of an indigenous American culinary tradition than pizza, so it's perhaps fitting that Goldman has paid homage to the principle in financing his company. So far, most of the $1.7 million he has spent has come from savings he amassed before his calamitous foray into fast-food chicken. There was a Japanese steak house, which he sold, and there were those 15 years at Arby's. Gregg Pancero has added his own $250,000 or so for a sliver of equity. Goldman won't say how much deeper his own pockets are, but he admits, "I don't have as great an access to capital as I would like. I'm a restaurateur. I am not a financial guy."

Given that, Goldman says he will suppress his more ambitious streak and grow slowly, using cash flow to finance his own expansion and choosing franchisees very carefully. "Maybe one of the franchisees will want to become a joint-venture partner," says Goldman. "But I'm not going to start looking at their financial qualifications ahead of their experience. You can self-destruct if money starts becoming more important than the quality of the concept."

Goldman has developed the Pizza Now! concept with an eye toward fast-food history. So perhaps it's fitting to draw on the past for some insight into the challenges ahead. Back in the mid-1960s there were four fast-food restaurants in the Cincinnati area called Barney's Drive-In. Oddly enough, the owner of them was not named Barney. His name was Philip Goldman.

What happened to Barney's Drive-In stands as a cautionary tale for these early days at Pizza Now! By the late 1960's McDonald's, Burger King, and others were well heeled enough to compete fiercely. By 1969, recalls Goldman, "I started looking for something else to do."

Now, jump ahead to the fall of 1990—or sooner—when McDonald's will decide whether to roll out its own pizza nationally, adding 10,000 new pizzerias. McPizza would be available only after 4:00 p.m. and would cost more than any drive-through competitor. And McDonald's huge promotional budget would likely lift pizza sales everywhere—for a short time. After that, well, no one who knows the business would append the word *benevolent* to this particular giant.

If McDonald's doesn't cut into Goldman's niche, there are plenty of others who could. After all, nothing about Pizza Now! is terribly tough to copy; the cooking technique, the siting strategy, and even the special software take simply money and ingenuity to develop. What's to prevent Pizza Hut from attacking Goldman head-on, or at least sideswiping him with an ad campaign promoting *its* fresh ingredients? "A lot of people may have this idea," concedes Goldman. "But the difference between me and them is that I am doing it."

True, getting there first counts for something. But getting big fast is what's required to complete the equation. And, as Goldman admits, he doesn't have much access to capital. Nor does he have reserves of experienced management. The two members of his management team were barely *born* when he first got into the restaurant business. "Our money has to go into building restaurants, not people," he says. It's worth noting that Rally's launched its training school even before cutting the ribbon on its 10th unit. There are other questions. Is Pizza Now! filling a market need, or is it just something new? And consumers aren't the only group Goldman has to fret about. Those who have $325,000 to invest may not want the kind of active involvement Goldman envisions.

Still, during a recent sunny—as always, in Phoenix—lunchtime, eight people are sitting outside, munching individual pizzas. Four more are at the take-out window. And a van is just swinging into the drive-through lane. "Tell me there isn't a market for this," says Goldman defiantly. "I'm not going to put Domino's out of business and I don't want to be the next McDonald's. But if we do what we do well, there will be room for us."

His comparatively skimpy resources, Goldman asserts, may give him the biggest advantage of all. "The other companies are selling something else at the same time," he says. "For me, it's not like, `Let's test this and drop it if it doesn't work.' We'll test it, massage it, cajole it, and figure out its strong points. We'll make this work."

"I hate to throw cold water on somebody else's idea, but we saw the same numbers he sees, and we drew the same conclusions. The sales are just not there."

– Leo Kelleher

OBSERVER

JOHN CORRELL
Restaurant consultant specializing in pizza; founder of Pizzuti's, a two-unit restaurant chain in the Detroit area offering one-minute drive-through pizza, which he sold in 1984

Goldman seems to have done some good research on the drive-through industry. But I'm dubious that he can avoid the low-quality stigma that one-minute pizza has.

Attempting to position the product a notch above the competition is a very good marketing idea. But can he pull it off? Ultimately, pizza quality is not a matter of ingredients but of perception. When you take a product and push it through a drive-through window, the quality perception goes down. Goldman doesn't want to go deeper into delivery because of the competition, and that's smart. But how long before drive-through is full of intense competitors? Twenty-four to 36 months, maybe. It won't take Pizza Hut and Domino's long. And McDonald's is not too shabby, either.

So the only way he's going to survive is by outmarketing them on a neighborhood basis. He'll have to do a slightly better job than the rest at being customer responsive. And he needs to understand the importance of creating management and training systems. Rally's isn't successful because it has a better-looking box or burger. It all comes down to execution. When the competition gets fierce, that will be key. If he can pull this off, he's a pizza marketing genius.

COMPETITOR

LEO KELLEHER
Chief financial officer, RioStar Corp., which owns a controlling interest in Bambolino's Italian Kitchen, a 15-unit chain of drive-through pizza and pasta restaurants in Houston and Lafayette, La.

We've gone down the exact path he is going down, and we would not do it again. Franchising, for example, can be a major distraction. Selling 50 franchises in the next year—that is absolutely undoable. When you have a start-up concept, you are out there competing for franchisees. He thinks he'll somehow find the people who have the money; we didn't.

Even if he does, franchisees are looking for more upside than he can offer. Remember, there's nothing in the numbers for debt service. If the franchisee is getting $75,000 in cash flow, you've got to service his debt out of that for the first four to five years. After the debt service, he could easily be left with $35,000 on a $325,000 investment. Is that worth it? I don't think so. You could go get a $35,000 job at McDonald's. OK, so then you say, "But it's not just

WHAT THE EXPERTS SAY

$35,000, because you'll open a bunch of restaurants." Then you are getting into multiunit management, and for that you need people who are very experienced. And all of this is assuming $520,000 in sales, which is overly optimistic.

There's tremendous competition in pizza, and there's not that big a market for drive-through. We went the route he's trying to go, and we got rave reviews about the taste, but it didn't seem to make that much difference. It's still a very price-sensitive market. And the big players are on television all the time. You have to prop up sales with a disproportionate amount of advertising. We managed to offer franchisees a total turnkey investment cost of $180,000—we built our units off premises, too—and we found they could survive at $250,000 in sales. Still, only a few of our franchisees are really doing well; the rest of them we'll probably convert to company units.

I hate to throw cold water on somebody else's idea, but we saw the same numbers he sees, and we drew the same conclusions. The sales are just not there. We're a couple years further down the road, and I would advise him to cut his losses and try something else.

FINANCIER

BRUCE RAUNER
General partner, Golder, Thoma & Cressey, a Chicago venture firm with an investment in several fast-food franchises with drive-through operations

It sounds like Goldman's got a lot of relevant experience, and it's nice that he's had a failure before. If you learn to be cautious but still optimistic, failure can be a good thing.

Still, I was troubled that his background is roast beef and chicken, not pizza. Gregg Pancero apparently is the one who really understands pizza, and our bias is that once you find people who are important to the success of a venture, make them full partners. Goldman should do more to make Pancero part of the team.

Goldman is trying to do major pioneering on several fronts, which is one reason we wouldn't want to invest. Pizza really is a dinner item; nobody's made it a successful lunch item. You can eat burgers while you're driving—pizza you can't. And with pizza, there's a wide variety in tastes: while to some degree a burger's a burger, with pizza the crusts can vary, the sauce can vary, and it's hard to come up with a product that will appeal to a wide audience—unless, like Pizza Hut stores, you're in a location where you're the only pizza around.

What's more, consumer perception of quick pizza is pretty negative; I wouldn't want to be fighting it. And I wouldn't want to bet a lot of money that Goldman will be the first to pull it off.

174   RESTAURANTS & FOOD

He's in Arizona and opening single outlets in northern and southern California—that to me is very dangerous. Especially if you're pioneering: You've got to go for a cluster, focus on a market or two, become a well-known, proven performer there, then go elsewhere. He shouldn't be franchising yet, anyway. I don't think franchisee money should be venture money; you ought to have something that's demonstrated to be reasonably successful.

Bottom line, though, is how it tastes, and if your review is right and it's not any better than Pizza Hut, then the odds are pretty low that the company will succeed on even a modest basis.

COMPETITOR

RICHARD SHERMAN

Chairman and president of Rally's Inc., operator and franchisor of 230 drive-through hamburger restaurants in 24 states; former president, Church's Fried Chicken; former executive vice-president, Hardee's

He is in a crowded field—just as we are—but there's a significant opportunity because pizza has such a low food cost.

Goldman was known as a good Arby's operator, and he's somebody we respect. You can see by his commitment to the software and having it in place that he has thought about what is necessary to achieve speed. But his operating costs should be significantly lower, and he needs to pass that through his menu. If I were Goldman, I would want a business that could succeed without delivery, to keep the cost structure down. He might take out a register and some labor. And he needs to look at whether the menu is limited enough. Maybe he should offer only one size of pizza. I'd urge him to keep things as simple as possible.

His prices are not low enough. He ought to use price to get people to try his product. It's tough to communicate quality through the marketing clutter. If he wants me to go there, he has to give me a compelling reason. Drive-through is not enough. People don't like to admit it in marketing surveys, but they will go if something is a buck cheaper. I'd copy what Pizza Hut serves for lunch as closely and as legally as I could, and I'd be 25% cheaper.

If he looks at everyday lower prices and then gives people something extra, like "zesty" tomato sauce and better packaging, it could work. Phoenix is one of the most challenging markets in the country. If he can succeed there, he ought to be heartened.

PLAY MONEY

Currently the hottest fad in town,
Wall Street Games Inc. must choose among three
long-term growth strategies

BY ROBERT A. MAMIS

Henry Hilliard

Last October, bull-marketers were taught an expensive lesson in complacency. But at least one investor closed out that infamous month with an impressive gain. Taking long positions in Blockbuster Entertainment, MCI Communications, and Microsoft, then hedging with a short position in IBM, a gutsy 21-year-old improved his personal stake by nearly 20% in one month. Not bad for a beginner—except that the certificates involved had no more negotiable standing than houses on Boardwalk.

His—and millions more—ersatz shares are held in computerized safekeeping at the offices of Wall Street Games Inc. (WSG), a newly

Timothy DeMello, founder of Wall Street Games Inc., in Wellesley, Mass.

founded corporation in Wellesley, Mass. The company's own stake is expected to produce about $460,000 in sales for fiscal '88, its first full year; for '89, a 360% leap to more than $2 million is projected. And no play dough this: Those numbers represent genuine coin of the realm.

Via the 12-person trading room of WSG, would-be investors get a vivid feel for the techniques of investing in stocks by actually going through the steps. Every month, WSG's computers disgorge a ranking of the winners and losers among the 3,000 or so players of its initial product, a game called The Blue Chip Edition. It's not a game in the joy-sticking sense of the word, though. That shibboleth comes from its creator's belief that Wall Street itself is "the greatest game in town"; therefore *his* should be second greatest, since, as art does life, WSG imitates the authentic version.

And therein lies its essentially solemn mission: to educate the masses—or, perhaps more often, the classes. Under WSG's aegis, novices and students learn to play the market like the big boys, only they don't lose like the big boys. Of course, they don't win like the big boys, either, but perhaps celebrity—a mention in the newsletter WSG mails to players—is its own reward. As fanciful as the concept is in practice, it was far more so in the spring of '87, when the simulated brokerage operation existed only in the agile mind of Timothy A. DeMello, then a real six-figures-a-year stockbroker in Boston. That March, 27-year-old DeMello quit an L.F. Rothschild vice-presidency to work out the details of the intricate product he envisioned. Between then and September, when WSG's first product was declared ready, DeMello designed the aspects of interactive play, enlisted a software expert to execute them, hired a suite in a mainline suburb of Boston, set up a toll-free phone line and an electronic call distributor, leased a battery of computers, hired a battery of workers to run them, and raised enough money through a private offering to pay for it all.

Why spurn real life for make-believe? "I was tired of those news items that said Mrs. Jones lost her fortune because she didn't know what she was doing and some broker supposedly misled her," WSG's founder explains. "How come she *didn't* know? It was her money." Concern for widows and orphans aside, DeMello, an '81 graduate of Babson College with a B.S. in finance, founded Wall Street Games mostly because he was inspired by such business heroes as Ray Kroc and Fred Smith who had been inducted into his alma mater's Distinguished Academy of Entrepreneurs. "I wanted to get involved like they did, but when I got out of school I didn't have enough money to start my own company. So I went into the brokerage business," DeMello relates. "After six years I decided it was time—but what to do? I noticed that most entrepreneurs didn't

EXECUTIVE SUMMARY

THE COMPANY:
Wall Street
Games Inc.,
Wellesley, Mass.

CONCEPT:
A simulated stock
market, enabling
college students,
financial-services
trainees, and
individual investors
to play the securi-
ties game with
mythical money

PROJECTIONS:
Profitable from
start. Second-year
sales of $2.1
million with pretax
profit of almost
$500,000

HURDLES:
Picking the right
market from among
retail, academic, or
training; creating
demand beyond fad
appeal; servicing
uncertain volume

start things they knew nothing about. Well, I knew financial markets."

As it happened, a number of colleges— Ohio State, Texas Christian, and Babson among them—were considering courses in which business students handle a portion of the college's endowment as a learning experience. But since only a few students at a time could do the hands-on managing, that left millions more still learning the hands-off textbook way. A rightable imbalance, De-Mello was alert to note. "On the one hand, here were these investors who needed to be educated, and on the other, students who needed a practical education. I looked around the office and wondered what would happen if I were to duplicate this stuff. Let everyone get burned or make fortunes, receive statements, initiate phone calls, talk to brokers, order stocks—only don't use actual money. If I could deliver a stock-trading product at the right price and make it realistic, the market was sure to buy it."

The idea found embodiment as a slender box the size of a typical computer-game package. For a hefty $99 retail, you don't even get a pair of dice, only an 800 telephone number, a stock-symbol guide, and $100,000 in bogus buying power. Yet at first DeMello toyed with an even heftier price, hoping potential users would recognize value in the lessons that lay behind it. However, he conceded, to launch the concept "I had to have a product that was priced under $100, because no matter how great it was, it wasn't going to find a mass market at anything higher."

A player dials in during the market day, asks for quotes and last-sale prices, buys or sells, and rings off. WSG's computers are networked both to a database for posting and retrieving customer information and to a roof satellite antenna that pulls in up-to-the-minute stock-market prices from the NYSE, the Amex, and NASDAQ. The system automatically logs activity and generates statements, which the postman brings every month in bright green envelopes that won't get lost in the detritus of workaday mail.

THE FOUNDER

Timothy A. DeMello

Timothy A. DeMello founded Wall Street Games Inc. exactly six years after he was graduated from college with a B.S. in finance. In the interval he, along with thousands more young, upward-moving professionals, had managed to climb several rungs of the financial community's ladder. DeMello successively became a vice-president of Kidder, Peabody & Co. and of L.F. Rothschild, handling individual and institutional accounts—just the ticket to a dull, six-figures-a-year existence. Handily, by the time repercussions from the October crash thinned the ranks of other investment-banker aspirants, the personable and persuasive DeMello, then 28, had already departed Wall Street to develop and market his own less hazardous version of it. By then he had learned his own lessons well. Most of the capital for the venture came from former clients and fellow brokers; DeMello threw in a mere $20,000, signed a debt instrument to secure another $50,000, and kept 86% of equity in the company for himself.

But why not simply buy a newspaper, note your stock picks, and see how they come out later—a savings of some $98.50? "People have been trying that for years," DeMello scoffs at such cut-rate competition, "but they lose concentration. If you've just been given $100,000, you have to keep doing something about it. You need a regimen. You need to talk through the procedures. If you write it down from the paper, are you going to bother to figure out your daily interest on a margin loan? You have to be hit with a statement every month. We give you the discipline."

At the end of the summer, when The Blue Chip Edition was ready to ship, DeMello coached his two-person (now five) senior staff, "Let's not spend money on advertising until we find out who our customer is. For all we know, it could be 10-year-old kids who end up playing this thing." (A few do, it turns out.) With no promotional to-do, WSG threw open its doors on September 1 and waited to see who walked in. "The strategy was, let's hope it generates some publicity. All we did is declare it available."

As luck had it, just before Black Monday, WSG had been mentioned in *Business Week* of September 28, and *New York* magazine had run a captioned photo in its October 19 edition. Then came the dive, and in the gloom the financial press knew where to turn for a droll sidelight. On October 22, *The Wall Street Journal's* front-page "Business Bulletin" column led with an item on the "swamped" condition of the Wall Street Games phones. Associated Press wired a feature, DeMello shuttled off to "The Today Show," and various cute pieces about how

WALL STREET GAMES INC. PROJECTED OPERATING STATEMENT

	Fiscal year ending 9/30/88	Fiscal year ending 9/30/89
SALES		
Game sales	$385,000	$1,875,000
Sponsor fees	75,000	250,000
Total sales	460,000	2,125,000
COST OF SALES		
Game packages	40,000	140,000
Direct labor (service)	12,000	156,000
Toll-free phones	11,000	150,000
Monthly mailings	19,000	115,500
Postage & shipping	8,250	52,000
Sales commissions	12,500	125,000
TOTAL COST OF SALES	**102,750**	**738,500**
GROSS PROFIT	**357,250**	**1,386,500**
OPERATING EXPENSES		
Payroll & related	162,000	197,000
Rent	54,336	61,128
Insurance	6,024	7,500
Equipment & furniture leases	39,840	72,000
Equipment maintenance	1,200	7,500
Quotation service	10,140	30,000
Stock-exchange fees	6,480	22,000
Advertising & promotions	20,000	250,000
Promotional awards	0	150,000
Telephone	4,600	8,800
Legal services	3,200	20,000
Professional services	8,500	18,500
Travel & entertainment	2,100	18,000
Research & development	5,000	25,000
Office supplies	1,500	3,500
Interest expense	3,100	22,000
Miscellaneous	2,500	6,000
TOTAL EXPENSES	**330,520**	**918,928**
NET INCOME BEFORE TAXES	**26,730**	**467,572**

WSG's "customers" lost "millions" popped up in scores more places.

WSG's switchboard started smoking. "Brookstone called and asked, 'Can you make money selling us games at $50 each?' " DeMello remembers, understanding that that was the best retailers could pay and still get their 100% markup. "I don't know," he told them, "but I think we can." Waldenbooks ordered it; American Airlines, TWA, and Haverhills put it in their catalogs; Marriott's Host International vended it from airport video kiosks. "Don't miss what could be the newest, funkiest, hottest, most challenging toy product for 1988!" advised the Toy Manufacturers of America, apparently misperceiving Blue Chip as Green Slime. Coming into 1988, WSG was becoming entrenched in retail, the market DeMello least expected—or, for that matter, wanted. "But we were getting good orders," says DeMello, "so we just let it happen. We could afford to do it, because we'd have the use of the money: We were shipping boxes that cost us $4, and taking in $50." It was found money.

But not *riskless* money. Having only a few weeks' experience in the habits of end-users, DeMello could only hope that the direct costs and variable expenses per game would be in line with the price received. When it came time to service the game, were players' phone calls going to average a minute each or 10 minutes? What if more phoned in from California, the most expensive WATS zone, than from New York? What were the trading patterns—would WSG have to open earlier, stay later, hire more phone answerers, install more lines?

It's essential to structure play so it requires only a 30- to 45-second phone call, DeMello calculates. Indeed, subsequent months have proved that The Blue Chip Edition's biggest variable expense is the toll-free line, to which is assigned $12 per game per year. Because charges tick irrepressibly upward at 6-second intervals, the software, phone-switching routines, and playing rules are designed to keep them at a minimum. "If a client asks what stock he should buy," DeMello trains his brokers, "you reply, 'If we gave advice, it wouldn't be a game.' "

As for labor costs, ordinarily significant in a service-oriented operation, WSG is sitting pretty, with many of its unregistered reps coming from Wellesley College, right around the corner. Others come from nearby campuses. Each is paid on a part-time basis at $5 an hour with no benefits—a worse deal than dishwashers get in this high-employment corner of the country. Because of the technology behind his $99 ceiling, "I had to have cheap labor," DeMello insists. "Yet at the same time I need someone capable of responding to complicated questions. That's why I decided to locate where the colleges are. Money isn't a high priority with students; more important is a learning experience and something they can put on their résumés."

An added benefit of a stock-market facsimile is that workers need be employed for only six and a half hours a day—the interval the stock market is open. Not only that, but DeMello has received requests from university co-op programs for WSG to take on apprentices at no pay at all. The prospect of *absolutely* cheap labor is alluring, but he admits he'd feel guilty. Still, that's nothing a good psychiatrist or unexpected margin squeeze couldn't overcome.

The low cost of WSG's labor is a function of the high cost of its decor. WSG could be run out of a warehouse across the tracks and customers wouldn't know the difference, but students wouldn't go to work there. This way, they're impressed. "They feel like they're at a trading desk," says DeMello.

To lend the premises the atmosphere of a bona fide operation, WSG doles out $2,976 a year for an overhead ticker, although the instrument has as little bearing on procedures as a ficus plant. For the 3,300-square-foot premises, Wall Street Games pays close to $20 per foot. That's not unusual for Wellesley Square—the difference being that at WSG's decorated digs, no shoppers come in to browse.

"Now we have to step out of internal development and get into marketing," DeMello realizes. Although so far 80% of game sales have been through retail, The Blue Chip Edition's shelf-life actuarial tables aren't convincing. When WSG peddled product at New York City's International Toy Fair in February, its price scared buyers away. Retail stores that carry it tend to place it in a games section beside popular items that sell for much less, and it doesn't do well. "In the long run," DeMello predicts, "the campus and training will constitute the bulk of our business."

DeMello has opted for the former. "Some people insist training is the biggest market, but college business is something we always want to be involved in, if only because of the nature of the beast: New-customer turnover is 25% a year, and word-of-mouth advertising is very cheap on campuses. There are 7,000 colleges and some 12 million students, 30% of whom take business courses. If we produce a product for them at $40 per semester, even if there are only 30 students in a course, the numbers are huge." Catching on in a syllabus is a blessing that extends product life—forever. WSG adapts playing time to fit a semester's requirements, and gets professors (rather than bookstores, where "the markups would hurt us") to enlist the paying customers. The campaign already has been so successful that a trickle of students even ordered themselves fresh playing time after their classroom allotment expired.

After them, however, the deluge. This fall, as many as 26,000 more students are expected to pay $49.95 each to enter WSG's collegiate investing contest. Armed with the usual $100,000 worth of gossamer, entrants will trade the market for four months. If they're particularly good, they won't just find their names on some obscure list: The top 10 will divvy up $62,000 in WSG-provided ante.

In his marketing plan, such as it was, DeMello had intended to establish this campus contest in '88, then go after cash-paying sponsors the next year (see box, "Financials," page 180). But sponsors couldn't wait that long. Before summer even began, AT&T had grabbed the title (the event is now officially called The First Annual AT&T Collegiate Investment Challenge) for $200,000 in cash and advertising; Dow Jones had arranged for a scholarship tie-in; and Reebok International had signed up to provide merchandise awards. "This is big for us, credibility-wise," DeMello grants. "AT&T, Dow Jones, and Reebok are definitely three top companies."

By mid-June, WSG had enlisted participants from some 500 campuses in the United States, Canada, Mexico, and England, at which point DeMello decided he'd better limit enrollment before it overwhelmed his ability to service it. And that's only one promotion. Next spring comes a three-month, cash-prize contest, with a $150 entry fee, marketed and promoted with Players International Inc. The response so far has been spectacular, reports DeMello, looking toward yet another sizable piece of change—and an apparently lawful one in at least 44 states, WSG's attorneys have advised.

Because of such easily placed sales and the possibility of more (WSG has been considering concentrating on such would-be clients as the American Association of Individual Investors, the American Association of Retired Persons, and even Wall Street brokers), DeMello so far has been content to exist without a sales force. "That will kick in in year three, when we have other products," he plans. Until then, DeMello himself insists on doing the selling. "If I had a full sales force going after every market we could possibly get into, and they all hit, I couldn't service all the business," he explains. "I'd rather find out where we're headed and directly identify every market, *then* put together a sales force and tell them this is what you can sell. We have to make sure we have the core of it right before we can expand." On the other hand, DeMello is willing to second-guess himself: "Maybe we should have the sales force first. If I could throw in $50,000 to increase sales 20%, I definitely should."

While promotions seem to be catching on by themselves, equally fertile but tougher ground awaits in the training market. So does a higher pricing structure, inasmuch as a training course isn't particularly price sensitive. "Employers know that just to put an employee on a plane is a $500 expense without adding in anything else," assesses DeMello. "We can train them through self-study." Several corporations already have solicited WSG, among them multiservice financial institutions that must familiarize customer-service staffs with the stock market. In Boston, National Financial, a Fidelity Investments company that processes brokerage orders for correspondent banks on the side, has been asked by some of the banks to set up dummy accounts as teaching vehicles. But fearful that the fakes might get mixed up with the real thing, National Financial refused and is now reviewing WSG's proposal to set up a riskless program through its trading desks.

And if pure training works out, won't training cum promotion do even better? In the fall, as part of the Fidelity deal, WSG is proposing to stage such an amalgam for 500 employees of the brokerage arm of New York City's Irving Bank Corp. While the employees sop up training through game play, they also vie for a substantial cash prize. Corporations with employee stock ownership plans also are WSG's fair game. Wide-scale employee education helps the employer in the end, the pitch goes, because ESOPs are a cheap source of capital.

DeMello ought to be familiar with cheap sources of capital, having seeded his enterprise with $20,000 of his own, then offered outside investors 20% of the company for $500,000 in May 1987. Simple arithmetic appraises DeMello's share of Wall Street Games at close to $2 million even back then. And there were no products, no prototype, and no assets; what's more, start-up charges of about $65,000 (of which software design alone ate up $35,000) had yet to hit the books. There was, however, a reassuring written pledge from key personnel (the chief executive officer, treasurer, and sales manager—each in the person of one Tim DeMello) to work full-time for two years at $60,000 a year plus a bonus of not more than 10% of EBIT (earnings before interest and taxes). Since the second year's EBIT was estimated to be $375,000, that would give key personnel another $37,500 and put DeMello back close to six figures.

"My plan was not to go for debt financing," he explains. "I knew there had to be a certain amount of equity, because if I went in and tried to do the whole thing on debt, no bank was going to give me enough. So I figured, let's get the equity taken care of first to show it's in line, and then the bank will respond positively." (Subsequently, the bank did, extending $250,000 in a line of credit, of which WSG has used $100,000— its only debt.) Over the next three months, DeMello doggedly hawked stock, accumulating commitments from fellow brokers and old clients.

He stopped when he got to $325,000, concluding that it was enough to proceed with.

Many variable costs haven't settled in yet, but DeMello feels he has understated them in the '89 projections, which are based on selling 35,000 units. Labor is well controlled, because, as DeMello notes, "If we don't sell product, we don't use the students." And if they do sell product, there's no problem, either: In June alone, 26 job applicants were turned away. Shipping will go up as product is freighted to more than 500 campuses. Sales commissions also will rise noticeably: WSG pays campus reps $5 to $10 per game sold for the college competition. As demand for service increased, DeMello hired a full-time director of computer operations. To pay for expanding operations, this time around DeMello intends to do some debt financing. The reason is sound enough: "If I have $300,000 committed from sources like AT&T, it would be crazy to go out and dilute the stock by selling more equity."

In any event, DeMello has been busy upgrading the verisimilitude of the original version (an uptick restriction for short-selling has been added, for example, and stop and limit orders are upcoming), and is considering exotic variations such as options, futures, and commodities. Hence the leap in '89's R&D budget (see box, "Financials,"page 180). Again, big-name partners such as the Chicago Mercantile Exchange have expressed interest in joining in. Indeed, given more computing power and employee expertise, a player's options and futures portfolios might be linked to his equities portfolio, demanding intricate total-income solutions. Add to that the prospect of a worldwide market for a WSG game that is playable round the clock, dealing in securities of Japan and England as well as the United States, and growth possibilities seem endless.

But they're not. For one thing, 24-hour world trading would require 24-hour local service. Will low-paid employees be responsive—or even show up—at 2:30 p.m. Tokyo time? Won't players run up the WATS line trying to determine the difference between Matsushita and Mitsubishi? Even professional brokers are intimidated by trading soybeans and pork bellies, and as players surely would make more demands on WSG's services. Right now, DeMello calculates, the company can accommodate 48 terminals with 48 students each answering 250 phone calls a day. That's 12,000 "plays" all told, wedged in with utmost precision.

By now dialing-for-fake-dollars habits have become predictable. A typical participant is very active his first month, moderately active the second and third, then eases off markedly. Right now less than 10% of The Blue Chip Edition's 3,000 players call in each day, so total usage is barely two hours. Thus 98% of capacity is unused. Indeed, some periods are so dull that DeMello often sends the troops home early.

However, that pace should quicken once the cash-award promotions hit WSG's trading floor. Each contest likely will strain services for three or four months running, which leaves DeMello a potential of only three sponsored promotions per year. Ironically, one presently in the works is a simulated-investment competition among real stockbrokers, bringing his concept full circle—and possibly closing it.

"The trouble with WSG's concept is that learning happens only when real dough is on the line. A game isn't going to teach people. The only thing that will do that is life."

—John Spooner

CUSTOMER

RALPH KIMBALL
Lecturer, Babson College, Wellesley, Mass. Uses WSG's The Blue Chip Edition in course on securities analysis

I've used The Blue Chip Edition for two semesters, and the first semester went very smoothly—students liked it a lot. In the second semester the students liked the game itself, but there were transaction errors. Records showed purchases of the wrong stock, or stock that students claimed had been bought didn't show up, or the wrong number of shares were recorded. I think as the volume has gone up, there's been some decline in the service.

If that's so, DeMello's got a real problem, especially in the education market. A large number of errors kills the aspect of realism and creates ill will on the part of professors. If I assign the game, I'm essentially vouching for its quality. If there are lots of errors, I can't go on assigning it.

But it *is* the right market, especially if WSG can broaden the product. I use it only in my introductory courses now. For advanced courses the game needs options and futures, and more than the allotted $100,000 in funds—make it $10 million, say—so a student could act as a portfolio manager rather than a private investor. But the price is right. Most college textbooks are $30 to $60, and if a student is paying $1,000 tuition for a course, another $45 for WSG doesn't seem too far out of line.

The education market offers a customer base that's continually renewing at a low market cost. There are several thousand professors of finance in the country, and DeMello will have to figure out how to get to them. But the nice thing is that once you've got professors on, you don't have to go back and resell them every quarter. I teach four of these sections a year, and each course has about 40 people—that means I deliver 160 customers per year. *That's* where WSG can come up with a sustainable customer base—not from onetime promotions in catalogs.

CUSTOMER

JOHN D. SPOONER
Stockbroker; senior vice-president at Shearson Lehman/Hutton

DeMello did a wonderful job. It's well thought out, packaged very well, and easy to understand. As a learning tool, it's terrific. But I just don't see the demand. There is zero need for it among my customers. Most of them are passive. They *want* me to do it. Sure, if I lost money for them they'd ask why, but a game isn't going to teach them. The only thing that will do that is life.

The main problem with anything

that deals with money in a hypothetical way, whether it's betting on horses or playing the stock market, is that unless you're emotionally involved, it's not valuable. When it's play money, you're not emotionally influenced. To learn anything, you have to have put real dough on the line. Students can say they were up 400% in a college course on the stock market, but the result would be different if they had their own money at risk.

Another problem for WSG is timing: Nobody cares about the underlying product right now. Wall Street is in a full-fledged depression. The average investor, even one with plenty of money, is buying CDs or staying in the money market. The atmosphere is one of fear, anxiety, or at least indifference. I think we may be in this climate for quite some time. If at first the game was bought as a fad, that thrust is now completely taken away. DeMello might as well paint the windows of his brokerage office black, because right now nobody cares.

The college market is viable. But how much is marketing going to cost? I think his projections are way off, given the climate. Even college stock-market courses tend to decline in periods when nobody cares. So he's in for some tough sledding. There already have been layoffs on Wall Street, and you haven't seen the half of it. The average stockbroker isn't even making $200 a week. It's not a glamorous job anymore.

This is a business you can't force. At most, you can cut prices, advertise, reposition. But you can't make people buy stocks—for real or for pretend—when there's no appetite for it. I would hate to start a business with something that may be out of favor for a long time. DeMello is obviously a true entrepreneur. He's going to make it big in one direction or another. But this isn't the one.

MARKETER

JOSEPH CORNACCHIA
President, The Games Gang Ltd., marketers of Pictionary; turned down DeMello's request to market The Blue Chip Edition

This is a tough call. I think WSG's product is well done, but I can't tell whether it's going to be successful or not. When Tim showed us the product, we were fairly excited at first to take it into our line and sell it to stores. Then we estimated the number of phone calls each player would generate and realized we could get into a real jam if we sold 200,000 or 300,000 units over the next two years. Tim says that not everyone calls, that the phone calls dry up after the first month. Well, if that's the case, then it's not going to be successful. I told him I still think it's a great product, but maybe he should rethink it.

To me, he's selling $100 worth of smoke—the phone calls. And if Tim's right about usage patterns, the player is going to figure out he's paying a lot of money for phone calls he's not using. That's what I thought was wrong. I would bring out the game for much less and have people pay an extra charge for the toll-free calls, or pay for the calls themselves.

The game needed testing. What has to be determined is whether the public will respond to the product and have fun playing it. Is it a game or an educational tool? *I* perceived it as a game, because the stock market is a game. If the public sees it that way and is willing to spend the $100 or so, it will be successful. If, on the other hand, it's educational, then the educational emphasis should be reflected in its packaging and accompanying materials—it should teach you about the stock market. Then say, "By the way, if you want to play with fake money, for another $5 or $10 you can join up and get monthly mailings and an account, and you can phone in and play the market like it really *is* the market." Tim's had it in Brookstone, and my guess is it didn't sell. I don't think it can work at retail.

I had my men survey some of the top buyers, and the price scared them. We as a game company could sell it at $16 [wholesale], which is the new standard price; it used to be $20 for Trivial Pursuit, but now it has slipped back.

If professors accept it, people in schools take it to their friends and talk it up, and the game starts to generate its own excitement—what we call legs—maybe it will succeed big. My guess is it won't, but you don't have to set your sights on half a million games a year. If he keeps his overhead low, he can make a good profit at 5,000 to 10,000 a year. But he's going to have to do a lot of hard work to earn his money. Can he peddle it to the schools? He'll do best selling it himself, because he's a good salesman. He can't let someone else peddle that product; it has to be sold personally. He might burn himself out in a couple of years, but by then he might have something going. If he's hitting his magic 35,000 to 40,000 units a year, that's the time to add the option game and other products, and he'll have himself a nice business.

CUSTOMER

MARY THORN
Vice-president of education and training, Kemper Financial Services Inc., Chicago

From a corporate-training standpoint, the amount of time the game takes is what's most troublesome. The point of training is to get the employee productive as soon as possible. When you're in the classroom doing two days of training, maybe a week of training, you have to collapse real-life experience so that people see the results of their choices far faster than WSG lets you.

There are ways around the problem, though. WSG could establish a division that customized its products—the way software companies do—for the training program at any given company. Along with a leader's guide and other training aids, the customized game might include look-up tables or something computerized that would simulate a year's play in stages that would take just hours.

Still, it would be tough. I'd advise him to stick with the college market, and forget businesses.

OPERATOR

JOSEPH GEKOSKI

President, Strategic Management Group Inc., Philadelphia, creators and marketers of computer-based business simulation games

The concept is great. It's a very powerful learning tool. The biggest opportunity for WSG is not in promoting the product at retail but selling it as a training vehicle. That's where DeMello can gain his greatest leverage. Our experience has been that the college market and the retail market are tough. Both are price sensitive and require customer knowledge.

There are some things I'd be concerned about, though. One is that the college students answering the telephones can't provide feedback. All they're doing is taking orders, like a discount broker. I recognize that if they did more, his phone costs would go up, which means he might have to charge extra for an auxiliary service that would include consultation. But people are going to want to know what they did right and what they did wrong. That's the key to making it a successful training product. What dis-

tinguishes a training product from simply a game is that not only do you learn from the playing experience, but you get to deal with an expert and ask questions. For that reason, I'd consider developing a seminar or courseware around the simulation.

I'd also be worried about the boredom factor—he says people lose interest after a couple of months. On the one hand, as calls fall off he won't have as much fulfillment expense, but on the other, the game would be more successful if it sold for $39 or $49. That price would buy a quarter of a year, rather than a year, and if people were really into it, they could resubscribe, maybe for $25 the next quarter. If they're real good at it, maybe they would win free play, like on a pinball machine. The packaging and advertising have to convey very clearly what the product does, that there's something viable in the box.

If WSG can make this game work, it'll be in good shape. I can see it moving into other things, like commodities and options trading. Simply as a product line, there are opportunities for growth.

HOT SEATS

Building Eurostyle chairs
for the corporate elite

BY JOHN CASE

Andy Goodwin

This can't be the place. That was my first thought. We'd already driven 30-odd miles west from Grand Rapids—down bumpy back roads, past cornfields still stubbly with last season's cuttings, apparently heading straight for the shores of Lake Michigan itself. Now Dick Keener was pulling his red Oldsmobile into a tiny parking lot in front of a small, drab, shedlike building. The image didn't quite fit. Keener's new company was planning to make high-design, very expensive office chairs, the kind a glitzy New York interior designer might order for a new corporate conference room. Somehow I expected to see a high-design, very expensive—yes, even a little glitzy—installation.

My mistake. I must have spent too much time among the splashy start-ups of Silicon Valley and Route 128, where the first order of busi-

Cofounders Leif Blodee (left) and Richard Keener on site at Keener-Blodee Inc.

THE COMPANY:
Keener-Blodee Inc.,
Holland, Mich.

CONCEPT:
Make and sell
stylish, expensive
office chairs,
pitching quality of
craftsmanship and
uniqueness of lami-
nated-wood design

PROJECTIONS:
Fifth-year sales
of $6 million with
$1-million pretax
profit. Profitable
from year one

HURDLES:
Stagnant market;
pleasing the tastes
of architects and
interior designers;
getting products
through the sales
and installation
chain with no com-
pany sales staff

ness is to rent a building with manicured lawns and smoked-glass doors. In the office-furniture industry, I soon realized, you can work out of a barn, so long as it's within reach of a truck and a telephone line. And the less you spend on high-priced land and fancy buildings, the more you can spend where it counts—on design, tooling, and marketing. This was the place, all right: Keener pointed to the muddy field out back, where the outlines of a 12,500-square-foot factory were staked in the dirt. In just a few months, he said cheerily, a preengineered steel plant would be erected there, and Keener-Blodee Inc. would be ready for production.

Production! Getting there, admittedly, was taking longer than Keener had expected. In June 1986, at age 57, he had taken early retirement, ending a 31-year career with American Seating Co., a large manufacturer based in Grand Rapids. By January of '87 he had grown tired of "Europe and golf," and had begun talking with longtime friend Leif Blodee (pronounced Blo-DAY), a Danish-born architect and furniture designer, about the company they had often imagined starting. Maybe now was the time. Both men's children were grown. Old age was still a decade or more away. They knew—and were known in—an industry.

"Eight to 10 million in 8 to 10 years," thought Keener, envisioning a pleasantly symmetrical sales goal. Then sell the company and retire.

Over the next several months, the partners' plans began to take shape.

When an insurance agent opens a new office, he's likely to drop by an office-furniture dealer's showroom and pick out desks and chairs himself. When an insurance *company* opens a new office, it hires an interior designer (or an architectural-design firm) and gives the designer a contract for the whole shebang. The designer, in turn, develops a "spec"—instructions to the corporate purchasing department about the types of furnishings needed to execute their design. The folks in purchasing then place orders through a network of manufacturers, reps, and dealers who specialize in commercial and institutional furnishings.

The "contract furniture" business, as it's known, is the industry in which Keener and Blodee had spent their careers—and in which they proposed to start their new company.

Not that they intended to take on the giants. Big manufacturers such as Steelcase, Herman Miller, and Haworth—all of them headquartered in western Michigan—dominate much of the contract market with endless lines of desks, chairs, and the ubiquitous slotted-panel, "open-plan systems" used to turn unbroken office space into "componentized" cubicles. But there are plenty of niche players in the industry, simply because a designer doesn't impress that special client by specifying, say, yet another Steelcase conference-room chair. Let's get something a little nicer looking, she might think. Let's get something . . . in wood! Warm, natural, elegant in its lines, yet well crafted and highly functional.

Keener and Blodee were counting on just such a train of thought. For them, high-design wood-and-upholstered chairs made a natural product line. Blodee already had some drawings on his worktable, even a couple of hand-built samples. Tooling and equipment costs would be lower than with steel or plastic, and gross margins would be relatively high.

Nor did this particular niche seem overcrowded. A few modest-size U.S. manufacturers—such as Westin-Nielsen and The Gunlocke Co. (recently acquired by Chicago Pacific)—were doing pretty well; so was Rudd International, a Washington, D.C.-based company that imports stylish Scandinavian furniture. But the dropping dollar was already beginning to hurt the imports. Besides, Keener knew from his days at American Seating that designers were always looking for something new and different.

Different, he figured, is exactly what Keener-Blodee would give them. Unlike most domestic manufacturers, the company would work exclusively in laminated wood. Laminates are stronger than comparable

---

THE FOUNDERS

Richard N. Keener
cofounder, president, and CEO

Age: 59

Worked at American Seating Co., 1955–1986, in sales and sales management, then as president and general manager of $58-million operating division... B.S., University of Wisconsin, 1950

Leif Blodee
cofounder and executive vice-president

Age: 60

Owner/operator since 1982 of Leif Industries, small manufacturer of lounge seating systems for American Seating Co....independent designer since 1967....previously product designer at Herman Miller Inc. and elsewhere... B.A., Institute of Technology, Aalborg, Denmark, 1951

KEENER-BLODEE INC. PROJECTED OPERATING STATEMENT
(in $ thousands)

	Calendar year 1989	Calendar year 1992
SALES	**$1,700**	**$6,000**
COST OF GOODS (including overhead)		
Labor	440	1,310
Materials	580	2,050
Total cost of sales	1,020	3,360
GROSS PROFIT	**680**	**2,640**
Gross profit/sales	40%	44%
SELLING EXPENSES		
Commissions	180	650
Marketing materials	80	120
Travel & entertainment	20	40
Royalties & miscellaneous	60	210
Total selling expenses	340	1,020
GENERAL & ADMINISTRATIVE		
Salaries	160	360
Other fixed costs	40	120
TOTAL G&A	**200**	**480**
OPERATING PROFIT	**140**	**1,140**
FINANCE COSTS	**80**	**140**
NET PRETAX PROFIT	**60**	**1,000**
Net pretax profit/sales	3.5%	16.7%

thicknesses of solid wood, and thus permit long, lightweight, curved members—a "European look" effectively captured by Blodee's designs. Finely detailed joinery, traditionally associated with European craftsmen, would reinforce the continental image; so too would Keener-Blodee's marketing materials, right down to the accent marks gracing the two founders' names on the company logo. But the prices, turnaround times, and reliability would be all-American.

"Everything's designed to give the idea we have a European heritage," says Dick Keener. "Designers love the European style; they just can't get it. We give them the look, but we're made in the USA."

If he was right about the concept's appeal—and some early evaluations from designers convinced him he was—creating the new company would be simply a matter of building these highly crafted chairs economically, then persuading the interior designers of America to specify the products of a new, untested supplier. Oh, yes—and raising money. Something close to half a million dollars, Keener thought, would do the trick.

MANUFACTURING. Most of Keener-Blodee's products will be made of laminated oak. "Sixty percent of [wooden] office furniture is oak," explains Keener, "and our products have to fit in." But customers will be able both to specify finishes and to order upholstery fabrics from the widely used Maharam catalog and others. Maharam ships the fabric to Keener-Blodee's factory; inventoried parts are assembled and finished; the chairs are shipped. Turnaround time: six to eight weeks.

That process is little different from any other chair manufacturer's, though most companies are now offering partial-selection, "quick ship" programs, with chairs delivered in a couple of weeks. But Keener and Blodee are counting on fine construction as well as European styling to distinguish their products in the marketplace. In their plans for manufacturing, they hope, lies a competitive edge.

Take the "A" chair, for example, a light, stackable chair that will be among the company's first products. The legs are 14-ply laminates, continuously curved. A tapered maple insert holds the crosspieces that support the seat. The crosspieces are morticed into the maple, then anchored in place by both glue and by tiny wedges, much like those in an ax handle. Just the kind of craftsmanlike detail, Keener says, that designers will love.

But Keener and Blodee aren't budgeting for many highly skilled Old World craftsmen; nor would their production schedule allow for much in the way of hand labor. And until they get bigger, it wouldn't be economical to buy the numerically controlled machine tools that could make all the complex cuts automatically. So Blodee, a tinkerer and inventor with several patents to his name, has rigged up some intricate and effective jigs and fixtures. Using them, he says, even a semiskilled worker can quickly cut a perfectly tapered mortice and a perfectly shaped tenon. He has already developed a machine to make the cuts for the wedges and a custom-made press to drive them in.

"The uniqueness of design and construction gives us a product

COMPETITIVE ANALYSIS

	Keener-Blodee 1989	Projections 1992	Industry average
Sales	$1.7 million	$6 million	$22.7 million
Gross profit/sales	40%	44%	25.3%
Pretax profit/sales	3.5%	16.7%	3.3%
Unit sales	7,100	24,300	NA*
Number of manufacturing employees	22	60	NA*
Sales/employee	$77,273	$100,000	NA*
Independent sales reps	11	15	NA*

*Not available

with integrity that designers will respect," asserts Keener. He also believes competitors would find it a difficult design to knock off: they'd either have to ignore the fine detail or produce an outright copy, which he thinks customers wouldn't buy. "Designers would recognize a knock-off as not the same chair," he scoffs.

If things go according to plan, such integrity will not come at too high a price. The partners have budgeted labor costs at a base rate of between $7 and $8 an hour, and are planning on spending only $135,000 for additional machinery in year one. These numbers, in turn, allow for competitive pricing of products. The "A" chair, for example, will list for between $316 and $460 depending on fabric, roughly comparable to Westin-Nielsen's wooden stacking chair at $270 to $500. Even with the 45% to 55% discounts that are standard in the industry, Keener-Blodee's gross manufacturing margins will average roughly 40%.

MARKETING. To a novice in the business, Keener-Blodee's marketing challenge might seem well-nigh intractable. Too new to interest dealers, too small to set up its own show-rooms, the company must somehow catch the eyes of customers who are pressed for time and swamped with product offerings. What makes that task merely hard, rather than impossible, is the fact that designers do indeed watch for new items. "We're not buying a service, where we have to stay with the same people," says one. "We're buying a product, and we want to know what's new, what's exciting visually."

Keener, who had worked in marketing much of his life, put togeth-er the marketing plan. Beginning nearly a year ago, he interviewed 40 manufacturer's reps, eventually signing 8. By the end of 1988 he plans to add 3 more, which will give him coverage of virtually the whole country. Why would a rep sign on with a small start-up? Credit the founders' long experience—and reputations—in the contract-furniture business. "I've known Dick Keener for 22 years, Leif for maybe 10," says George Forbes, whose rep firm covers the Philadelphia area. "Dick came out with ideas and programs [at American Seating] that made my company very successful, and Leif has designed some great furniture."

The reps will call on designers, "schlepp the chairs out so they can sit on them" (as one put it), and arrange for display at their own or other local showrooms. Once the chairs are in production, they'll also take orders and make sure the product gets to the right place at the right time. Since Keener expects the typical order to be anywhere from a dozen to 50 chairs, there's little need for the elaborate warehousing and staging services provided by dealers. But some reps plan to work through local dealers anyway, if only to maintain good business relationships. If volume grows significantly, dealers may eventually play a bigger part in the distribution system.

Keener-Blodee isn't planning any national advertising for the moment; nor will the company be an official exhibitor at this month's Neocon, the industry's mammoth trade show in Chicago. (The partners are taking a hotel suite instead, and will have their reps visit with potential customers and designers in tow.) But they are spending some serious marketing money. Later this month, 3,000 copies of a glossy purple three-ring binder will be imprinted with Keener-Blodee's mauve-and-white logo, then filled with elaborate product information, including fabric and finish selections. Next the company will do a two-part staggered mailing to individual designers in every firm recommended by its reps, introducing its first two products. When the reps make their follow-up calls they'll have the new binder in hand, and they'll have sample chairs at their disposal.

The goal: getting the binder on designers' shelves, and the name Keener-Blodee firmly implanted in their minds. The cost for the entire marketing program: $85,000. To Dick Keener, anything less ambitious would have been self-defeating. Keener-Blodee is targeting a high-end customer; cut-rate marketing efforts would have conveyed exactly the wrong message.

FINANCE. When Keener started looking for money, everyone said he'd have no trouble finding it. Today, he reflects on that oft-heard statement. "It ranks up there with `The check's in the mail,' " he sighs.

Keener put up more than $200,000 in cash. Blodee, who was running a tiny job shop making upholstered-foam furniture for American Seating, contributed his company's building and equipment. By August they had a commitment from FMB-First Michigan Bank for $300,000 in capital financing (new building, new equipment) plus a $250,000 line of credit.

But Keener knew he needed at least another $150,000—preferably $200,000—for development capital. Money to complete the marketing program. Money for molds and fixtures. Money to hire a couple of draftsmen and an office manager. The partners weren't choosy about the form of investment; they just didn't want to give up control. No matter: For months, they got nowhere. Conversations with an investment manager representing the investment group of Marshall Field V looked promising but fell through. Talks with private investors located through the Grand Rapids-based West Michigan Venture Capital Group foundered on the control issue. Eventually, Keener-Blodee got a commitment from a new state-sponsored investment corporation known as Arcadia BIDCO, for Business & Industrial Development Corp. But the terms of the deal struck Keener as too costly: BIDCO would lend them $100,000 over nine years plus another $100,000 in five-year convertible debt. If the company grew according to plan, buying out BIDCO's equity in the fifth year would cost the founders roughly $650,000.

Early this spring, Keener's brother-in-law suggested he put together a package for the Small Business Administration. Keener broached the idea to FMB, which promptly agreed to fold in its own commitment. The new plan: FMB would put up about $203,000 on the new building and equipment, plus a side loan of $162,000 on Blodee's old building and equipment. The SBA would provide about $162,000, the two founders would kick in another $40,000, and four outside investors would add $25,000 apiece. Total: around $650,000 plus the agreed-upon line of credit. All the financing would be straight debt, repayable over 15 to 20 years, and the SBA portion would carry a favorable interest rate.

The SBA's local committee, in Holland, approved the application on March 22, 1988, then sent it on to Washington. The bank has given its approval, and Keener was expecting the final OK as *Inc.* was going to press in May 1988.

This, says Keener, is all the money they'll need for full-scale operation. "There's a significant safety factor built into all our estimates," he says, "and there are plenty of items we can delay spending money on if sales come in under projection. In fact, we could finish the first full year with sales 35% under plan, lose money, and still be OK on cash flow."

For all of Keener's confidence, there's no doubt that the delay in finding financing has slowed up the company. "Quite candidly, they've been dragging their feet," said David Olson, who represents Keener-

Blodee in Minneapolis. "They're not going to get any specifications until product is available." That was in late March; once the money is in hand, the task is to get the marketing program under way, get samples into the reps' hands, and get ready for production—quickly, yet with each step well coordinated. The reps can't be out selling until that building has begun to go up.

Longer term, the challenges are of a different sort. Any new business faces the possibility that its founders have simply guessed wrong, or that things won't work out the way they hoped. But Keener-Blodee faces three particular hurdles that reflect the risks of its industry:

A no-growth market. Shipments of wood seating, according to Commerce Department figures, have been flat. Unlike start-ups in growing industries, therefore, Keener-Blodee can succeed only by wresting market share from the competition. On their side: the declining dollar, which makes imports more costly. Working against them: a trend toward consolidation. Competitors such as Gunlocke (recently bought by Chicago-Pacific) and Stow & Davis (now a division of Steelcase) have deep pockets.

The idiosyncracies of taste. Since one chair in a given category is pretty much like another, Keener-Blodee's major selling point is styling. Will the designs catch on? Designers shown photos of samples reacted enthusiastically ("Love it!" "Nice form and flow"). But it's an industry whose fads seem to defy description, let alone prediction. "The European look is very popular right now," one expert told *Inc.* Nonsense, said another—everyone's looking for traditional styling. Place your bets.

The fickleness of fashion. Designers' never-ending quest for the new gives K-B a window of opportunity. But those who live by novelty can die by it. Product life cycles in the industry, acknowledges Blodee, run four to five years. He hopes his designs will last longer. If they don't, the company will have to introduce more new products, with corresponding risks.

In this business, even success can have its perils. "We have two nightmares," says Keener with a laugh. "One is that we get no orders at all. The other is that we're swamped with orders and can't handle the volume." Fully staffed, Keener-Blodee's plant will have an annual production capacity of roughly 13,000 pieces. Most manufacturers would just farm out excess pieces; this one may not be able to. When Keener approached a local chair-frame maker to discuss the matter, he was dismissed out of hand. Looking at the samples, the fellow growled, "That's European style. I wouldn't begin to know how to make it."

Ah, well. You get the idea that the two men would rather face Nightmare Number Two than Nightmare Number One. A few years down the road, if the company is as successful as they hope, they even plan to build a wholly new factory—custom-designed by Leif Blodee. I expressed an interest in the plan, and Blodee proudly got out a little drawing he had made. The building looked stylish; modern; costly.

Maybe even a little glitzy.

"This is not a growing market segment. For them to expect to be able to whack 7,100 units out of somebody else's hide is a gross miscalculation. Not minor; gross."

—Justin J. Thompson

ANALYST

WALLACE EPPERSON JR.

Senior vice-president, Wheat First Securities, Richmond. Specialist in contract-furniture industry

For starters, they're facing some real shifts in the industry—some helpful, some not. After double-digit growth from 1975 to '85, the contract business hit something of its own recession, thanks mainly to tax reform. Uncertainty about how rules would end up for depreciation and investment tax credits meant buyers couldn't predict their real cost of product. There was a tremendous deferral of buying. So the industry saw a bit of a shakeout and the first signs of a serious consolidation as some of the players got weak and there were buying opportunities.

Consolidation resulted in the loss of lots of independent distribution avenues, making it much tougher to start up in this business today than it would have been three or four years ago.

On the other hand, business seems to have been picking up over the past 9 to 12 months, partly due to deferred demand—though there's still not enough business to go around.

Also helping the contract industry rebound is the well-publicized glut of office space. Because most of our country's metro areas are overbuilt, the logistics of office setup have been transformed. Back in the early '70s, people would get a contract from GM or GE or IBM, and it would be for two and a half years hence, because the building would have to be constructed. Today, with all the space that's out there, moves can take place immediately, putting speed and timeliness of delivery at a premium. It will be a big plus if K-B can be as flexible and fast as it promises.

Now the downside. Like any start-up in this business, K-B will be competing under one significant disadvantage: the inability to have control of its sales organization. The reps handling Keener-Blodee will have a number of products in their bags, which means that too often they'll be thinking about somebody else's product, not K-B's. One of the first things I'd recommend to these guys is to move as fast as possible either toward getting single-bag reps, captive reps, or working toward some form of captive distribution or alliance. Distribution is going to be much more of a key, much more important to the success of their company than they appear to believe. It'll be the single most difficult issue they'll face.

ANALYST

JUSTIN J. THOMPSON
CEO of Business Products Consulting Group, Centerport, N.Y., consultants to the contract-furniture industry

This is not a growing market segment. For them to expect they're going to be able to whack 7,100 units out of somebody else's hide is a gross miscalculation. Not minor; gross. I think they've got a big problem with that number.

Other problems: (1) Blodee has done a nice job designing the chairs, but what he perhaps hasn't seen is the need for all the variations—the whistles and bells—that a designer will invariably require from a supplier. Unupholstered options, stain-color options, chairs with table arms or armrests. If you don't have a broad offering within your product line you greatly reduce your ability to take market share from somebody else. Keener-Blodee's competitors will be tough—they can do all those things, and there are plenty of them. Probably 8 or 10 other manufacturers produce chairs that are visually similar, have similar construction systems, and carry about the same price.

(2) They'll have a hard time holding "spec." Selling the architecture and design community is only half the job; designers don't order, they prescribe. Then the corporate client's purchasing department places the order. The designer will specify, for instance, "a chair by Keener-Blodee or equal," only to have the purchasing agent sub the job not to Keener-Blodee but to somebody else whose product is close enough.

So the art orientation that starts at the design level doesn't follow all the way down to the purchasing agent and the dealer. At the purchasing level there's a series of influential people that K-B's sales reps have to be sure they're contacting. The reps might sell designers on the beauty of this European design, the integrity and quality of its construction, only to see the hard-won specification slip through their hands when the order is made at the corporate level. It won't happen every time, but the potential is there.

(3) Another red flag: Why in God's name are they planning to hire an office manager? That's a manifestation of big-company myopia. A company like this needs the principals to be the office managers. It's the principals who need to maintain one-on-one contact with the reps, the designers, the specifiers. They need to communicate their vital interest. The last thing they should do is relegate the day in, day out operation to someone who takes a check at the end of the week and goes home.

Are they going to make it? They have a tough row to hoe. I strongly urge they rethink their sales projections based on the limited depth and breadth of their product line. Even if they do make it, it won't be at 7,100 units a year.

DESIGNER

CAROL GROH

Founder of GN Associates, a New York City interior-design and graphic-design firm

Design quality has got to come first, and I think their stacking chair of bent wood is quite beautiful; I think it will sell well. The armchair, however, I find ugly. I don't think it's well designed. The stacker is cleaner, neater—it has visual appeal *and* functional value. The armchair doesn't. The lacquered chair is interesting, but looks as though it might be uncomfortable because of the low back. Still, I think they've scored with the stacker.

They've done some other things right, too. I like the fact that they realize they've got to spend big bucks on marketing. If you're a new company in this industry, marketing is all you've got. And their approach is very good. You've got to spend to get your name out there initially, and you've got to get your product to the right market— designers and architects. They seem to realize how important it is to get the right brochures, the right photographs, the right dealers to represent them. Their emphasis on the presentation of their image is smart.

They're overselling the Euro-influence, though. I don't think that many people care about the claimed European connection. Call the designs "bentwood." It's beautiful. Besides, designers *can* get European products. They're not that unusual. So Keener-Blodee won't make it on the European pitch alone.

If they can really perfect this whole bentwood approach, there's something else they should consider: bringing in well-known designers to do a design, in prescribed materials, for Keener-Blodee. I don't think Blodee himself is the answer to all of the world's design needs. The sooner they realize that, the better. More and more companies are going to key designers to do this sort of work for them, and royalties are minimal, around 2% to 4%.

I think they'll do well. They've had experience, and there's no substitute for that.

DESIGNER

VINCENT CAFIERO

Principal in Vincent Cafiero Designs Inc., an Irvington, N.Y., design and consulting firm

They suffer from what a lot of people suffer from: thinking big. It's a real interesting problem. In the process of starting up, a certain kind of thinking is encouraged; the bankers want to see big schedules, you push for big clients, and the tendency is to pump high top-end projections into your plans. Nowhere along the line is someone saying "back off," or that the most important thing in the first year is survival. And in this case that danger is increased by Keener's years of experience in a large, successful company. Large companies condition you—force you, in fact— to think big. Which is the opposite of what Keener-Blodee needs.

Keener-Blodee can make it, *if* they can keep things under control.

THE SMALL CHILL

Can a start-up marketer sell proprietary appliances to
college dorms and budget motels?

BY ROBERT A. MAMIS

Brian Smith

I n September 1989 the Associated Press sent out a story about a novel kitchen device that had begun shipping the month before. "The next thing I knew," relates the contrivance's inventor, Robert P. Bennett, "my brother phones from Alaska—he just saw my picture in the local paper. Then ABC News calls up, and Paul Harvey describes it on radio, and Cable News Network airs a TV item; we're in *USA Today*, the *Chicago Tribune*, *The New York Times*. I personally was interviewed live at least a dozen times." The most-asked question: Are students *really* going crazy over the thing?

So crazy, Bennett predicts, that they will pay for some $90 million worth of them over the next five years. On top of that, Bennett is looking to collect $55 million from motels, another $5 million or $6 million from housing projects, and lesser six-figure amounts from the army and navy, business offices, and trailer camps. Indeed, in this, his first full selling year, Bennett anticipates revenues of

Robert Bennett, founder of MicroFridge Inc.

more than $15 million, with net profits after taxes close to $1 million.

If everything goes as planned, every cent will have come by way of one rather unimposing item barely the size of a two-drawer filing cabinet—the refrigerator-freezer-microwave oven that his new company, MicroFridge Inc., makes and markets. But couldn't any of us go to the corner discount store, purchase a compact fridge and a midget microwave, and spend less than the $429 that Bennett's tripartite unit sells for? Sure, but we'd likely end up with less capacity than his collective three and a half cubic feet—nor would the components be spliced into the energy-saving circuit that is the MicroFridge product's sine qua non.

It's this now-patented circuit, initially devised with the help of some engineering friends, that positions MicroFridge for the customer niche Bennett spotted back in '86—anyone occupying cramped living quarters that are served by marginal electrical wiring. The current-limiting switch rules over the power draw of each component, so that when the 500-watt microwave is in use, the refrigeration system is automatically shut down. Even under multiple use, demand never exceeds a modest 10 amperes, and the appliance therefore can be plugged into an ordinary household outlet without blowing fuses.

The largest markets Bennett felt couldn't help but respond to a sales appeal centered on size and safety were hotel/motels and college residences.

(1) Motels: About halfway down the old road between Boston and Providence is MicroFridge's original hospitality-industry research lab: the lobby of a Super 8 Motel. There, Bennett polled guests. Would they be willing to pay an extra $3 to have a MicroFridge unit in their room? Yes, a startling 79% replied—particularly since this place is in the middle of nowhere.

"Our segment of the lodging market is the economy and limited-service part, not executive suites," concluded Bennett. In budget facilities, restaurants (if any) close early, and late checkers-in can get little to eat beyond a bag of nacho chips. Put a MicroFridge in, charge a few dollars extra, and the unit's paid for in three months. Ninety nights @ $3 = $270, and the hundred dollars or so more comes from the front desk, which vends popcorn and other microwave foods at high margin to captive guests. Given a room's full occupancy, a motel can make more than $1,000 in its first year per installed unit. That's 300% ROI—and the useful life of the humble appliance is presumed to be a good seven years.

In 1989 there were some 1 million rooms in establishments with limited or no restaurant service, and, trade sources estimated, that sector was growing at close to 10% per year. Bennett expects to put a MicroFridge in 2% of those rooms in 1990, yielding sales of nearly $7

THE COMPANY:
MicroFridge Inc.,
Sharon, Mass.

CONCEPT:
Make a miniaturized combination refrigerator-freezer-microwave with a proprietary device that enables it to run off one plug in an ordinary household outlet, and market it for use in college dorms and budget motels

PROJECTIONS:
Pretax profits of $1.5 million on sales of $15 million in 1990, the first full selling year; sales of $30 million in 1991

HURDLES:
Securing enough capital to keep product flowing steadily from manufacturing subcontractor to wholesale distributor; establishing solid market position before competitors—big or small—enter the niche

million. By 1993, he predicts, he'll sell his units into 5% of the expanding market, for revenues of about $21 million.

(2) College residences. Fire statistics make for scary stories—and easy selling. The National Fire Protection Association reports that an average 1,600 fires per year broke out in school, college, and university dormitories from 1983 to 1987; a MicroFridge-commissioned poll claims that some 90% of students use hot plates, although most universities forbid them. "They're going to cook anyway," Bennett reminds purchasing agents, "and *our* unit has no exposed heating element."

Besides, don't administrators want to attract paying customers? Parents don't have big families anymore, Bennett argues, so there's money behind the fewer children they do have. "Our push is for the school to put one in every room, which makes sense for the school. With their buying power, they can own the units inexpensively and rent them out." The school controls heavy-wattage appliance usage and reduces its liability exposure, and savvy administrators can enhance income in the process, stocking cookables in school-owned convenience stores and vending machines.

Based on its own market survey (substantiated by a test mailing to students at California's Whittier College, which resulted in a combined purchase and rental response rate of 12%), MicroFridge projects these campus revenues: $6.3 million in 1990, based on supplying 4% of the students at the 250 schools the company expects to reach, and almost $40 million in 1993, the result of supplying 7% of the students at 960 schools.

Those aspirations may seem giddy, but Bennett reminds doubters that "MicroFridges already are spreading across the country. If your school doesn't have them, your students won't be enjoying the quality of life they can get somewhere else." And, it's implied, they may choose to *go* somewhere else.

THE FOUNDER

Robert P. Bennett, president and CEO

Age: 33

Family status: Married, one child

College degrees: Bachelor of applied mathematics, University of Maine; master of engineering management, Northeastern University

Typical workweek: 50 hours

Equity held: 40%

Outside board of directors: Not yet

Businesses previously founded: None

Last job held: Regional sales manager at small computer company

Most interesting characteristic of ownership: Can't stop thinking about it. Perturbs wife, because difficult to have conversation that doesn't relate to MicroFridge

What used to be concern: Running out of money

Present concern: Getting sales numbers up

Why line of business chosen: Sought a product, any product, to leverage sales abilities with; could just as well have been shoes

MicroFridge Inc. was incorporated in August 1987, capitalized with $35,000 from Bennett, then age 31 and regional sales manager for a $44-million computer company. An additional $25,000 came cumulatively from two soon-to-be-active partners: Procopio Soriano, then 45, vice-president of sales at the computer company that employed Bennett; and Edward J. Ward, then 35, an M.B.A. who was manager of the engineering staff of a research firm. Bennett became MicroFridge's president and CEO, Soriano its VP of sales, and Ward VP of operations. None of the first-round capital was spent on management salaries: Even with the alluring projections their studies endorsed, no principal rushed to quit his full-time job. First they had to make sure they could deliver the little device at an appropriately little price.

Novices at hard bargaining for hard goods, the partners arranged to travel in pairs as they searched for the right supplier, lest one tyro alone be tempted to give away too much. They contacted General Electric, Amana Refrigeration, and other domestic manufacturers but could stir no interest. So they tried Samsung Electronics and similar off-shorers, and "within five minutes," Bennett recalls, "we were talking to someone in charge." Eventually, Sanyo E & E Corp., in San Diego, the

MICROFRIDGE INC. PROJECTED OPERATING STATEMENT
(in $ thousands)

	1990	1991
NET SALES	$15,033	$29,695
Cost of sales	12,428	25,286
Gross profit	2,605	4,409
Percent gross profit	17%	15%
OPERATING EXPENSES		
Salaries, wages, & benefits	459	914
Advertising, direct mail, & trade shows	75	115
Travel & entertainment	88	124
Professional services	55	66
Depreciation & amortization	62	106
Building occupancy, office expenses, & misc.	84	108
TOTAL OPERATING EXPENSES	823	1,433
Interest expense	292	130
NET INCOME BEFORE TAXES	1,490	2,846
Percent net income before taxes	10%	10%

U.S. affiliate of Japan's giant Sanyo Electric, agreed to produce the unit. In March '88 Bennett began negotiating terms. "They have 70% of the compact-refrigerator business in this country," says Bennett in affirmation of the ultimate relationship with Sanyo. "They're a recognized leader, and that helps us, because who the heck is MicroFridge Inc.?"

MicroFridge would pay $170,000 for special tooling and molds, and put up $100 for each unit in advance of manufacture, which would take about four months from order to delivery. Units would be landed FOB San Diego, 3,000 miles from MicroFridge's corporate home in Sharon, Mass., in two parts, which would be drop-shipped across the country. When they got to their destination, the purchaser was to hitch them together with eight screws.

Neither those screws nor any other part of the 87-pound, 43 1/2-inch-high unit is fabricated in the United States. The microwave component is assembled in Singapore and the refrigerator-cum-freezer in Tijuana. Manufacturing-wise, all that the 7 employees (including management) who constitute the entire pay structure of MicroFridge can do is admire the cost-effectiveness of cheap labor. (Hourly pay in Tijuana starts at about 80¢.) According to plan, at the end of 1991, MicroFridge will be employing 15 people at most, yet will have shipped some $30 million worth of the unit. "That's the beauty of subcontracting," Bennett beams.

MicroFridge was paying $270 for each unit at the end of 1989. But the five-year contract grants Sanyo the right to readjust the price in response to changes in costs of labor, currency, and material. The exposure doesn't worry Bennett. "If the yen-to-dollar goes in the wrong direction, we can get penalized," he admits, "but this business is competitive and has a history of stable pricing. And ours isn't so difficult a product that they can't keep moving it into countries with better labor costs." In March 1989 an exclusive agreement was signed. Sanyo cannot sell it to anyone else in the world.

"For someone to knock us off now," Bennett claims, "not only would they have to provide the circuitry, they'd have to build a separate freezer box from scratch like the one Sanyo already has." Therefore, he calculates, MicroFridge will be unopposed in the marketplace for perhaps two years, maybe longer. "If we turn ourselves into a $35-million-a-year company, someone will go after us," he grants. But by then, MicroFridge will have cemented a brand-name advantage.

The initial price the partners established for direct sales was $369, and when a dude ranch owner in Wyoming sent in cold cash after having seen notice of the machine in a trade magazine, they exulted, "This product is a no-brainer!" But, admits a now-wiser Bennett, "We definitely mispriced it early." And often. Shortly thereafter, retail was raised to $389, and a few weeks later, in September, to gain more operating margin it was boosted to $429. A yet higher price—$499—was being tested at year's end. "Sooner or later we'll hit a ceiling," he pledges. "But we don't know where that is."

Then there was the question of how to move the merchandise, whatever the price. The choice was between big-margin, highly profitable sales on a direct basis without large volume, and selling at lower margins to distributors, making less money but getting the volume. Bennett opted for the latter, rather than face the costly prospect of building his own direct sales force, credit department, and warehousing and service operations. "We don't want to carry inventories, and we don't want to carry inns in Vermont," he ruled. Nor did he want his own people having to be the ones going around handing out $10 discounts for units that arrived dinged or dented. Let the distributors contend with that. Net profit would be lower, but, if revenues climbed, in the end who would care? "When you're positioning a company for a public offering or a buyout," Bennett argues, "revenues is the significant number."

Also among the presumed benefits of tying into distributors

(which MicroFridge charges from $309 to $323 per unit, depending on how many they order) is the rapid cash flow their prompt payment throws off. Appliance distributors make profits on rapid inventory turns and getting the money in fast, and then take advantage of manufacturers' discounts. "One percent net 10 tempts them," Bennett learned, "but 2% net 10 is guaranteed." The lowest credit rating of any distributor MicroFridge has considered is AAA-2—reliable payment within 30 days. Eventually, the plan goes, MicroFridge receivables will consist only of those from its distributors.

Bennett intends to blanket the map with distributors, to whom he will hand over existing house accounts. As of the end of '89, the company had signed up seven independent distributors—in New England, the MidAtlantic, the West Coast, Ohio, Michigan, and Florida, plus one who deals with the military. Accounts elsewhere will stay on a direct basis for the time being.

Where a distributor is in place, MicroFridge passes on qualified leads generated by one full-time, in-house telemarketer. "That's another thing you get with a distributor: follow-up," the salesman in Bennett savors. In turn, distributors "love" the affiliation, he claims, because the appliance opens discrete markets they've never had before, such as schools, hotels, and office-food services. And in making end-user sales rather than selling to a dealer, distributors enjoy from three to five points more margin than the 15% they customarily work with.

For its part, the company backs up distributors' sales with joint marketing. After contracting with its first major distributor last July, $50-million, 18-salesperson Choquette & Co., in Seekonk, Mass., MicroFridge got it moving by designing a mailing piece that was sent to 4,000 hotels in New England. The response was so positive that in August, for the first time, the by then full-time partners began paying themselves salaries.

Last June MicroFridge raised $100,000 through a private placement of equity, at that time bringing the company's capital base to $221,000 (including a loan from the founders of $61,000). But it could hardly be called a base, since the sum had already been spent on start-up activities, some $50,000 going to legal fees, $6,000 to the market study, and much of the rest to appearances at national trade shows. How, then, to pay Sanyo its $100-per-unit down payment, never mind the $170,000 for tooling?

The latter could wait a bit; the former couldn't: By July, Micro-Fridge had booked orders for 2,400 units. A Korean trading company offered to finance them, and Bennett signed on for $170,000 credit at 2% of the amount financed plus an annualized $3/8$ of a point over prime.

MicroFridge's first order went to Sanyo for 1,700 units. The rest was backlogged. When the Korean company "tried to get higher rates out of us," Bennett reports, "we dumped them." For its second order, MicroFridge switched to Transamerica Commercial Finance Corp. at 1% plus 4 points over prime. "It may seem expensive, but it's very short money—only days at a time." And Sanyo agrees. With the less burdensome terms, Sanyo rescinded its $100-in-advance demand. A third equity placement completed last November for $350,000 ought to relieve the rest of the credit crunch.

Raising private money—most from relatives and friends—has been comparatively uncomplicated. "The concept is easy to grasp—after all, it's not gene-splicing," explains Bennett. Initially, however, the partners hoped to get funding from venture capital firms. "They wanted at least half," Bennett complains, "and were prepared to wait us out until we were absolutely desperate. So we said forget it, we'll operate on a shoestring." On purpose or not, the strategy continues to bring in just enough capital to take the business to the next stage. Even after last fall's sale of $15-a-share equity, the three original owners still owned 70% of the company—at an investment of 56¢ a share.

That round at last made MicroFridge bankable, confirms consultant Peter A. Chapman, 55, a small-business specialist whom the principals brought in as treasurer and part-time CFO last April. Even though MicroFridge still owed Sanyo $170,000 for the tools, the company probably achieved the positive net worth status that commercial banks require. Soon, some loan officer should be willing to extend conventional debt financing for round four. When that happens—maybe late this year—MicroFridge will be off the inventory-financing factor's costly hook.

Until then, a current $1-million credit ceiling will impede MicroFridge's ability to satisfy distributors' demands for product. For example, the line will nearly have been used up paying for 1990's first two shipments—1,700 units due to arrive this month and 3,400 to arrive in March. When the company opted to forgo warehousing in favor of frequent production runs, it had to learn to live with Sanyo's four-month lead time. Forecasting had better be accurate, because coming into 1990, operating expenses were running close to $50,000 a month. Bennett projects that 40,000 units will be sold in 1990, and demand beyond that may have to be placed in backlog. If demand gets *too* brisk, distributors probably will be put on allocation—a resolution they're apt not to like.

Clearly, Transamerica's financing can carry MicroFridge just so far. It must move ahead cautiously, since every new distributor likely will want a few container-loads (at 220 MicroFridges each) to start with, and putting them on hold won't do, thanks to the expense-free power of the press. "At first we were having a hard time finding distributors," Bennett relates. "But publicity has created a condition where distributors are calling us."

In just one week late in '89, a Boston-based 35-outlet office-supply chain purchased 220 units from Choquette and committed to 220 more, and the University of Massachusetts another 232. The torrent caused Bennett to conclude that New England, which he estimates is about 8% of the national market, was starting to gel. That left 92% of the country yet to come on with equally strong demand. It also caused Choquette president Normand Choquette concern, lest MicroFridge not be able to keep the product flowing. "And I don't know what the cure for that is," he grants, "because *we* sure can't inventory it that deeply." On the other hand, Choquette isn't about to drop the hot line: "We only need to deliver 2,500," says Choquette, "and we go over $1 million in billings."

Another budgetary concern is that MicroFridge—not Sanyo—must stand behind each unit. This it does nationwide through an autonomous appliance fixer, Sanyo Fisher Service Corp., which bills MicroFridge each month. MicroFridge's *pro formas* show conservative allowances for the service contract, but, says Bennett, "we're no longer getting that failure rate. We did for the first few hundred, and we said, Hey, send them all back, we'll give you new ones." Now cofounder Ward travels to manufacturing sites to monitor quality. But in case something slips by, on the back of each unit is a sticker with an 800 number that leads directly into Bennett's office. "It may be made by Sanyo," says Bennett, "but it's the MicroFridge name that's on the line."

Because they aren't actual manufacturers, Bennett prefers to conceive of his enterprise as a "research-and-development and marketing company." Indeed, already similar other would-be geniuses are dropping by with ideas. Among them: a portable microwave that dries clothes in 15 minutes and can also be used for cooking. The aspirants show up with their prototypes and patents, but Bennett has to turn them down. "Right now we have our hands full," he tells them.

Indeed, they do—with more piling up. To broaden its sales base and cut off competitive inroads, Chapman would go international, taking advantage of secure patents in Japan and other key countries. Already, MicroFridge has been contacted by a housing authority in Saudi Arabia, inquiring into a possible 40,000-unit deal. And several Canadian distributors have also evinced interest.

If no ambitious entrepreneur (or GE, for that matter) rips off the product, perhaps someday the MicroFridge name will become a household word. Before then, the company has to pass its break-even point, estimated to be 15,000 units, and settle into positive cash flow. And that prospect appeared achievable in the not-too-distant future. As of last December the government had granted preliminary approval of the unit's specs for the military, and more than 30 colleges across the country had put in significant orders, as had Econo Lodges of America, Super 8 Motels, and Howard Johnson Hotels & Lodges among motel chains.

Bennett is convinced that in Sanyo he has found the world's lowest-cost subcontractor. What with its shoestring financing and disdain of warehousing, MicroFridge's major hurdle remains securing adequate capital to keep the flow of cooler/heaters coming from abroad in timely fashion. One big distributor out of inventory is apt to force one little marketer out of business.

WHAT THE EXPERTS SAY

"I don't believe it would be that difficult to build something similar without copying. A major appliance maker could come up with its own product in six months."

—Stephen Nickerson

FINANCIER

G. BICKLEY STEVENS II

General partner, Eastech Management Co., Boston, a venture capital firm that chose not to fund MicroFridge Inc.

The reasons we declined are that it was quite different from the high-tech venture deals that we ordinarily look at; plus it had an inexperienced management team.

The positives were the patentable product and the exclusive tie-in with Sanyo, which to me were very powerful. The product was complete, there was a large potential market, and there could be high profits if sufficient units could be sold. I was intrigued and believed they'd end up selling over 50,000 per year. I admit there was limited evidence to support that case, other than my own reference checks and the results of Bennett's market study—which, frankly, was quite limited.

On the negative side was an entrepreneur who didn't have much experience. He was bright and I liked him a lot, but the whole team had little knowledge of the marketplace. And it was essentially a distributor business with inherently low margins and relatively high cash-flow risks. It would have required a fair amount of hand-holding if we got involved.

Because of their inexperience, it makes a lot of sense to use only distributors and not keep house accounts. Any time you have house accounts, you create problems with your distributors. Right now Bennett has enough other risks that he shouldn't yet risk his distribution channels.

Competition is a concern; definitely, he will have some. But I think Bennett's right—he has a near-term advantage. If he can control his growth, he may be able to pull it off. Bringing in a CFO as they did was very, very important.

COMPETITOR

STEPHEN NICKERSON

National product marketing manager, Samsung Electronics America Inc., Saddle Brook, N.J. The $15-billion Samsung Electric sells microwave ovens and compact refrigerators into domestic, college, and hotel/motel markets

Bennett's two markets aren't as broad as he thinks, but there's no doubt this product should be very successful within them.

However, he's presented a very aggressive picture and maybe hasn't been careful enough in considering things outside his control that will influence his company's performance. For example, while it's true that MicroFridge could be attractive to his targeted motel chains, which are trying to differentiate themselves, it's an area of the industry that's based on being no-frills. Yet for the MicroFridge-in-your-room deal to work for guests, these motels will have to provide things to cook or cool. Will a no-frills hotel want to keep food in stock? And who's going to service that food supply? How is Bennett going to make sure hotels are hooked up to food distributors?

I'm not an engineer, and Bennett apparently has the patents for the current-switching device, but I don't believe it would be that difficult to build something similar without copying. A major appliance maker could come up with its own product in six months. If a brand-name company like GE decides to get into the business, it will most definitely affect his five-year plan. People feel more comfortable with a name they know. The GE name on the same product, even if it's more expensive, would sell. I'd guess that big-company interest will depend a lot on MicroFridge's success. Bennett's probably got a two-year lead on his competitors, which gives him somewhat of an advantage. But no matter how big he builds the MicroFridge name in those two years, a GE name or an Amana name is bigger than he'll ever get.

CUSTOMER

ROGER TREADAWAY
Vice-president of purchasing, Days Inn of America Inc., Atlanta, operator of 950 economy-class motels throughout the United States

The MicroFridge people identified a big market—college kids. Motels will also pick up on it, especially the suite properties. I'm willing to look at it, and I think most destination and commercial properties will have an interest in this type of product. The switch is the key to the whole thing. You could buy the appliances separately, but Micro-Fridge has only one cord. You don't have to have the three pieces spread across the room. You can have them in one location.

We also have a lot of motels along highways, and once people—especially older people—get into their rooms, they want to stay in their rooms. They don't like to go out, because they don't know the area. If you have microwave food and equipment available, you're going to increase the value of your accommodations, and most people won't have a problem with paying $3 more.

CUSTOMER

LARRY DURST
Business manager, housing division, University of Michigan at Ann Arbor

MicroFridge would have a problem here, because we still have a policy that microwaves are not permitted in the students' rooms. Cooking in the students' rooms is prohibited; it's one of those fire safety issues that's been around for many years.

But Bennett may have a good argument that a microwave can allow you some safe cooking in a student's room. We're interested in student services, so if in fact we can do it safely and students want it, then we'll be discussing it more in the next year or two. Still, we have not seen a group of students saying they want to have microwaves in their rooms. And that usually has to happen before we consider doing something like this. These days we're encouraging students to have computers, which is probably one of the reasons we'll stick tough with the microwaves for a while. If you had a microwave and a refrigerator and two computers and a hair dryer all in the same room, we'd have some concerns.

If we did bring in units like this, I'd be worried about buying from a new company. You've got a refrigerator and a microwave that's totally redesigned. Bennett says the product life should be seven years, but this power switch has never been done before. Will that microwave last seven years or will it last three years? And if the microwave goes bad, what do you do with the refrigerator? This is a new concept, and there's more risk involved in buying something that you haven't seen on the market.

"PLASTICS!"

Alan Robbins is betting everything he owns that the world will pay more for picnic tables, mailbox posts, and speed bumps if they're made from recycled plastics

BY PAUL B. BROWN

Jack Van Antwerp

Yes, he's heard the career advice line from *The Graduate.* ("I just want to say one word to you: *plastics.*")

And yes, he's gotten used to the jokes about his business's name (The *Plastic* Lumber Co.?). And no, he doesn't mind them at all.

You see, if you're Alan E. Robbins, 43, a sense of humor comes in handy.

You need one, given what he wants to do with the rest of his life. Robbins, a charming father of five, wants to make wood obsolete. Maybe concrete, too.

It's not quite as silly as it sounds.

Robbins is president of the Akron company, which takes recycled plastics—milk jugs are a primary source of raw material—and turns them into everything from mailbox posts, picnic tables, and speed bumps to retaining walls at Sea World.

Alan Robbins, founder of The Plastic Lumber Co. in Akron

And no doubt there's a desperate need for someone to do something with what the industry calls postconsumer (used) plastics.

With Americans producing 160 million tons of solid waste a year—that's better than three pounds per person per day—landfills are beginning to overflow. And while plastics account for only 7% of those garbage heaps by weight, they make up 13% of their volume. Anything, even a mailbox post, that can reduce that amount of trash is something to be wished for.

The problem is that a lot of people have been rubbing on the genie's lamp for a long time. The first reported use of recycled plastics dates back to the 1930s—a Du Pont chemist with a sense of humor used some postindustrial plastics to make a length of fence—so the idea is not exactly new.

And Robbins is not exactly without competition. The notepad holders, in-and-out trays, and trash cans produced by Rubbermaid Inc. are made in large part of recycled plastics. Plus, companies such as Du Pont, Dow, Amoco, Mobil, and Occidental have all begun joint-venture projects aimed at making recycled plastics widely available.

But despite the growing interest, there are two major reasons why the idea of recycled plastics has not caught on—and Robbins must deal with both.

First, there's no consistent source of raw materials. Recycling is still not mandatory nationally, and even those states or towns with recycling programs don't always require that plastics be left by the curb, believing—mistakenly—plastics can't be recycled. (They can. But since traditional recycling methods can't guarantee the purity of recycled resins, recycled plastics are not used in packaging that comes in direct contact with food.)

Cost is the second reason that everything from marina docks to highway dividers is not yet made from recycled plastic. If you use recycled plastics as a substitute for virgin ones, as the carpet industry is doing, you'll save money.

But if you use recycled plastics to replace materials such as wood

THE FOUNDER

Alan E. Robbins, president

"I've been preparing for this my whole life," says Alan E. Robbins, referring to the company he started last year. Given that he's constantly discussing and/or handling such materials as polypropylene and high-density polyethylene, you'd think he was talking about years of toil in the chemistry lab. He's not.

Robbins, a former industrial-technology major who "finished in the upper 98% of my class; thank heaven for that other 2%" at Miami University in Oxford, Ohio, is talking about how the past 20 years have equipped him to run his own business.

He began work in Oxford running restaurants (good for learning how to manage people) and went on to run a mom-and-pop supermarket (people skills again, inventory control, marketing). From there Robbins worked as a headhunter (telemarketing, selling) and eventually a stockbroker ("great financial training"). Before starting The Plastic Lumber Co., Robbins was director of merchant sales for Rondy & Co., an Ohio-based reprocessor of scrap rubber and plastic.

"Everything I've ever done has led me to running The Plastic Lumber Co.," says Robbins, who is putting his money where his mouth is. In budgeting his salary for the start-up, he took about a 50% pay cut—to $55,000 a year. Since November, given the company's slower-than-expected start, he's been working for free.

and concrete, the economics change. Robbins's picnic tables and parking stops cost up to twice as much as those made from traditional materials.

While that's a problem, it's not an insurmountable one, says Robbins, who has worked as everything from a restaurant manager to a stockbroker (see box, "The Founder," above). His sales pitch stresses that since plastic lumber and plastic concrete last longer than their traditional counterparts, they're actually cheaper over the long haul.

Besides, as Robbins points out, the potential market is huge. In 1989, only 250 million pounds of plastics were recycled, yet the demand for materials that plastics could replace was thousands of times greater, according to Robert A. Bennett, associate dean of the college of engineering at the University of Toledo. For example, last year Americans used some 3 *billion* pounds of treated lumber, and roughly 7.4 billion board feet of wood just to build pallets.

Robbins is not looking to replace all that wood—just a splinter of it.

And he's convinced his timing is right. Some 20 years after the first Earth Day, taking care of the environment is suddenly fashionable again. Everyone from McDonald's to Dayton Hudson department stores is using seedlings as a sales promotion tool. *Time* magazine made

"Endangered Earth" its planet of the year, and George Bush will tell anyone willing to read his lips that he is "the environmental President."

Even the plastics industry has gotten into the act, creating impressive-sounding task forces (The Council for Solid Waste Solutions) and running commercials during the Sunday morning news shows explaining that it, too, wants a cleaner environment. When you have politicians and *Fortune* 500 CEOs tripping over themselves to be ecologically correct, it's relatively easy to get people to listen—for a little while, anyway—when you tell them you're selling products made out of recycled plastics.

Robbins is making the most of the opportunity. Early on he hired a public relations firm that has made his company better known than his sales would justify, and the attention is beginning to pay off. "We're getting inquiries from businesses and governmental units we never knew existed."

When he returns those calls and letters, Robbins is quick to stress the advantages his goods offer. Products made from plastic weigh less than concrete (that means fewer injuries and workers' compensation claims), require less maintenance (unlike wood or concrete, they don't need to be repeatedly stained or painted), and are virtually impervious to the weather.

Plus, plastic lumber can be sawed, nailed, drilled, glued, and bolted just like its wood counterpart.

In 1989, convinced he was onto something, Robbins hired Ken Boersma, who had worked at another plastics company on recycling, to create a proprietary extruding machine, and The Plastic Lumber Co. was born.

MARKETING: Robbins started with a great idea—he'd let his market tell him what his sales, positioning, and pricing strategy should be. Unfortunately, the market is speaking with about as much clarity as was heard from the tower of Babel.

And the message that is getting through is certainly not the one Robbins expected.

Before opening his doors last September, Robbins knew his potential market was huge. For example, anyone with a parking lot might need The Plastic Lumber Co.'s car stops (the rectangular bar that keeps a car from taking up two spaces) and speed bumps. So Robbins tried to narrow the field to places where he'd have the easiest time making the sale.

"I figured we should go after universities and municipalities," says Robbins. "With landfills being close to capacity, government seemed a natural. The universities also seemed a good fit, given the environmental appeal of the product.

"I thought there might be a consumer market as well. I could see selling our picnic tables through hardware stores. And I knew there'd also be a commercial application—things like pallets—but I wasn't really going to chase that hard at first."

What happened? Commercial sales now account for virtually all of his revenues.

Why? Because the huge marketing advantage Robbins thought he had—that he's using only *recycled* plastics—produces nothing but yawns when he explains it to schools and government.

Yes, they quickly acknowledge, using recycled components is a good idea. Now let's talk price.

The moment that happens, Robbins is on the defensive. His parking stops cost about $22.50, or about 50% more before installation than those made out of concrete. His picnic tables are easily twice the price of their wood counterparts.

But, Robbins argues, those prices are misleading. You must look at the *long-term* costs of using plastic versus concrete or wood. "Somewhere around 5 to 10 years out, we actually become cheaper, and we get more so every year after that, because there are no maintenance costs."

That may be, but his product is still more expensive initially. Cost savings over a product's lifetime can be a very difficult idea for schools and especially municipalities—which are used to awarding contracts to the lowest bidder—to understand.

Robbins's marketing thrust isn't misguided. The biggest company in this tiny field is getting a very large part of its revenues from a municipality. But at $3.5 million in sales, Hammer's Plastic Recycling Corp., in Iowa Falls, Iowa, can afford to have a marketing staff. Hammer's people met continually with city of Chicago park department officials, for instance, to answer their questions, eventually working out a deal for landscape ties for playgrounds and plastic slats for park benches.

But Plastic Lumber Co. is woefully undercapitalized. There's no money for a marketing staff. In fact, there's not much of a staff at all. Robbins and Boersma had a falling out, so the entire company consists of Robbins, his administrative assistant, and the four plant workers who actually turn out his product.

If you're running the plant and front office, and also chasing every sales lead that comes in, you don't have a whole lot of time to spend educating some civil servant about the long-term advantages of plastic lumber. While there are growing signs that states and municipalities may be willing to exempt recycled products from the traditional bidding process, that hasn't happened yet.

THE PLASTIC LUMBER CO. OPERATING STATEMENT

	1990	1991
SALES	$495,000	$2,075,000
COST OF SALES		
Raw materials	222,000	913,000
Direct labor	44,500	186,750
Rent	21,132	23,000
Electricity	11,535	48,349
TOTAL COST OF SALES	299,167	1,171,099
GROSS PROFIT	195,833	903,901
Gross profit %	40%	44%
EXPENSES		
Production	53,120	150,568
Marketing	42,000	72,000
General & administrative	55,000	114,684
Finance costs	15,000	14,737
Depreciation	10,529	41,736
Other	13,400	24,000
TOTAL EXPENSES	189,049	417,725
NET INCOME	6,784	486,176

Fortunately for Robbins, businesses get the concept right away. Some 80% of The Plastic Lumber Co.'s revenues come from a placement in a building-supply catalog.

But that's not the kind of sales mix Robbins was looking for. For one thing, he's now overly dependent on that one distributor, and for another, selling to businesses just about locks him into commodity status.

When Robbins was punching numbers into his Lotus spreadsheet, trying to forecast potential profit margins, he assumed he would average 20% pretax profits. In part, he'd do that by keeping his costs low—while Robbins budgeted raw materials cost at 44% of sales, labor was expected to be just 9%. But he also expected he'd fetch a premium price for his products.

First off, he thought he'd get a bit more for shaping that recycled plastic into picnic tables and the like. "After all, every time you punch a hole or screw in a bolt, you're adding value, and people are willing to pay for that," he says. And given the unique nature of his goods plus the lack of competition in the field—financing for recycling companies has proven hard to come by—Robbins figured people would be willing to pay a little extra for something that was environmentally on the side of the angels.

Well, some consumers might. And so might some universities. But businesses tend not to be that altruistic. "Purchasing agents are trained killers" is the way Robbins puts it. So far, pretax margins on the speed bumps and car stops he has sold to commercial accounts—businesses tend not to buy Robbins's value-added products—have been lower.

Bothersome as this is, at least Robbins knows there's a market for his paving products. With plastic lumber. . . well, let's quote the business plan: "The plastic lumber market can only be considered in its infancy."

To be honest, no one knows what kind of recycled plastic products—if any—the market wants, and that's an important point, because when it comes to recycling, there is plastic and then there is plastic.

Some companies, such as Wellman Inc., headquartered in Shrewsbury, N.J., have chosen to specialize. Wellman deals almost exclusively with polyethylene terephthalate, which is used to make soda bottles. Empty soda bottles are traditionally recycled into things like carpet fibers and the linings of parkas and sleeping bags.

The problem is that the equipment needed both to recycle polyethylene terephthalate and to convert it into usable products is expensive. The Plastic Lumber Co. avoids most of that cost by being less fussy about the plastics it uses. It either buys raw materials or cleaned and sorted scrap, which is then melted down and extruded.

However, since the resulting plastic is a blend—a catsup bottle, for example, which might be part of the company's raw materials mix, is made up of five to seven different plastics—it's impossible to predict the quality or strength of the resulting products.

That's why the company focuses on making simple products in which the specific properties of the plastic are not important.

Robbins started by selling mailbox posts and picnic tables because they are relatively easy to make. "We're not all that skilled as craftsmen," he says with a shrug. He'll be more than happy to add to the line—within the limits of his plastic's quality, of course; making a plastic four-by-four to support a swing set would be out of the question, for example, because its strength would not be up to code. But first he needs the market to tell him what it wants.

Ironically, Robbins is finding himself with more time to listen than he expected. His products turned out to be very difficult to sell during cold weather. Nobody is going to go and put a speed bump on the ground when it is 20 below zero, and very few people go looking for picnic tables when they have to shovel their way out the front door. "I didn't realize the extent to which we would be affected by the weather," he says. "Next winter we will concentrate our marketing efforts on the southern part of the country and on building inventory."

That assumes that (1) he'll have a better handle by then on who his customers are and what they need and (2) his money will hold out.

CAPITAL: If Plastic Lumber doesn't make it, it won't be because Robbins overspent on decorating. As you walk into Robbins's fifth-floor offices in downtown Akron, you have to hurdle the tires strewn about and duck under stunning pictures of elaborate food displays. Robbins sublets from his brother-in-law, a commercial photographer who does a lot of work for area food and tire companies. Says Robbins: "By sharing space with him, I didn't have to worry about going out and buying fax machines and copiers."

The same sense of frugality exists throughout the company. Robbins drives a 1982 Oldsmobile diesel that had been in mothballs. He pays $2 per square foot—about half the going rate—for his production facility in an old tire plant that Ohio is trying to turn over to small businesses. And by marrying interest from a CD to a term loan in a linked-deposit program, Robbins has borrowed $154,000 at about prime.

But the money is going quickly, thanks to a combination of lower-than-budgeted sales and cost increases primarily caused by problems with the extruder. "We've had to rebuild the chilling system and the molds a few times," says Robbins. "What has happened, given the cost overruns, is that we've gotten one machine for the price of two."

The upshot: The company lost $55,000 during its first three months. And when sales failed to come close to forecasts this past January and February, Robbins reduced salaries and eliminated his public relations program and most of his advertising. The Plastic Lumber Co. is still losing money.

With Robbins having contributed about his entire savings, and the banks reluctant to loan any more, what is needed—and soon—are additional equity investors. (When the company was formed, Robbins sold stock and options totaling 24% of it to a friend for $50,000.) "We've been putting off looking for outside funding," says Robbins. "The better shape we can get the company in before offering stock, the higher the valuation will be. But we are now starting to hold serious meetings with venture capitalists."

The question is, of course, whether the money will come in time—and in sufficient amounts. Even if it does, there are other problems. Is it reasonable to expect university administrators and civil servants to be farsighted? Will they pay higher prices today for savings tomorrow?

And what about Robbins's embryonic marketing program? There's little doubt that someday there will be a huge market for products made from recycled plastics, but which products?

And even if Robbins does figure out which products the market wants, can he muster the technical expertise to make them? Good questions all, says Robbins, who remains sanguine nonetheless. "We'll be OK."

We'll see.

"It's a common mistake to think people are going to buy products just because they're environmentally correct. You can't rely on that kind of altruism."

— Nancy Pfund

FINANCIER

NANCY PFUND
General partner, Hambrecht & Quist, a San Francisco venture capital firm; co-manager of its $17-million Environmental Technology Fund, which has a position in a recycling company

I think Robbins was correct in perceiving there's a tremendous market opportunity here. The concept of the business, broadly defined, is sound; there will be exponential growth in the waste-minimization segment of the market.

But I think Robbins has made things difficult for himself by focusing on the lower end of the business. By taking mixed plastics and making something that can't be used for much because of the tensile strength, he's artificially narrowed his business opportunities to the commodity level. Recycled products with the characteristics of virgin materials—that's where money will be made. If I were Robbins, I would upgrade the technology and therefore the end product.

How do you do that? He needs to get some help where he doesn't have the background or the inclination. He's got marketing contacts and distribution experience; he should weave that into some kind of relationship with a plastics recycler with a little more know-how. He does have a little business there

that could feed into the activities of another firm. There are all kinds of options: a co-marketing arrangement or a subcontractor or OEM relationship. He's certainly got a lot of energy and enthusiasm, which could be put to better use.

One of the common mistakes is to think people are going to buy products just because they're environmentally correct. You can't rely on that kind of altruism. It certainly can help. But people are very dollars-and-cents oriented. Recycled plastics products do not have to be more expensive than what they're replacing, and in the long run they can't be. In the long run they have to be cheaper.

If Robbins is lucky, maybe he can bring in the top line, but I think his costs are going to increase. The company is very thin, and he can't run a business effectively and wear all the hats at the same time. But he does have the option of finding someone who will work with him. He's developed a market and has some customers, which is an asset that should be valuable to someone.

OBSERVER

THOMAS J. PENRICE
Director, Plastic Consulting for Strategic Analysis Inc., a Reading, Pa., firm

I'm very bullish on Robbins's idea and his chances for success. I think his sales forecast is actually quite modest. And there may even come a time when his raw materials cost—which is relatively high now—could be negative. As communities collect all this plastic, they're going to need somebody to take it off their hands.

However, there is a major problem. He has seriously underestimated his marketing costs. If he uses the $72,000 he has budgeted (on $2 million of projected sales) to hire a marketing person—and he'll pay at least that to get someone qualified—there won't be any budget for mailings and travel. You have to go to the trade shows and network.

Eventually there'll be many viable consumer and industrial applications for recycled plastic products. However, Robbins's company must first survive the next several months. Instead of letting his customers dictate his marketing approach, I would begin by working directly with major producers of plastic resins—the Dows and Du Ponts—and work out a deal where they would give him the plastics they can't use in their recycling programs, the commingled plastics, and see if they would be willing to buy the picnic tables and the like from him. These companies all have active recycling programs and are eager to promote recycling. Once the applications are demonstrated to be practical and cost-effective, however, Robbins has got to reach a broader market.

BRIAN HARPER
Technical director, Hammer's Plastic Recycling Corp., Iowa Falls, Iowa, The Plastic Lumber Co.'s largest competitor

They're going to be struggling to stay alive unless they do something clever, and there doesn't seem to be anything clever on the horizon.

First, the company is grossly undercapitalized. And it's not spending the little money it does have on the right things. It's marketing that drives companies that make plastic lumber, yet Robbins has scaled back his marketing efforts to save money. He needs large orders to survive, and without a marketing budget, he's going to be hard pressed to get them.

Even with a marketing budget, he would seem to be in trouble because he doesn't have a marketing strategy. He's going with the flow, and that's a big mistake. There is no inherent market for plastic lumber; you have to create one. I think Robbins believes—as a lot of companies that are no longer in business once believed—that his product is so good that people will fight to buy it. That's wrong. It's always been wrong.

But in addition to overestimating sales and underestimating marketing expenses, he has another problem. There is no depth of technology. Ken Boersma has left. Who's going to replace him?

If I were running their company,

I'd go out and recruit a good marketing man and a good technology person, but I don't see how Robbins will be able to attract the money he'd need to do it. When potential investors visit the company's offices and see the lack of staff, they're going to conclude the company is close to broke. The venture capitalists won't trust the company with their money, and customers won't trust it with their orders.

Plastic Lumber is where we were four years ago, but we had marketing and we had technology people who allowed us to create new products. They have neither.

CUSTOMER

GLENN TROWBRIDGE

President, National Association of County Park & Recreation Officials; park and recreation director for Clark County (Las Vegas), Nev.

New products have to do something above and beyond what old ones do. There are a hundred manufacturers of picnic tables and speed bumps out there already. If Plastic Lumber came out with, say, a vandal-proof bench you could wipe spray paint off of, now we're dealing with something. But customers already have long-term relationships with manufacturers, and they're not going to set them aside just because somebody says, "Hey, I've got a newer product." I'm approached at least once a month by picnic-table manufacturers; it's an incredibly competitive field.

Robbins will have to prove his claim of extended life expectancy— he can't just come out and say it costs more but is going to last twice as long. The documentation seems absent at this point.

If the company isn't competing on price it's going to have to convince customers to raise the standards of what they spec—for instance, to require that benches last six years—and then the company will have to prove that its product meets those standards. Convincing buyers and architects to stop specifying one product and specify something more stringent, on the basis that it's better for them, is an uphill battle. But that's how the game works.

MUSCLING IN

*Joseph J. Bianco, founder of American
DreamCar Inc., is betting that America is ready for
$20,000 reconditioned Mustangs and GTOs*

BY ROBERT A. MAMIS

nvestment banker Joseph J. Bianco sold his sports-car importing operation to General Motors Corp. in 1987. Confronted by middle age and without a company to play with, the self-admitted auto fanatic was nostalgic. "I owned a '67 Camaro when I was a kid," he moons, "and I loved that car." So using himself as the typical customer, he designed a business that would "bring back cars that were everyone's dream when they were young," he says.

Brisk as the market for classic vehicles was and still is, Bianco found no one doing what he envisioned—buying up old specimens from the late 1950s, '60s, and early '70s, completely reconditioning them, and selling them by the thousands through licensed dealers. Such a company could breathe life not only into his own beloved Z28, but also into the other whimsically gewgawed muscle cars beloved by baby boomers—GTOs, Chargers, Mustangs, Road Runners, even Cadillacs, each a pow-

Founder Joseph Bianco still dreams about his first love: his Chevy

erful (250-horsepower on up) representative of the country's last great automotive era.

On that premise, in November 1988 American DreamCar Inc. (ADC) was formed. But authentic restoration, because it's so hopelessly slow and expensive, was left to romantic purists. American DreamCar's coldly commercial version restores the aged hulks on an assembly line, a half dozen at a time. Costs are kept down by standardizing parts, and profits kept up through systematized production. That way, Bianco figured, margins should come in above those of today's new machines—way above, once economies of scale kick in.

The challenge of kicking in those economies before the money runs out has fallen to an industry lawyer named Robert Gil Seasonwein, first enlisted by Bianco to check out the legal ramifications of selling reconstructions on a like-new basis. The idea wouldn't be feasible if the cars' reconditioned but nonetheless old motors had to meet emissions regulations for new cars or if their battering-ram chassis had to comply with current safety standards. Nor would it do if, starting out under another's brand name and still looking very much like it, a product labeled American DreamCar got ensnared in trademark and fair-use bickering. When Seasonwein came back in favor of proceeding, Bianco hired him to do just that and faded into the background as the company's chairman and largest shareholder.

Spurred by $1.75 million in seed capital that Bianco's initial equity placement coaxed from a handful of believers, CEO Seasonwein searched for manufacturing facilities. He settled on Cleveland, where in August 1989 American DreamCar moved into 29,000 square feet of leased factory space. Although other cities had cheaper real estate, none proffered Cleveland's main lures: local suppliers and inexpensive skilled labor. Last July, ADC was employing some 20 skilled laborers at an average wage of about $14 an hour. If paying salaries of $30,000 a year sounds untenable to manufacturers in other industrial areas, doubters should note that ADC's first help-wanted ad for auto-shop specialists drew 60 inquiries, and the company has not yet found it necessary to run a second.

The finished ADC product, although unabashedly a rehab, boasts not only a body that is identical to the original (accompanied by original title) but also an engine that outperforms it. In fact, argues Seasonwein, who worked his way through law school as an auto mechanic and car salesman, a DreamCar is likely to be reassembled more precisely in Cleveland than it was originally assembled in Detroit. That's one justification for showroom stickers that range from $19,995 to $27,995, of which ADC receives three-quarters.

After a muscle car is acquired, it is eviscerated. The engine it arrives with is sometimes reconditioned, but most often unceremoniously junked and replaced with a one-size-fits-all Chevy 350—no Schwarzenegger, but acceptably brawny nonetheless. Its transmission, suspension, brakes, shocks, steering box, and other mechanisms are likewise gutted and modernized. It is given tires, a sound system, and air-conditioning; each model's decorative kitsch is authentically revived, and its body is stripped bare and painted. All that takes place in a handful of specified work areas—disassembly, power train, and such—until it arrives at final assembly, where the body is put back on and the car rolled out the factory door.

Meant as much to be motored as admired, the now-gleaming hybrid—cosmetically '60s, mechanically '90s—is promoted in sales material as "the best of both times." Whatever marketing boost is needed beyond ADC's generic brochure is up to individual dealers to provide. Even though it hasn't yet been determined whether there is a market for such cars,

THE FOUNDER

Joseph J. Bianco
chairman

Age: 40

Source of idea: Fond reminiscences of Camaro from youth and a suspicion that many other drivers shared the nostalgia

Equity (held separately by wife): 26.2%

Workweek: 5 to 10 hours

Salary: $5,984

Education: Yale Law School, 1975

Outside directors: Yes

Other businesses started: British Performance Car Imports Inc., general partners with Lotus Performance Cars, 1982; sold 1986. Van Allen Capital, 1983; dissolved 1986. Fulcrum Capital, now called Whyte Lyon & Co., 1987. Sentex Sensing Technology Inc., 1983. Cognitive Systems (cofounder), 1981

FINANCIALS

AMERICAN DREAMCAR INC. PROJECTED OPERATING STATEMENT
(in $ thousands)

	1992	1994
Units sold	400	1,200
Man-hours/car	152	127
REVENUES		
Average unit price	$19.75	$19.75
TOTAL REVENUES	**7,900**	**23,700**
COST OF REVENUES		
Core-car & major components cost	5,031	14,674
Labor cost	886	2,215
TOTAL DIRECT EXPENSES	**5,917**	**16,889**
Overhead*	1,082	2,380
TOTAL EXPENSES	**6,999**	**19,269**
PROFIT	**901**	**4,431**

* Includes rent, utilities, telephone, accounting, legal, leases, insurance, travel, and marketing

Seasonwein says that whenever the concept was shown to a target audience—aged 35 to 60—people were wowed by the product and the affordable price.

ADC has no intention of competing in the primary-transportation market. The strategy is to gain a fraction of an undefined but obviously large and still-growing market—*Road & Track* recently reported that 38% of its readers owned pre-1968 cars—by pitching DreamCars as head-turning showmobiles. Seasonwein himself cruises to ADC's Bethesda, Md., headquarters in a yet-to-be-reconditioned '57 Bel Air Sports Coupe.

In addition to concerns about the continued availability at reasonable cost of the company's basic resource—the original cars—Seasonwein has to juggle typical manufacturing factors such as labor, shipping, inventory, and distribution. He also must worry about committing to prices of finished products whose costs are not all that predictable. In its first six quarters ADC spent $1.2 million of working capital. But $200,000 a quarter is a snail's pace compared, say, with John De Lorean's luxury-sports-car start-up 10 years ago, which devoured $15 million a quarter during its 16 quarters.

But unlike De Lorean Motor Co., ADC's aspirations are quite modest. Its goal is to be breaking even by the end of its second fiscal year this month, a delicate balance that, at the least, will require the output and immediate sale of 24 cars a month. ADC's *pro formas* show annual earnings of $900,000 on sales of 400 cars by 1992 and more than $4.4 million on 1,200 cars annually by 1994 after a proposed expansion, yielding a pretax margin of 18.6% (see box, "Financials," page 232).

Eventually, ADC intends to remanufacture a car for $12,300 on average, including a core-vehicle acquisition cost of about $4,000 and a direct-labor allotment of some $1,850. As early estimates have proved less realistic, the company has adjusted its expected labor costs. "Twenty minutes into doing our first car," recounts Timothy L. Cline, ADC's one-person middle-management team, "we discovered our initial numbers were wrong." The guinea-pig vehicle ate up 1,000 man-hours of direct labor, a cost of $14,000. To speed up the learning curve and output, four outside subcontractors were hired to rebuild a car each, so ADC could determine how best to proceed. Not one car was completed. "We paid dearly to find out one essential," says Cline, "that we have to have complete control over everything."

At the end of May 1990, after six months of trial-by-error engineering of its reassembly techniques plus one month of line production, the average time devoted to each vehicle still was 773 man-hours. That factor must be lowered to 161 simply to break even. Then, presuming that can be achieved and held, ADC will have to steer around a number of other potholes, some as yet unseen, to maintain even moderate levels of income.

Here is a selection:

Will the supply of car bodies dry up? It's not likely. Muscle cars were manufactured by the millions, and even if the lion's share lie rusting in junkyards, ADC needs but a minuscule percentage. If one model becomes too expensive or scarce—as Bel Air convertibles have—production can switch to still-plentiful types such as Chevelles, Gran Sports, or 'Cudas. The rule is that a dealer wanting delivery has to take whatever is going through the factory, which depends on whatever ADC's buyers happen to have acquired.

Rather than rely on just in time purchasing and the willingness of owners to part with their suddenly coveted heaps, ADC could stock up on vintage machines. But if they're stored outside, Seasonwein frets, they may be vandalized; if kept inside, they'd occupy valuable cubic footage. And hoarding a meaningful number would tie up serious cash. Besides, he says, "accountants attribute overhead to cars that are in inventory, and it drives your inventory costs up."

Will replacement parts be hard to find? Possibly. So far, so good, though. Even after 20 years body parts such as fenders remain available off the shelf, because such replacements were produced in the same large quantity as the dented cars they're sculpted to fit. And if a part is not in stock, some original equipment manufacturer likely has tooling to stamp out an order.

As for elusive trim pieces such as tail-fin bezels or hood ornaments, the worst that can happen, foresees Bianco, is that the company will have to make its own. Far from being distressed, he views such a lack as a growth opportunity. "Think of a subsidiary called American DreamCar Parts!" the entrepreneur muses. One of ADC's suppliers, Year One Inc., of Tucker, Ga. (#308 on the 1988 *Inc.* 500), sold more than $8 million worth of muscle-car accoutrements in 1989 alone.

Will working capital run out? Unlikely, as long as there are car fanatics—or bargain hunters. To sweeten the first round, each investor was offered an American DreamCar for $1,000. Bianco's intention was to use the first $1.75 million to stay in business long enough to get product flowing. After 18 months or so the plan was to raise more through a public offering. In July 1989, however, some cash came from an unlikely source. Bianco was approached by a public corporation with $600,000 lying idle in its treasury. Through a reverse merger, the shell, an entity called Access Capital, in Bethesda, acquired an interest in ADC, after which the corporate name was changed to DreamCar Holdings Inc. Its only holding is American DreamCar. In exchange for about 18% of the original company, ADC gained both an easy chunk of second-round capital and a public market.

Even so, the aggregate $2.35 million threatened to approach zero well before the operation could become self-sustaining. In March 1990, therefore, a second private placement for up to $1.25 million more in working capital got under way. With virtually no debt (as of April 30, 1990), ADC could look to the public for a flotation; its NASDAQ symbol is DCAR. However, this past summer its 52 million common shares, not to mention an overhang of warrants, were trading for around 50¢ each, at which price the stock market valued the company at more than $26 million. Talk about American dreaming.

Will the concept be rejected by retailers? Quite the opposite. One attraction of taking on the ADC line is that a dealer can enjoy a markup of 25%. Compare that with the recent estimate from the National

Automobile Dealers Association, which brooded that between 1990 and 1997 new-car dealers will realize an average 0.4% return on sales.

In fact, scores of would-be ADC dealers have been held at bay ever since three prototypes—a '67 GTO, a '57 Bel Air, and a '69 Mustang— were unveiled at a trade show in Las Vegas last February. Instead of the handful of queries ADC expected, 160 dealers showed interest, says de facto sales manager Cline, some begging to buy the show cars on the spot, despite Big Three prohibitions against their franchisees' carrying off-brand lines. Overnight ADC's problem became not one of representation but of supply: How can you sign up dealers if you have nothing for them to deal?

As of June, 9 dealers had already been enlisted of the 15 or so ADC intends to end up with nationwide in its first phase. Each was a new-car dealership, an ADC criterion. One, Dream Cars of Connecticut Inc., was established in Milford specifically to handle ADC products. Its reasoning, as expounded by owner George DeLauri, "I decided this was a good market area. Fairfield County is one of the richest in the country, and there's a return to nostalgia here—'60s restaurants, old-car clubs, and so on. I had been thinking of putting something together ourselves to sell restored cars like these, but after I saw American DreamCar in Las Vegas, I realized I couldn't do it for the same dollars. And I wouldn't have the quality or the backing of their warranty."

Will demand fall short? You don't need to sell many cars to make money. Bianco's importing company was moving only about 250 a year to the United States before GM bought it, for example. Even if those cars happened to be exotic Lotuses from England, which went for considerably more than domestics, the principle is the same: low volume, big margin. "They'll be popular," DeLauri predicts, "but not as popular as 10 a month." Dream Cars of Connecticut will be content to sell 4 a month, he says.

Is the price too low or too high? Your guess is as good as theirs. Seasonwein discusses how prices were determined: "To make it more like a new car than a used car, it was important to standardize the retail price. Real car manufacturers determine where they want their car to be in the marketplace and work backward from there; they have to shave costs off the car if it's too expensive to make a profit. We went at it the other way. We knew approximately the acquisition cost of a core car and what it would cost to buy parts. We thought we knew—and didn't, but have figured it out since—how long it would take to tear one of these cars apart and put it back together. From that, we ballparked what it would cost to add the parts and shove it out the door."

ADC first thought it could sell its cars at $12,000 to $18,000—a good price since that was less than half what their collector-car counterparts were fetching at auction. Another lesson the learning curve demonstrated was that no profit could be made at those levels. Suggested retail was cautiously jacked up. "We've purposely been going slow, because I don't want to put us in a position where we price ourselves too high and have to give rebates," says Seasonwein. "The day we give rebates is the day I'm out of here."

Another of Seasonwein's realizations was that "when you strip down the body to bare sheet metal, that's the moment of truth; you have to live with what you get." Sometimes you have to live with patches of plastic putty where metal used to be. One reason for raising prices is that ADC now pays more for higher-quality core vehicles than planned.

If it flies, will there be competitors? Without doubt. There's no secret to selling these cars, Cline grants. But there is a secret to modifying them efficiently. So secret that when ADC brings dealers to Cleveland, visitors aren't allowed to take pictures.

Will it take time for economies of scale to be realized? Maybe. Even in the tiny universe of the six or seven different models that ADC focuses on at a time, it has already established sources for thousands of replacement parts. Although ADC is a national account with a few OEMs, such as its engine remanufacturer, it has been seeking more. But at only 240 to 400 cars a year, qualifying for discounts and favorable payment terms isn't yet a given.

Will needed expansion be too expensive? Probably not. ADC is looking for a 50,000- to 75,000-square-foot building with acreage to expand into and has already contacted the mayor's office and the Greater Cleveland Development Corp. in search of it. "They like what we do and where we do it," says Seasonwein, who intends to set up an industrial revenue bond in an enterprise zone around Cleveland, thus qualifying for tax abatement and public funding.

Can the business be run from 600 miles away? We'll see. It's inefficient, but it keeps the CEO happy. Why doesn't Seasonwein leave Bethesda for Cleveland? "Because I like it here," he says with resolve.

What a strange and powerful force is nostalgia: older and older stuff changes hands at higher and higher prices, and buyers never run out, it seems. Indeed, the Americana market has shown little sign of fizzling, neither in autos nor in baseball cards, carousels, Coke, comics, and on down the alphabet of coveted native memorabilia.

Bianco's revivals, however, aren't authentic nostalgia, adding another layer to the considerable challenges the company already faces.

Like many other manufacturers, ADC must attend to such conventional details as finding adequate yet reasonably priced facilities to grow within, attracting and keeping skilled labor, and lowering labor costs to sustain the pricing levels it has committed to. It also has to solve some inherent problems such as establishing and transporting a steady stream of base components, standardizing disparate parts from hundreds of outside vendors, and tying into a dealer network ruled over by giant competitors.

It also must convince 1,200 consumers each year that its neither-fish-nor-fowl artifact is better than the real thing. If it can't, CEO Seasonwein may be in a position to offer you a nice '57 Bel Air Sports Coupe in good condition. Cheap.

Research assistance was provided by Anne Murphy.

"American DreamCar's outstanding problem is that its gross margins are too low for a manufacturing company."

– Benjamin M. Rosen

COMPETITOR

ALAIN CLENET

Manufacturer and marketer of custom cars, 1975–82. Founded ASHA Corp., an automotive-development company in Santa Barbara, Calif., 1986

The venture has a lot of merit, and I completely agree with its point of view. The formula is not to make a collector car, but a nostalgia car. Nobody makes good money restoring cars. And buyers won't care if the car isn't absolutely authentic. They want the car they always wanted, and suddenly it's available with the reliability and comfort and service that collectors' cars do not have. But it's a hell of a lot to control, mostly because of the training. When I was in manufacturing, there were 360 parts vendors, and we had more than 4,200 parts numbers—for one model alone! If I were in American DreamCar's shoes, I would stick with only three models: the Mustang, the Camaro, and the GTO. They were a reasonable size, and they're in plentiful supply.

But how can it be done economically? Twelve percent return is not enough. ADC would do better with progressive integration, which means going vertical (manufacturing subcomponents). And I doubt that 160 man-hours is possible. Maybe something like 200 when it's producing 1,200 a year. Also, it has to have specialists purchasing the cars, because a car full of holes ends up costing twice as much. It should focus on the West Coast, since that's where the cars without rust are. But cars it buys there will be tagged with a good $500 in extra transportation [to ship back to Cleveland]. Therefore, location becomes important. It would have been easier to handle everything from California. In lieu of enlarging the company centrally, eventually it could repeat the same system in other locations; that is, if the first is successful.

OBSERVER

MATT DELORENZO

Editor, AutoWeek, *a magazine for car enthusiasts, Detroit; published article pointing out American DreamCar's deleterious effect on collector market in April 1990*

The notion of recapturing one's youth with an updated old car is appealing. Given the success of the Miata, which rekindled interest in the 1960s and '70s sports cars, there's no doubt that American DreamCar will do the same for the muscle car, especially in that the reliability of a new car takes away the nostalgia-oriented driver's basic fear that the thing won't run. Collectors have bid up the prices of real muscle cars to, in some cases, way more than an equivalent American DreamCar, and that'll work to support its market.

The downside is that the market is based on a fad, which this current trend may be. It can vanish as quickly as it appeared. And buying an American DreamCar will be a onetime deal. At those prices, there won't be much repeat business. When owners tire of their toys—which really is what they are—used DreamCars will compete with new DreamCars. If and when the fad dies off, you could have an oversupply. It'll be interesting to see what happens after the company sells a couple of thousand.

FINANCIER

BENJAMIN M. ROSEN

Founding partner, Sevin Rosen Management Co., a New York City–based venture capital investor in more than 40 start-ups; has his own collection of Americana memorabilia

The idea is clever. But my gut reaction is that there are flaws in its concept of the nostalgia market. No doubt people are willing to pay premiums, but only for an authentic article. When the article is ersatz, value and price and market probably get diminished. I don't have a real feeling for [the market for refabricated nostalgia cars], but it may be big enough to support the idea.

Looking at it financially, American DreamCar's outstanding problem is that its gross margins are too low for a manufacturing company. I'm afraid it's underestimating what the below-the-line expenses are. It hasn't budgeted enough for harder-to-visualize items such as general-and-administrative, sales, and marketing costs. Even as its projections look to 1,200 units, it doesn't show enough gross profit to support what I think will be true overhead. For example, since it's trying to create a new market rather than exploit an existing one, the costs associated with setting up a dealer network may come as a surprise.

This means that ADC's cookie-cutter financial model for manufacturing and marketing a car, if adjusted for reality, is not attractive to a professional investor. Therefore, the company may be in a bit of a financial bind. A positive aspect of its shell financing is that it got cash on reasonably good terms. On the other hand, a private placement would have to be for far, far less than the public valuation, and that would have implications for public shareholders. It would be very hard to do a public financing, given the state of the company.

That ADC doesn't have debt is appropriate to this stage; it's hard for a company that's losing money as it'll be for a while to absorb debt-service cost. Therefore, it should be able to continue to get financing for the operation from friendly sources, who obviously have been willing to make necessary leaps of faith until the financials prove realistic.

MARKETER

JIM WANGERS

Created and promoted the concept of the muscle car while at Pontiac's ad agency in early '60s; wrote lyrics for hit song "GTO"; now runs own firm, Automotive Marketing Consultants Inc., in Detroit

Needless to say, I'm an enthusiastic backer of the concept, notwithstanding some difficult business aspects. If there was one thing Detroit was good at, it was piling on horsepower. American DreamCar is bringing that era back, along with a level of quality that consumers at least think they remember. Given the drivability of its cars, the company might attain a level of acceptance, of snob appeal, that could rival Japanese or German cars.

ADC should continue to restrict franchises to about one per major-market area, maybe 40 altogether in the country. An attractive aspect of an ADC franchise is you're looking at only a couple of hundred thousand dollars to get it off the ground. You don't have to stock hundreds of cars like everyone else.

Supply may be more limited than realized, and the company may face a serious setback as popular cars such as GTOs and 442s get thinned out. Thanks in part to ADC itself, owners today are asking $8,000 for beat-up '69 jobs that would have sold for $1,500 just a year ago. I was a little surprised the company didn't take some of that first capital and go out and buy what it could so it would have a bunch of cars to work with. There's no question that the average cost of basic units is going to increase significantly.

The company's got to move quickly to deepen the line. It's an unfortunate selling premise for a franchisee to be told it has to take what it's given. In a revival atmosphere, buyers have serious preferences and little patience. Right now ADC can't predict when it'll be able to deliver certain choices. If it offered five or six key models and could build any one on order in a month, that would be acceptable. I realize I'm spending money ADC doesn't have, but it's what's needed for growth.

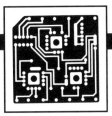

MADE IN THE U.S.A.

Can appliance-control maker
ACT Inc. become both the low-cost producer
and *the high-quality provider?*

BY TOM RICHMAN

Mark Segal

I n a business in which success has eluded the likes of Texas Instruments, National Semiconductor, and Motorola, Wallace Leyshon, the founder of two-year-old Appliance Control Technology Inc. (ACT), optimistically expects his company to succeed.

In an old-line industry in which potential customers—companies with familiar brand names such as Whirlpool, Tappan, and General Electric—usually take years to incorporate new product features, Leyshon brashly claims ACT can get its components designed into products within months.

In competition with rivals who do their manufacturing in Singapore and other low-wage locations, Leyshon confidently predicts that he'll beat their product quality, service, *and* prices by using stay-at-home U.S. labor.

Is Leyshon naïve? Just hopeful? Or does he know something that the others don't?

Wallace Leyshon, founder, president, and CEO of Appliance Control Technology Inc.

EXECUTIVE SUMMARY

THE COMPANY:
Appliance Control
Technology Inc.
(ACT), Addison, Ill.

CONCEPT:
Manufacture
electronic controls
cheaply enough to
break into midline
appliance market
(where they haven't
been used before);
achieve low-cost
production goals
by introducing
standardization, a
changed sales pro-
cess, and onshore
manufacturing to an
industry that has
embraced none of
the above

PROJECTIONS:
Profits in 1989
of $1.4 million on
sales of $18.9
million; 1991 sales
of $62.2 million

HURDLES:
Getting big-company
appliance makers to
change their habits
in the ways ACT's
concept calls for;
keeping onshore
manufacturing costs
competitive

ACT, Leyshon's first solo business venture, designs and manufactures microproces-
sor-based controls for major kitchen and
laundry appliances—the electronic buttons
and panels you use to make them work. The
challenges confronting the company are
prodigious. Its customers are the large, conservative U.S. and European corporations
that manufacture the appliances, and persuading decision makers at such places to
take a little company's claims seriously is a
major hurdle for Leyshon and his crew. And
the almost-revolutionary ambitiousness of
those claims does not make clearing that hurdle any easier.

ACT, promises Leyshon, 39, who has
education and experience in management
and engineering, will be the low-cost producer of electronic controls. Aggressively reducing its price will not only assure his company's entry into the market, he says, it will
greatly expand the size of the market by
helping to make electronic controls price
competitive with old-style electromechanical
knobs and dials. But at the same time that he
touts his company's lower prices, Leyshon
claims that ACT delivers measurably higher
quality than the competition and demonstra-
bly better service. And one other thing:
Leyshon says that ACT will make the entire
appliance industry more responsive to consumer demand by changing the working
relationship between vendors and their
appliance-manufacturing customers.

That's an awful lot of challenges for any
company—but especially the youngest in the business—to take on all
at once.

In 1986 Leyshon was running Motorola's electronic appliance-control business. While Motorola was the market leader at the time, appliance controls were just a small part of its booming automotive and
industrial-electronics group, whose main business was producing computer controls for the automobile industry. Leyshon's division shared a

Wallace C. Leyshon, president and CEO

Age: 39

Before founding ACT, he was business director of the electronic appliance-control division of Motorola Inc., which had sales of more than $30 million, head count of 584 persons, and sales, engineering, and manufacturing facilities in the United States, Western Europe, and East Asia. He has a B.A. from Ohio University and an M.B.A. from DePaul University.

Somewhere along the line, Leyshon turned into a fervent industrial patriot—which may explain his near obsession with onshore manufacturing. Bob van Dusen, vice-president of sales, recalls a call he and Leyshon made to the U.S. plant of a Japanese appliance manufacturer. "The Japanese told us we weren't smart enough to redesign their control," says van Dusen, "and you could just see the little American flags starting to pop out of Wally's head."

---

manufacturing facility with its parent group, which meant that Leyshon had only dotted-line control of that function so far as his products were concerned. When Motorola management decided to move the entire manufacturing operation to Taiwan, Leyshon took issue. The move offshore, along with his feeling that Motorola wasn't adequately funding his end of the business, precipitated his departure.

In December 1986 Leyshon incorporated ACT, headquartered in Addison, Ill., a western suburb of Chicago. Eventually, some of his former Motorola colleagues joined him: Brian Althoff, engineering manager at the appliance-control division, became ACT's vice-president for engineering and R&D. Les Jones, director of quality at the Motorola unit, became vice-president of quality assurance in the new business. In March 1987 the Electrolux division that makes Tappan microwave ovens wrote a $3-million-plus purchase order to become ACT's first customer. In September of that year ACT produced its first controls on a single, $1-million automated assembly line. Now, more than a year later, the company is operating two lines and contemplating a third.

Leyshon wooed Tappan with promises of lower prices, higher quality, and better service, the same line he uses on other prospective buyers. The issue is whether ACT can deliver.

Leyshon predicated his venture's early survival on its ability to drive the price of electronic controls down, thereby expanding the potential market and quickly building ACT's volume. Major appliance makers produce more than 45 million of the so-called white goods for the U.S. market annually. In 1986, maybe 15% of those appliances incorporated electronic controls. But 60% to 75% of the unit volume in any

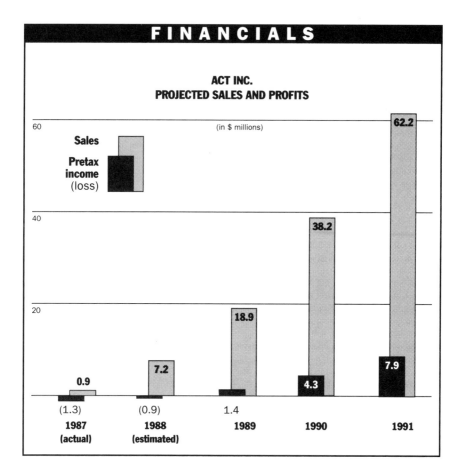

FINANCIALS

ACT INC.
PROJECTED SALES AND PROFITS

(in $ millions)

Sales
Pretax income (loss)

	1987 (actual)	1988 (estimated)	1989	1990	1991
Sales	0.9	7.2	18.9	38.2	62.2
Pretax income (loss)	(1.3)	(0.9)	1.4	4.3	7.9

appliance line, Leyshon's research revealed, is in the midprice models, which electronics still hadn't penetrated. That's the market he wanted ACT to get into. By 1991, according to his projections, it will be worth some $750 million in the United States alone. There was also the European market, about the same size, to compete in.

To meet his objective, Leyshon elected to use three strategies. The first involved design and engineering; the second, manufacturing. And the third, maybe the riskiest, involved selling and marketing.

Before and during Leyshon's management, Motorola's appliance-control group had concentrated on designing products that were proprietary to each of its customers. ACT's design, Leyshon decided, would aim for increased standardization. That doesn't mean that its controls will look alike to consumers who buy, say, different brands of microwave ovens incorporating the ACT product. They won't even look the same from model to model within the same brand. Higher-priced ovens will still have more features—a defrost cycle or a meat-temperature probe, for instance. But in the ACT design scheme, underneath the touch pad, there's the same chassis, same microprocessor, and the same components mounted on the same printed circuit board. The differences lie mainly in the software that's embedded in the microprocessor chip and in the panel face presented to the user. ACT's first product replaced 12 separate controls Tappan had been using on its family of microwave ovens with just 2 standard control models—one for domestic ovens and the other for export. The electronic ACT product was priced at $16.80, about 12% less than the competitor's electronic control it replaced.

Standardizing its products within and even across appliance lines—from clothes washers to dishwashers, say—will reward ACT and its customers with substantial cost benefits, Leyshon argues. Instead of buying a million each of 10 different electronic components, for instance, ACT can buy 10 million of just one and get the higher volume price from the component maker. That's an important savings, since as much as 70% of the cost of the control is in materials. But nearly as significant in the Leyshon scheme are the savings reaped from lower inventory costs and shorter lead times. ACT and its customers will have fewer different parts to inventory; Just in Time inventory demands will be easier to meet.

If his design strategy breaches industry practice, Leyshon's manufacturing strategy violates all conventional wisdom. It's cheaper to manufacture in the United States, he insists, than to chase low-cost labor overseas. Cheaper in the high-wage United States? Yes, the way Leyshon figures costs.

First, he says, forget direct labor. It's not an issue. With automatic-insertion machines doing 70% (and eventually more) of the assembly work on ACT's PC boards, direct labor constitutes less than 10% of product cost. Anything the competition saves on direct labor overseas, says ACT engineering vice-president Althoff, they spend on duty, shipping, and airfreight: "It's a wash, we think."

In fact, from the point of view of engineering and manufacturing, there's *no* good reason to go overseas, *no* savings at all. An overseas plant requires additional management personnel. "We don't need a communications person at each end, a customer-service person here talking to a scheduler there; we don't need a plant manager there and a division manager here. All those communications are gone. One guy," says Althoff, "replaces two." Travel and hotel bills add up. At other companies, Leyshon has seen those T&E expenses come to $1 million a year.

But more important than all of these considerations, in the eyes of ACT's management, are the operational advantages to having engineering and manufacturing under the same roof. Those advantages, they argue, show up in product quality and service delivery.

Designer Jeff Krasnesky's CAD/CAM system and manufacturing's assembly lines are separated by one wall and a few paces in ACT's headquarters and plant. "I can't tell you," says Leyshon, "how critical it is to have those people able to work closely together." Communications, says Althoff, "is the biggest advantage. Manufacturing can walk into Jeff's office and say, `Here's a problem.' With Motorola's plant in Taiwan, they can't send their Jeff over every time they have a problem, so the design center may never hear things like `This doesn't fit,' or `We're having to insert this by hand.'"

If he has a problem on the line now, says quality vice-president Les Jones, he can take it right to engineering, "and instead of Band-Aiding it, we can fix it." More than a year into production, ACT estimates a field failure rate of 0.25% on its controls, which is, according to Jones, "better than any other manufacturer." More impressive, the *actual* failure rate, Jones claims, is running 0.029%.

Customer service is also easier to deliver from stateside. "In this business," says Bob van Dusen, vice-president of sales and marketing, "the next generation could be tomorrow, and customers want it yesterday. If you go overseas, you're 16 weeks on the boat. If you're on the East Coast and I'm in the Midwest, I'm 14 hours away. . . . I've taken a truck to Atlanta in the afternoon and gotten it there for the 7:00 a.m. shift."

ACT's domestic manufacturing strategy will lift skeptical eyebrows. But its protocol-defying marketing plan, in contrast, could irritate people who are important to the company's success. It's gutsy because it seeks efficiency at the expense of tradition.

Remember, ACT is not selling its product directly to consumers or even to retailers. It's simply a vendor to appliance manufacturers that may market their own brands or act as original equipment manufacturer (OEM) suppliers to such retailers as Sears, Roebuck & Co.

Traditionally, according to ACT's managers, vendors work from specifications. Sears, for instance, will tell Whirlpool's marketing people that it wants a new washer. The marketing people will generate ideas for product features based on Sears's suggestions, hand their ideas to the engineering department, which writes the specs and gives them to purchasing, which puts them out to bid. So, maybe 8 or 12 months after Sears decides it wants a new washer, the control maker finally gets a look at what the OEM's marketing people think Sears wants.

Now, maybe the vendor can make a control with the features Sears wants and for the price Sears wants to pay, or maybe it can't. And maybe it has a completely wrong-headed notion of what Sears wants, given the number of people the idea has passed through. Or maybe Sears would want something different if it knew what the new technology could do and what its costs were. The point, says Leyshon, is that the current process leads to "wholesale miscommunication" and takes entirely too long.

Instead, for key components, the manufacturer's marketing people and the vendor's marketing people and, if Sears is involved, its marketing people, too, should sit down in the same room at the outset. They could make all their trade-offs then, and everyone would be working with the same information. That, says Leyshon, is how the Japanese and Koreans do it.

And that's how ACT is trying to do it. "My target," says van Dusen, "is the vice-president of marketing. He's the one guy you've got to sell. If you sell him, the VP of engineering is going to be predisposed to buy."

"We think it's important to American industry that everybody do this," says Althoff. "In Japan they can work out design issues in a week. In the United States it takes a year. The industry has to shorten the cycle."

But Leyshon and van Dusen have to persuade marketing VPs to talk to them, and they've got to assuage purchasing's hurt feelings. Whomever they talk to first, it's still purchasing that signs the POs.

In Leyshon's analysis of the competition his two-year-old start-up will face, Far Eastern companies don't yet play a big role. Japanese and Korean microwave makers do supply controls for ovens manufactured in their own U.S. plants. And a couple of Asian firms have contracts to supply U.S. appliance makers. But except for microwaves, offshore appliance makers have found entry to the U.S. market tough for two reasons. Their own domestic appliances are very different from those sold here, so they can't practice in their home markets on designs that are salable in the United States. Second, Leyshon's business plan points out, U.S. appliance manufacturers have kept their labor productivity quite high ($115,000 to $130,000 in sales per employee versus the U.S. manufacturing average of $64,000) and their costs low. Consequently, they don't provide the same wide price umbrella for imports that other industries—autos and machine tools, for instance—do.

Nor does Leyshon's plan anticipate much competition from semiconductor makers. Texas Instruments and National Semiconductor tried and failed to capture significant shares of the appliance-control market. They never took the time, in Leyshon's view, to understand the old-line industry they were trying to sell to.

ACT's chief competition comes from two groups of firms: electromechanical-control makers trying to convert their products to the new technology and electronic-equipment makers.

The first group knows the market well, he concedes, but he holds that it is difficult for companies organized around one technology successfully to make their own products obsolete by converting to a new technology.

The second group he takes more seriously. Motorola, which was the market leader when Leyshon left the company two years ago, has fallen behind a relative upstart, Digital Appliance Controls Inc. DAC is headed by its founder, Peter W. Sognefest, the man who originally put Motorola into the appliance-control business in 1977. Sognefest left Motorola in 1984, when he was promoted out of the job he had and wanted to keep. Like Leyshon two years later, he launched his own company. With projected 1989 sales of $25 million, DAC claims it will hold the largest single share of the electronic-control market next year. But unlike ACT, DAC manufactures overseas, sells its products through OEM purchasing departments, and stresses proprietary design and quality over standardization and low pricing.

The total U.S. and European market for appliance controls of both types now runs some $2 billion a year, about equally split between each side of the Atlantic. By 1991, Leyshon projects, electronic controls will account for close to half this market, and ACT, his business plan predicts, will have grabbed about 12% of the domestic market for electronic controls. It will also be competing in the European market, although just how European sales will be handled is still murky.

Capital does not seem to be a current problem for Leyshon, which is not to say that raising it was easy. It wasn't. Chicagoland is no Silicon Valley, Route 128, or Research Triangle when it comes to financing start-ups. "You mention start-ups in this community," Leyshon says, "and nobody wants to talk to you. Real estate people, for instance, treat you like dog poop." He launched the company largely on the expectation that he would be able to attract investors. Indeed, with the first purchase order in his pocket, he was able to sell a first round of equity financing in early 1987 to raise $1.1 million. And with several months' production under his belt and a respectable order backlog, he raised an additional $2.2 million in a second round that closed in May 1988. A large portion of the second-round financing came through a venture capitalist, but even so, Leyshon and his key managers together have managed to retain 48% of the equity in the company. He expects to finance growth through cash flow and a line of credit. No further equity offerings are planned.

Estimated sales for 1988 were $7.2 million, less than half of his original business-plan projection, but not bad for a company's first full production year. ACT lost an estimated $900,000 in 1988, down from its $1.2-million loss in 1987—its first, partial operating year. Projections call for a $1.4-million profit in 1989, when sales, by the company's rosy predictions, will more than double. In fact, by 1991, Leyshon projects sales greater than $60 million, more than eight times 1988 revenues.

Besides the microwave controls sold to Tappan, ACT has added Maytag's Magic Chef division to its customer list. And it has development contracts in laundry and dishwasher products for Sears, Frigidaire, and White-Westinghouse.

But one thing isn't working as he planned. In his business plan, Leyshon said ACT would find eager customers among Japanese microwave-oven manufacturers with plants in the United States. After all, he reasoned, having a domestic supplier would help satisfy those manufacturers' Just in Time inventory demands. And the appreciated yen was making Asian-produced controls expensive to install in U.S.-made products. But the Japanese weren't as eager as Leyshon thought they would be—or should be.

"It's a joke," he says, "I don't think they're the least bit serious about doing business with American companies. . . . The yen has appreciated 50% in two years, and I'm still not doing business with them. The economics don't add up."

"Almost all its competition is manufacturing overseas. It's hard to believe only Wally Leyshon has been able to figure out how that isn't smart."

—*James West*

FINANCIER

JAMES FITZPATRICK
Principal, Canaan Venture Partners, Royalton, Conn., formerly General Electric Venture Capital, experienced in electronic-control business with GE, Texas Instruments, and Motorola

I think ACT's notion of building on-shore is right. It's absolutely correct that labor costs are a minuscule part of this product. Manufacturing in the United States should provide ACT with an enormous advantage.

Will ACT succeed? I don't know. You've got a very experienced team, people who know what they're doing. But I'm concerned that they may be trying too many things at once. A good company, a good entrepreneur, a good venture really does one thing very well. And here they're proposing to use a new design approach, a new marketing approach, and the onshore manufacturing approach—three big bites. I don't think they're wrong on any of them, but if they flunk in any one area, they're in trouble. I'm not sanguine about their ability to survive, but I hope that they do.

COMPETITOR

PETER W. SOGNEFEST
President and CEO, DAC Inc., Hoffman Estates, Ill., electronic-control maker with 1988 sales of $15 million

I believe it will be very difficult for ACT to overcome the many obsta-cles that lie ahead. Leyshon started his company after less than six months' experience managing the appliance-control business at Motorola. It is difficult to learn any business in six months. Leyshon is on the right track in focusing on service and quality. However, a lowest-price strategy is seldom successful, especially when coupled with a high-cost factory (ACT's U.S. factory versus competition in Singapore and Korea). He's right to have a U.S. factory, but he also needs an offshore factory to meet the total needs of the appliance business. His major competitors, companies like mine, have factories in both places. And the DAC U.S. factory cannot compete with the DAC Singapore factory.

During my 20 years in this business, I have never seen Leyshon's sales approach work over the long term. The supplier must serve the needs of his customer's purchasing and engineering departments. The customer's purchasing and engineering departments are quite able to work with their own marketing organizations. It is necessary to sell to those who give the order in this market.

I think there'll be a capital problem, too. ACT has raised $3.3 million and plans to grow to $18.9 million through retained earnings. However, just licensing the required technology has cost my company $750,000. ACT will also need these licenses. If ACT has similar licensing costs and cumulative losses through 1988 of $2.1 million, it won't have a lot of money to support growth. Contrast this with $16.1 million in equity raised by DAC to reach $25 million in 1989 sales. The numbers suggest that much more equity will probably be required.

CUSTOMER

JAMES WEST

Executive vice-president, marketing sector, WCI Major Appliance Group, Columbus, Ohio, which buys from ACT and other control suppliers

Their sales approach is working here. Marketing people are working with ACT along with the purchasing and technical people. Can others copy that? I think they can, but at this point most haven't. This is a great marketing strategy for getting new business, but it's not without risk. What happens when you get the new business? A year after a control goes into a design, the purchasing guy is going to take that wonderful new system that ACT has developed with the marketing and engineering people and take it out for quotes—"OK, industry, have at it, beat this price." That's the nature of the industry. It's very cutthroat. Given that, ACT will be in the position of continually having to defend business that it's already gotten. Your ability to gain business is only as good as your ability to keep business, and you do that only by keeping costs down and prices competitive—great relationships won't do it. They've got a tough, competitive road ahead.

It's uncomfortable to think about how much of its competition is overseas. It's hard to believe only Wally Leyshon has been able to figure out that that isn't smart. But I'm relying on what he's said to us, which is that direct labor is indeed no more than 10% of product cost, and that's more than offset by the longer supply-chain issues. He's very committed to this made-in-the-U.S.A. strategy, and I'm on his side—I hope it works. But he *is* all alone on that one.

FINANCIER

KYLE LEFKOFF

Venture associate, Colorado Venture Management Inc., Boulder, Colo.

The company's credibility, I think, is excellent, evidenced by a $3-million purchase order from Tappan before the first venture financing. To our minds, that's a real feather in Leyshon's hat. Because a guy who comes to me and says, "Hey, I've got this new product, would you be willing to put up some seed capital, and by the way I have a $3-million purchase order on the table," is a very impressive guy to us. That's the kind of guy you love.

Also, the entire team comes from what was the industry leader in the business, Motorola, so they're not reinventing this business. They've already made money at it; they just want to do it for themselves now instead of for a big company. And that's a story that appeals to a venture capitalist.

The projections look reachable given the size of the market and competitor DAC's experience. DAC reached $25 million in a couple of years. It got big fast, and venture guys like to see that, too. Here's a company that is, in a sense, an analog to ACT, and it shows that little companies can get into this market and make it work.

Would I invest? Obviously, it depends on price, but the answer would probably be yes. It looks like a good deal. I would have liked to have gotten in on the first round, not the second. I think ACT will get to pretty significant revenues fairly soon; the numbers are achievable. The plan is aggressive, but it has a team that looks like it can do it. Even if the company gets to $15 mil-lion the third year, that's pretty good. Do I think the company will succeed? Yes. My definition of success is 10 times the investment in five years, and I think they'll do it.

One nagging question, though: Why is ACT in Chicago? This business could be anywhere. If I needed to build a factory, I'd go looking in the boonies and see who'd give me the best deal. There are places that would love this business. It's basic, hard-core, nonpolluting manufacturing. States like Colorado would have rolled out the carpet for him, given him a free building and equipment grants and tax breaks.

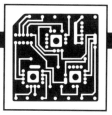

SEEING RED

He who laughs last, laughs best—so Randy Wise doesn't mind the inevitable reaction when he tells people about his contact lenses for chickens. That's right, for chickens

BY BRUCE G. POSNER

Ann States

Say what you will about the notion of chickens wearing red-tinted contact lenses—and just about everyone, including Johnny Carson, has said *something*. To Wise, it's a matter of simple economics. A commercial egg farm is a commodity business: The price of a dozen eggs is set by the market, and the expenses—for feeding and housing the chickens—are almost impossible to alter. Your average egg rancher makes do with profit margins on the vanishing side of thin.

According to Randy Wise, the red-tinted lenses cause changes in the behavior of egg layers. They eat less, produce more, and don't fight as much. The lenses will remake the economics of egg farming, raising gross margins by 400%.

Wise, a 40-year-old Harvard M.B.A., thinks the contact lenses made and marketed by his company—Animalens Inc.—will change the rules. Over the years tests have shown that chickens wearing red-tinted contact lenses behave differently from birds that don't. The chickens are

Randall Wise, founder and CEO of Animalens Inc., in Wellesley, Mass.

THE COMPANY:
Animalens Inc.,
Wellesley, Mass.

CONCEPT:
Make and market
red-tinted contact
lenses for egg-laying
chickens, altering
their behavior so
they will fight less,
eat less, and pro-
duce more eggs—
increasing egg-ranch
profitability

PROJECTIONS:
Eventual pretax
net margins of 25%;
1989 sales of
$329,000; 1992
sales of $24 million

HURDLES:
Persuading histori-
cally conservative
egg farmers, operat-
ing on thin margins,
to risk money up
front for an un-
proven product;
sustaining the com-
pany in the face of
slower-than-expect-
ed product accep-
tance; defending an
easily copied prod-
uct from competi-
tors likely to enter
after the market has
been opened

calmer, less prone to pecking and cannibalism; the mortality rate is lower. For a variety
of reasons, some not fully understood, they
also tend to eat less feed while producing, on
average, the same size and number of eggs as
other chickens (even a bit more). In financial
terms, Wise predicts, the savings from all this
improved behavior will add up to a *quadru-
pling* of chicken-ranch profit margins. And
once farmers know that, Wise figures, he'll be
off and running.

He could be sitting on a gold mine. The
U.S. population of commercial egg-laying
chickens—layers—is currently around 250
million. Because it isn't practical or safe to recycle old lenses at the end of a layer's yearlong productive lifetime, chicken farmers
would buy new lenses every year and install
them in new birds. Once a few key egg producers adopt the product, Wise thinks others
will follow out of fear of what would happen
if they didn't. "Nobody will want to be left behind," he says. The lenses might also be sold
to farmers whose business is breeding chickens. And down the road, Wise believes, there
are opportunities for related products. Though
he'll begin in this country, the global market
could be 24 times the size of the domestic one.
And the U.S. market alone, at a lens price of
15¢ a pair, says Wise, is $37.5 million.

You can't achieve the same advantages
by using red lights, Wise maintains, because
many chicken houses use natural light and
would have to be completely rebuilt. Even in
closed houses, red lights would be difficult to
operate with and costly to run.

There aren't many new businesses that have been on the drawing
board as long as Animalens, in Wellesley, Mass. In the early 1960s Wise's
father, Irvin, was managing a chicken ranch north of San Francisco and
became involved with a California start-up that planned to sell a highly
unusual product: contact lenses for chickens. The start-up's founder, a
medical supply salesman, had known a local chicken farmer who had

Randall E. Wise, CEO

Age: 40

Randy Wise's decision to sell contact lenses for chickens is not the result of a sudden impulse. He's been preparing for this since he was a teenager in California.

Back in the early 1960s, his father, a chicken rancher, got involved with a similar venture. The idea then was to reduce the cannibalism of egg-laying chickens with a lens that distorted their vision. The business flopped, but the goal—improving the economics of egg production—is something Wise didn't stop thinking about.

At Harvard Business School during the early 1970s, he wrote a popular case study that evaluated his father's ill-fated experience and outlined the opportunity for a new company. It explored the economics of egg ranching and examined the options for marketing the new lenses. Even today, the case (which sells about 6,000 copies annually) is used in business schools all over the country to highlight pricing and marketing questions.

Wise hoped to launch the business right after business school, but he couldn't get the financing. "Investors had a hard time relating to egg production," he recalls. Fifteen years later, with money in the bank, he's raring to go again.

Wise thinks the odds of success have improved with time. For one thing, plastic molding technology has moved way ahead. Chicken farmers, too, are a little less resistant to newfangled ideas than they once were. And, having built one successful business, Wise believes he knows how to build a second. Initially, for example, he's got a team of just three full-time employees, and he's resisting every impulse to spend money in advance of sales. "I'm a lot smarter than I was when I wrote the business-school case study," he says.

So what does he worry about? These days, Wise says, the biggest danger may be overconfidence. "The way I see it, the next 12 to 18 months are critical. As much as we believe in this, we have to sell it. You can't believe it's going to happen until it actually happens."

some birds with cataracts and had discovered that the vision-impaired chickens were easier to handle than their sighted counterparts. It dawned on the salesman that there could be a market for a lens that blurred the vision of chickens. The company was called Vision Control Inc.

Vision Control—which for a short period employed Wise's father full-time as vice-president and his mother part-time—did write some orders. But the lenses, molded out of plastic, were inconsistent: They tended to irritate the birds' eyes, and though designed to be permanently installed, many of them popped out. The company soon went out of business, but not before the principals collected a good deal of data. When the lenses fit, Wise remembers, the product performed beauti-

ANIMALENS

255

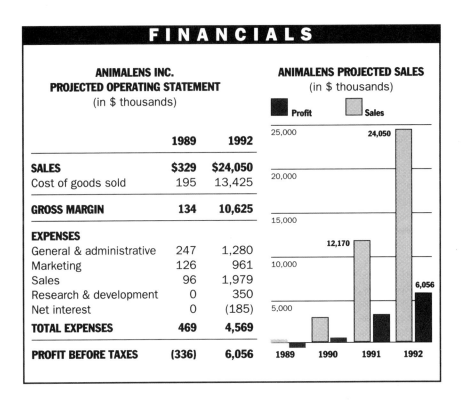

FINANCIALS

ANIMALENS INC.
PROJECTED OPERATING STATEMENT
(in $ thousands)

	1989	1992
SALES	**$329**	**$24,050**
Cost of goods sold	195	13,425
GROSS MARGIN	**134**	**10,625**
EXPENSES		
General & administrative	247	1,280
Marketing	126	961
Sales	96	1,979
Research & development	0	350
Net interest	0	(185)
TOTAL EXPENSES	**469**	**4,569**
PROFIT BEFORE TAXES	**(336)**	**6,056**

ANIMALENS PROJECTED SALES
(in $ thousands)

■ Profit   ▢ Sales

25,000 · 24,050 · 20,000 · 15,000 · 12,170 · 10,000 · 6,056 · 5,000

1989   1990   1991   1992

fully. "The chickens were easier to handle and they laid more eggs."

In the fall of 1966 Wise went East to attend the U.S. Merchant Marine Academy, and in 1972 he started business school. He encountered many opportunities there, but the contact-lens business had hooked him. In fact, during his second year at Harvard, he investigated the market for a company he proposed would follow in the footsteps of Vision Control; the research became the basis of a business-school case study still in use. Like the original lenses, the product he had in mind would impair vision. What was the potential? He didn't project sales. But, if successful, Wise said, "We will have revolutionized the business of animal behavior in much the same way that IBM revolutionized the processing of data."

When Wise tried selling the idea to venture capitalists, nobody bought it. For one thing, he hadn't pinned down details as to how the lenses would be produced and how much they'd cost. The venture capitalists were polite, Wise says. "But they tended to see it as a shaggy dog story." He was 25 and inexperienced.

Instead of abandoning the idea, Wise kept it in the back of his mind for almost 15 years. During that period, he held a series of high-paying consulting jobs, specializing in marine transportation. In 1981 he founded a graphics software company in Boston. All the while, Wise did his best to keep informed about the chicken business. He read *Egg Industry* magazine and other poultry trade journals. And he commissioned research into a new lens design—one that relied on color instead of distortion. "Hardly a week went by when I wasn't thinking about contact lenses for chickens," he says.

Each year thousands of business-school students were exposed to the idea through the case study. Wise says it wouldn't have surprised him if someone had beat him to the punch. It was a concept waiting to be executed. But to his relief, nobody ever touched it.

Between 1979 and 1984, when Wise incorporated Animalens, he invested nearly $15,000 of his own money. In 1985 and 1986, when he sold his graphics software company to Lotus Development Corp. for a reported $12 million to $15 million (he owned about 20%), he put up another $100,000 to pay for prototypes and new molds. For the design work, he retained a well-known professor from Virginia Polytechnic Institute named A.T. Leighton Jr. The challenge, says Leighton, was to get the right depth and thickness of lens. The lens had to stay in the bird's eye for life. In January 1988 Wise felt they had a product that overcame the design flaws of the earlier lens—and one that fell within the cost parameters he had targeted. The patent application was in the mail. Wise was ready. Now all he had to do was sell it to the chicken farmers of America.

Consider how the typical egg producer makes money: He buys a 17-week-old pullet for $3.25. Then, over the course of the next year (the normal productive life of the bird), he spends some $9.40 maintaining it—$7.60 on feed and another $1.80 or so for housing, lighting, and labor. His cost per bird: around $12.65. The average egg layer produces 21 dozen eggs in its year of work, which, at 60¢ a dozen to the farmer, generates $12.60 a year. If the farmer is lucky, he'll net another 25¢ by selling the chicken once its production falls off. In this example, the gross margin is a scant 1.6%.

Like many businesses, the commercial egg trade has undergone tremendous changes over the past two decades. What used to be a good-sized chicken ranch—say, 100,000 birds—hardly counts by today's standards. Given cost pressures, the most competitive producers have sought economies of scale—big farms can, for example, mix their own feed. Currently there are about 50 egg farms in the United States with more than a million chickens; among them they manage nearly 55% of the country's almost 250 million layers.

Even the big guys have been hurt by recent trends. Americans have been eating a lot fewer eggs; since 1960 per capita consumption has plummeted from 335 to 235 per year. And despite the efforts of operators to hold the line, the costs of feed, labor, and overhead have been climbing. All this would be fine if egg farmers could keep on raising prices. But the price of a dozen eggs is continuously squeezed by oversupply. So every year farmers are driven out of business.

From the point of view of the individual egg rancher, there are very few opportunities for cost savings. Over the past decade, the farmer has brought on all kinds of automated equipment to minimize his labor needs. The modern-day chicken house is filled with Rube Goldberg–like contraptions: cage systems, feeding and watering systems, egg-packing systems. Eggs are shipped to market without being touched by human hands. So what else can farmers do? They can fiddle around with feed additives and look for genetic improvements. Smart operators are already doing these things.

But nobody—*nobody*—is using contact lenses.

Randy Wise figures he has three key selling points on which he can build his case. The first one—that the lenses reduce cannibalism—is something he's known since the 1960s. The calming effect of the color red has been corroborated again and again over the past several years by research on light and color at agricultural universities. The other two benefits—that lenses reduce feed consumption and that they increase egg production—have been noticed only more recently. Supported by fewer tests, they're more controversial. "Basically," Wise says, "we try to figure out what the rancher is most concerned about. But we like to talk about all three."

Dealing with the effects of pecking, he notes, has been a chronic problem for egg farmers. All chickens normally establish a social hierarchy, or pecking order, though some breeds are more aggressive than others. When one bird bleeds, the other birds peck at it. Ranchers can lose up to a quarter of their flock to such cannibalism. They mitigate the results of this behavior by beak trimming. The procedure, better known as debeaking, uses a hot knife to cut off the tip of the beak. Debeaking, which costs from 3¢ to 5¢ per bird, doesn't solve the problem. Chickens still peck, Wise says, but less harmfully. The procedure reduces the 25% mortality rate, but it can still run as high as 12% to 15%.

"Since the red lenses absorb all colors but red," says Wise, "the chickens can't distinguish blood, because everything looks red. If the chickens don't see blood, they don't peck." In tests, Wise notes, the mortality rates for birds wearing red lenses dropped to less than 8%. And some of those deaths could be attributed to causes other than pecking. On 1,000 birds, farmers could save from $120 to $150, just as a result of reduced mortality. That's at least 12¢ per bird.

The effect of the red lenses on appetite results in even greater savings. It was first documented in a 1986 test at Virginia Polytechnic Institute. The researchers found that birds wearing lenses ate an average of 7% less than the control group. Wise says that the experiments in other locations confirm the same levels of feed savings, in some cases greater. "Because [chicken] activity is lower," he says, "the chickens don't need to eat as much." Using the 7% figure, a farmer could save around 54¢ per bird per year, or more than 4% of the annual investment—a savings that would go straight to the bottom line.

But the biggest surprise is on the production side: Chickens that eat less don't produce fewer eggs. Birds with lenses do tend to be a bit leaner, Wise says, citing the Virginia Polytechnic study and several other commercial trials. But the number of eggs they lay—and the size of those eggs—doesn't change. "The tests show that, if anything, production goes up by 1% to 3%," Wise says. For the average egg farmer, a 1% increase means another 13¢ of revenue for every bird—another boost to profitability.

Altogether, Wise argues that the savings add up to a significant shift in the cost structure of egg production. Obviously, the value of these benefits fluctuates with the market. But right now he talks about savings in the neighborhood of 80¢ per chicken—practically 4¢ for every dozen eggs. Not bad if you consider the cost of a pair of lenses: 15¢ if you sign a three-year contract (18¢ or 19¢ otherwise). Animalens estimates that, based on an installation rate for two people of 150 pair per hour, operators should be able to install them for approximately 10¢ per bird. On 100,000 chickens a farmer would spend around $25,000 to save two to three times that. We're talking about a gross margin increase from 1.6% to 6%—not chicken feed.

So why aren't ranchers lining up at Animalens's door?

Wise admits things haven't taken off as quickly as he hoped they might, but he says he isn't worried. "Any time you're introducing something that's new and different, there's a natural lag." People need to get used to the idea, he explains.

In February 1988 Wise attended the International Poultry Trade Show in Atlanta, accompanied by his father and two associates. From a small booth, they showed a video and displayed the lenses for the first time. They met lots of chicken people and collected business cards, but nothing concrete developed. "People would say, `We're not ready to do anything now,'" Wise recalls. "They wanted to see more data." The reaction to a $60,000 marketing campaign last summer—which included a glitzy mailing to the top 200 egg producers and two-page ads in several poultry magazines—was lukewarm as well. Lots of inquiries, but most of the discussions have led nowhere.

In some cases, chicken farmers think that Animalens's story is too good to be true. Some operators are skeptical, for instance, about the installation. "I don't think handling the birds and installing lenses can be as simple as they say," offers a poultryman from Iowa. Wise, however, sticks to his guns. "Yes, it's labor intensive," he says. "So is vaccinating. But two people working together can do 1,200 birds a day. I've done it myself."

Many ranchers question how the product will perform in their specific setting—say, a 700,000-bird operation in North Carolina. Given variations among breeds and management practices, Wise says one can't know for sure. "We tell ranchers to run their own trials." Animalens offers to help farmers design the trials and will assist in the initial installations. "If, based on the test, there's no savings," Wise says, "a rancher would be stupid to buy the lenses for his whole flock."

A few ranchers have told Wise and Animalens's sales vice-president Jim Collier, who came to Animalens from the computer industry, that they'd gladly test the lenses if Animalens provided them for free. "We won't pay that kind of money until we know they work," says the manager of a million-bird operation in Georgia. A few months ago the company was willing to make deals to generate more data; it provided a few hundred pairs of sample lenses, for instance, to an egg farmer in Connecticut. But now Wise opposes the idea of giving away product. "We want to work with guys who show a level of commitment." When people pay, he thinks, they'll try harder to realize the benefit.

Until last fall Wise thought that ranchers would be jumping at the opportunity to test his product. He still thinks that once ranchers test the lenses and are sure that they deliver, they'll buy them on a larger scale within a year. Wise had wanted dozens of trials happening simultaneously at farms all over the country. These farmers' decisions might influence others to adopt the product without additional tests. But it hasn't worked out that way. Why? Because the first step—getting farmers to do the trials—is taking a lot longer than Wise expected.

The product is now being tested in a few locations. Last December a major ranch in northern California began trying the red lenses on 20,000 birds; smaller field tests are being conducted in Connecticut, Oregon, Florida, and Virginia. There's an academic study in progress at Purdue University.

The company will pass a major milestone, says Wise, when the folks who are testing shift to full-scale adoption. "Having a few happy customers is a lot different from having three or four tests with good results."

Ultimately, Wise thinks, egg farmers will act in their own interests:

If it's known that a few ranchers are achieving superior results with the lenses, others will follow. From that point on, he thinks, the job of selling will get easier. "It's not like there are 2 million potential customers. In the United States there are fewer than 200 major farms. They'll know how to find us, and we have a directory with their names and addresses."

Given the delays, Wise doesn't expect sales to materialize much before the end of the year. In 1989 he figures the company will lose about $336,000 on sales of $329,000. But it will turn profitable in the middle of next year, he thinks, once test results are circulated. In 1990 Animalens will be a $2.5-million company; in 1992 a $24-million company, with pretax earnings of $6 million. The 1992 number may be conservative, he says. "It's based on selling to less than half of the commercial ranches in the States and only about 5% of the worldwide market."

Until early 1988 Wise was bankrolling virtually everything himself. In addition to $100,000 of equity, he personally guaranteed a $175,000 credit line. Since then he's managed to raise a total of $825,000 from private investors (mostly friends and professional contacts). He still owns 55% of the company.

The rate at which the product takes off will determine how much additional outside capital Animalens needs. Because things are running behind schedule, the company has been tightening its belt. The vice-president of marketing was recently let go. On January 1 Wise and the three other employees took pay cuts ranging from 15% to 25%.

When the lenses begin to sell, Animalens wants to be ready. Wise has contracted the manufacturing to a Massachusetts plastic injection-molding company, and he's been accumulating inventory. With six machines cranking away, the plant can make about 80 million pairs annually, enough to generate $12 million of revenues.

As a matter of policy, Animalens intends to stay away from independent sales representatives and build a dedicated sales and service staff of its own. Eventually, Wise hopes to place sales-service representatives in satellite offices—first in the United States and later in offices overseas. Not many, he says; perhaps 10 or 15. But he refuses to do anything until the revenues start to materialize. "I've learned from earlier experience that you shouldn't spend it until you've got it."

That's where things stand. Randy Wise thinks he's got an awfully good shot at changing the way that egg farmers do business. "That's what kept me from letting this idea die," he says. He's put up a lot of his own money and convinced many of his friends to do likewise. In Wise's mind, it's not whether his product will succeed, but when.

The only people who haven't signed on yet are the people who will determine the outcome: the ranchers themselves. Wise thinks he's on the right track. "Chicken farmers aren't known for jumping the gun," he comments. Whether he'll be able to win their confidence before he loses his own remains to be seen.

> "Their mistake was to think purely in economic terms. They said, 'Here's an industry that needs our product because cost savings should automatically be embraced.' They lost time."
>
> —*Ray A. Goldberg*

FINANCIER

DAN TESSLER
Partner at Tessler & Cloherty Inc., a $50-million venture capital firm in New York City; former president of a feed-supplement company

The basic economic premise that the business addresses is a reasonable one, but I sense that Wise and his people have miscalculated the uniqueness of their selling proposition from the point of view of the people they're selling to. Wise seems to believe this product really can and should sell itself, because it's so overpoweringly valuable and important that customers shouldn't be able to resist it.

Well, I think the reality is that producers in this field are constantly bombarded with ideas for improving their cost/output ratios. A lot of these products come with the same pitch: "Your margins are very low, this can decrease your cost, so it'll multiply your profits by a lot. Buy some." I think Wise doesn't have enough respect for the volume of such opportunities that are presented to producers, who are very conservative people. They have a complex system, which works. And they don't take altering it lightly.

I think Animalens probably needs to spend a good deal of money sponsoring extensive, repeated field trials, putting together a database that encourages leading producers to say, "It really is worth doing my own test."

I think it will be very hard to sustain the 25% pretax margins that are projected. These farmers who work for pennies a bird are people who force their suppliers to work for pennies per bird, or minimum possible profit. And that pressure backs up through the entire system in the poultry industry. If you don't have a real proprietary position—and you don't if you're not selling anything more than an injection-molded plastic product—then you can be sure that there will be alternate suppliers.

My guess is that Animalens needs more money to do what it expects to, but I'd probably not invest. If it were a clearly proprietary and protectable product, we might be interested. As it is, it looks like a one-shot nonproprietary technology.

I think Animalens as a product may well succeed—if it works and if it produces the kinds of benefits to cost outlined in the article. Whether the company will succeed is not necessarily the same question.

OBSERVER

FREDERICK S. NICHOLAS
Executive vice-president, Avian Farms International Ltd., a chicken-breeding company, Winslow, Maine

The best thing Wise could do is live with the people who are testing the product and do whatever he can to help things run smoothly. It will take a lot of hand-holding. The success of any test depends on more than the product—it's how the rancher is managing the product. So the company needs to have people working for it who can get in the chicken houses and put lenses in and help farmers any way they can. I'd put the money there, not in advertising. If the tests work well, things will happen.

Will the company be successful? I certainly don't see it happening as fast as Wise does, even if the lenses provide all the benefits he says they will. You're up against the standard resistance of a low-margin industry, in which products that don't work can turn you from a profit to a loss.

ACADEMIC

JOHN B. CAREY
Associate professor and extension poultry specialist, North Carolina State University, Raleigh, N.C.

It seems to me that Wise should be talking in greater detail about the way the lenses work. I don't think it's enough to tell egg farmers that the product saves money. They're used to hearing that from folks with suits and briefcases, and they're pretty skeptical. They'll want details about the physiology or they won't believe it.

Wise will also have to provide more detail about the installation. Two people installing 1,200 pair a day may seem fast to him, but it sounds like a snail's pace to me, particularly when you're talking about chicken houses with 100,000

birds. It means you'd need about 20 people doing nothing but putting in lenses for around eight days straight. Even if the labor cost only works out to 10¢ a chicken, not every rancher has access to that kind of manpower.

Is there a market for these lenses? Assuming that they're relatively easy to install and they stay in place, I imagine there is. Right now, though, it's an awful time to sell anything to chicken farmers. Many of them can't afford new birds—it's all they can do to cover their losses. Even when the industry recovers, I don't foresee the market penetration Wise does. It will have to be really obvious to the farmers who don't use his lenses that competitors have an advantage over them.

INDUSTRY SPECIALIST

RAY A. GOLDBERG
Professor of agriculture and business at Harvard Business School; a director of several companies, including a poultry-breeding business in Glastonbury, Conn.

The most glaring weakness I see with Animalens is that Wise didn't think through the whole question of how new ideas get adopted.

In every segment of agriculture, you've got leaders. The whole psychology of change is based on example. If you get one well-known and successful farmer doing something new—and being satisfied with it—that's 10 times more valuable than getting others who aren't industry leaders. These guys should have looked at the poultry industry and asked, "Who are the three leading university researchers?" And they should have done the same thing with chicken ranchers and convinced one or two of them to try the product. Their mistake was to think purely in economic terms. They said, "Here's an industry that needs our product because cost savings should automatically be embraced." They lost time.

In the best of times, egg production is a high-volume, low-margin business. As a group, farmers have been losing money over the past year. It's very difficult to take on new technology when you're squeezed. Farmers, for example, won't buy fertilizer when they're losing money, even though it's obvious that they should. But the industry should be recovering over the next 12 months. Animalens should be using this period to make sure the tests are done properly so that the credibility is there when the industry improves. If the tests confirm what they've been saying, I think they have a viable shot.

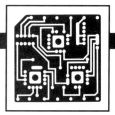

HOUSE CALLS

*Can Buddy Systems Inc. persuade
doctors, insurers, and patients to accept its
new home monitoring device?*

BY ANNE B. FISHER

Northbrook, Ill., is a Chicago suburb that is in most respects as blandly middle-American as Wonder Bread—not a place where many folks know when Chinese New Year begins, let alone celebrate it. But at the headquarters of Buddy Systems Inc., in a Northbrook industrial park, the frigid February day when the Year of the Dragon ended and the Year of the Snake began was the occasion for a festive stir-fried lunch party, where most of the guests—including several Buddy Systems engineers and the company's founder and president, Thomas Manning—chatted in Mandarin. Of the six technical staffers at Buddy Systems, four are Chinese immigrants. "Their academic qualifications are excellent," explains Manning, who

Thomas Manning, founder of Buddy Systems Inc., in Northbrook, Ill.

began learning to speak Chinese during a stint in Taiwan in his junior year of college. "But beyond that, they've made some really impressive sacrifices to come to the States and be educated here and get established here. So they are highly motivated people who have something to prove to themselves and to their families. If you can find someone with something to prove, hire them."

It's an apt remark. Buddy Systems, which Manning started in early 1985, is a company with something to prove—namely, that its product can dramatically cut the cost of caring for patients with congestive heart failure and other serious chronic illnesses without compromising the quality of the care those patients get. The company's product is a computer system, sold to doctors' groups and home-care agencies, that allows health-care professionals to monitor the vital signs of patients who have been sent home from the hospital but are still in need of observation. The system in effect delivers an electronic house call. The patient uses a computer console, chummily known as "Buddy," to measure and record his or her own blood pressure, weight, heart rate, electrocardiogram, and other data, which are then transmitted to the doctor's office and the home-care agency via telephone hookup and printed out for evaluation by doctors and nurses.

The only such machine commercially available now, Buddy is designed to let people go home from the hospital sooner, at a savings of hundreds of dollars a day. And by taking care of routine testing that would otherwise be done by a visiting nurse, Buddy greatly reduces the number and length of nurses' calls—another significant savings, since each runs $60 or $70. In contrast, depending on the use each doctor and patient makes of it, Buddy costs between $17 and $30 a day.

The idea of developing a cost-effective home monitoring system occurred to Tom Manning—a Harvard graduate with an M.B.A. from Stanford—during the five years he spent as a consultant in the Chicago office of McKinsey & Co. Manning's clients were companies in the health-care industry, where cutting costs is nothing short of an obsession. In 1983 Medicare and Medicaid, by far the biggest health insurers in the United States, began to crack down on the ever-soaring cost of medical care, which had reached a colossal 10% of the gross national product. Instead of paying hospitals and doctors on a cost-plus basis— which meant reimbursing whatever the medicos saw fit to spend and then some, no questions asked—the feds set strict ceilings on the fees they would henceforth shell out for any given treatment. So in order to keep their doors open, hospitals had to start thinking and acting like businesses. They scrambled to find ways to cut costs while they rustled up new sources of revenues, including new departments that oversee

EXECUTIVE SUMMARY

THE COMPANY:
Buddy Systems Inc., Northbrook, Ill.

CONCEPT:
Make and sell a computer monitoring system that delivers an "electronic house call," enabling doctors to keep track of the patients whom hospitals are being forced, by a financial crunch, to send home sooner than they used to

PROJECTIONS:
A 1989 loss of $400,000 but profits each year thereafter, with 1991 sales of $9.6 million yielding after-tax income of $902,000

HURDLES:
Getting doctors to use a device that involves no direct observation of patients and that may raise liability concerns; getting major insurers to routinely reimburse for use of the system; sustaining operations over what may be a longer-than-anticipated product-acceptance and sales cycle

the care of patients in their homes. Manning observed that one result of all this upheaval was a tendency to release patients, in the rather flippant phrase some industry insiders use, "quicker and sicker"—and more in need of clinical supervision.

Moreover, partly because of the aging of the U.S. population, health-care costs seemed likely to keep right on climbing. They've risen more than $140 billion since 1983. Health-insurance companies have been hard pressed to make ends meet: The Blue Cross and Blue Shield Associations reported a net loss of about $1.1 billion in 1988, which was an improvement over their $1.9-billion deficit the year before. Nor does relief seem near. According to figures released by the U.S. Health Care Financing Administration and analyzed by Sanford C. Bernstein & Co., in New York City, the nation's medical bills rose an average of 8.6% a year between 1982 and 1987—but from 1988 through 1992, the cost of getting well is expected to go up at a 12% annual clip. A product that could help cut medical costs without compromising quality, Manning reasoned, should be an answer to a health insurer's prayer.

The idea for Buddy Systems gradually took shape as Manning advised McKinsey clients on how to survive in the harsher and less forgiving world Washington's new cost-consciousness had wrought. "One pattern that emerged right away was the tremendous movement of patients from high-cost sites like hospitals to low-cost, decentralized locations," he recalls. "Home care was growing fast. The main issue, which nobody was looking at in any systematic way, was how doctors could keep tabs on their patients who'd been sent home." Medical technology, meanwhile, had spread from hospitals to doctors' offices, and consumers were becoming less leery of electronic gadgetry. A home computer that would be

Thomas J. Manning, CEO

Age: 34

When Tom Manning started Buddy Systems in 1984, he was in effect moving from an ivory tower into the trenches. Since 1979 he had been a consultant in the Chicago office of McKinsey & Co., advising top management of health-care companies about how to adapt to a fast-changing business environment. It was in the course of that work that Manning spotted the trend he is attempting to exploit with Buddy Systems: the shift from costly hospital care toward treating more patients in their homes.

Before he joined McKinsey, Manning worked his way through Harvard, where he received a B.A. with honors in East Asian Studies in 1977 and earned an M.B.A. from Stanford in 1979. While at Harvard he helped run the $1-million-a-year Harvard Student Corp., an undergraduate-run business that provides a variety of services to students and publishes the *Let's Go* series of bargain-travel guides. "That experience was the root of my interest in someday starting and running a business of my own," Manning says. He is founder of a newly formed network of entrepreneurs in the Chicago area. The group, whose 18 members are founders and CEOs, meets every six weeks to talk about the issues and problems facing growing businesses.

easy for patients to operate by themselves and would instantly provide doctors and nurses with essential medical information seemed logical.

By late 1984 Manning, then 29, had made up his mind to start a venture that would develop and market such a system. But first, just to make sure it was workable, he took two weeks of vacation from his job and interviewed dozens of doctors and computer technicians. What kinds of data did doctors need to assess the condition of a patient, sight unseen? And could a computer be designed that could measure and transmit the right stuff? Manning got a crash course in both medicine and electronics. "Then I got some good advice from a colleague at McKinsey," he says. "He told me not to overanalyze it, or I'd lose the excitement that could make it work."

With that in mind, in December 1984 Manning quit the consulting business. He set up shop in the basement of his house, living on his savings, scrounging $25,000 in seed capital from friends, and huddling with engineers to come up with a viable product. From the outset, Manning concentrated on meeting the needs of the growing number of health-care agencies and doctors who were trying to treat patients at home. Those customers' biggest concerns: how to cope with a shortage of nurses and how to gain a competitive advantage over other home-care providers, for-profit and nonprofit alike. If his product could satisfy those needs, Manning figured, he could sell the system to home-care providers who would then amortize or absorb the initial cost, as they were already doing with other types of medical equipment.

Throughout the spring of 1985 Manning and two technical consultants toiled in the basement and came up with a working prototype for a system that would be cost-effective and easy for patients to use without professional help. At the same time, Manning wrote up a long-term strategy for his new company and set out to pitch it to potential investors.

An early encounter with venture capitalists taught him what he now wryly calls the Rule of Halves. After a frustrating six-hour meeting on a Sunday afternoon in New York City—a get-together he had hoped would yield $50,000 in working capital—Manning flew home empty-handed and crestfallen. "But a few days later I decided not to take no for an answer, and I called them back. They gave me $25,000, half of what I'd asked for," he says. "When you have a totally new, untried product—where there are no competitors to compare it with, and you're really trying to invent a market that doesn't exist yet except as a hypothesis—venture capitalists tend to give you half of whatever you say you need." The Rule of Halves.

The venture capitalists' initial hesitation was understandable. Not only was Buddy Systems pioneering a whole new market, it was doing so in a business that demands more patience than most. Any new medical device must win approval from the Food and Drug Administration before it can be sold. With equipment such as Buddy, gaining that crucial green light could take at least a couple of years of testing, paperwork, and clinical trials, all while operating costs are mounting and before a single sale is made.

To some investors, Buddy has seemed worth the wait. In all, the company's total capitalization reached $4 million as of April 1989. In mid-1986, while Buddy was still in the R&D stage, a couple of investors forked over $100,000 each, and Buddy Systems moved out of Manning's basement and into a real office. Manning even hired a few full-time employees. But like the cash-strapped hospitals that inspired his venture, Manning ran a tight ship. The company's walls are decorated with colorful crayon art commissioned from a local class of second-graders. The furniture was bought at auction secondhand—"which was eerie," Manning notes, "because these auctions were held at the sites of businesses that had failed, so you had these intimations of mortality"—and employees hauled their own desks and chairs back to the office in a rented truck. To save still more nickels and dimes, employees doubled as janitors; they took turns cleaning the bathrooms and taking out the trash.

FINANCIALS

BUDDY SYSTEMS INC. OPERATING STATEMENT
(in $ thousands)

	1989	1990	1991
REVENUES			
System sales	$0	$4,667	$7,486
Recurring (parts, maintenance)	0	1,024	2,158
TOTAL REVENUES	**750**	**5,690**	**9,644**
COST OF GOODS SOLD	**400**	**2,584**	**4,480**
GROSS PROFIT	**350**	**3,106**	**5,164**
% gross profit	47%	55%	54%
OPERATING COSTS			
Sales & marketing	0	1,073	1,859
General & administrative	0	838	1,071
Research & development	0	567	744
Depreciation	0	64	102
TOTAL OPERATING COSTS	**750**	**2,543**	**3,776**
Operating costs as % of sales	100%	45%	39%
OPERATING INCOME	**(400)**	**563**	**1,388**
Income tax	0	197	486
NET INCOME	**(400)**	**366**	**902**
Net income as % of sales	0%	6%	9%

Like many infant electronics companies, Buddy Systems has kept its labor force and capital expenditures small by building its machines from parts made by outside suppliers. In Buddy's case, that is more cost-effective than it might seem. The computer consoles have thus far been manufactured in such tiny volumes—by the dozen, not the thousand—that the cost of producing its own basic components would be too high for Buddy Systems to bear. Although Manning wants to be able to do more manufacturing in-house as the company grows, he has concentrated up to now on doing meticulous final assembly, testing, and quality control.

"In medical products, for obvious reasons, quality is absolutely crucial," Manning says, "so we want to keep close control over that. And the biggest challenge was finding the right people to do prototypes for us. You need a component maker who's willing to do top-quality work in very small volumes and who'll be patient with you while you keep modifying and refining the design." Noting that manufacturing has rolled along with only minor glitches, Manning adds, "One thing we've learned is that it's important to diversify. If you rely too much on any one vendor, and it has a period when it's overloaded with demand, that sets you back. When it gets behind, you get behind. So it's crucial to have an alternate supplier lined up."

By late 1987 Buddy Systems computer consoles were doing well in clinical trials with the cardiology and home-care departments of Chicago's Rush Presbyterian St. Luke's Medical Center. With FDA approval just around the corner at last, Manning was getting ready to start selling Buddy to large, well-established home-care agencies and doctors' groups around the country. For the long-awaited marketing phase of his strategy, he had planned to ask his backers for a new round of financing. So on October 1, 1987, Manning once again began calling on venture capitalists, hat in hand. Then came the crash on October 19. "Overnight, investors who had been encouraging us were suddenly behaving like commercial banks," Manning says. "They wanted low risk. And they wanted to make loans, not take on equity investments."

Those were dark days in Northbrook. As Buddy System's bank accounts dwindled, marketing took a back seat to scratching around for capital—which finally came in February 1988, when a team of investors led by pharmaceutical giant Johnson & Johnson put up $1.2 million. Manning's contract with J&J prohibits him from discussing the terms of the deal, but when huge medical-products companies back start-ups, they usually have an option to buy part or all of the business. The closest Manning will come to explaining why he waited so long to approach companies like J&J for money is to say, "Corporate backers, generally, have other expectations than the purely financial, and there's more potential for conflict." In his particular deal, though, he claims that "J&J brought very little baggage."

In any case, by the time J&J rode to the rescue, Manning had been forced to lay off 11 employees, their departure marked by a tearful staff meeting, and morale was badly bruised. "We had done very careful— and, up to then, very accurate—projections of our cash flow. But in the wake of the Crash, it was clear we hadn't left ourselves enough slack," Manning says now. "We had to pick ourselves up off the floor and focus on a very limited set of objectives. We're just now getting back on our feet. The main task was, and is, to learn the best ways to reach the customer and get market acceptance for the product."

The effort to make Buddy as user-friendly and as salable as possible has already led to some changes in the computer system's design. For one thing, there's the name Buddy. Early on, Manning called his company Biometrix Inc. But a focus group of nurses, asked to comment on the machine while it was still being developed, said that when people are ill, frightened, and newly released from the hospital, they need friendly reassurance, not high-tech dazzle. Manning's wife, Ellen, who has worked extensively with chronically ill children at the Rehabilitation Institute of Chicago, suggested renaming the company Buddy Systems.

The computer's name in turn shaped its—pardon the expression—personality. The data-entry key on the console's simple four-button keyboard is labeled BUDDY. Each time a patient is supposed to enter information, the instructions on the screen direct him or her to TOUCH BUDDY. Patients seem genuinely to like Buddy—especially now that it's taken to speaking plain English. In the beginning, the computer was programmed to ask patients to enter yes or no for such symptoms as edema and palpitations. Buddy now inquires about swelling and heart flutters instead.

So far, Buddy has been used by 64 patients—most of whom are suffering from heart problems—under the care of 22 different doctors, for a total of 24,216 operating hours. The prognosis is good: The system not only won FDA approval and a U.S. patent, but users are impressed with its performance. Patrick Smith, a cofounder and president of New England Critical Care Inc., a rapidly growing national home-care company, began experimenting with Buddy in the summer of 1988. The company now has a dozen doctors using Buddy to monitor patients, and Smith expects to add more networks. "The biggest difficulty is hesitation from doctors, not over the system itself, but over whether cardiac patients ought to be treated at home at all," Smith says. "The medical community traditionally is slow to accept new modes of treatment. But once that acceptance is there, rapid growth can follow."

Buddy's ultimate success also depends in part on whether insurance companies will agree to cover its cost. If not, home-care agencies may be reluctant to install the system. Over the long run, Buddy is cheaper than any alternative at about $20 per day for each patient, but the initial investment that home-care providers must lay out—up to $90,000 for a system that can handle 10 patients simultaneously—may prove unappealing if insurers turn thumbs down.

"Insurance reimbursement is a big hurdle for any venture in health care these days," Paul Judy observes. A former CEO of the securities firm A.G. Becker & Co., Judy was Buddy's first major backer and now sits on the company's board of directors. "The key is to get yourself wired in with the big, reputable home-care organizations that are already submitting a lot of insurance claims and whose judgment the insurers trust. And the fact that Buddy is designed to reduce costs, at a time when that is so critical, is a real advantage."

Getting wired into the claims system isn't simple, and it takes time—anywhere from six months to two years, depending on whose estimates you believe. But Buddy Systems's quest for widespread acceptance, and the insurance dollars that will come with it, is picking up speed. With more than 5,500 separate home-care agencies and about 15,000 doctors' groups in the United States, the company can't hope to make its pitch to every one. Instead, Manning is aiming to get national distribution by forging contracts with large regional customers who will buy and use hundreds of systems in dozens of states as part of their existing treatment programs. That plan has two advantages: It obviates the need for Buddy Systems to hire a big in-house sales force, and it will disseminate the product in enough places, with enough established claims-filing groups, to grab insurers' attention. Manning is now negotiating with 12 such megacustomers. He predicts that at least 3 of them will sign on by the end of 1989. To date, though, he has sold only two of the $90,000 systems.

Further down the road, Manning anticipates other as yet unexplored uses for Buddy's technology. One possible market is drug manufacturers, who could use a Buddy-like system to keep track of patients in clinical trials of new drugs. Another potential customer base is nursing homes, where Buddy could reduce the need for costly nursing staff by helping residents do routine tests themselves.

In Manning's view, tapping such potential will require a twofold effort. "We need to keep listening to our customers' reactions and suggestions," he says. "And we need to respond by continuing to innovate. If we can refine Buddy and perhaps come up with new versions of the system to meet different needs, we can remain the leader in the field even after new competitors come in."

For a man who still has a lot to prove and whose own projections don't show Buddy turning a profit until 1990, Manning has lost none of the excitement that made him quit McKinsey. It's contagious, too. Walter McNerney, a past president of Blue Cross/Blue Shield and currently professor of health policy at Northwestern University, has advised Manning since Buddy System's birth. "Tom really believes in what he's doing, and his energy and enthusiasm have gotten this thing as far as it is now," McNerney says. "If it keeps passing muster with the medical community, as it has so far, it's got a good chance of succeeding." Once McNerney's former employers and their ilk agree to foot the bill, Buddy could be a $200-million baby.

Research assistance was provided by Leslie Brokaw.

"I'm concerned about barriers to entry. It would seem that someone in the EKG business, a Hewlett-Packard or somebody, could knock this thing off. And they have a whole lot more resources."

—Peter Santeusanio

FINANCIER

PETER SANTEUSANIO
Partner at Hambro International Venture Fund, a $150-million Boston venture capital firm; has been on boards of three companies selling to doctors and hospitals

I think Buddy Systems has a next-to-impossible task in selling to doctors. Consider the question of liability. If patients stay in the hospital, then the liabilities are shared by the nurses and the hospitals; if they go home, potentially more of the liability falls onto the doctor. And the last thing in the world doctors want is more liability.

I'm also concerned about barriers to entry. It's not clear what's patented here. The people at Buddy allude to patent protection, but I think the barriers are, at best, questionable. Much of their data—blood pressure, weight—can pretty easily be gathered in other ways. Maybe the EKG is the one thing that they could put some barriers around, although I'm not sure. It would seem that someone in the EKG business, a Hewlett-Packard or somebody—and there's fierce competition in this industry—could knock this thing off. And they have a whole lot more resources.

I question Buddy's ability to market without a large direct-sales force. I would say they're going to have to establish credibility and a reference base with doctors—and that's expensive and takes a lot of time. You have to sell direct. The selling expense budgeted in the financial projection is not a particularly large percentage of sales, and I think that's unrealistic.

I think it's impossible to make money at this business in a year. Buddy Systems is going to have to put 50% to 100% of the top line into selling. In companies like this, sales costs are very high initially—I don't see any way it can put money on the bottom line next year. Which is not bad; a venture capitalist is going to look at this and say there's no way they *should* be able to. But that they're showing they can ramp up that bottom line in a relatively short period of time suggests to me a significant. . . I don't know if the word is naïveté or ignorance or what. It calls into question whether they realize what has to happen to be able to sell to this market.

CUSTOMER

ARTHUR J. BERMAN
Director of medicine, Lawrence Hospital, Bronxville, N.Y.; past president, Westchester Academy of Medicine

What they've done well is simplify the procedure and recognize the market in terms of patients who may have difficulty even recalling when to take medications and who find any kind of machine or high-tech instrument threatening.

But would I recommend it be purchased? I don't know that I would. Physicians are conservative in that they make decisions based on judgment, and they may feel that judgment is interfered with by having just a few pieces of paper and bits of information to make decisions on. We need clinical information: whether the patient is short of breath or looks ashen, whether the lungs are clear. Doctors need to feel they know what the patient *looks* like. I'm not sure how big a hurdle this will create for Buddy Systems.

It's not the cost that might present a problem; for a hospital I think $90,000 is small potatoes. I just don't think general hospitals, especially given the question of physician confidence, will want to get involved with it unless they see it as a business venture they can profit from. It might do OK, but it wouldn't be anything I'd think every patient discharged with a cardiological problem would use.

CUSTOMER

KATHEEN DODD

Corporate director, home-care services, American Nursing Resources Inc., an Inc. *500 nursing-care company in Overland Park, Kans.*

Providing another high-tech product in the home is creative and quite ingenious. I see the future of patient management moving from an acute-care setting into a home setting. But I wouldn't buy this system. I don't see that we would have any incentive whatsoever to put it

in our agencies. They would either cut down the number of visits I would be able to charge to a payer for the nurse or add to my costs for the person I've got to have in my office to call patients and process the information.

HMOs, however, *could* have a real need for this. They could determine the cost benefit of paying for a system to be put into a patient's house and then subcontracting a home-care agency like ours to monitor it. That way, the HMO would be paying for it, and we'd just help provide their services.

I can almost assure you Medicare is not going to pick up the bill for these systems. HMOs are much more sensitive than Medicare to the cost-containment arguments. Their livelihood depends on how judicious they are with their fiscal management. Medicare will see the systems as adding to the already high cost of managing the Medicare population. *I* think the cost-effectiveness argument has a lot of validity, but the federal government doesn't deal in reality. It's possible for Manning to get it to see the cost-savings benefits, but it's going to take a long time.

CUSTOMER

LAWRENCE I. SOSNOW

President, Patient Care Inc., a $23-million chain of home-care agencies based in New York City

Manning is way out in front in terms of timing. Other companies are beginning to develop systems like this—AT&T is working on one—but he has the advantage of getting there first. The second thing he did right was recognize the labor shortage home-care agencies are dealing with. This machine can save nurses' time, which helps spread the available labor over a larger number of patients.

But I'm concerned that insurers aren't reimbursing home-care providers for use of this system yet. To get Medicare or Medicaid reimbursement, you have to have generated a lot of convincing data; you must be able to *prove* that this will save money. For Manning to build a statistical track record, he may have to approach the insurers on a case-by-case basis at first. That is, go straight to an individual patient's carrier and say, "Here's proof that if this patient goes home from the hospital and uses this system, you'll save X number of dollars."

Making that case is partly a matter of getting the right personnel. Manning should hire somebody with a lot of experience working with insurers, who really knows the reimbursement business. Manning himself doesn't have the background—the credibility—to approach insurers. He probably doesn't have the time, either. But it's essential. Without reimbursement a lot of potential customers won't make the purchase.

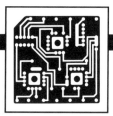

DECISIONS, DECISIONS

*Unschooled in the ways of commerce,
scientist Michael Kuperstein finds himself the owner of a
technology with unlimited applications. Now all he
needs to do is choose the right niche*

BY EDWARD O. WELLES

B etween the business plan and the marketplace lies the reality, as Michael Kuperstein has discovered since opening Neurogen Laboratories Inc. in January 1988. When idea meets customer, things change. Fate intercedes. Markets open, close, and shift. All this surprised Kuperstein, who never intended to turn his grant-funded research operation into a business in the first place, let alone worry what his key markets would be. Those intentions didn't last long.

Kuperstein, then 34, with a Ph.D. in brain science from the Massachusetts Institute of Technology, had motives more academic than mercenary in starting Neurogen Labs. He couldn't find a good tenured job at a university in the Boston area, so he set up Neurogen in Brookline, Mass., as a private institute to further his research on neural networks—computer solutions based on how the

---

Neurogen's technology enables computers to read handwritten numbers

278   BUSINESS PRODUCTS

brain works. Conventional computers are programmed with expertise that lets them perform specific tasks. Neural network computers, meanwhile, are programmed to learn from experience and figure out the correct course of action—much as humans use their brains.

Soon after Kuperstein got the lab up and running in early 1988, the angst started to surface. "My first thought was, Oh, no, what do I do now? How am I going to survive?" When would the grant money dry up? As Kuperstein got deeper into the research, a way out presented itself. "Gee, there's a lot more here than I first thought. The opportunity to commercialize what I was doing was tremendous." It was time to think not just about science but about business. In August 1988 Neurogen grew a mercantile arm, Neurogen Inc. Kuperstein suddenly found himself an entrepreneur—albeit one with a problem. Owner of a proprietary technology with seemingly limitless applications, he had to choose which to pursue. Where was Neurogen's market?

Kuperstein had to find a customer.

Neural networks have applications in four basic fields, two of which—robotic control and pattern recognition—were options available to Neurogen. In robotic control, neural networks guide robots, making them more versatile in a factory setting because the robot can actually learn from its environment and modify its behavior. In pattern recognition, neural networks use computer-imaging technology to identify anything from targets to tumors.

For Kuperstein, this is where the road first forked. If Neurogen were to survive as a business, he had to make a choice and travel down one path or the other.

Kuperstein chose pattern recognition. The choice might seem odd. The year before, Kuperstein had developed the world's first neural network robot. He had garnered a lot of praise and press for doing so. But by the time Neurogen was up and running, the robot wasn't. It was still a prototype. Getting the robot into production would take more time and money than Neurogen had. Even though his heart lay with the robot, Kuperstein knew he could get to market much faster with a pattern-recognition product.

But what exactly would that product be?

Kuperstein had no idea. Instinctively, he set out to copy another computer-imaging company's product. He would create an electronic stylus with which stock traders could record transactions. The nation's stock exchanges would be his market. But in the midst of his research a serendipitous, eureka sort of moment interceded, presenting Kuperstein with an application that others had yet to crack—the

EXECUTIVE SUMMARY

THE COMPANY:
Neurogen Inc.,
Brookline, Mass.

CONCEPT:
Develop and market
a technology that
enables computers
to read handwritten
numbers

PROJECTIONS:
Sales of $800,000
in 1990, $20
million in 1992.
Break-even in first
year, aftertax profit
of 11% in 1992

HURDLES:
Establishing a
presence in the
product's large,
bureaucratic mar-
kets, among them
banking, credit-card
companies, and
the U.S. Postal
Service; lack of
market research

recognition of handwriting by a computer.

Within two weeks after that revelation Kuperstein had completely refocused Neurogen's mission and written a program that could recognize four characters. He was on his way to devising a computer program that could read handwritten numbers. Kuperstein knew this could be done in a relatively short period of time with a limited amount of money. Kuperstein stopped thinking about styluses and the stock market.

By April 1989 Kuperstein had a production prototype of a product called Inscript. He also had added two more employees. Arthur Gingrande Jr. became Neurogen's vice-president of marketing and sales. Jerry Fisher became vice-president of product development. Neurogen Inc. was formed with Kuperstein, Gingrande, and Fisher as the company's founders. Betweeen June and February the three of them raised $200,000 privately to keep the company going.

Inscript is a deceptively simple-looking device, a collection of off-the-shelf semiconductors mounted on a PC board along with Neurogen's proprietary software. This simple array, however, masks the considerable brain work programmed into the software. Added on to any IBM-PC/AT–based scanning technology, Inscript can read virtually any handwritten digit at the rate of 15 characters per second. It can do so as long as that digit is "segmented," or not touching another digit. It can also read dashes, periods, and commas.

Now how could the company begin to find its niche? Where were Inscript's customers? The problem for Neurogen was they were everywhere. The company—unknowingly at first—had stepped into a megamarket, the forms-processing industry.

Americans write 50 billion checks a year. They charge everything in sight, each time attaching their signature to a telltale set of numbers. They fill out countless forms—medical, insurance, taxes. They annually send 170 billion pieces of mail to one another, each bearing a simple five- or nine-digit zip code. This torrent of paper needs to be processed by someone.

The companies this unenviable task has fallen to have come to rely on an army of key-entry operators, drudge workers engaged in a dreary task. For them the tedium is unrelenting. For their employers the cost of all this labor is equally onerous. They would like nothing better than to cut the human being out of the paper loop.

Neurogen's product had manifest appeal. For some 25 years giant technology companies had been laboring to solve the riddle of handwritten character recognition. Now Neurogen, a comparative gnat, had seemed to do so with Inscript—and at a reasonable price. The PC board, the software that drives it, and the necessary support from Neurogen cost a client $60,000. Volume users need more than one board, but they also get volume discounts. As a general rule, buying Inscript entails a onetime, nonrecurring expense that, Kuperstein claims, a user can earn back in four to nine months, depending on the volume of data processed.

It fell to Arthur Gingrande to open up the market in the spring of 1989. "We figured that if I showed this to enough end-users we'd find out where the demand was," he recalls. "We wanted to let the market tell us what we ought to sell. Then we'd react. It was a case of dynamic positioning."

The company had no precise list of who would want Inscript and in what order. "There was no market research available on this," says Gingrande. It did, however, foresee seven large markets into which it could sell: banking, insurance, sales ordering, credit-card companies, mutual funds, the U.S. Postal Service, and the Internal Revenue Service. Getting a foothold in these big industries seemed impossible, given that Neurogen was little more than three guys in a second-story walk-up office.

As Neurogen set about getting into the market, it imagined that the banking industry would offer the "the quickest entry point," for two reasons. First, banks had the necessary volume. They process checks by the carload. Volume translates into huge labor costs. Neurogen could clearly save banks a lot of money.

Second, the banks by dint of their size and needs also had another critical characteristic. They had invested in the necessary "enabling" computer technology that Inscript needed in order to integrate into the banks' systems.

Yet for all that recommended the banks to Neurogen, they lacked a certain intangible—the willingness to take a risk. Recalls Gingrande: "They would say, 'IBM is already taking care of this for us,' or 'Banctec already has the problem well in hand.' I'm not sure they really understood what we had."

Undeterred, Neurogen shifted its focus. It pitched those banks' vendors, the systems integrators and value-added resellers that sold computer solutions to the banks. "They were all interested in our technology," says Kuperstein, "primarily to see how far along we were. And by the nature of the questions they asked us we could deduce how far along *they* were." The answer, Kuperstein believed, was not far.

Neurogen then went back to the banks to put pressure on them through their vendors. "We told them we could deliver what they wanted today," says Gingrande. This time the banks, with their vendors' endorsement of Neurogen, took notice. Their interest was further piqued by a very favorable review of Inscript in a leading industry newsletter that had appeared in the interim.

But then a technical problem intervened, one that Neurogen had yet to allocate much of its scarce resources toward solving. When people write a dollar amount on a check, they often crowd the numbers. They fear that someone else might insert an additional digit. On checks, many handwritten numbers touch. In the jargon of the pattern-recognition business, they are "unsegmented." No machine has yet been able to pull two overlapping numbers apart and identify each of them fast enough to satisfy customers. "We were really naïve," recalls Gingrande.

This rude discovery confronted Neurogen with a hard choice. It could plow its limited resources into solving the overlapping character problem, and thereby crack the primary and hugely promising check-processing market. But doing so meant neglecting other, more accessible markets. The alternative was to develop other markets and put banking on the back burner until the company had more resources at hand.

That's what Neurogen did.

It took us a long time to find out a simple fact," says Arthur Gingrande. "The attitude a person has about a form determines how legibly he will write on it." The banking experience got the founders at Neuro-

NEUROGEN INC. PROJECTED OPERATING STATEMENT
(in $ thousands)*

	1990	1992
SALES	$800	$20,000
Cost of sales	280	7,000
Research & development	160	2,400
Selling and general & administrative	200	3,000
Customer support	160	4,000
TOTAL EXPENSES	800	16,400
OPERATING PROFIT	0	3,600
Taxes	0	1,400
PROFIT AFTER TAXES	0	2,200
% profit after taxes	0	11%

* *Inc.* estimates based on Neurogen forecasts and market information

gen to debating a now-obvious question: If check writers were paranoid, then who, when it came to writing numbers on a form, was not?

The answer came at an electronic imaging trade show in October 1989, when Neurogen and a large sales-order entry company—which was looking for a faster way to process its forms—bumped into each other.

When Kuperstein, Gingrande, and Fisher studied the sales-order forms, they liked what they saw. The forms had a separate box for each character. The numbers *had to be* segmented. They realized that sales-people had the opposite motivation of check writers. They need to write clearly so the order gets entered correctly and they get paid a commission.

In the order-entry company, Neurogen had a live contact. A development contract between the two companies resulted. Neurogen, in return for a fee, would try to customize Inscript so it would integrate with the larger company's technology. In the course of the work, a potentially lucrative secondary market opened up for Neurogen.

Neurogen's partner in the form-reading effort, it turned out, also printed and corrected standardized tests. With Neurogen's help, it could redesign the answer form—and potentially remake the standardized-test industry. It made little sense to have rows of five small spaces arrayed across the page, with the student marking just one. If a system that could read a handwritten number was available, it would be simpler to have the student write one of five numbers in just one space. This would save paper. It would also diminish every student's nightmare: recording a page full of wrong answers by improperly aligning questions and answers.

Banks had seemed a hot market and had not immediately panned out. Sales order-form processing was down the list and standardized tests scarcely conceived of in Neurogen's first business plan; yet those markets suddenly seemed full of promise. The U.S. Postal Service, meanwhile, fell somewhere in between.

Neurogen had always considered the post office a potential bonanza. One hundred seventy billion pieces of mail go through the system each year, each with a five- or nine-digit zip code. Letter writers tend to be more like salespeople than check writers. Write the zip code neatly—no numbers touching—and the letter will get there. Technically, this market seemed within reach.

But as promising as the post office seemed from a volume standpoint, it was positively daunting as a bureaucracy. It was an institution wrapped in red tape. Dealing with the post office meant a long ramp-up time on any project, something a small company like Neurogen could ill afford. On top of that, the post office has three different sections that see to its various procurement needs.

Neurogen decided it couldn't afford to penetrate the post office on its own. Its strategy would be to find an enabling partner—a bigger, savvier company that already serviced the post office. Neurogen could ride the coattails of such a systems integrator.

Through a chain of contacts, Neurogen found Scan-Code Inc., a systems integrator that sold systems to companies that put bar codes representing nine-digit zip codes on first-class letters. Two years ago Scan-Code didn't exist. The company had formed quickly after Congress passed legislation privatizing parts of the postal system. Under the new law, the government paid private companies 4¢ for five-digit zip codes and 5¢ for nine-digit zips it presorted.

Introduced by Scan-Code, Neurogen got a two-hour meeting with a postal rate commissioner and an assistant postmaster general and got its chance to show off the technology. The post office gave Inscript 2,000 handwritten zip codes to read. Inscript rejected 30% for being mechanically unreadable and in need of human handling. Of the remaining 70% it read 99.5% correctly. The newer, faster Inscript is capable of reading 80% of five-digit codes, and of that 80%, 99% would be read correctly. Scan-Code and Neurogen now have a development contract to work on mail-sorting solutions.

Another market presented itself when a year ago a major credit-card company announced an effort to upgrade its technology in order to read handwritten characters. After a year spent probing the bureaucracy of this large company, meeting with one vice-president after another, and demonstrating its technology, Neurogen landed a development contract.

In the process, Neurogen kicked over another possible market. It assumed that the technology available for reading typewritten characters—optical character recognition (OCR)—was mature and adequate. That was not really true. New typefaces, photocopies, laser printing—all resist recognition by machine. So do the imprints made by the embossed numbers on credit cards after they have broken down with use. Neurogen's technology can read this "degraded" type. This submarket, called OCR cleanup, is one that Neurogen had totally ignored at the outset. Now it accounts for about one-quarter of its business.

Neurogen now has seven employees. It added two software engineers in March and hired a chief executive officer, Robert Tabor, in April. Tabor's job includes honing the company's mission and revising the business plan. He will try to determine which leads thus far are promising, which are dead ends.

In rethinking what its business should be, Neurogen has recently targeted six major market niches it wants to fill. These are, in order of their current accessibility: forms processing, OCR cleanup, credit-card processing, the mail, remittance processing, and check processing.

Next, the company identified the enabling technological developments that would have to occur before it could penetrate each niche. These developments were then put on a time line, so Neurogen could guess what niches would open up in which order.

This process accomplished two things. It made it easier for the company to allocate its scarce resources in solving various technical problems, and it helped determine how much capital Neurogen would need in order to meet the timetable.

By this fall the company expects to have raised a round of financing from venture capitalists totaling between $1 million and $3 million. "We need a cushion," says Kuperstein. "Right now we're in a position of strength. We can raise money on our terms, not theirs."

In the meantime, his company will begin generating sales revenues. Neurogen, which made its first sale and installation last February, projects sales of roughly $800,000 in 1990. The company thus far has prospects for 23 separate installations. In 1991 Neurogen expects sales to grow to $6 million. Kuperstein bases this figure on having 5 to 10 volume customers placing orders of anywhere from $500,000 to $2 million each. That projection works out to a gross of between $2.5 million and $20 million. Kuperstein reasons that $6 million is appropriately conservative.

Those sales, a number of them to *Fortune* 500 companies, will create a critical mass and give his company legitimacy, believes Kuperstein. Other large customers will then surface. Sales in 1992 will jump to $20 million, $40 million the year after, and $75 million the year after that. At $75 million, Neurogen expects to have between 30 and 40 customers placing orders of between $1 million and $2 million.

Kuperstein will not disclose the company's profit margin, other than to say that at the outset it will be "very large." He bases this on the belief that Inscript is a unique product for which there is considerable demand. "Our pricing policy is based on the labor savings we will provide." Currently, the cost of each document processed by a human in a large company ranges between 0.5¢ and 1.5¢. When you're a big bank or credit-card company, that adds up fast. Kuperstein has based Neurogen's financial projections on the experiences of two hypergrowth companies, Microsoft and Sun Microsystems. The cost of sales in software product companies such as Microsoft is quite low, so gross profit typically exceeds 50%.

At $800,000 in sales, Kuperstein allows, "we're breaking even." He adds that in this first year of sales, Neurogen's major cost—engineering and manufacturing—will amount to only between 12% and 15% of gross sales. As time goes on, competition will doubtless intensify and margins will come down.

Hiring a CEO will allow Michael Kuperstein to assume a role, along with the chairmanship, that he's more comfortable with, that of chief technologist. Much of his time will be spent doing research—in order to assure his company a future. Kuperstein envisions the research side of the business, Neurogen Labs, growing to about 10 researchers and forging a symbiotic relationship with Neurogen Inc. Neurogen Labs has already received seven grants totaling $400,000 from government agencies to further its work on neural network robots. Kuperstein sees licensing its inventions to Neurogen Inc., which will then reciprocate with royalty payments—which, in turn, will contribute to the funding of further research.

Kuperstein doesn't worry about falling behind on the technology— so vital to keeping the company from being a one-product phenomenon. He is an editor of the two best-known journals on neural network technology. "I know the field. I'm at the pulse of the community."

"Michael's famous," says Arthur Gingrande. "He's one of the top people in his field. We have drawers full of résumés from people all over the country who want to work with him."

Kuperstein projects an assurance that borders on arrogance. While he knows of perhaps 30 to 40 small companies in neural network technology, he is not worried. He says, in fact, they are off the mark. Almost all, he claims, are providing "tools"—neural network technology. Neurogen, by contrast, says Kuperstein, offers "solutions"—the harnessing of neural network technology to resolve specific problems.

As for the goliaths, Kuperstein isn't worried about them, either. He plans to get far enough ahead of them that they will be moved to forge strategic alliances with Neurogen, not squash it. At the moment, Neurogen seems to have that edge. At a recent imaging trade show—the largest one of the year—Neurogen shared a booth with Citicorp. Both Kuperstein and Gingrande found it mildly embarrassing to find people flocking to their display booth, oftentimes leaving representatives of Citicorp with little to do but twiddle their thumbs and stare into space.

That kind of attention leaves Michael Kuperstein, an academic with no prior business experience, brimming with confidence—something he doesn't lack to begin with. "When people see our demonstration they're blown away," he says. He believes he has something the world wants. Does that mean someday soon he sees himself presiding over a company in a large, gleaming building with hundreds of employees?

Kuperstein answers that one without a moment's hesitation: "Yup."

Stay tuned.

"I hope the CEO they've hired is market driven. These guys have to recognize that they can't just develop this technology and see who wants to buy it."

–Joseph S. Tibbetts Jr.

FINANCIER

PATRICK J. SANSONETTI

Managing partner, Advent International, a Boston venture capital firm managing $1.3 billion worldwide, with early-stage investments in high-tech companies

Looking at this deal is like evaluating a balance sheet: There's always some good news and some bad news.

Kuperstein seems to be approaching the organization of the company the right way. He's hired key operating people, and he's putting together a nucleus of development people who can attack more markets with this product line. He's smart to recognize that he is a technologist and hire a CEO to run the company.

But these guys are clearly chasing too many markets. What's happened—and this is not atypical—is they're being driven by the technology. They've got to get this down to one or two, maybe three markets, not six. They're trying to be too big too soon.

They've got to utilize good market research, and if they don't have it they should get it or hire expert consultants. A well-conceived product marketing plan would save them a lot of time and capital. It appears that they've been fooling around for a couple years looking for a market—a classic problem.

If I were investing, I would have the company concentrate on selling through the integrators and the value-added resellers; it's a good approach for this company. The product seems like it would be difficult to sell on a direct basis. The integrators and resellers would enable Neurogen to provide a focused product to the market, as opposed to technology looking for a market.

The banks, the credit-card guys, the check processors, and the post office don't want to deal with a mom-and-pop company. They want to have somebody install a system, keep it running, and ultimately bring in a new generation of product. A small company can't provide this security blanket.

Going from zero to $6 million to $20 million to $75 million is wildly optimistic. Also, basing projections on Microsoft's success is not realistic. Microsoft had significant revenues and profits because it attacked a very fast-growing, broad-based market—it had IBM in its camp. These guys don't.

I think the company will succeed, but it's going to take it longer and require more capital than Kuperstein thinks.

COMPETITOR

MICHAEL THIEMANN

Vice-president for new-business development, HNC Inc., San Diego, a $10-million manufacturer of application products that use neural networks

Most of the applications they've targeted are operations oriented, and those people tend to be hard-nosed and conservative when it comes down to buying anything. That's bad, because I think this is a young company selling a lot of sizzle while other people are selling steak—solving customer problems in very difficult operations areas. Making broad claims without being able to back them up with something that can be used immediately at the operations level might cause Neurogen a lot of trouble.

I think they've underestimated the character segmentation problem. It's not an area you can plug an engineer into for a couple weeks and get a solution. IBM has been working on it for about 25 years, using a lot of resources, and hasn't solved it.

If they can solve the segmentation problem as well as the character-recognition problem, then they can package that into a product that is very high value added. But as things stand Neurogen is offering only a piece of the puzzle. In making his growth forecasts, Kuperstein likens his company to Microsoft and Sun Microsystems. Well, they were offering the lion's share of the total solution. Neurogen right now isn't.

FINANCIER

FRED HANEY

Senior vice-president, 3i Ventures, a venture capital firm in Newport Beach, Calif.

Kuperstein's attitude toward venture capital, and how appealing the company will be to VCs, seems slightly cavalier. I suppose it depends on how proprietary the technology really is, but technology is moving very rapidly in this world, and they could get leapfrogged by a competitor. And there's a market acceptance risk: They're attacking large, high-volume markets with cost-sensitive applications, and that's a sell that will take some time. So I don't think it's as close to a slam dunk as the founders seem to think.

Bottom line, I think the company's managers have a dilemma. I've got the sense they would like to bootstrap the operation—not raise too much capital, not bring on too many people, not build up the infrastructure, not give up a very large percentage of their stock. If that's the case, then they really need to focus their attention on one market, one application, and carve out a very strong competitive position in that small niche area, at least initially.

I think each of the six specific markets is probably perfectly legitimate. If anything, I would worry that they will not be easy to track. People may be quick to buy one system to test it and see how it works, but the real test for the company will be whether it can sustain itself until customers start to make multiple purchases.

OBSERVER

JOSEPH S. TIBBETTS JR.

Managing partner, Price Waterhouse's Entrepreneurial Services Center, Cambridge, Mass., a provider of business advisory services to start-up and early-stage companies

The good news for this company is in the recent events, the hiring of a CEO so Kuperstein can stay on the technical side of the business. The CEO needs to be a real business planner and a good tactician. These guys need to recognize that they can't just go out and develop this technology and see who wants to buy it.

After all, they are not only trying to go out and compete. They are on a crusade as well. They have to convince huge customers, who are ingrained in their ways, that what they're doing makes sense. The best way to do it would be to convince an intermediary, a systems integrator, to work with them. They'd have to give up margin, but it's worth giving up some margin to get the business an intermediary can bring.

But they're still doing market R&D. They've let two years slip by, and they still don't know what their market is. Making the discovery about banks and the problem with characters touching when they did is such a fundamental mistake. And the niches they've identified are so huge. It's a misnomer to call these markets niches. They need to focus. Instead of trying to do six different things, they need to stop and say, "This is the one place where we think we can make a dent in the market" and go for it. If they don't, the lack of funds, given what they're trying to do, will kill this company.

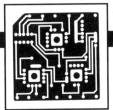

DOWN IN THE DUMP

We're quickly running out of room for our solid waste, and innovative companies like Rusmar Inc. stand to get rich. But can this start-up first navigate through a maze of government regulations?

BY JAY FINEGAN

L et's talk trash. In fact, let's talk 160 million tons of trash—the amount Americans throw out every year. And let's talk about an opportunity.

Anyone who remembers Long Island's vagabond garbage barge of a few years ago knows that the country is fast exhausting landfill space. In 1978 there were some 20,000 landfills. Since then nearly 14,000 have closed. Some got full; others were shut down by regulators. About 6,000 remain, and strict new laws will close 2,000 of those in the next decade. What's worse, so few new landfills are being built—they're difficult and costly to site—that national disposal demands may outstrip capacity by the late 1990s. Northeast and Great Lakes urban centers might run out of

Paul Kittle (right), founder, and Paul Russo, VP and general manager, Rusmar Inc.

THE COMPANY:
Rusmar Inc.,
West Chester, Pa.

CONCEPT:
Exploit the landfill crisis by making and selling a patented foam to replace the dirt spread daily over dumped garbage, saving landfill operators space and money

PROJECTIONS:
Small profit on 1990 sales of $2 million; pretax profit of $1.5 million on 1994 sales of $7.8 million

HURDLES:
Persuading regulators to approve foam's use; convincing operators of its cost-effectiveness; battling giant 3M, which has introduced a competitive product

space by 1993. Speeding the crunch date is a regulatory requirement that landfills, each night, cover the day's trash with at least six inches of soil. The intent is sensible. The soil controls odors, litter, and vectors, landfill speak for insects and rodents. The trouble is, the soil consumes as much as 30% of landfill capacity. In some places soil itself is so scarce that landfill operators are buying farms just for their dirt. A landfill manager in Ventura, Calif., is actually trying to buy a mountain.

Enter Rusmar Inc., a West Chester, Pa., start-up aiming to replace all that soil with a patented, shaving-cream-like foam. If ever a product matched a need, you'd think, this is it. The foam is biodegradable, environmentally benign, and just as effective as soil in suppressing odor, litter, and vectors. In most cases it is cheaper than dirt and much easier to apply.

But most important, foam occupies virtually zero space. It breaks down to the landfill equivalent of bathtub ring. By reducing the need for soil, it can extend landfill longevity by years and thus increase profitability.

According to Rusmar's calculations, for instance, the average landfill requires at least 185 cubic yards of soil for daily cover, space that could generate about $5,800 in revenues if used for trash instead— or more than $1.5 million a year. If soil must be purchased and transported, at costs of up to $12 a cubic yard, landfill expenses run even higher. As the crunch worsens and garbage-truck dumping fees escalate, the value of landfill space will rise, and the economics of using foam will grow more compelling still.

Yet however urgent the landfill problem appears, founder Paul A. Kittle stumbled on it almost by accident. In 1985, after pitching a plan to use foam to control odors at hazardous-waste sites, Kittle was approached by a listener. "If you do foams," he said, "why don't you invent one to cover landfills?"

Kittle was skeptical. He had come out of the University of California at Berkeley in 1963 with a Ph.D. in chemistry. Between stints with

Rohm & Haas and ARCO Chemical, he'd worked at Apollo Technologies, a small specialty-chemical manufacturer in New Jersey, where he first became intrigued by foams. By the early 1980s he was a self-employed headhunter of technical talent. Foam technology, though, still fascinated him to the point that he'd obtained a patent for a foam to control coal dust and was working on one for odor suppression.

But landfills? Landfills would require a covering that holds up overnight, and foam doesn't last that long. At least not the foams in existence at the time.

But Kittle was convinced the landfill opportunity was real. He didn't mind the idea of holing up in a lab to tinker with the problems it presented. "I think if you are a well-trained Ph.D. chemist and you want to see if you can cut it, then you try to invent a technology and take it to the marketplace and make it a success," he says.

He rented a small space in West Chester and went to work. Methodically, Kittle mapped out the requirements. The material had to be a water-soluble, single-component product, so it could be sold as a concentrate and delivered by tank truck. It had to be so innocuous in its chemical composition that no one would question its safety. And it had to be so cheap that a landfill could cover a square foot of trash for 5¢ or 6¢. Ideally, there should be no question that if you used it, you'd save money.

Cut to September 27, 1988, Kittle's 50th birthday and the date his dream began to jell. On that day a group of five Philadelphia investors committed $1 million—half in debentures, half in equity—taking a 55% stake in Rusmar, named after Kittle's parents, Russell and Mary.

Over the previous few years Kittle had struggled with "hundreds of gremlins," he says, to invent and perfect a foam he called AC-645.

When tested, it formed a complete barrier to odor and vapor emissions for up to 36 hours. And he'd managed to make it from environmentally harmless ingredients, chemicals commonly found in cosmetics, detergents, and shampoos. "You could eat this stuff," he notes, "and the worse that would happen is you'd get a case of the runs."

The capital infusion allowed Kittle to get serious. He moved into a larger facility in West Chester and hired Paul Russo, an energetic chemist he'd worked with at Apollo Technologies. Russo, then 36, had experience in management and sales, and would handle everything from strategy to marketing. "Most people thought this would be an instant success," Kittle recalls. And why not? The market looked like a natural. His business plan, projecting first-year sales of $3 million, practically oozed optimism. Rusmar, Kittle thought, was on its way.

Russo, as he came on board, was more guarded. He knew that foam faced a rocky reception. Rusmar had to persuade two kinds of customers: the landfill operators who would decide whether to buy the product and the government regulators who had to approve the product. Though introducing any new technology is tough, it can be hellish in the landfill area.

It wasn't as if Russo could win blanket permission from the Environmental Protection Agency to begin selling foam. The EPA sets the macro standards for landfills but leaves micro regulation to the states. And some state regulatory agencies, mostly byzantine bureaucracies, issue permits for use of such products as foam on a case-by-case, site-specific basis. They'd have nothing to gain by issuing permits to landfills and everything to lose if, once approved, the foam had an unforeseen downside.

Landfill operators could easily grasp the value of the product. But would they go to the mat with the state agencies? Not likely. The agencies had enough to tangle with already. On a community-popularity scale, landfills rank near the bottom. Sure, your trash has to go somewhere—preferably somewhere far away. To complicate matters, landfill operators were now facing new national regulations requiring the installation of pumping systems and liners to protect the groundwater, a tremendous burden. They didn't need a fight for foam permits.

The landfill scene itself was diverse and problematic. Russo's best targets were the large landfills in urban areas of the East Coast, Midwest, and West Coast, those taking in 500 to 10,000 tons a day with fees upward of $65 a ton. He estimated their number at 300 to 500, constituting a potential market of $45 million to $75 million a year—if the landfills could get permits.

Even beyond securing permits and convincing customers of foam's

FINANCIALS

RUSMAR INC. PROJECTED OPERATING STATEMENT
(in $ thousands)

	1990	1994
REVENUES		
Chemical foam compound	$725	$6,472
Application equipment, sale/lease	1,269	1,285
TOTAL REVENUES	**1,994**	**7,757**
COST OF REVENUES		
Chemical foam compound	248	2,542
Application equipment	385	795
Commissions	128	729
TOTAL COST OF REVENUES	**761**	**4,066**
GROSS PROFIT	**1,233**	**3,691**
GENERAL & ADMINISTRATIVE	**1,225**	**2,148**
EARNINGS BEFORE INTEREST & TAX	**8**	**1,543**

benefits, though, was the challenge of getting landfills to buy or lease the necessary application equipment. Foam for industrial use can't be sold in cans. It requires a large, specialized piece of machinery, outfitted with an air compressor, a pump, hoses, a solution-storage tank, and a manifold. Machines like that cost $100,000 to $150,000 depending on size, and you don't buy them off the shelf—they have to be built. Early on Kittle had designed and fabricated a couple of units that are still operating at hazardous-waste sites in the South. And the cost wasn't outrageous by landfill standards. "They pay $250,000 for a big dozer," says Russo, now the company's vice-president and general manager, "and earth movers go for around $350,000." Still, that was big money for a start-up. And Russo couldn't sell any foam until he could build the machines for sale or lease.

To top it all off, foam—specifically its application—had a poor reputation. The marketing and technology rights of the first company in the field, a California outfit called Sanifoam, were acquired by 3M in February 1989, shortly after Russo joined Rusmar. At a test application in Chester, Va., the 3M/Sanifoam gear proved so troublesome that landfill operations manager James McCook decided not to use it.

"It would take four or five hours of maintenance after using the system for a 30-minute application," McCook says. "The chemicals would solidify in the machinery, and they'd have to disassemble all that stuff to clean it out. This just wasn't practical."

It was here that Russo perceived an edge. Though 3M's entry into the field was threatening, it also served to legitimize the market. Rusmar's single-component foam was about half as expensive as 3M's double-component product, and it didn't jam up the equipment. "This is a process-driven industry in which machinery and its ease of use is key," Russo says. "Landfill guys don't care about the foam. They see the device—that's what they use. So the real object of the sale becomes the equipment. You are selling them a machine that will help them solve a problem. It just so happens that along with the foam machine comes the foam chemical."

The chemical itself, with R&D costs largely past, could be a money machine all its own. It could generate gross margins of 70% or more, enough that Russo would need only six sales to reach break-even. An average landfill covers 10,000 square feet. At 6¢ a square foot at a depth of three inches, foam sales to the landfill would reach about $150,000 a year. Six customers like that would yield revenues of $900,000 a year, enough to sustain Rusmar. But in Pennsylvania, which requires six inches of foam depth, six customers would provide $1.8 million a year, growing the company even faster.

Pennsylvania was the obvious place to start. Rusmar was already there, and as it is a tough regulatory state, any successful field trials might help crack other markets. Soon after taking the job, Russo traveled to Harrisburg to meet with officials at the state Department of Environmental Resources (DER).

"The regulators need to be sold on this like anybody else, and the way to sell them is to get them involved," he says. "I asked what it would take to get the foam approved, and they described this incredibly long and complicated process. I asked if we couldn't just do a demonstration. It would give the department an opportunity to see the technology and also give some landfill operators a chance to see it in action."

William Pounds, a senior DER official, agreed. He cleared Rusmar for a June 1989 test at a landfill near Philadelphia. Russo made sure regulators from other regions attended. Among them was Rick Watson, engineering manager of the Delaware Solid Waste Authority, who liked what he saw. He gave Rusmar permission to conduct a small-scale test at Delaware's Central Solid Waste Facility. That went well enough that the facility conducted a successful full-blown, six-month trial, and by the end of June it had agreed to buy the Rusmar system.

When the results of the Philadelphia test proved satisfactory, the DER allowed Rusmar to conduct a second test last December. This one took place at the huge Empire Sanitary Landfill Inc., a privately owned facility near Scranton. Empire is a 600-acre, double-lined, state-of-the-art operation that can handle up to 5,000 tons of trash a day—some 250 trucks' worth.

"We did test strips, and we did our best to make the foam fail," says Ronald Sturgeon, Empire's engineering director. "It was bitter cold, but it didn't freeze. We put it on a sunny slope, and it didn't slide away. Strong winds barely budged it. It did everything that soil did—it just worked beautifully." Empire liked the product so much that it has applied for DER permission to use it on a regular basis.

"It's definitely going to be a benefit," Sturgeon says. "This landfill has a life expectancy of 25 to 38 years, and we think the Rusmar product will extend that by about 2 years. We charge from $48 to $62.50 a ton, so we'd be saving a lot of expensive airspace. It will also free up our trucks for other work."

Rusmar is speculating boldly on the Empire project. It has built a $200,000 foam-application unit to do the job—a self-propelled, tracked number that looks like a cross between an army tank and a fire truck. It's a gamble: Empire will purchase the machine, but only if it gets the state permit. Russo is doing everything in his power to make sure it does, including much of Empire's permit-application work.

Should the Empire contract proceed, Russo plans to parlay it into a major sales edge. Meanwhile, he is pressing on with a vigorous one-man sales crusade in the New England and MidAtlantic states. And he's not neglecting the huge hazardous-waste market—the thousands of chemical lagoons and industrial-waste piles that might need foam sporadically to control toxic vapors and odors. Rusmar has already been awarded the odor-suppression portion of the Boston Harbor cleanup project.

But as Russo sees it, the steady, long-term payoff is in sanitary landfills. He has enlisted the help of a sales rep in Irvine, Calif., to work the West Coast's large but highly regulated landfill market. And he's buttressed that with videos, a direct-mail campaign, and ads in trade publications.

Those efforts have generated some action. Not least is a technology sale and license agreement with Japan's Hodogaya Chemical Co., which will bring Rusmar some $300,000 a year while Hodogaya test-markets the foam in Japan and much more if it blossoms into a fully realized program. That was a significant coup for Rusmar, and Russo made sure it made the local newspapers. "Foam Firm Does Bit for Trade Deficit," read one headline—heady stuff for the tiny outfit.

R usmar operates out of a 16,000-square-foot garage that had been vacated by a trucking company. The whole company is 10 people. In addition to Russo and Kittle, there is an office manager and a young, Berkeley-educated chemical engineer named David Manlowe. Three jacks-of-all-trades craftsmen assemble the pneumatic foam units (PFUs)—the application machines—and provide technical field support. Kittle, whose work attire runs to jeans and flannel shirts, spends his days producing chemicals. The garage is stacked high with drums of supplies from the likes of Dow Chemical Co. and W.R. Grace & Co.

All in all, it's a modest crew to be pitted against mighty 3M, an $18-billion giant that has the deep pockets to play the regulatory waiting game. For now at least Rusmar has the funding to hang in there, but it hasn't always been easy. It cut quickly through the first $1 million—Kittle had dug himself $500,000 in debt developing the product and building the first couple of machines. "We were not cavalier, but perhaps not as cautious as we should have been," Russo confides. "Things got real hairy with the investors—they thought we'd be at break-even in three months."

In October 1989 Kittle was issued a method patent on his foam and the method of dispensing it. That was critical. "There are only a certain number of things that make foam," Kittle says. "The patent makes a broad claim to incorporate as many of these raw-material sources as possible. It's always possible that someone else could invent a brand-new molecule that foams. But how much is it going to cost to produce that, compared with the raw materials that we've got claimed in our patent, for megaton quantities? So it gives us a lock, if you will, a corner on the market for the lowest-cost raw materials. The patent protection is very important, because the chemical world runs on patents."

But start-ups run on money, and Rusmar was in desperate straits last winter. In a bit of serendipity, however, it received $500,000 from A. Duie Pyle Inc., the West Chester trucking company whose garage Rusmar is leasing for $7,300 a month. That infusion gave heart to the original investors, who ponied up an additional $200,000. When the dust settled from the stock reshuffling, Kittle, Pyle, and the Philadelphia group each emerged with about a third of the company.

Last summer Rusmar was courting financial institutions, trying to secure an equipment-construction line of credit to build the PFUs. At the same time, a West Chester bank came through with $120,000 to fund construction of two small foam machines for hazardous-waste applications.

But Rusmar is hardly out of the woods. It badly needs a sales force but can't yet afford one. And it has yet to form an alliance with one of the so-called waste majors—unlike 3M, which has made a cooperative agreement with Waste Management of North America, an operator of 128 large landfills. It's not for lack of trying. Russo has pitched Browning-Ferris Industries Inc. (BFI), Laidlaw Waste Systems Inc., and other landfill biggies to no avail. "I'd love to have one of those," Russo says. "But I can get by selling to the Empires and Delawares. What we need now is credibility and respect."

Still, that's the sort of thing that troubles venture capitalists who have traipsed through Rusmar's garage. "You take a company like BFI—these are rational people," says Rick Defieux, an environmental specialist with Edison Venture Fund, in Lawrenceville, N.J., who looked at the deal. "When they show no interest, you have to wonder why. It makes you think there's something missing."

That something may be rain resistance, no minor detail to landfill operators. While 3M's foam can't be easily applied in a heavy rain, it does form a leathery surface that allows for runoff if rain falls on it after application. That's part of the trade-off for its cumbersome two-component mix. Rusmar's AC-645 can't survive a driving downpour. But then, the Rusmar product appears to be easier and faster to apply, and that's no minor detail to landfill guys, either.

But no matter how the votes come in, Rusmar believes, there'll be enough landfill business to keep both companies happy.

"The problem [for Rusmar's managers] is that any success they do have will require a substantial marketing effort, and right now their marketing is grossly insufficient."

– Rick Defieux

CUSTOMER

JOHN CONAWAY

Solid-waste manager, Ventura Regional Sanitation District, which runs two landfills in Ventura County, Calif.

Rusmar looks to have a good product, but here in California the permit process will be a big pitfall. I'd be using Rusmar's foam right now if it weren't for the regulatory nightmare. We have a severe capacity crunch. But any time you file for a major operational change here—and foam would fit into that category—you need new permits from three separate agencies.

It would cost us more than $1 million just to apply for them, given all the monitoring and documentation they require. I can easily see being required to do a very complicated and expensive series of groundwater tests and surface/air emission tests. Some of these are fly-emergence tests, where you have to get people to come out and actually count the number of flies that emerge prior to using the foam and then after using it. And even then there's no guarantee we'd get approval.

FINANCIER

RICK DEFIEUX

General partner, Edison Venture Fund, Lawrenceville, N.J., a $40-million venture capital firm with a half-dozen investments in environmental companies

If you'll excuse the pun, this company looks pretty good on the surface, but you might find some problems as you dig deeper. It has developed a good product with tangible advantages in application. The problem is that any success it does have will require a substantial marketing effort, and right now its marketing is grossly insufficient. Paul Russo cannot do this alone.

For one thing, trimming the cost of daily cover is not the landfill operator's primary concern today. In many sections of the country, a valid permit in the waste-disposal business is tantamount to a license to steal; this is a very, very profitable industry.

What these landfill guys want to do foremost is keep their permits intact. Cost cutting is less important than staying in compliance with changing regulations. If Rusmar expects to sell its foam on the economics, then the numbers have to be very strong and show an overwhelming benefit. For some landfills, too, switching from soil to foam cover may precipitate a regulatory review of the entire landfill, which no operator would be eager for.

The second reason I think this company needs a substantial marketing effort is that landfill cover is not the regulators' number-one concern, either. Because foam is not environmentally beneficial—it's basically just environmentally equivalent to soil—regulators aren't particularly motivated to spend a lot of time on something that's just going to improve a landfill operator's pretax margin. They have a lot of other issues to think about.

Finally, Rusmar is facing formidable competition; 3M is very capable of outselling it, with Rusmar's rain-resistance disadvantage as a lever.

If Rusmar increases its direct-sales force, it needs very knowledgeable people and needs to focus on two or three or four states and do a full-court press on those agencies. If it simply can't afford to do that, then it's got to get an alliance with companies that know both the operators and regulators—engineering consulting firms, maybe, that know how to deal with regulators.

I thought the revenue line was not outrageously unrealistic. The bottom line, I think, is that it has a shot at building a successful company, but it's got its hands full.

CUSTOMER

RICK WATSON

Engineering manager, Delaware Solid Waste Authority, which operates three state-owned landfills

We recently completed a six-month test of Rusmar's foam at one of our main landfills, and we've decided to stick with it on a full-time basis. The combined cost of the foam and the application machinery is actually slightly higher than soil. Each month we spend $6,200 to lease the machine and about $7,500 on foam. If you looked at it strictly on a daily cost basis, you could not justify using the foam.

What makes it worthwhile is the space savings. Landfill space is tough to get, and we need to maximize what we have. At the landfill where we tested it, soil takes up 30% of the volume. We think the foam will extend the life of that site by at least 10%. The reason it's not longer is that you can't use foam every day. If rain is forecast, you have to revert to soil. You have to use soil on weekends, too. We found that we used the foam an average of 16 days a month.

An extra benefit is labor savings. It takes the crew close to three hours to cover a day's garbage with soil, but only 30 to 45 minutes to do the job with foam. We had experience with Sanifoam before, on a test basis, and it was a pain to apply.

The foam was OK, but the machinery jammed up and created a lot of extra work to clean it out. Rusmar's machinery is very easy to use, and it doesn't jam. That's really one of its strongest selling points. The people who have to use it really like it.

Our main concern is dealing with a start-up. We're concerned that if we buy the application machinery at a cost of $120,000 or so, then we're taking a chance—but Rusmar has offered to minimize that risk by leasing the machinery instead.

CUSTOMER

GARY STEEDE

Manager, Outagamie County Landfill, Appleton, Wis.

I don't agree with the evaluation of Sanifoam, the 3M product. We've used it for five years and never had the kind of problems described here. We're happy with it, and our maintenance has never taken more than an hour.

Still, I would have inquired about Rusmar's foam if I'd known about it. They're talking 5¢ or 6¢ a square foot, whereas we're paying 12¢ to 13¢—so right there I'm interested. But I wasn't even aware that the product existed, and we've been using foam coverings for years. Rusmar needs advertising. It needs to get into more trade shows and publications like *Waste Age* and *Public Works* to make the operators aware this product is available. Otherwise, it's going to have a hard time selling.

It also hasn't addressed the critical question: how long its foam lasts. It mentions 36 hours. The foam we're using now lasts a minimum of three days, and I wouldn't want to go any less than that. We have to alternate our active area every day, so duration is a big, big factor.

A WHOLE NEW GAME

At birth, it's already bigger and richer than most businesses ever get. But like many start-ups, America's first all-sports daily newspaper is gambling on a hunch

BY EDWARD O. WELLES

Ken Kerbs

rank Deford's favorite color is purple, a hue that does not match his prose. A writer for *Sports Illustrated* for 27 years, Deford has been chosen six times as national Sportswriter of the Year. He has also written 10 books and done sports commentary for both TV and radio.

Despite the acclaim he had garnered as America's de facto dean of sports writing, Deford, by the time he was pushing 50, had come to feel the dread that rises in any magazine writer embarking on the same sort of story one too many times. By February 1989 Deford was ready for a break. He had his house on the market and was looking forward to a year in London, during which he would finish a novel. But then came the call from Peter O. Price.

Price was the publisher of *The New York Post,* and in February 1989 he was a harried man. The paper was about to launch its first Sunday edition. After that, Price was looking forward to a well-earned vacation,

---

The National *expects daily circulation of 200,000*

THE COMPANY:
The National,
New York City

CONCEPT: Publish a national daily sports newspaper

PROJECTIONS: Losses of about $16 million in first year, break-even in fourth year; 1 million circulation and pretax profit approaching 14% in about five years

HURDLES: Getting people to buy another newspaper; providing competitive coverage with a smaller staff; sustaining up to $100-million loss before break-even

the opportunity to lie on a beach somewhere and give his mind a chance to empty out. But before he went, Price *had* to talk to Frank Deford.

When Price called, Deford protested he was on deadline; he couldn't talk. Price persisted—five minutes, Frank. Deford relented, and Price went over to *Sports Illustrated*. "Here's the concept, Frank: a sports daily for the United States."

"It'll never work."

Price wanted Deford to edit this mythical paper, and he needed Deford's decision fast. Price himself had a decision on his hands, thanks to a high-stakes offer by someone else hungry for an answer.

That person was Emilio Azcarraga—the owner of, among other properties, a media company that controls 90% of Mexico's television programming. As influential as he is rich, Azcarraga is reputed to be worth at least $1 billion. In November 1988 he had met Peter Price, and the subject of national sports daily papers came up. Other countries had them, said Azcarraga, why not the United States?

Price replied that America was a "confederation of city-states," each with a loyalty to its local institutions, including sports teams. A sports daily would require marrying local and national coverage. That required talented people and state-of-the-art technology. That required satellites in space, bureaus and presses across the continent. That would cost a ton of money.

"I know," said Azcarraga. "We ought to do it." Price then said he had a handshake deal that obligated him to the *Post* for one year.

Last February, just as Price was approaching his first anniversary as publisher of the *Post*, Azcarraga called. That precipitated Price's urgent call to Deford and a detour to Mexico City on his way to a long-anticipated Caribbean vacation.

When Price met with Azcarraga, he threw out six numbers off the top of his head. These related to such issues as circulation, staffing, and revenues. The most mind-numbing figure was $100 million. That's what the venture would consume before the paper broke even three to five years out. Azcarraga, unfazed, asked, "Anything else?"

Price considered him blankly. "No."

"Let's do it."

Price, in semishock, protested. Maybe he should call his lawyer.

Azcarraga rolled his eyes. "You Americans are all the same. You always want to get lawyers involved." The next morning they signed a letter of agreement, giving Price enough time to catch a 10:00 a.m. flight and ring up Deford before his plane took off. "Uh, Frank, you'd better take your house off the market."

Unless you've spent the past six months crossing the Gobi Desert, you've probably already heard about *The National*. On January 31, 1990, the first copies of this amply hyped paper rolled off presses in New York City, Chicago, and Los Angeles. *The National Sports Daily* is published six times a week (Sunday through Friday). It costs 50¢ a copy and varies in length from 32 to 48 pages per issue. Initially, single-copy sales will account for all the circulation income, which will contribute 75% of the paper's revenues. Advertising income will make up the balance.

The National is a hybrid. It carries sports stories of general interest wrapped in eight pages of intensive, up-to-date reportage about the local heroes. In New York, for example, the lead stories detail yesterday's fortunes of the Yankees, Giants, Islanders, Rangers, and Knicks, written by beat writers assigned to cover those teams on a daily basis. *The National* runs columns and cartoons. It has an editorial page and a gossip page. It has a full-time two-man investigative team. It intends to write about the business of sport.

The National is meant to convey the immediacy of a tabloid and the permanence of a magazine. It is printed on a heavier-weight newsprint. The brightness factor—contrast between type and page—is more than 70%, while the typical newspaper falls somewhere in the 55% to 58% range. About one-third of its pages are in color. The black ink is low rub, designed not to come off on your hands or the inside of your raincoat pocket.

By the end of its first year *The National* hopes to have added as many as another dozen bureaus to its initial three, reaching audiences in the 15 largest markets in the country. By the end of the second year, coverage and availability will peak at 25 markets, comprising about 85% of the national market.

One key element in *The National's* strategy hinges on Peter Price's belief that "Sports is like entertainment. It requires some stars." *The National* has put together a firmament's worth, a number of whom are pulling down six-figure salaries. Besides Deford, these include John

Feinstein, author of the basketball best-seller *A Season on the Brink.* Then there are Scott Ostler and Dave Kindred, prized and prize-winning columnists from *The Los Angeles Times* and *The Washington Post,* respectively. The paper's executive editor, Vince Doria, came from *The Boston Globe,* whose sports section is often considered the country's best. The best paid in this highly regarded bunch is Mike Lupica, a sports columnist who had a wide following at *The New York Daily News.* He is making a reported $300,000 a year, putting him right up there with your basic journeyman infielder hitting .235, lifetime.

So who will buy *The National*? The company has done scant market research, but Peter Price nonetheless has a vision of his archetypal reader. That person is likely a man, an avid and learned follower of the sporting scene, a connoisseur of sorts. (*The National's* radio spots have run, among other places, on classical music stations.) Conversely, Price asserts: "The hard-core sports fan is *not* our audience. The fan is a junkie. The fan buys *USA Today* for the stats because he must have them. He eats them for breakfast."

Price hopes for a daily audience of some 1 million readers within about four years. "At that level we're making money," he says. "And we're also the fourth-largest daily newspaper in the United States of the some 1,800 out there."

But how exactly does Price intend to make this leap of more than faith? In projecting readership, says Price, "we've tried to be very conservative." In its first year *The National* expects daily circulation of about 200,000 in its three markets (100,000 in New York, 50,000 in Chicago, and 50,000 in Los Angeles). Those three markets comprise about 15% of the national market. Thus, extrapolating from that, once *The National* goes truly national it will be read by about 6.6 times more readers, or some 1.3 million.

What's the logic behind those numbers? Price bases his conservatism on the New York metro market, where 5 million papers are sold daily, and *The National* need capture only a 2% share. Some of these 100,000 readers will replace their daily paper with *The National.* Most will buy it in addition to their daily paper.

But is the typical *National* reader really a diehard, a six-days-a-week, 52-weeks-a-year buyer? No, says Diane Morgenthaler, the paper's circulation director.

How often then?

"I don't know, but the less frequent buyer, the guy who reads us two or three times a week, will make or break us."

So how many of those readers are there?

"I don't know. That's a multimillion-dollar question."

The National's conservative numbers begin to look less so when the
scene shifts to Los Angeles, where people commute by car and the old-
fashioned newsstand is as rare as snow. Add to that the substantially
lower circulation base of daily papers than New York's (2 million versus
5 million), high ratio of home delivery versus single-copy sales, and the
Sunbelt fact of life that people have less time for the newspaper and
more for TV.

Frank Herrera, vice-president of Hearst Magazines, considers The
National's circulation figures "wildly optimistic." He points out that
there are 3,000 magazine titles muscling one another for space on the
nation's newsstands. Of those, only 40 circulate more than 1 million
copies. Most of these titles have built readership slowly over the years
and are backed by huge promotion budgets. Herrera also notes that pro
football, for example, has a huge TV audience—and no widely circulating publication to match.

Another skeptic is Glenn Guzzo, former executive sports editor of

FINANCIALS

THE NATIONAL PROJECTED OPERATING STATEMENT
(in $ thousands)

	Year 1 (Launch)	Years 3–4 (Break-even)
Number of markets	15	25
Average daily circulation	225,000	740,000
Number of employees	250	450
SALES		
Circulation revenues	$35,100	$115,440
Advertising revenues	11,700	49,474
GROSS SALES	**46,800**	**164,914**
Cost of sales		
Circulation/ distribution	10,530	34,632
Ad expense	3,276	11,544
Production (paper, printing)	9,828	38,326
GROSS PROFIT	**23,166**	**80,412**
EXPENSES		
Salaries & benefits	18,750	36,000
Promotion	10,000	10,000
General & administrative	10,764	34,631
NET PROFIT (before taxes)	**(16,348)**	**(219)**

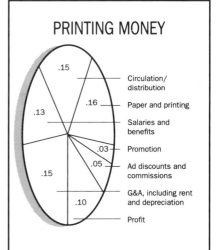

PRINTING MONEY

- .15 — Circulation/ distribution
- .16 — Paper and printing
- .13 — Salaries and benefits
- .03 — Promotion
- .05 — Ad discounts and commissions
- .15 — G&A, including rent and depreciation
- .10 — Profit

Total revenues from one copy sale is $.77

If *The National* reaches 1 million circulation, its year-five projection, and hits a 65%/35% circulation to ad revenues ration, each copy would generate $.77.

The National, April 1990

*Source: *Inc.* estimates, based on information from *The National* and industry sources

---

The Philadelphia Inquirer, now assistant to the vice-presidents for news at KnightRidder Inc., the *Inquirer*'s parent company. He says that for *The National* to reach its projected circulation figures in cities like Los Angeles it may have to go to home delivery. "That's extremely expensive and a tremendous administrative burden. If the demand [on the street] in Los Angeles is 20,000, would that encourage them to take on the cost of home delivery [to sell the additional 30,000 copies]? That's a decision a lot of big corporations wouldn't want to have to make."

The National's strategy is to invest heavily in talent and technology in an effort to add as much value as it can to a commodity product—sports information. In addition to paying top dollar for marquee names,

The National has poured a lot of money into a state-of-the-art electronic publishing system. This is a system that beams copy via satellite to the paper's hub in New York, where stories are edited and pages made up. That information is then beamed back to print sites around the country.

The National also seeks to outsource as much of the labor and headache of running a paper as possible. Unlike USA Today, which owns two-thirds of its printing sites and fleets of trucks, The National owns none. It will contract for printing and delivery in each market. "We don't want to get into the trucking or printing business," says Tim Lasker, The National's assistant publisher. "Our philosophy is to run a lean, clean machine."

The National also has no national distribution network. It has instead entered into a service contract with Dow Jones & Co. to distribute the paper and process the paperwork. (A distributor does not physically distribute the paper. It acts as an adjunct marketing force, ensuring the paper is reaching the right retail locations in the right quantities and then seeing that returns and payments are handled smoothly.)

In its first year The National expects each copy of the paper to generate roughly 67¢ of revenues (50¢ from circulation, nearly 17¢ from advertising). About 14¢ of that total will be consumed by production (paper, ink, press time), another 20¢ by circulation, distribution, and commission. The National will thus take in about 33¢ per paper. With a projected daily circulation of around 225,000 the first year, that amounts to about $23.2 million. That sum will be more than consumed by salaries and benefits (almost $19 million) and promotion ($10 million). From there The National goes deeper into the red.

General overhead and administration—which includes such items as capital equipment, rent, free-lance fees, travel, satellite time, and accounting support—will account for about 23% of gross revenues, or nearly $11 million. This includes the cost of depreciating equipment and an allowance for bad debt. In its first year of operation The National will lose at least $15 million.

Price expects his paper to break even probably around its fourth year of operation. What will circulation be then? Price will say only that the number is somewhere between 500,000 and 1 million. The National's likely break-even figure is about 740,000 (see box, "Financials," page 308). At 1 million circulation the paper's gross profit should be around 14%. Since The National will be printing the paper at multiple sites and selling fewer than 50,000 copies in most markets, it will likely achieve few economies of scale as circulation rises. Its large variable costs—production, distribution, administration—will continue to rise. Above 1 million circulation, though, the differential between revenues and fixed costs begins to widen, as more and more copies of the paper are sold and advertising revenues increase to about 35% of total revenues.

But getting from zero to 1.3 million looks tough. *USA Today*, after all, has spent about eight years and $500 million building circulation to its present 1.7 million—and even now is barely breaking even. Price and company, by comparison, intend to spend $100 million to get to 1.3 million circulation and hefty profitability.

Nonetheless, Al Neuharth, founder of *USA Today*, thinks *The National* might have a chance. This, after all, is a subject he has considered. "A sports daily was one concept we looked at 10 years ago before we started *USA Today*," says Neuharth. "I thought the concept was good, but in the end we went for a general-interest publication with an emphasis on sports." He adds: "Our sports section has hooked by far the highest percentage of our readers, maybe higher than the other three sections combined."

Another affirming journalistic force is Dow Jones, publisher of *The Wall Street Journal* and distributor of *The National*. Dow Jones not only has clout at the newsstand. Its name lends credibility to *The National*'s efforts; its sales force ensures that bills get paid on a timely basis. In return, *The National* has something to offer Dow Jones—the potential for a great fit. The *Journal*'s market research reveals two interesting facts. First, 98% of the *Journal*'s readers read a second paper. Second, next to business news, the *Journal*'s readers are interested in sports.

Every wholesaler that takes *The Wall Street Journal* in New York, Chicago, and Los Angeles will also take *The National*. In addition, a good number of wholesalers who don't distribute the *Journal* have taken *The National*. This considerable interest is reflected in what is known as the draw—the number of copies the wholesalers take.

At the outset *The National* projected its daily draw at 250,000, assuming about 70% of those papers would be sold on day one. Two weeks before the newspaper was launched, wholesalers, who had been talking to newspaper and magazine retailers about their customers' buying habits, came back with another number. They told *The National* to raise the draw to 380,000.

Interest in sports has mushroomed in the past decade. Attendance records continue to be set. The airwaves grow ever-more saturated with sporting events and sports information. Advertisers see sports as a great vehicle to reach a prime audience—affluent males between 25 and 54.

The National hopes to be the print version of this phenomenon—a pipeline to this hard-to-reach audience. Before it had published even a single issue, the paper had signed commitments for 1,200 pages of paid advertising for 1990. At $9,800 per full-color page in all three editions of

The National, the paper offers its advertisers low out-of-pocket expense. (Incremental discounts would lower that number further.) Advertising sales director Peter A. Spina says *The National's* strategy is to cultivate charter advertisers that will not see large increases in cost per thousand as circulation picks up. *The National* might continue to look like a bargain to loyal advertisers for years to come. *USA Today* (circulation 1.7 million) charges $66,000 per color page. *Sports Illustrated* (circulation 3.1 million) charges $113,000.

Another facet of *The National's* strategy is to rely initially on circulation for 75% of revenues, and advertising the balance. (With most magazines the ratio is about 50-50.) This will take pressure off the ad pages. Spina will not be forced to chase advertisers. Rather, he can court—and showcase—blue-chip advertisers that do not often advertise in sports publications. It is a given that *The National* can wallow in beer, cigarette, and automobile ads. But keeping those advertisers in check and enticing an IBM or American Express into the paper will be key. Charter advertisers thus far include Philip Morris, Panasonic, Minolta, AT&T, Nike, and Sears Roebuck. Those companies may have come in because *The National* offers advertisers another advantage: the pass-along factor—how many readers see each copy. *The National* is projected to have a pass-along number between 2.5 and 3. This compares favorably with daily newspapers, which are in the 1.2 to 2 range. Moreover, daily papers reach a mass audience. *The National* reaches a choice slice of the market.

The National also offers urgency. A color ad can run within 48 hours of being placed. It produces, as well, a hard-core audience, its ranks uninflated by discounts, free alarm clocks, and promises that the bill isn't due before the next millenium. *The National* is a demand buy. The reader plunks down his two quarters to buy the paper—now.

The National has announced that it will spend $10 million its first year to promote and advertise the product, but one newspaper executive finds that number low. "To successfully launch a national newspaper and have it become known, you've got to spend between $30 million and $50 million in the first three years." Given Emilio Azcarraga's deep pockets, promotion may be the least of his worries.

If things go according to plan, in two years *The National* will be in 25 markets. That's 25 bureaus sending copy and photos back to New York. That's New York editing the package and making up the pages to be sent on to 25 print sites, from which the paper will be taken by 25 fleets of trucks—all in the space of about four hours. That's so many contracts to negotiate, so many suppliers to be relied on, so many snowstorms to endure. "The biggest problem will be the linkage," admits Peter Price. "There are so many individual pieces that have to work together."

Down the hall in another corner office, looking out over a prime block of Fifth Avenue, Frank Deford, smoothing his purple tie, projects none of this angst. Deford, with his graying swept-back hair and pencil mustache, projects a swashbuckling air. He has never been an editor before, never worked for a newspaper. He seems bemused by this role that fate has handed him. "Right now it's a little vague who our readers will be," says Deford. This seems to excite him. He continues the thought, a bit of wonder now rising in his voice: "The product I know will be terrific. The technology seems to work, and we know we can distribute it. But at the end of the food chain, will Mr. Sports Fan reach down into his pocket, put half a buck on the table, and say, `Give me a *National'. . . ?"*

"The real question is how deep are Mr. Azcarraga's pockets—or how big is his ego, pick one. If his pockets are deep or his ego is big, then I think over time *The National* can succeed."

–Ron Reilly

COMPETITOR

BRIAN TOOLAN

Assistant managing editor,
Philadelphia Daily News, *a sports-driven tabloid relying mainly on street sales; former sports editor*

The National will have to force itself into the customers' hands every day. The only way it can do that is by breaking news, having information other papers don't have, and looking terrific. It's impossible to have compelling, exclusive material six days a week, 52 weeks a year. To sell 1.3 million copies per day they're going to have to *average* 54,000 sales in each city. In Philadelphia, the fourth-largest newspaper market, *USA Today* sells between 17,000 and 22,000 papers a day, and that's after eight years and tons of promotion dollars.

This paper is also going into markets where the best daily newspapers are. *The National* is going to be outgunned in every instance. In Chicago, New York, and Los Angeles, it will have bureaus with 10 to 12 staffers in them, competing with papers with staffs of 40 and 50 in just the sports departments.

I think it's a misjudgment to place entertainment value on writers. People in New York know who Mike Lupica is, but if you asked 100 people in Denver or St. Louis who he is, they wouldn't know.

Writers build a reputation by writing about local issues, teams, and personalities.

Finally, *The National* also incorrectly believes that the notion of a national sports daily is reinforced by there being more sports on television and radio. In fact, *The National's* reader is being *wooed* by TV and radio, which have never been more sophisticated, informative, and appealing than they are now.

ANALYST

KEN NOBLE

Media analyst, Paine Webber, New York City; has watched newspaper and magazine properties for 23 years

This may look like a newspaper, but economically it is a magazine. That means it'd probably be better off with a cover price of $1. The higher price would demonstrate to advertisers that indeed the audience is above average and therefore desirable. It would also enable it to generate profit sooner.

I'd also consider trying out the paper in one city at a time. That lowers the investment cost and allows it to test the concept in one market before committing to the next. By going national quickly, they've created a splash, but I'm not sure how much that splash is worth.

It's going to be tough to obtain the circulation numbers with a newsstand approach. Street sales are erratic because buying a magazine on the newsstand is an impulse buy. The newsstand circulation of magazines has been declining for years now, in part because of increased competition for what space there is. The magazine industry is going very much toward subscriptions. That attracts advertisers because it offers a more stable audience.

CUSTOMER

RON REILLY
Senior vice-president/executive media director, Ogilvy & Mather, Los Angeles; has bought ad space in The National *for clients*

The key to the paper's success will be selling its editorial excellence. *The National* hired some very good writers, and it needs to continually push that, because that will keep it attracting the audience it wants—upscale, not kids or statistic fanatics. To do that, it should continue to promote Deford, do advertising that features the editorial staff.

The financials are somewhat optimistic on when they'll turn profitable. That's not a problem, though, as long as the pockets remain deep. It's refreshing to see people who still understand the value of a brand: that you can still create something with long-term value. *Sports Illustrated* wasn't profitable until its 19th year, but Time Inc. continued to invest in it and today has a valuable franchise.

The advertising revenues for year one are reasonable. *The National* will not have great difficulty attracting advertisers, because the audience it expects is an appealing one. Down the road, ad sales will be guided by the actual readers of the publication and the health of the circulation—will people continue to buy it, or will it become a sporadic purchase? Will the circulation be stable on a day-to-day basis? I don't think it will; I think they'll see significant fluctuations.

Will they succeed? I believe that they have a good chance of succeeding. They've hired a good staff. It will not be a success like *People* magazine, which hit big almost instantaneously. The real question is, how deep are Mr. Azcarraga's pockets—or how big is his ego, pick one. If his pockets are deep or his ego is big, then I think over time it can succeed.

COMPETITOR

THOMAS G. OSENTON
President and CEO, The Sporting News, *a St. Louis–based sports weekly with 730,000 circulation*

They've identified a market that has a great deal of vitality: advertising pages in the sports category have grown significantly over the years; the number of newsstand sales generated by the sports category has grown in the past several years, as has the number of subscribers in the category. Major-league attendance each year has been reaching record levels.

But *The National* is asking people either to add this source to their reading list or replace something else with it. I don't know that people have the time to add it.

Can it replace *The Wall Street Journal*? *The New York Times*? *USA Today*? You have to get almost market specific and person specific. To speculate is tricky—there was so much speculation about whether ESPN would succeed or CNN or *USA Today,* and they all generated an interest and an audience.

I don't view *The National* as a threat because *The Sporting News* isn't daily. Our mission is to give retrospectives and previews of the sports world on a weekly basis. As a result, the time spent with each publication will differ greatly. A daily is designed for readers to move in and out of and then toss away; a weekly is slower and more thoughtful. Our relationship with the reader is very different, and from the standpoint of the appeal to the advertiser, more attractive, because we have the attention of the reader for a longer period of time.

BROADCAST NEWS

Can positioning yourself as the low-cost producer work in television broadcasting?

BY JILL ANDRESKY FRASER

Ann States

own in New Orleans, the business community was surprised—shocked, even—when it heard that a new television station was preparing to set up shop. After all, the local economy was hurting; advertisers were few and far between. And the Big Easy had five commercial TV stations already, some of them barely managing to break even. Who was this New York City hotshot, the town elders asked themselves about WCCL-TV founder and chief executive Barbara Lamont, who thought she was going to move into New Orleans and carve herself a piece of its already-shrinking pie?

Then came the crabs. There were hundreds of the little crawlers, fresh and gritty, straight from Lake Pontchartrain. Packed in cardboard boxes that were discreetly labeled "perishable—open immediately,"

Barbara Lamont, founder of Crescent City Communications Co.

they were hand-delivered on a single day by WCCL's staffers to the heads of every single advertising and media-buying agency in the area. The locals took notice.

It was an unusual introduction to one of the most unusual entrepreneurs this city has seen in a long while. Lamont, 50, speaks seven languages, including Mandarin Chinese and Yiddish, and comes to TV-station ownership with a résumé that includes a stint as an international cabaret singer. She's insatiable when it comes to taking on new challenges. After 20 years as a successful broadcast journalist in New York City's high-profile radio and TV markets, Lamont led a team of 23 to Nigeria, where she managed the state-owned television network. A 1984 military coup sent her home via a tortuous northern escape route to the city of Kano, where she caught the midnight flight to Paris. Somewhere along the way she decided that it was time, finally, to think about going into business for herself.

But what a business she chose. Independent television stations, or "indies"—stations unaffiliated with any of the three major networks—have been on a roller-coaster ride since the early 1980s, when new owners and financiers started flocking in, convinced that an FCC license to build a TV station was a license, plain and simple, to print money. And for a while they were right. Thanks to investment tax credits, accelerated depreciation, and some of the other tax goodies available before 1986, backing a new station could be lucrative for investors—even if ad revenues, the heart of TV-station viability, were sluggish or market shares small. Given those incentives, it's not surprising that the number of independent stations in the United States rose from about 250 in 1984 to some 400 today and now account for around 25% of all TV-station revenues. "The hard part was getting the FCC license. The rest used to be easy," says Lamont.

Not anymore. After tax reform wiped out those breaks for investors, indies were forced to become something more than a clever tax play. To attract needed capital they had to start making money the old-fashioned way—by taking in more cash (in ad sales) than they spent (on overhead, transmission and selling costs, and program creation or purchase). All the new stations only made things tougher; increased competition for the syndicated reruns, movies, and original programs that indies buy for broadcast led to higher prices, sending programming costs ever upward.

Still, Lamont—resettling stateside after her Nigerian escape—saw an opportunity in operating as the low-cost TV station in a low-cost city. (She chose to apply for the New Orleans license instead of Tampa, the other available FCC slot, because its market seemed to be close to bot-

EXECUTIVE SUMMARY

THE COMPANY:
Crescent City Communications Co./WCCL-TV, New Orleans

CONCEPT:
Launch an independent TV station as the low-cost producer in its market, seeking profitability more by controlling expenses than by building audience and ad revenues. Develop cash flow of $3 million to $4 million in six years in order to sell the station for up to $40 million

PROJECTIONS:
Losses in year one, ending June 30, 1990, of $1.9 million; profits in 1991 of $175,000 on net sales of $3.9 million. Positive cash flow in 1991 of $1.2 million

HURDLES:
Building enough of an audience on bargain-basement programming to attract projected ad revenues; getting carried on the cable systems that control access to New Orleans viewers; securing enough capital to hold on until cash flow turns positive

toming out, with plenty of real estate and construction bargains available.) Her business plan concentrated on controlling fixed and operating expenses as the key to profitability, rather than the more typical industry approach of building audience share and subsequently raising advertising prices. It would be OK if her programming didn't bring the viewership other stations got; she wouldn't need as much ad revenues as they did to cover costs. "I decided to run my television station like a lean, mean radio station," Lamont declares.

Lamont's strategy focused at all times on building cash flow, which in the TV industry is seen as the ultimate indicator—rather than net aftertax profits—of a station's viability and market value. (It's worth noting that WCCL's cash-flow formula is controversial. Unlike most stations, WCCL considers program amortization a noncash expense, leading to a more attractive cash-flow figure than standard industry accounting would yield.) The reason for her focus: Her goal is to sell most or all of WCCL-TV to investors after six years, for what she hopes will be between $27 million and $34 million, or 10 times projected cash flow—about the multiple that TV stations currently fetch.

OPERATIONS: Barbara Lamont figured she was coming into the market at a good time. Most of her competitors were locked into the kind of longer-term, high-cost programming contracts that were popular in the mid-1980s. But she would be free to buy whatever shows came on the market cheap. In addition, New Orleans's economic problems gave her room to bid down her construction costs.

She wound up spending about $3.6 million on land as well as transmission and

THE FOUNDER

Barbara Lamont, president and CEO

Age: 50

Source of idea: Former employer suggested she apply for a TV license after the FCC streamlined its procedures for minority applications

Personal funds invested: $1 million

Equity held: 66%

Other businesses started: Notel Inc., a teleport (satellite transmission facility) in New Orleans, in 1988

Other jobs: Reporter, WINS-AM, WNEW-TV; writer/reporter, CBS network, all in New York City; anchor, WNEW-TV; producer, ABC radio network; director of operations, Nigerian Television Authority

Typical workweek: 94 hours

Outside board of directors: Yes

What I lose sleep over: Money

Sources of inspiration: Mother, husband, Winston Churchill, Shirley Chisholm

Why I did this: "Because I want to earn $5 million before I'm 55 years old in order to ensure myself a comfortable lifestyle for the next 60 years."

broadcast equipment—a good price, thanks to bargains such as the state-of-the-art production equipment that she bought, slightly used, after it had been deployed at the Seoul Olympics. Lamont's offices, set up in an old glue factory in an industrial corner of the city, are equipped with furniture, computers, and even stationery that she bought at a bankruptcy auction.

Lamont won't disclose precise cost figures for WCCL's programming, but she says that she paid about one-tenth what her competitors typically spend. As a result, her 20-hour programming day is littered with well-worn oldies like "Kojak" and some best-forgotten dogs such as "Dobie Gillis" and "Airwolf." As a result, WCCL projects annual expenses of $2.2 million. "Most people coming in with this kind of station and equipment would run costs about three times ours," she claims. To cover her yearly nut, she figures she'll need about a 4.5% market share and nearly $4 million in sales.

As the third indie in a crowded market, Lamont doesn't expect to achieve those numbers quickly. She projected net ad sales of about $1.7 million for her first operating year, ending June 30, 1990; that would translate into a net operating loss of $508,000 and—after taking into consideration fixed expenses such as loan interest and equipment lease costs—an aftertax net loss of $1.9 million. But by fiscal 1991 she expects to achieve her 4.5% market share and to report operating profits of $1.6 million (aftertax profits would run about $175,000). Keeping the focus on cash flow, she hopes to turn a first-year negative of $816,000 into an impressive $1.2 million in positive cash by year two.

By year six, when Lamont expects to put her station up for sale, she's counting on about $8 million in net sales and at least a 6% market share. That would translate into about $2.4 million in aftertax profits and, better still, nearly $3.5 million of positive cash flow.

MARKETING: But getting from here to there will take more—much more—than tight control of WCCL's purse strings. Lamont must figure out how to carve a niche for her station in a market that was already saturated without her. (Most midsize cities like New Orleans, which is the 35th-largest TV market, have three network affiliates and only one or two indies.)

Lamont turned for help to a man she considers one of the marketing geniuses of the industry—George Stantis, a veteran of more than 30 years in the management of independent as well as network-affiliated TV stations. The pair faced some real obstacles: The New Orleans market, depressed as it is, is heavily dominated by one station, owned by Loyola University, a Jesuit institution with less incentive to show a profit and thus able to keep its commercial spot prices low. To make matters worse, the two non-network independents that WCCL planned to tackle were owned by the Tribune Co. and TVX Broadcasting Group Inc., backing that gave them the kind of marketing, programming, and staying power that a thinly capitalized station like Lamont's just wouldn't have.

Lamont and Stantis decided to position the station as the city's "local" alternative—not as improbable as it might sound, since Lamont and the Jesuits are currently New Orleans's only home-based television-station owners. To build up their local image fast, Stantis adopted a logo mascot: a well-known French Quarter mime who looks like Charlie Chaplin with shocking-red hair. His image was eye-catching, especially when WCCL splashed it for three months across city billboards, complete with a 22-foot spinning cane. "We came to town and tried to sell some sizzle," Stantis says.

They had no other choice, because there weren't going to be any market-share numbers to speak of, perhaps for quite a while. After all, it takes time to attract viewers to a new station. And WCCL faced an even tougher battle precisely because Lamont had done such an admirable

CRESCENT CITY COMMUNICATIONS CO. (WCCL-TV)
PROJECTED OPERATING STATEMENT
(in $ thousands)

	Year one June 30, 1990	Year two June 30, 1991
NET SALES	$1,738	$3,859
OPERATING EXPENSES		
General & administrative	272	294
Accounting & traffic	145	157
Sales costs	339	366
Engineering	353	381
Promotion	273	295
Operations & programming	864	758
Total operating expenses	2,246	2,251
Net operating profit	(508)	1,608
OTHER EXPENSES (FIXED)		
Long-term debt—land	69	68
Loan interest	275	259
Equipment loan/lease	415	443
Amortization & depreciation	663	663
NET PROFIT (LOSS)		
After taxes	(1,930)	175
Aftertax profit margin	—	4.5%
Cash flow	(816)	1,150

job of penny-pinching on programming: her competitors could pull viewers in with shows such as Oprah Winfrey's and Arsenio Hall's while she ran cheapies on the order of "Room 222." Unfortunately, many potential advertisers decided to wait for proof of at least a 3% rating before they would consider buying into a show. And WCCL has been able to score that only at scattered time periods as recently as August, when official July ratings were issued.

The reason for WCCL's rating-share shortfall actually has less to do with its programming than it does with a Supreme Court ruling that put an end to an FCC regulation known as "must-carry." The regulation had required cable operators to carry every television station located within a specified area. Now cable companies have the right to decide whether to carry a station, which they do on purely economic grounds.

Some indies have closed up shop to conserve cash and hope for congressional intervention, but Lamont, always a fighter, decided to tough it out and try to build market share without the help of must-carry—despite the fact that one of the city's two major cable carriers, the one that serves the desirable, upscale Jefferson Parish, has only recently reconsidered its earlier refusal to carry her station. "I went home feeling pretty devastated when I found out that we were the only local station they had decided not to carry," Lamont recalls. But then she and Stantis launched a lobbying campaign aimed at every relevant government official from the Jefferson Parish city council all the way up to Congress, even targeting representatives from Atlanta, where the cable carrier's parent company is based. At press time, the two were waiting for the carrier to make a commitment to carry WCCL-TV.

Meanwhile, Lamont has been forced to be imaginative—to put it mildly—in her efforts to build audience share by "counterprogramming" the existing offerings from the network affiliates and indies. In a time slot where all of the other stations are showing the news, WCCL schedules a game show. Or if there are situation comedies on the other stations, WCCL will offer an action show. The goal is always to provide an alternative to what the competitors offer.

Local programming, particularly sporting events, is clearly the best way to capture audience share and advertisers quickly, but it's costly to produce; also, most of the desirable sports events are already contracted for. WCCL managed to score one touchdown when Lamont negotiated her way into an exclusive five-year contract to produce and syndicate the Bayou Classic, the Superbowl of black-college football games. And she has just followed her WCCL-produced show, "Step by Step Cosmetic Surgery," with a new entry, "Saints' Better Half," which takes a weekly "intimate" look at the tumultuous (she hopes) home lives of New Orleans's professional football players.

Lamont and Stantis also have been forced to be inventive about selling their ad time. And that doesn't just mean offering good discounts—which of course they're doing. "We're reaching out to a lot of advertisers who have never tried television before; we can produce their commercials for them right here in our own production studio," says Stantis. So far, results are positive. One locally based store concluded that increased sales paid for the cost of producing and running its WCCL commercial six times over.

The pair scored a real coup—and won credibility—this summer when they convinced a major national ad rep firm, Blair Television Co., to take them on as a client. But the question now is whether they can attract national advertising to a sluggish market: net ad revenues in the city were only $75 million in 1988, not much better than the $58 million netted in 1983.

FINANCE: While Lamont's marketing problems are large, her financing difficulties have often seemed insurmountable. WCCL lost some of its original investors in 1985. "I went to all the big Wall Street firms looking for new backers—but nobody wanted to hear anything about an independent television station, especially one in Louisiana," she says with a laugh.

But by then the company had spent nearly $1.5 million on lawyers' fees and settlements to other applicants for the same frequency (the procedure encouraged by the FCC in such cases). So Lamont had no intention of giving up her hard-won license. Instead, she gave herself a crash course in government incentives for entrepreneurs—especially minorities, since she's black—and came up with a shrewd substitute for all those nifty tax breaks that TV-station investors had lost. She offered her backers minority tax credits (MTCs), which allowed them to earn tax-free dividends on their WCCL investments, the first time MTCs had been used for a television start-up.

The tax breaks helped her attract seven investors at a time when her FCC license was her only asset; in return for some $250,000, investors bought about 5% of Crescent City Communications Co., WCCL-TV's operating company. That tided Lamont over until she could obtain about $3.5 million of land, construction, and equipment loans. While waiting for her airdate—which finally came on March 19, 1989— she convinced First City Texas bank to give her $2 million of working capital collateralized with her personal assets. (In all, the bank holds another 20% of Crescent City's stock warrants.)

Lamont was on a roll. She got the state to name her office/production site an enterprise zone. This status frees her from state income and corporate franchise taxes until 1993 and lets her skip some state sales and use taxes during construction. She also qualifies for a tax credit every time she creates a new job.

But WCCL is still running out of money, thanks to negative cash flow that's been about $150,000 monthly. Lamont's original projection of fiscal year 1990's negative cash in the range of $800,000 was already looking too low by October, when cash was in the red to about $500,000. It isn't an expense problem—she's been keeping labor costs, for example, about 20% below budget. The trouble is ad dollars, which are coming in slower than expected.

So Lamont has decided to sell another 15% stake in the company, which would cut her to about 51% ownership. The deal was still pending at press time in December 1989, but Lamont hoped to raise another $2 million, thanks in large part to the advantages offered through the minority tax credits. "It's going to give me the money to pay my bills," she says. "That's how I'll hold on until I build the market share I need."

Can she raise this new round of financing? Undoubtedly, given her high-level contacts in the media world and New Orleans's business community. But will it help her hold on long enough to build an audience and turn her station profitable? Will she ever have the programming that viewers want? It all remains to be seen. But, says Wilbert "Bill" Tatum, publisher of the New York City–based black newspaper *New York Amsterdam News*, and one of her earliest investors, "if energy, commitment, talent, and competence can make any venture work, then Barbara Lamont is the person who can do it. I have complete faith in her abilities."

She does have her work cut out for her. Still, Lamont is more than capable of inspiring those around her with her boundless energy and enthusiasm. "I don't want to sound naïve," she confesses from her tiny, windowless office, speaking above the WCCL shows that play from morning till night on her office television set. "But I feel as though we've already succeeded—just by winning the FCC license, getting on the air, and building something with a high asset value."

She smiles. "It's not that everything else will be easy. But I do believe we're going to make it."

"Starting with low program costs sounds sensible, but when the available low-cost programming is so bargain basement that you really can't generate an audience, then you're in a catch-22 situation."

—*Bill Ross*

CUSTOMER

PETER MAYER

Chairman, Peter A. Mayer Advertising Inc., a New Orleans agency. Has convinced some clients to buy time on WCCL

Lamont has done several things very well. She has a first-rate staff, which is important; her staff has sold the advertising community. And she has created community awareness—people know that there's a WCCL and that it's broadcasting.

Now not so good: She has very poor programming. It's just trash, the dregs. You can't just buy old shows and plop them on the air; that day is gone. We've bought time for some of our clients because there are areas we're interested in; "CBS This Morning" is one of them. Although it has a minute audience, the cost of the spots was reasonable. There are things that we can cherry-pick, but that's not enough.

I think it's urgent that Lamont create a niche in the market with WCCL, and if I were in her boots, I would definitely slant my station toward the ethnic market. I would broadcast stuff of interest to the black and Latin communities—New Orleans has the audience to sustain that. And she's got to get a couple of the current, viable shows that other people are picking up and at least have something to base a promotion around.

I definitely think advertisers would support an ethnic station; we vigorously support two black radio stations and one Latin radio station, and they're doing very well. There are advertisers who want that audience, and I think she could do it in television. Sure, that'd mean more investment, because you'd have to get a local news staff, but right now she's just what everybody else is, but not as good.

I don't think she's going to make it without finding that niche. I admire the hell out of her, but she's really going into a storm here, and the market's not getting any better.

COMPETITOR

BILL ROSS

Director of sales, WGNO-TV, a Tribune Broadcasting station in New Orleans

Lamont's assumptions about ratings, market share, and selling out for $30 million to $40 million a few years down the line—they're all way off base. We're looking at negative growth this year, with next year flat or maybe having slight growth.

She's built the station on the premise of three-point audience share and $4 million of ad revenues, and there's really no way that she can achieve those figures. In reality, because she's not on all the cable systems, she's got to double the actual viewing in the homes she reaches to a 6% share in order to get that three-point share of audience in the whole New Orleans market. And that's virtually impossible, because you're looking at two strong independents—us and WNOL—and there just aren't programs that she can afford that will garner that kind of audience. Anything that gets an audience has already been taken in the market, or it's way too expensive for us, WNOL, and any of the network affiliates—and therefore way out of Barbara's league.

So put yourself in her shoes. How do you get where you want to go, ratings-wise, without having the programming to get there or the available outlets to reach the people you have to reach? If you look at her strategy on paper, it makes sense; it would work theoretically because any start-up station, unless it's backed by a huge company with deep pockets, has to go in with low program costs and build its way up. But when the programming that is available is so bargain basement that you really can't generate an audience, then you're in a catch-22 situation.

It's not the best time to put on an independent station, especially in a market where you already have two strong independents and a strong cable carrier that you're not on. I think it would take almost a miracle to have a new profitable station in this market.

I wish Barbara luck. But she may have picked the wrong market to do it in.

OPERATOR

GEORGE COLES

President and chairman, WCOM-TV, Mansfield, Ohio, an independent that went off the air while waiting for "must-carry" legislation to be reinstated

If WCCL were my station, I would have started out doing local news briefs and an "eyes and ears of New Orleans" show. The more local programming you do, the more people become aware of your TV station because they see your truck and reporters at school-board sessions, Kiwanis Club meetings, and high-school basketball games. That's the way for Lamont to get on the local cable carrier—by doing so much local programming that the local audience demands to see WCCL, even if it means knocking someone else off the system.

I also think Lamont is wasting time and money on Blair Television. She doesn't need a national rep firm, because the national market is a pure numbers game; the big ad agencies won't go along until WCCL can demonstrate market share. And the way to do that is by concentrating attention and spending on local programming—which, incidentally, is the way to bring in revenues from local advertisers.

Would I invest in WCCL? Absolutely, if I had the capital and time to watch my investment. New Orleans is a great market; the economic downturn is just a cyclical thing. The big picture in New Orleans is all that ad money that's not being spent on television.

Lamont is right to go after those dollars by producing so much local programming that advertisers feel they can't afford to ignore WCCL.

FINANCIER

BILL COLLATOS

General partner, TA Communications Partners, Boston, a venture capital firm specializing in media, including independent television stations

Good local programming can help, but remember: It's easy to overvalue it. Local shows usually don't bring in much audience, because they're specialized and often get lost in the shuffle on cable systems. The exceptions are news shows, which bring in the audience but are very expensive to produce. So I think Barbara would be better off moving into good-quality, mainstream syndicated programming as soon as she can afford it.

I like Barbara's marketing strategy. The third independent in any market has got to face some hard facts: Other independents are usually well established and there's usually a fight over cable space. The fact that she's got "CBS This Morning" is fabulous, because anything that can convince people to turn on her channel is a step in the right direction.

This is too small a deal for us to consider investing in. But Barbara has shown remarkable resourcefulness and a refusal to give up. I think she'll be the determinant in whether or not the channel succeeds, and I would not bet against her.

PLAY BY PLAY

*When is a great product not
a great business? Maybe, just maybe, in
the case of SportsBand Network*

BY LESLIE BROKAW

Dan Bryant

What no one disputes about SportsBand Network, an in-your-ear audio program for fans at golf tournaments, is the sheer intuitive appeal of the idea: No one who hears about it doesn't love it. Combining play-by-play commentary and features, Sports-Band provides spectators on the course with as much information and entertainment as television coverage offers couch campers at home. Now fans watching Tom Kite make birdie on 15 can at the same time hear, through a special Walkman-like receiver and earpiece, about Lee Trevino eagling the ninth. SportsBand erases the single biggest frustration of anyone who's ever attended a golf tournament: It tells you *what's going on.*

What's more, no one who's actually listened to SportsBand argues that it's anything but a top-rate production. The technical quality is

SportsBand Network cofounders Theis Rice (left) and Frank Mitchell

superb. The 30-member crew of engineers and broadcasters are pros and put on a clean, exhilarating show.

So: a good idea; a well-executed production. Then why has it been so tough to turn SportsBand the Product into SportsBand the Business?

Credit the $2.3-million question: Who's going to pick up the check? Between production costs and overhead, $2.3 million is what SportsBand must bring in just to break even. Do you ask individual spectators to shell out five bucks each to rent a receiver? Do you charge tournaments $100,000 to enhance their events and let them bundle the service into ticket packages? Do you seek a corporation willing to plunk down $1 million for the privilege of being the title sponsor (for example, "The *Inc.* Magazine Broadcasting System coming to you on SportsBand")? Do you do a combination? Which do you do first?

Those are the questions Frank Mitchell, president and chief executive officer, and Theis Rice, chairman and chief financial officer, have struggled with over the past three years. Who's the real customer for a service that at first glance offers benefits to so many? Who should pay, and how do you convince them to do it?

"When the SportsBand concept came to us, it was not a new idea," says Art West, director of promotions for the Professional Golfer's Association Tour. "But it *was* a buttoned-down, polished presentation." That was in the spring of 1986. Mitchell and Rice had been running an oil-and-gas-drilling business in Dallas since 1983, but having learned about past attempts at on-site tournament broadcasts, they approached the PGA Tour to see if it was interested in trying the idea again.

Mitchell had spent a few years playing professional tennis and knew a bit about the world of sports marketing (see box, "The Founders," page 331). He was intrigued by the idea of setting up a company that could serve three customers: the golf spectator, the tournament operator, and the corporate advertiser seeking to buff the company image. The obvious appeal of the product itself was so strong and so diversified that he didn't expect revenues to be a problem. "I'd been around sports sponsorship," says Mitchell. "I knew the kind of dollars that are spent."

The Tour was interested. In 1981 it had introduced electronic scoreboards to the courses, and since then had been investing heavily in building hilly "stadium" golf courses so spectators could see better. Developing a broadcast to make viewing still more enjoyable was something Tour officials had considered, and when Mitchell said he was willing to spend SportsBand's money to pursue the idea, they pledged not to sign other broadcast agreements while he went to work.

With $75,000 invested by Rice and his two sisters early in 1986, Mitchell consulted a radio engineer who suggested using an open por-

EXECUTIVE SUMMARY

THE COMPANY:
SportsBand
Network, Dallas

CONCEPT:
A mobile audio
broadcast for
spectators at golf
tournaments and
other events, using
Walkman-like
receivers to deliver
the sort of commen-
tary and entertain-
ment that TV view-
ers are used to

PROJECTIONS:
1990 pretax net
of $2.2 million on
revenues of nearly
$5 million; 1993
profits of $5.7
million on revenues
of $11.9 million

HURDLES:
Persuading
tournament opera-
tors to underwrite
SportsBand in order
to have broadcasts
at their events;
persuading potential
sponsors that buy-
ing a SportsBand
affiliation makes
sense for prestige
and image, though
it can't be justified
by standard media-
buy criteria

tion of the FM band—and by October 1986 SportsBand had secured special temporary authority from the Federal Communications Commission to send out low-level signals over golf courses via a mobile transmitter and antenna tower.

Next, Mitchell set out to put together a broadcast prototype. The lawyer who helped SportsBand approach the PGA Tour had spent several years working at National Public Radio, and he pointed Mitchell toward a former colleague there, Steve Rathe.

Rathe and his New York City–based production company had coordinated other multisite broadcasts, including the New Orleans Jazz and Heritage Festival, and he was game to see what would happen when he combined "the public-radio crew, the Dallas oil folk, and the golf crowd." He signed on for a $450 daily consulting fee.

By the fall of 1986 SportsBand had a system ready to test at an actual tournament. Rathe contracted with a group of 20 professionals—including Carol Mann, a Ladies Professional Golf Association Hall-of-Famer and an NBC reporter—and headed for the J.C. Penney Mixed Team Classic, in Largo, Fla.

The operation went beautifully. The tournament director wrote the Tour that SportsBand was exciting and would be welcome to return the next year.

The Tour liked SportsBand's demo tape and in early 1987 began negotiating a licensee contract, structured like its deal with network television: The Tour would deliver a group of tournaments at which SportsBand could broadcast, and SportsBand would pay a rights fee.

The agreement, however, had to be approved by the Tour's tournament policy board, and that's when SportsBand hit its first snag. At the June 1987 meeting of the 10-member committee of players, business-people, and officers of PGA of America, the players bluntly said they weren't sure this was such a good thing. What if a player was set to putt, and something dramatic was announced over the system? Would everyone listening gasp in unison? Or cheer? Just what kind of effect would this information have on the crowds and the game? Before they could approve it, they wanted to see three more tests in the fall—and large-scale ones, too, with thousands of receivers at each course.

It was a reasonable request, but for Rice and Mitchell a daunting one. Here it was the middle of 1987, the point at which they'd presumed they'd get the final go-ahead. They'd been buying equipment, paying consultants, gearing up to start making money later that year. Instead, they were going to have to dig up more money for the test runs—a good $200,000 since, as Rice remembers, "we were going to go into those tests loaded for bear. People three deep with equipment. I wanted to make sure that *nothing* went wrong at those tournaments."

The company's tab to date was close to $500,000—Rice had been regularly loaning personal funds on an as-needed basis—and it had yet to bring in a dime. But they knew they could find more capital and agreed to the policy board's request.

Rice and his sisters continued borrowing against $328,000 in certificates of deposit that made up their savings; an uncle loaned him $300,000 to be paid back when it was convenient. The company

FINANCIALS

SPORTSBAND PROJECTED OPERATING STATEMENT, 1990
(in $ thousands)

GROSS PROFIT FROM TOURNAMENT BROADCASTS (15)	$3,927

EXPENSES

General & administrative	$ 828
Inventory loss (8%)	324
Depreciation	145
Total operating expenses	1,297

OPERATING INCOME	**2,630**
PGA Tour's percentage of income	405

PROFIT BEFORE TAX	**2,225**

Annual revenues (above) are based on per-tournament projections (right). SportsBand anticipates netting about $250,000 at each event.

1990 P&L PER TOURNAMENT
(based on 15-event schedule)

REVENUES

Title sponsorship (based on $1-million title divided by 15 tournaments)	$66,700
Presenting/commercial sponsors	57,600
Tournament operator's fee (for cost of production)	75,000
Tournament fee (for share of corporate overhead)	22,500
Tournament receiver rentals (20,000 units @ $1.50, prepurchased by tournament)	30,000
Other receiver rentals (by attendees with unbundled tickets; 3,000 people x 3 days x $5)	45,000
Retained rental deposits (when customers trade $3 deposit for corporate premium)	30,000
Broadcast sales (updates to radio networks)	5,000
TOTAL TOURNAMENT REVENUES	**331,800**

COSTS

Labor & production costs incurred by broadcast subcontractor, Murray Street Enterprise	$47,380
Additional contract engineering staff	4,900
Receiver distribution	8,520
Expenses of Dallas personnel in attendance	4,200
Fee to PGA Tour	5,000
TOTAL TOURNAMENT PRODUCTION COSTS	**70,000**

NET INCOME FROM TOURNAMENT BROADCAST	**261,800**

got a bank loan of $138,000 against its hard assets. Mitchell sold some oil interests to kick in about $175,000 in cash and credit.

In the fall of 1987 SportsBand broadcast at three tournaments. "We saw firsthand," Mitchell says, "the future of this product." Contrary to the players' concerns, the audio play by play seemed to have a calming effect on the gallery, and in December 1987 the tournament policy board unanimously approved the system.

Mitchell and Rice went back to the Tour in January 1988, expecting to pick up the agreement negotiated a year before and simply put pen to paper. But its officials had become more intrigued with SportsBand. "The broadcast raises the value of a tournament ticket, which is important to us," says the Tour's West. The Tour offered a new proposal: Why not rework our relationship as a joint-marketing venture? The Tour would sell SportsBand sponsorships to its stable of corporate partners and help with operations and advance work. In return, it would get $10,000 per event to split 50/50 with each tournament, and a percentage of SportsBand's revenues—15% to start, increasing to 30% over the life of the contract.

For Mitchell and Rice, it sounded perfect. The affiliation would lend them leverage and prestige in the world of big-bucks corporate sponsorship, which they envisioned SportsBand entering. And it would help them address the question that they'd been mostly avoiding: how to make SportsBand pay.

At that point—early 1988—Mitchell and Rice were counting on three sources of revenues: receiver rentals, sale of tournament updates to such radio networks as the Mutual Broadcasting System and NBC, and corporate sponsorship. Their business plan outlined a 1989 schedule of 20 tournaments and $4.2 million in revenues; receiver rentals at $5 each to 10% of the crowd would make up 35% of sales, updates 20%, and corporate sponsorship 45%.

Selling the receivers to spectators and developing relationships with radio networks seemed to Mitchell and Rice challenging yet doable marketing tasks; market research with listeners at one tournament showed interest among spectators to be high, and Mitchell had already begun talking with radio people. But they guessed that finding sponsorship through cold calling would be enormously difficult, and that the PGA Tour, which had so successfully sold itself, could prove invaluable. "The PGA," figured Mitchell, "is a 900-pound gorilla to do our marketing for us."

SportsBand's title sponsorship would be priced at $1 million, for which a company would be incorporated into the program's name and get its logo printed on the receivers and SportsBand trucks, uniforms, and promotional materials. Secondary, or "presenting," sponsorships for individual tournaments would go for tens of thousands of dollars, depending on the prestige of the event. There would be commercials, too, but only in conjunction with such features as health tips, and they'd be made to sound like part of the broadcast.

Were the prices realistic? Mitchell and Rice didn't know, and the Tour was guessing; mostly they were working on instinct and a sense of what the market would bear. SportsBand would ask corporations to be visionary. If you believe in the concept, they'd say, help us get launched—and you'll have a lock on affiliation with this unique and eventually prestigious medium.

Most media buys, however, are not made on instinct alone. Advertising-placement decisions center on how many impressions are presented to how many people how many times; sports marketing usually works the same way. "When you don't put a calculation on it, it's harder to sell," says Bill Neff, director of sales at Advantage International, a Washington, D.C.–based firm that matches sponsors with events. "The sophisticated clients now ask the hard questions, although they didn't for years."

SportsBand, reaching maybe 30,000 fans a day, couldn't sell on the numbers, but Mitchell was convinced that "sports marketing is, has been, and always will be an emotional, impulse buy." And with some 3,900 businesses plowing $2.1 billion into events from golf tournaments to marathons, according to "Special Events Report," a Chicago newsletter that tracks sponsorship; with major sponsorships for weeklong tournaments running $500,000 to more than $1 million; with companies already pouring tens of millions of dollars into golf; and with the Tour's assurances that the pricing was in line, Mitchell figured sponsors would take the lure. "There's nothing that's going to be closer to people at these events than my broadcast," he insists. "Wouldn't common sense tell you that if you give sponsors a *talking* sign, which can bring their affiliation to life, it would be of value? Much more so than hanging a banner."

SportsBand signed a five-year contract with the PGA Tour in the spring of 1988, and for the rest of the year Art West and another member of the Tour's promotion department made sponsorship introductions. Mitchell and Rice built a staff at their Dallas headquarters, planned a 1989 schedule, and raised additional capital through a private offering— getting $1.15 million in $25,000 units from 35 limited partners for 35% of the company.

At the end of the year SportsBand broadcast at two tournaments, underwritten by RJR Nabisco for $50,000 each. Mickey Nutting, a vice-president at Sports Marketing Enterprises Inc., which advises RJR Nabisco, says that while he initially considered the idea "a gimmick" back in 1986, he'd come around to it by the end of 1988. "I was impressed by those two shows. The receivers were used extensively by people out there." SportsBand seemed to be a good thing to tie into hospitality packages, he says, and was a good forum for pitching individual brands of RJR Nabisco products.

Entering 1989 SportsBand had 13 full-time employees, including engineers, operations coordinators, and marketers. Most of the on-air and production people remained contracted through Rathe's company, and Carol Mann had become the company spokesperson. Everybody connected with SportsBand had been given a portion of stock.

Twenty tournaments were scheduled. Eight sponsors, including Nabisco and Gatorade, had signed on for packages of commercials at $36,000 to $65,000 each, about $400,000 collectively.

But for the most part the business plan wasn't falling into place. The title sponsorship was unsold, and by June only two presenting sponsors had signed on. SportsBand was fighting an uphill battle, says Mitchell, because "when people first hear of it, they think `radio,' which translates into a tiny media buy. They don't initially understand the system."

In addition, no agreement had been reached with radio networks for update sales. And after a couple of tournaments, Mitchell and Rice even concluded that receivers were not going to be as easy to rent as anticipated. "We had to educate people," says Rice, "and the only thing that seems to sell SportsBand is SportsBand." They began offering free receivers on Fridays, and charging just $2 rental on Saturdays and Sundays.

By March Mitchell and Rice decided that revenues were not going to be anywhere near what they'd anticipated for the year, and they began reevaluating their plans. First, they'd need to raise an additional $2.5 million to make up the 1989 shortfall and continue operations. Second, they began to look at alternate ways to market the receivers in the future. Could tournament directors be talked into including receivers in the price of their tickets? That would solve the rental problem and make the network more attractive to sponsors by ensuring spectator usage.

At a meeting that month of the American Golf Sponsors (the directors who work year-round to plan their tournaments), Mitchell, Rice, and the Tour made their proposal: Here's a service that your attendees will love, they argued, but we need your help to get the receivers into their hands. Why not raise ticket prices $5 to incorporate SportsBand into the price of entry? We'll take the first $30,000 and split the rest with you. And we'll all be partners: You'll have this great service at your event, we'll have our service at least somewhat premarketed, and we'll all share the profits—the PGA Tour will pass on part of its portion of SportsBand revenues to each tournament that signs on.

Some tournaments expressed skepticism at the plan. "I'm not receptive to raising prices," says Jim Lyle, tournament chairman for the 1990 Nissan Los Angeles Open. "Some companies buy 500 or 600 tickets, and if you raise them $5 each, you're talking about a substantial amount of money." Others seemed affronted that SportsBand assumed they'd raise prices just to pay for a radio program instead of to make capital improvements or increase their purse. Still others raised a different question: What if we like SportsBand enough to promote it and include it in our tickets, but want to pass on the cost to a corporate sponsor? How do we figure out how much to pay you?

By June Mitchell and Rice had revamped the plan again, and this time the difference was more dramatic. Go ahead and find the money however you want, SportsBand said, but we'll need a minimum of about $100,000 to broadcast at your events.

In a letter to tournament directors in late June, Mitchell explained that from each tournament, SportsBand would need $75,000 for production costs, $22,500 to help recover "a portion of the Network's general and administration expenses," and $1.50 for each receiver distributed. If, for example, the tournament wanted to incorporate receivers into 20,000 of its most expensive tickets, it would pay SportsBand $127,500. If the tournament got a sponsor to pick up the tab, SportsBand might offer the company airtime as part of the deal.

It was an abrupt switch, shifting the bill from sponsors to tournament directors and making SportsBand's presence contingent on tournaments' participation as marketers and partners. "Frank and I always dreamed of being part of the ticket. We always knew life would be easier that way," says Rice. But now, they'd decided that an arrangement they'd once thought would be nice had become *necessary*.

"We had thought that by hanging out our shingle and putting out a bunch of these receivers, we could develop, slowly but surely, a following of spectators," says Rice. "We thought that word of mouth and the press coupled together would generate some pretty good penetration. And we weren't really right about that."

What's more, he says, the company had found it couldn't *afford* to grow slowly. "We're in a market for three or four days," says Rice, "and we don't get to come back for a full year. So if you convince somebody to use it this time, it's not the same as convincing somebody to use it today and then 10 days from now. It's pretty critical to become part of the ticket."

Under the new strategy, SportsBand's break-even revenues would be virtually guaranteed up front by the tournament directors. All the sponsorships, at-the-door receiver rentals, and ancillary broadcast sales, though, would be gravy—potentially a lot of it. Next year's projections call for the company to have expenses of $2.3 million against revenues of almost $5 million—37% of which, or the bulk of the margin, is still expected from sponsorships.

As of July Rice and Mitchell planned to spend the summer meeting with tournament directors and corporate sponsors, trying to sell them on the idea. Not until the tournaments fall into place will SportsBand go back to actively pursuing sponsors.

The SportsBand operation, meanwhile, went through a serious retrenchment as the new plan was being unveiled. Having done nine broadcasts between January and June, Mitchell and Rice decided to halt the rest that were scheduled and resume broadcasting only at tournaments accepting some variation of the proposal. "We've done enough broadcasts to demonstrate what this is, its reliability, its consistency," says Mitchell. "If SportsBand's going to be done, this is the level we insist it be done at or else it's not worth doing. It's just hard to keep justifying losing money at tournaments." In negotiating, though, Mitchell says he's "not going to be hard-nosed about it," expecting to cut deals with each tournament to accommodate individual operations.

Mitchell and Rice loaned at least $200,000 more of personal funds to the company and continued talking with individual investors and an investment banking firm about selling equity in SportsBand. "There's a definite end to what we can personally bring to this company," hedges Mitchell, "although we're not at it." With the staff trimmed to eight people as of July and monthly overhead down to about $33,000, Rice says they've got enough money to carry the company through 1989 while setting 1990 plans in place. If they get a half-dozen tournaments signed on for next year, Rice says he's confident he could find a quarter-million dollars from private investors this fall.

This is not where Mitchell and Rice had expected to be, going through yet another year of sales and marketing. "Is it frustrating? You're damn right it is," says Rice. Would he do it all over again? "Today my answer would probably be no. Hell, I was 34 when we started this business, and now I'm 70. It's just tough. It *is* tough."

After a moment he reconsiders. "That's probably not true. I probably would do it again. But I know there are still a lot of hurdles to clear, and I know they're big ones. And at some point you want to be able to look back and see you've already cleared all the hurdles, and now you're just running straight."

While they're mostly focused on making the idea work with the PGA Tour, Mitchell and Rice have been discussing a contract with the Ladies Professional Golf Association, and talking with Championship Auto Racing Teams and the United States Tennis Association about SportsBand broadcasts at their events. They've licensed a SportsBand organization in Canada to operate the service at sporting events. American golfing, they say, is just the start for their company.

But questions remain: Will tournaments agree to become partners? SportsBand has to convince operators that the promotional value of the broadcast justifies raising ticket prices or shifting more costs to sponsors—and that they don't have to lose money in the process. Tournament directors do seem enamored with having a broadcast at their events, but remain skeptical of the cost. Mitchell and Rice may have to settle for crafting a middle ground with each tournament.

Will sponsors see SportsBand as something worth buying into? MCI Communications special-promotions director Donald L. Campbell says that his company "has an awful lot of money invested in golf already, and whether it's worth putting out more money, I'm just not sure." On the other hand, Ernest J. Renzulli, publisher of *Golf Illustrated* and a sponsor this year, notes that companies buying SportsBand "may not be getting many people, but boy, you're getting the cream of the crop." And it's a captive audience. "Other buys may cost less," Renzulli says, "but with SportsBand you're getting five hours in someone's ear."

"We're still in a chameleon state," says Rice, "still trying to figure out how to sell and market this thing." Echoes Mitchell: "This just has never been a project that lent itself to absolute quantification. It's too new; it's going into such uncharted waters. You can guesstimate, you can intelligently propose how things are going to work, but until you get out and do them, you don't know. That's the way this project's always been. And continues to be."

"I'm sold on the idea, but you have to look at the financial side of what SportsBand is offering. It's hard to seriously consider its current proposal."

—Mike Stevens

OBSERVER

JUDY LAFRENIERE

Director of sales, Sponsors Report, a sports market-research firm specializing in media analysis, Ann Arbor, Mich.

A million dollars for their title sponsorship, I don't see happening. For that kind of dollar investment, a company could sponsor an event and have it all to themselves. They could entertain clients, get television exposure—the most important thing for almost all corporate sponsors—and get print exposure. If you sponsor an event, you're bound to get covered across the country, if not with articles, then at least with box scores. Well, with Sports-Band, you're going to get no print exposure.

Given the average attendance for SportsBand's events and using a formula where we put a value on the impressions that are generated, there's no way a company's going to get $1 million worth of exposure. SportsBand would reach 450,000 people, and I'd value it at $138,600—obviously, not even close to $1 million. Now, say SportsBand included its title sponsor's name in every piece of print advertising and radio advertising it did, then it would improve the impressions count and maybe take the value up to $500,000. But $1 million is just too high a number to be attractive to sponsors.

OBSERVER

LESA UKMAN

Founder and editor, Special Events Report—*an international newsletter that tracks events, Chicago*

What's happened is these guys have put all their resources behind their product, but spent no time or money on creating demand for it. They say fan interest—unit rentals—has been low not because of the idea but because "we haven't educated them." I agree. They should have launched a publicity campaign at the same time SportsBand was being introduced, even though it was only a test, so people going to the event could have anticipated it and understood its benefits.

Until there's audience demand, there's nothing there for sponsors. Even then, SportsBand has to think about offering far more than just on-site spectators. Sponsors aren't using golf just to reach the ticket holders. They can reach a much larger audience through TV broadcasts of the events. What you can do, once SportsBand is a proven attraction, is tie it into sales promotions: Test-drive a Cadillac and receive a coupon for a free SportsBand. One could argue that a Cadillac dealer can already do that with tickets to the tournament, but maybe Sports-Band will become really hot—it's new and sexier than the tickets. So it's an attraction. Maybe you propose to American Express that card holders get a free SportsBand; that's a way for Am Ex to create a sense of privilege. SportsBand has got to go to sponsors with these kinds of thought-out packages, but it has to create fan demand first.

I think asking tournaments to package SportsBand with tickets is totally absurd and unrealistic. There's no reason for the tournaments to do it; they're not going to sell more tickets because SportsBand is there. So asking tournament organizers to mark up their tickets $5 with no guarantee of return doesn't seem to me an enlightened proposition.

Tournament directors are used to people paying *them* a fee to be affiliated with the event. SportsBand is not only unwilling to pay them a fee and unwilling to say, "This is a great service, let us go out there for free and rent our units to your fans," they're saying: "Underwrite a portion of our costs." They've gone three steps the other way.

If the SportsBand folks depend on tournament directors as the main revenue source, I don't think they'll succeed. But if they can market the service to the audience and then bring it to sponsors as part of a tournament-sponsorship package, there's a good reason for hope. But doing that will take a year or two more of start-up cost and time.

OBSERVER

MIKE STEVENS
Tournament director, MCI Heritage Classic, Hilton Head, S.C.; currently considering SportsBand's pitch for bringing the service to next April's Heritage

I'm sold on the idea, but you have to look at the financial side of what SportsBand is offering. It's hard to seriously consider its current proposal. There will have to be some compromise on the company's side to make it more attractive, at least to this tournament. I don't want to negotiate in the magazines, but by "compromise" I mean that these guys might be off by at least a factor of two.

Right now we're looking to make SportsBand a revenue source for us. I might make a counterproposal by going back to SportsBand and asking for commercial airtime during their radio broadcasts that I, in turn, could sell to my corporate sponsors.

I think that in time a broadcast like this will be integral to golf—people will expect it—but I also think getting started will be difficult. You are probably looking at a five-year time frame.

CUSTOMER

ROGER BEAR

*Vice-president of planning and
development, Sports Marketing
Enterprises, which advises such
companies as RJR Nabisco on sports
sponsorship, Winston-Salem, N.C.*

I think they can make it. The way
they're trying to sell themselves
now makes a whole lot more sense
than expecting corporate America
to fund this whole thing through
sponsorship.

Before I'd recommend a Sports-
Band sponsorship to a client,
though, I'd have to see commitments from 15 tournaments. I'd also
have to have some kind of agreement that provides me with a guaranteed number of listeners, a way to
check that number, and a rebate if it
isn't reached. They can't provide
me with affidavits and proofs of
performance like radio—but they
can provide other kinds of proofs
of performance.

My advice to them would be sell
like hell. And stick to the plan
they've got now, because it'll work.
They're into this for a lot of pocket
money—you hate to see guys get in
this far and then make a major
change even though the major
change makes sense. They are really
gamblers, and it shows. But they
always had the right product, and I
think they've finally got it packaged
right.

CLASS PICTURES

*VideOvation is betting that today's
TV generation will want even their school
yearbook in video form*

BY BRUCE G. POSNER

Back in 1985, while working as an investment consultant to the Rockefeller family in New York City, Paul Gruenberg got a phone call from an acquaintance in California. The friend had recently invested in a young company that needed money. Did Gruenberg have any interest—or did he know anyone who might be interested—in video "yearbooks"?

Gruenberg agreed to look over a package of material. But nothing he saw suggested that it could become much of a business. "There was no market information. No financial or operating information either. It was a couple of pages of seat-of-the-pants stuff." The tape was like a home movie. "A kid from Duke had taken a video camera and shot a bunch of friends wrestling and drinking."

He put the idea out of his mind. But a few months later a funding proposal crossed his desk that cast it in a different light. By coincidence,

---

Paul Gruenberg, founder of Gruenberg Video Group Inc.

MEDIA

the proposal involved a publisher of high-school yearbooks. Gruenberg, who'd spent four years evaluating investment opportunities, was impressed with the characteristics of the industry, how steady and profitable it was. Three or four publishers, he learned, controlled about 90% of a $350-million market, much as they'd done for 20 or 30 years. As he saw it, "it was like an annuity." So long as they produced a good product, they were set.

The yearbook deal didn't materialize. But it got Gruenberg scratching his head. Was there a similar annuitylike opportunity in video yearbooks? With the right product and the right approach to production and marketing, his gut told him, there was. "I remember going home one night and telling my wife that *somebody* was going to figure it out." By January 1986 Gruenberg had quit his job and was working out of his Manhattan apartment, mapping out how he would be that somebody.

Four years and $3.3 million later, Gruenberg, a 40-year-old father of three, thinks he has a grip on what it will take to be a leader in what he believes may be a $500-million industry within a decade. In many ways Gruenberg Video Group Inc., doing business as VideOvation and located in Philadelphia, is modeled after the print yearbook businesses he'd once marveled at. First, it tries to sell middle- and high-school principals on the curricular and promotional benefits that video yearbooks can bring to students and schools. Once a principal has signed on, a field producer works with a faculty adviser and a team of students, who are responsible for shooting the raw tape. With VideOvation supplying equipment, training tapes, and field support, the goal is to produce a 30- to 40-minute video that brings back the school year's memories: the faces, the sights, the sounds. VideOvation sells the edited tape (which includes a "time capsule" of world events) to students and their parents for $29.95 plus a $3 handling charge.

Last year the company generated $134,200 by selling an average of 100 units at 43 schools; it lost about $1 million. But Gruenberg believes things will change dramatically over the next two years as VideOvation signs more schools, sells more tapes, and fine-tunes its operating methods. In the 1991–92 school year, he hopes to sell an average of 286 tapes at 833 schools. If he does, he'll earn $1.1 million on $7.9 million in revenues.

More than 95% of the country's 18,000 high schools produce printed yearbooks, and this year some 11 million students (about 65% of the U.S. high-school population) will spend in the neighborhood of $20 to $30 to buy a copy of the 1990 edition. But Gruenberg doesn't think he'll have to siphon business away from any of the traditional yearbook publishers to be successful. Rather, he believes there's a new cate-

EXECUTIVE SUMMARY

THE COMPANY:
Gruenberg Video Group Inc., d/b/a VideOvation, Philadelphia

CONCEPT:
Sell a video-production package of equipment, training tapes, and field support to middle and high schools to produce a video yearbook

PROJECTIONS:
Losses of nearly $1 million in 1990; projected earnings of $1.1 million on sales of $7.9 million in fiscal 1992

HURDLES:
Achieving market penetration with outside sales force; covering anticipated $1-million cash shortfall before break-even; overcoming reluctance of school principals to invest students' and faculty's time in production

gory of high-school memorabilia taking shape—one that takes advantage of the unique characteristics of video.

Already, Gruenberg notes, video has become part of the daily diet of most U.S. teenagers; they watch videotapes of entertainers, sporting events—you name it—for several hours a week. Up to now not many high schools (fewer than 1,000) have produced video yearbooks. But as more and more do, Gruenberg thinks that significant numbers of students—upward of 20%—will want to own both print and video yearbooks. It's only a matter of time, he says, before the numbers are truly interesting.

From his office on the 54th floor of Rockefeller Center back in 1985, it was raw numbers that caught his eye: 3 million Americans finishing high school every year, mushrooming sales of home VCRs and other video products. His first business plan described three different scenarios for how fast the market would develop. The most conservative of them anticipated revenues in the third year of $13 million. As Gruenberg saw it, he'd be producing his new-style yearbooks in 1,475 schools, shipping more than 440,000 tapes, earning more than $1.6 million.

On the basis of his projections, Gruenberg managed to raise $1.2 million of initial financing from 15 contacts in the investment world. Originally, he had approached the top two print yearbook companies, Jostens Inc., in Minneapolis, and Taylor Publishing Co., in Dallas. But neither was interested in providing seed money. This left Gruenberg with some obvious challenges. How was he going to get things rolling? And how was he going to differentiate VideOvation from the folks who were already in the market as well as those who would follow?

Gruenberg didn't realize then that there were three separate parts to the marketing puzzle that needed to be worked out. First, he had to define the product. Second, he had to find ways to sign up the schools. And third, he had to figure out how to sell tapes. Each posed a different

THE FOUNDER

Paul T. Gruenberg, president and CEO

Age: 40

Family status: Married, three children

Source of idea: Competitor's business plan

Personal funds invested: $175,000

Equity held: 26%

Salary: $75,000

Outside board of directors: Yes

Other business started: Antique and classic-car restoration business

College degrees: B.A. from Lake Forest College; master's in management from Yale

Typical workweek: 65 hours

Other jobs: Five years working for two venture capital partnerships

Typical workweek: 65 hours

Last vacation: A week in Maine last August

Favorite hobby: Formula Ford race-car driving

Why I'd quit: When it's no longer fun or if the initial assumptions about the market don't stand up

---

set of challenges. Only in the past few months has he felt that he has the basics figured out.

DEFINING THE PRODUCT: At the beginning, Gruenberg's idea was to have a school-based video product that was almost entirely created by the students. Instead of sending a professional video crew into high schools, like some mom-and-pop competitors were doing, he wanted to have the students, assisted by a faculty adviser, running the show—deciding what belonged on the tape and figuring out how to get it. Students, thought Gruenberg, had a feeling for the school and the people that would be critical to the appeal of the product; not only that, their labor was free. He didn't want a formula (30 seconds of this, 60 seconds of that) governing how they operated. "The idea," Gruenberg says, "was to have videos that reflected all the different ways kids are growing up." The company was going to furnish video cameras, tapes, and information on how to shoot. A team or class of students would do the filming. Everything else—the editing, the soundtrack, the in-school selling, and the distribution—would be up to VideOvation.

But could it really work this way? Could students without any professional video experience generate tape that was (a) interesting and (b) technically good enough to be edited without enormous amounts of labor? Gruenberg tested the idea at 11 schools in New England and the Midwest in 1987 and found, to his dismay, that the answer was no. "The early footage was a disaster," Gruenberg recalls. The cameras bounced up and down and meandered aimlessly; the content was often frivolous. Gruenberg recognized right away that his notion of the product had to change. "We had to teach students about video, or else we'd always be spending too much time on the back end of the process." In essence, they had to create a curriculum and a format for making the videos.

Today Gruenberg thinks he has a first-rate system for introducing students and faculty advisers to video. It didn't come cheaply. The company has invested more than $100,000 to produce a series of 15 video lessons designed by Howie Masters, a former producer and director of ABC's "Good Morning, America." (An earlier effort to create a written training text proved a total waste, notes Gruenberg; nobody read it.) The lessons begin simply (how to use the camera, how to shoot close-ups, how to use microphones and lights) and move along to more advanced topics (how to plan stories, how to review and select the best footage). To manage the process of assembling tapes, VideOvation has created a 19-segment format that's synchronized to the lessons. For each segment—fall sports, for example—students get simple instructions for what to keep in mind; they also get periodic deadlines for getting their cassettes back to the editing studios at VideOvation.

To differentiate itself from most of its competitors, VideOvation is attempting to position its program as a curricular tool as well as a product. Every school is assigned a field producer, shared by 10 to 20 schools, who assists students and faculty advisers on technical issues. Unlike field staff at other companies, whose main role is to sell, VideOvation's people have all studied filmmaking or video broadcasting in college, Gruenberg says, and have at least five years of professional experience. Obviously, this boosts the company's front-end costs: On top of the equipment, these personnel costs add $1,000 per school. But Gruenberg feels it's worth the money for at least two reasons. First, he thinks it helps the company control production costs and assure quality. And second, it becomes a selling point with principals who, he argues, in times of budgetary pressure seek cost-effective ways to enrich their school curricula.

SIGNING UP SCHOOLS: When he began, a more wide-eyed Gruenberg thought that lining up a few hundred high schools would be a walk in the park. After all, he wouldn't be asking principals to spend a dime (the students or their parents would do the spending), and he'd be supplying a worthwhile program. Who could say no?

But without a track record and references, Gruenberg found that

VIDEOVATION PROJECTED OPERATING STATEMENT
(in $ thousands)

	Fiscal 1990	Fiscal 1992
Net video yearbook sales	$563	$7,841
Interest income	14	61
TOTAL REVENUES	**577**	**7,902**
Cost of goods (copying, packaging)	82	952
Commissions	136	2,260
Total cost of sales	218	3,212
GROSS PROFIT	**359**	**4,690**
Percent gross profit	62%	59%
OPERATING EXPENSES		
Other marketing & selling costs	89	53
Field producer salaries, travel	193	1,280
Editing, postproduction	200	1,004
Headquarters		
Staff salaries, benefits	375	725
Building occupancy, other G&A	191	202
Depreciation	96	309
TOTAL OPERATING EXPENSES	**1,144**	**3,573**
Interest expense	97	0
NET INCOME BEFORE TAXES	**(882)**	**1,117**
Percent net income before taxes	—	14%
Number of schools	118	833
Tapes sold at each school	145	286
Total units	17,110	238,238

U.S. high schools weren't easy to sell. "We wanted access to the top decision maker—the principal as opposed to a business manager or activities manager," he says. It only made sense, he felt, to go after the person who had the power to assign faculty advisers; a good adviser, he thought, could make the difference between a successful school program and a dud. Unfortunately, principals, especially in the larger schools he wanted most, weren't easy to see. "In a lot of schools," he notes, "we couldn't get in the door."

When Gruenberg or the other employees did talk to principals, the feedback was often mixed. Many liked the idea of kids learning video—or so they said—but how exactly would it work? How much faculty time would it take? How much student time? And how might it undermine the popular yearbook? Because the VideOvation employees' experience with schools was so limited, they didn't have convincing answers. Most principals told them to come back when they did.

By mid-1988, Gruenberg thought the company was finally in a position to describe the program in detail. He and a staff of nine, including three field producers, had been working on an experimental basis with 28 schools; for the 1988–89 school year, they wanted 200 schools. To orchestrate the expansion, Gruenberg recruited a sales manager from a major publishing company who urged, among other things, that VideOvation try teaming up with one of the better-known yearbook companies to help sign up schools. It sounded fine to Gruenberg. He worked out deals with several sales representatives from Taylor Publishing, the number two yearbook company.

But the experiment was a bust. Gruenberg and others at VideOvation succeeded in getting renewal commitments from 25 of the 28 existing schools; but just 18 new schools joined the program, for a total of 43. "Only 4 or 5 of the new schools came from the yearbook reps," Gruenberg says. The problem, he feels, was one of access. "[The reps] didn't know principals—they knew yearbook advisers, many of whom were threatened by our product." Whatever the problem, it cost the company both time and money. With schools, he now knows, you need to have agreements negotiated by late spring or be prepared to wait another year.

On the theory that the wrong contact can be worse than no contact at all, Gruenberg and Bob Carl, a video-industry consultant, spent several months trying to identify other possible marketing partners. The question they asked over and over: Who had the principal's ear? They thought about suppliers of such products as class rings, caps and gowns, even athletic equipment; yearbook companies weren't even considered, Gruenberg says, because of their perceived lack of interest. Finally, just before Thanksgiving in 1988, they zoomed in on a company named QSP Inc., whose business is school fund-raising.

As the country's leader in the field, QSP, a Reader's Digest subsidiary in Ridgefield, Conn., specializes in helping principals raise money for everything from school equipment to team uniforms to class trips by getting students to sell magazine subscriptions, food, and gifts. Its field managers knew little about video. What they seemed to have—and what Gruenberg hopes to tap—is access to the top. Gruenberg is wagering that QSP field managers will be able to parlay their contacts and credibility into commitments from principals to participate in the VideOvation program. What began as a trial relationship was extended in June 1989 for one year; a new two- or three-year contract was being negotiated in March.

With the presence of a marketing partner, VideOvation is essentially out of the business of courting principals itself—and happily so, says Gruenberg, pointing to recent gains. During the spring and summer of 1989 fewer than 20 QSP field managers signed 85 new schools (double the company's previous clientele). This year QSP has assigned a lot more reps—about 150—and Gruenberg thinks it may sign 350 new schools by August. In addition to the East Coast from Maine to North Carolina, QSP will be targeting northern California, Illinois, Missouri, and Minnesota. "We're starting to get calls from principals who've heard about us from other principals," Gruenberg says.

Flattering as Gruenberg finds this, he is developing a set of criteria to make sure that schools aren't too costly to service. Among them: the size of the school (he wants to concentrate on high schools with no fewer than 900 students, where the opportunities for selling tapes is greatest); and where schools are located in relation to other VideOvation schools (the company is trying to cluster them in metropolitan areas in groups of at least 30).

S ELLING TAPES: The arrangement with QSP also provides VideOvation with new capability for selling tapes, which ultimately is—and will always be—the single most critical variable in this kind of business, says Gruenberg. He explains that producing a school tape costs about $2,350 before you make the first copy. The copies themselves, however, are ridiculously cheap; each copy costs about $4.80 for copying, labeling, and packaging. Commissions can run as high as $9 per tape. To break even, VideOvation needs to sell around 150 tapes at $29.95 at every school; whatever it sells above that is gravy.

Back in the days when the company was handling tape sales itself, the results were unpredictable and usually disappointing. Selling tapes was largely up to the individual field producers, who, with all their technical responsibilities, were spread thin. Sometimes they came close to breaking even by selling 100 or 150 copies (about 10% or 15% of a single school's potential market); other times, Gruenberg says, they'd sell fewer than 25 videos. "We'd spend all that money and get nothing back."

Now that QSP is running sales, the chances of getting stuck with a low-volume tape have all but disappeared. Before signing a school, notes John Davis, QSP's VideOvation product manager, field managers are expected to do as much as possible to cover their risks. First, they ask principals to guarantee purchase of 200 tapes. Failing that—and only a small percentage have said yes—they ask the principal to commit to holding at least one assembly that all students are required to attend, the sole purpose of which is to introduce the video program and to book orders. "QSP's business," Gruenberg says, "is running sales events and collecting money." If a principal will not agree to the assembly or if the event and follow-up activity don't generate sufficient orders (the target is 125 paid orders by October of the school year), the company may decide to walk away. "Our attitude," says Gruenberg, "is that the students have to indicate a tangible interest, or we can't afford to be there."

The commissions VideOvation is prepared to pay are nothing to sneeze at. But the benefits over handling sales internally, Gruenberg says, are becoming obvious not only in the speed with which VideOvation can get its hands on cash, but also in the overall acceptance of the product. "We used to struggle to get 10% of a student body. But now we only have a few schools under 20%, and a number are over 30%." In two or three years, Gruenberg thinks penetration in many repeating schools will exceed 40%. "We used to have a sales manager," he notes. "But we've recently let him go. Under this setup, he wouldn't have anything to do."

VideOvation operates out of a 5,500-square-foot office in a renovated parochial girls' school on the fringes of the University of Pennsylvania campus in Philadelphia. Its sparsely furnished space, which it rents at a below-market rate of $8,000 a month, is fitted with four fully equipped editing suites. The suites are staffed by free-lance video editors; rather than paying them by the hour, the company attempts to control its expenses by paying them a flat $1,000 for every master tape they edit.

The company payroll numbers 19, counting Gruenberg—10 are field producers assigned to the 118 schools VideOvation currently works with; the others are a vice-president for production, a production manager, a director of field operations, a managing editor, a producer, two secretaries, and a part-time controller. Payroll and other fixed expenses run about $80,000 per month, Gruenberg says.

Based on current levels of operations, Gruenberg expects to lose $882,000 on revenues of $577,000 during the 1989–90 school year. But sometime in the next 12 to 18 months, he expects to flip from losses to profits. The shift to profitability on a cash-flow basis will be achieved, he explains, by signing more schools, getting higher market penetration within schools, and lowering overhead by operating more efficiently.

With 118 schools, fixed costs don't get spread out much. But VideOvation could handle a lot more business, Gruenberg claims, at only modest incremental expense. Another 80 or 100 schools (which would generate a minimum of $395,000 in revenues), would be easy to absorb, he says. By adding extra shifts and hiring more free-lance editors, the company could get by with its existing editing equipment. Almost all the other staffing is already in place. "The most we'd need is two additional part-time clerical people," he says.

Gruenberg used to think that it would take around 375 schools generating revenues of about $2.2 million to reach break-even on a cash-flow basis—something he felt could be achieved during the 1990–91 school year. That goal was based on the assumption that the average penetration rate at high schools would be about 26%, that field producers would handle 20 schools, and that the equipment package would run about $1,150 for every school. But in recent months he's been pushing downward the number of schools needed for break-even, and he thinks it may go lower still.

As QSP field managers refine their selling techniques, the 26% penetration rate may be conservative, Gruenberg says. "At 30%, we'll only need around 300 schools." What's more, if the new schools are located close to one another, field producers may be able to handle more schools—perhaps more than 30. The company is negotiating with manufacturers of cameras and editing equipment for discounts or free equipment; it currently gets free tape from 3M Co. Gruenberg is also considering the sale of paid on-tape advertisements, which would drive costs even lower. "We're working a lot of angles—controlling costs and boosting penetration are the name of the game."

Gruenberg, who owns 26% of the business, admits that it's taken more time and more money to crack the market than he expected. In March, VideOvation was preparing to borrow $500,000 from its investors, who had already supplied $3.3 million in equity, to cover the anticipated cash shortfall for the next few months. Before the business becomes self-funding, Gruenberg figures he may need at least $1 million more. "How much we need really depends on what happens in the schools this spring." The student sign-up rate, the location of the schools, and whether the company can get breaks from equipment suppliers—each will tell part of the story.

Gruenberg says he's watched competitors of all types—from small independents to the big yearbook publishers—enter the video market. But he claims he isn't worried. "There is a huge number of schools out there. So there's plenty of room for three, four, even five viable competitors."

He's banking, too, on a loyalty factor: Once a school has worked with VideOvation and is happy with the results, he doesn't think it will change. "We're building barriers to entry for other companies whenever we sign and re-sign schools. Rather than steal our schools, they'll try to find new ones of their own."

And what about competition from schools that think they can make their own tapes? Gruenberg thinks that it's inevitable. But not many will actually do it—not when they figure out what's involved. Editing, he says, takes an enormous amount of time, which neither busy students nor their overworked advisers have—not to mention equipment and expertise. And who would do the packaging and selling? For uncertain benefits, he claims, few schools will want to take on the burden.

"We give students maximum creative control over the product without any of the back-end hassles." In the end, he hopes this approach will feel right to both principals and students. The future of his business depends on it.

WHAT THE EXPERTS SAY

"What does a school get out of this? These days a lot of school people are saying, 'Why should we do it unless we get 50%? Why should we try to make you money?' "

—*Rocco Marano*

CUSTOMER

RICHARD DUFOUR
Principal/assistant superintendent, Adlai Stevenson High School, Prairie View, Ill., with 1,900 students and no video yearbooks

I like the effort the company has made to involve students in the creation of the video and that it's created an actual curriculum—because principals always have to ask, "Is there an educational component to this?" If I were one of their sales reps, I'd really push that.

I think the biggest problem Vide-Ovation will have is its assumption that it's not cutting into the yearbook market. From the point of view of yearbook faculty advisers, that's not the case. They'll see it as a real threat to student interest in working on the traditional yearbook. We've had a couple different video companies try to pitch us, and our yearbook adviser was not in favor of it at all.

No principal in his right mind would guarantee the sale of 200 videos. And getting a principal to allow an all-student assembly to demonstrate this video is pretty unlikely, too. Just look at the controversy Chris Whittle got into by offering 10 minutes of news a day, free equipment, and televisions in every classroom in return for two minutes of commercials. There's a hue and cry about that. Imagine a principal saying, "Yeah, I'll take instructional time to have an entire student body sit as a captive audience for a sales pitch on this commercial product." Not many right-thinking principals would agree to that.

A better approach would be to simply offer this as a flat-out fundraising activity. To let, say, the junior class sponsor it. Then you charge $35, and the students keep $5. If the kids felt they could sell 200 or 300 videos, that's a lot of money, more than they'd make selling candy or pennants. Getting student leaders and a class adviser saying, "We can make this work," and approaching the principal would be a better marketing strategy.

OBSERVER

ROCCO MARANO
Associate director, National Association of Secondary School Principals, division of student activities, Reston, Va.

What the company did right was hook up with QSP. It went with somebody who really knows the school establishment and has the sales force to go and talk to principals. QSP's got a good reputation; it's a good organization for fundraising, and it's trustworthy.

I know that yearbooks are not looked on as a way to make money, but reading all this I wonder, What does a school get out of this? These days a lot of school people are saying, "Why should we be doing it unless we get 50%? Why should we try to make you money?" If Gruenberg is looking for a partnership with the schools, he may have to let them make money on it.

The company should consider offering varied services, not just one package. Some schools already do a fantastic job with video and may think, "We can't print our yearbooks, but we can probably edit our videos." They may not be top quality, but may be just good enough. So if schools have their own equipment, the company could provide training; yearbook companies, for example, hold workshops. Then even if schools get more sophisticated, they don't have to dump you.

COMPETITOR

MARTY ALLEN
President, Scholastic Video Inc., Exton, Pa., a one-year-old video-yearbook company; former marketing director for Jostens Inc.

Operating in the school market takes a lot of patience, and I think Gruenberg is finally beginning to see this. He's figuring out who to talk to, although in my experience the buying decision isn't very often made by the principal.

Structurally, I think he's making a mistake by having two sets of people—field producers and outside sales reps—servicing the same schools. At this point, it's important that schools build loyalty. They're going to be working most closely with the field producer, and that

person should have a very big stake in seeing to it that the school is happy and gets renewed. In the yearbook industry, sales reps handle both sales and service; their necks are on the line to get schools renewed.

Editors can make or break you in the quality of the final product. Gruenberg's chosen to use freelancers to keep costs down, but because he pays them a flat rate for the tapes they edit, the incentive isn't for quality but speed. If they can do something in 10 minutes, I doubt they'll spend an extra half hour to make an OK tape into a really great tape.

In terms of the overall market, I think he's optimistic. I doubt if we're talking about a $500-million market—it will probably be closer to $250 million or $300 million. The number of schools he hopes to sign is doable. But getting penetration within schools is going to be harder than he thinks. I think this will be a slow-growth industry in terms of unit sales.

FINANCIER

KEVIN DOUGHERTY
General partner, The Venture Capital Fund of New England, Boston, who in his former capacity as a commercial lender worked with yearbook companies

Gruenberg thinks they now have the right way to sell—and they might. But I'm skeptical. Whenever you rely on an outside group whose business is different from yours to do the sales, you have to worry about whether the partner will give it the attention it requires—and whether its interest will be diverted to something else next year. We see it all the time in the high-tech field: Something *looks* like a natural add-on product for a third-party selling organization, but it doesn't always pan out.

Is QSP's expertise the kind VideOvation needs most? QSP's business, as I understand it, is helping schools set up fund-raising drives; its bread and butter is really teaching sellers how to sell. To help VideOvation inside schools, it will have to get buyers to buy. Yearbook and ring companies already know how to do this, but I'm not sure QSP does. It's a very different skill, and it makes me wonder whether the company will get the penetration it expects.

I give Gruenberg a lot of credit for being flexible. He's been sharp enough to see what hasn't worked, and he's changed his marketing focus a few times. He hasn't been dragged down by a strategy that wasn't clicking.

Will he succeed? I don't take a lot of comfort in his financial projections. Investors already have more than $3 million in this business. If I were Gruenberg, I'd do what I could to make sure expenses are held down until revenues develop. If he can do that and react to what's happening in the market, I think he can survive. But I have real questions about whether this will be a $20-million business in three or four years, which is what it would have to be to justify all the investment.

THE RESULTS

What happened to
the start-ups? Did they
survive? Were the experts
right? Were you right?
Here are the answers you've
been waiting for.

THE TRUTH ABOUT START-UPS

Why does one new business succeed while another quickly perishes—and what can be learned from each? We revisited the 27 companies profiled in Anatomy of a Start-Up over the past three years and came up with some surprising answers

BY LESLIE BROKAW

Five bucks says we know your first question about the start-up companies we've profiled: How many of them are still around?

The answer, surprising to some, is a good two-thirds (although all but a handful missed their growth projections). Of the companies that aren't in business, some have failed in standard fashion, formally dissolving and closing their doors. And others have retreated in that more time-honored entrepreneurial way, collapsing back almost to square one, with a lone founder, encamped at a dining room table, continuing to pursue the long-held dream.

Other questions we hear: How are the companies that have made it *really* doing? What happened with the test site we read about, the expansion plan, the joint-venture idea? Did they end up raising that money? Who skipped town?

THE HARD PART

*Forget the strategic challenges a start-up presents;
the emotional ones can be worse*

Granted, leaving a $175,000-a-year job to start a business at home is probably not the prototypical entrepreneurial experience. Nor is doing that at age 27. Nor is pocketing about a million bucks, just a few years later, for 40% of the equity. Tim DeMello isn't representative of people who run four-year-old companies; he's been successful.

On the other hand, DeMello, founder of Wall Street Games Inc. (WSG), a marketer of national stock-market competitions, has struggled with at least one thing common to every company founder who sets out, as most do, utterly alone: an exposed and very vulnerable sense of self. "This is a way of life," DeMello explains, echoing countless others. "It's not a job, it's not a career, it's a way of life. I started a business for the sense of accomplishment, period." Trouble is, that sense of accomplishment takes a while to happen. And the lack of it can destroy confidence, summon doubt, and breed a paralysis no founder can afford.

"I came out of an environment with phones ringing a zillion times a day," says DeMello, who spent four years at Kidder, Peabody & Co. and two at L.F. Rothschild. "I believed if I reached for more, the rewards would be there, right then. I felt pretty confident of my skills."

He knew that new challenges— marketing, accounting, advertising— would tax that confidence. As difficult, though, was keeping his emotional balance without the support of a workplace. No more helpful, motivating colleagues; no more affirmations of personal worth from above (promotions, bonuses, commendations in the company newsletter); toughest of all, no more perspective of the sort you have when a job is something you do only at the office.

"When I started Wall Street Games, that was the loneliest period of my entire life. Those months I

And what about those so-called experts who comment at the end— who dissect a company's strengths and weaknesses? How often were those folks right, anyway? Are founders commonly blind to flaws that are obvious to informed and disinterested outsiders?

Finally, considering all the lost sleep, unfathomable debt, and enormous risk that come with starting a company, would any of those founders do it again? And if they would, then what—given the benefit of hindsight and the experience of surviving the occasional disaster— would they do differently?

But first, a bit of history. The Anatomy of a Start-up series made its debut in February 1988 with a profile of Video's 1st, a franchised chain of drive-through video stores founded by two former stockbrokers.

worked at home, I used to attack my wife in the driveway when she'd pull in, because I needed some form of companionship. Plus, you're focusing on something no one can truly appreciate. It's one of the scariest things in the world to sit there with an empty yellow legal pad and understand that nothing's going to happen unless I initiate it, so what in God's name do I do now?"

That vulnerability kept him from asking for help. "You don't want to try out your ideas on everyone, because you don't want a lot of people to say, `This is crazy.' You're going through so much self-doubt as it is, you don't need anyone else's. You end up waiting until the idea is totally together before you start presenting it. I think you've got to go through that stage, but it's tough."

When outside investors paid $500,000 for a 20% stake, WSG moved into the marketplace. DeMello added managers and a flock of part-time student workers to staff the telephones over which customers buy and sell mock stock. As the personnel and infrastructure grew and changed—

there are now 10 full-time and 125 part-time employees—so did the way the world dealt with DeMello. He started to become a star again.

"Perceptions are funny. In the office, new students will ask someone, `Can I meet Tim?' And it's like, `Yeah, you'll probably meet him next to the urinal.' But I used to think that way, too. We paint people to be bigger than life."

To maintain balance, DeMello says he "revisits the vision constantly" and doesn't look back on past victories—or even perceptions of victories. "I read the *Inc.* story only once. I remember saying to people, `It doesn't mean anything.' Hopefully it gives you a little boost of self-esteem, and you use it in your business if you can, but you go on."

Still, DeMello no longer feels like just another stockbroker. "I know how much work it was to get where I am—and I don't mean I think I'm at the top; as soon as I say something like that I'll crash in two seconds. But I feel I've done something that isn't that simple."

Video's 1st is now out of business, but the series continues to thrive; it has, in fact, become *Inc.*'s most popular. By the end of 1990, we had profiled 27 companies, doing our best to get into the minds of founders. How did they plan to compete? How did they calculate sales projections and profitability forecasts? How did they think they'd raise money, find staff, persuade customers to buy?

Now we'll see what happened to them. We've tracked them down, updated their stories (see box, "Where Are They Now?" page 372) and reassessed all that expert advice (see box, "Truth and Consequences" page 364). We've spoken to many of the founders—some bankrupt, some rich, most something in between—and examined their tales in a search for patterns. Did the start-ups beat have lessons to teach? Plenty.

• IF CASH IS KING, FLEXIBILITY IS GOD

Many of the challenges in the start-up process are utterly predictable. You need a good idea, and you need a market that has at least
marginal interest in that idea—even if that market doesn't know it yet.
You need good partners, unimaginable amounts of money, and the ability to charm in the morning and play hardball in the afternoon. Each
challenge has its own pressures, but it's clear from the outset that you'll
have to meet those challenges. Not only can founders foresee *which* challenges will come up, most can practically pinpoint *when*.

What has made or broken many of the companies we've watched,
though, is this: the ability (or inability) to recognize and react to the
completely unpredictable. To use enough managerial sense to plan and
anticipate, yet have enough street savvy to know when things are going
quite wrong. To be flexible, and not just in response to small surprises
but to really big ones—like discovering you're selling to the wrong customers or selling through entirely wrong channels.

Some companies even find they have to revamp from top to bottom in order to survive. They discover they're in the wrong business.

No Anatomy subject illustrates that kind of discovery better than
Buddy Systems Inc. When we wrote about it back in 1989, Buddy
Systems was a manufacturer of medical computer systems, providing
machines for cardiac patients to monitor vital signs at home. The company intended to sell to hospitals and home-care nursing companies. Last
year, when we checked in for an update, sales were slower than
molasses, but Buddy Systems was still making machines.

Today? Buddy Systems has metamorphosed into a *service* business—a provider of those very clinical services offered by the companies
it used to pitch to. Why did founder Thomas Manning make that kind of
fundamental change five years into development? Lack of success, partly, and inadequate financing. Target customers turned out to be "so
caught up with other growth situations that the cardiac application was
not the highest priority," he says. "It just didn't get the attention." That
miscalculation led to a cash crunch, and when a new investor group
offered $3 million if Buddy Systems would use its technology to become
a clinical-services provider, Manning took the plunge.

He argues, though, that Buddy Systems hasn't switched businesses. "The original conviction, that there is a need for telecommunication
between home and nurse and doctor, continues to be our guiding
vision," he says. He had always imagined going into the service business, but he originally abandoned the idea because of scarce resources.
The company now has contracts with clinics in Chicago and Cleveland.

Like Buddy Systems, Wall Street Games Inc. (WSG) went through a major metamorphosis. Timothy A. DeMello started the company as a toy business. Target customers for his securities game were general consumers and students; they purchased a box with instructions and an 800 number for buying and selling stocks in their mock portfolios. Because WSG was a standard retail product, DeMello had to confront the ensuing challenges of getting it onto store shelves and into college curricula.

No more. Like Manning, DeMello faced a crisis over what business could best be built on his idea—in this case, that of a fake stock market. Retail wasn't cutting it; the $99 game sat like a ton of lead next to Monopoly games and boxes of Pictionary going for about a third of the price. The college market meant having to resell to academics each fall and spring. So after "an agonizing analysis," DeMello repositioned WSG as a company that conducted investment competitions.

With the transformation, media heavies *USA Today* and FNN signed on as sponsors, offering updates on the top contenders and lots of publicity. Contestants registered with the company directly. DeMello's focus was making sure operations ran smoothly and sponsors were satisfied. Sure, WSG had to add prize money to its expense line, but the number of customers soared and revenues reached $7.2 million.

Same product—simulated stock market—but different business altogether. One consequence is that DeMello has come to see his database of customers as not just a list but a pipeline for more products and services, a distribution network. "It costs me $20 to get a college student to pay me $50," he says. "A 40% acquisition cost—pretty expensive. Could I get $60?" Already he's added a 900 number for contestants who want more details on their performance. He's also plotting completely different businesses—such as fantasy sports challenges—to feed into the network.

The marketplace pushed start-up after start-up to rethink strategy. MicroFridge Inc., with 11 employees, discovered that using wholesale distributors to move its combination microwave-refrigerator-freezer wasn't working as well as direct sales by "contract" salespeople might, so management chucked the original plan and began again. Rusmar Inc., which sells neutralizing chemical foam for landfills, didn't want to pursue hazardous-waste handlers since they wouldn't be annually renewing, but gave in when those handlers came calling. *The National*, the all-sports daily paper, scaled back its original vision of local coverage in each market.

Failure to act with that kind of flexibility would sometimes lead to a company's demise. Before it closed last year, Sanctuary Recording Inc. wasn't selling as much studio time as it needed to. Robin Halpin, who helped start the business with her husband, Tom Silverman, says they considered offering recording classes at night to fill the space. But with

Sometimes, a critic is a founder's best friend

We called them The Experts, or commentators; one start-up chief executive sniffed that they were simply pontificators. Whatever the tag, each one's assignment was the same: Read our start-up story and say what you think.

Our aim, of course, was to counterbalance the superheated plans of the founders we profiled (most of whom made seductively convincing cases for their companies) and to tell readers The Rest of the Story. The commentators pulled back the curtain a little, pointing out oversights, faulty logic, or calculations that raised positive thinking to an article of faith. And it's no wonder they weren't always popular. Whether competitors, academics, financiers knowledgeable about the industry, operators of similar businesses, potential customers, or editors of trade journals, the experts dumped hard reality all over somebody's dream.

Were they right? Yes, they usually were. The companies they received with heavy skepticism are the ones doing poorly.

More interesting than the experts' thumbs-up, thumbs-down verdicts, though, was that certain criticisms came up month after month, start-up after start-up. It began to seem as though there were intrinsic entrepreneurial blind spots. And the follow-up done for this article shows that 95% of the time the warnings—listed here—were wise.

■ Sales will not grow as quickly as founders project.

■ Miscalculations are usually made in what it costs to sell—including everything from salaries for salespeople to budgeting for conferences.

■ Most companies pursue too many kinds of customers or too large a geographic territory, or introduce too many products, given limited resources.

■ People with key experience ought to be given stock or some other incentive to keep them fully involved, and too often are not.

■ It's easy to let operating costs and overhead slide up, and too often that's what happens.

■ Selling someone once doesn't make that customer a loyal buyer.

Which category of experts was best? Hands down, the financiers—who, most frequently, were managers of venture capital funds with positions in companies comparable to the start-ups they were evaluating. Consistently, they got to the heart of the business under scrutiny, explain-

three other growing music companies, Silverman didn't have the incentive to work at developing Sanctuary Recording. "We didn't spend any time on the studio," concedes Halpin.

Says Buddy Systems' Manning: "To spend too much time overanalyzing the original plan is probably not productive. What comes out of this is that certain companies adapted well and certain companies didn't. The ones that *did* made adjustments—in investors, strategy, orga-

ing what its competitive advantage was and how to give it leverage. Sometimes they'd simply say that there didn't appear to *be* any competitive advantage. The financiers didn't flinch when it came to stating what to them was obvious.

An example: Bruce V. Rauner, a venture capitalist in Chicago, reviewed two companies, including O! Deli Corp., a franchisor of delicatessens. When he looked at O! Deli he said the founders' gargantuan projections for franchise expansion made them seem too top-line oriented. And the way they'd gone public, merging with a shell company trading on the pink sheets, might make it difficult for them to raise additional capital down the line. But just as troubling was the simple fact that no one connected with the operation had ever run a deli. The CEO had spent his career as a consultant, and as Rauner pointed out, "the start-up desert is littered with the bleached bones of former consultants." This business, he stressed, comes down to selling sandwiches, not franchises.

Today O! Deli has 21 shops; the prediction of 500 for 1993 now seems pure whimsy. The founders, bored with the deli business, left to start new businesses.

Perhaps the venture capitalists are good critics because they routinely do for a salary what we ask them to do for fun: figure out whether or not founders know what they're doing. Unlike consultants or industry observers or even customers, they inherently use a tough but telling criterion: Will this company make money for its investors? Are there people who want this product or service, and will the founders really be able to get it to them at a profit?

Other experts may not have been so consistently insightful, but their advice was always worth hearing. Operators of similar businesses or direct competitors, for instance, were good at cautioning against overestimates of swift market acceptance and assumptions about product or service uniqueness. They did, however, shy away from embracing new approaches. And in retrospect some of those new approaches worked—sometimes they turned out to be as good as, or better than, the tactics the "experts" were using.

Fact is, perspective like that provided by our experts comes pretty cheap. It's often readily accessible. And it's shocking how infrequently it's sought. There ought to be a rule—before you start a business, find 10 smart people who know the industry and ask them: How am I going to screw up? How else? How else? How else?

nization, product—from the simple to the complex. That adaptation spelled survival and success—or at least the chance for success."

• NOBODY LIKES YOUR PRODUCT AS MUCH AS YOU DO

Amazing to us, always, were the number of people who seemed to go into business with the barest information about the likelihood of making a living off their ideas—people who just assumed there'd be a market once they got off the ground. The most successful entrepreneurs worked hard to assess the need for their offerings; others acted on blind faith, and for them the start-up process has been particularly rocky.

Frank Mitchell, for instance, has spent the past six years committed to a gut feeling. SportsBand Network, a provider of radio play-by-play for spectators at sports tournaments, had a yearlong stint, complete with employees, copiers, and paychecks. But when the company failed to nail down a big corporate sponsor for 1990—an anchor sponsor that would be the pivotal source of revenues—it folded.

Mitchell contends that back in 1987, he had no choice but to barrel forward on instinct; he couldn't calculate the interest of potential corporate sponsors until he'd spent big bucks to produce the product. "Nobody would really take this seriously," Mitchell says. "You had to knock them over the head with it, let them see it and hear it firsthand. I would have loved to have researched and quantified this and sold it on market studies, but no one was willing to make the assumption it could be done."

That may be the case, but the result is that Mitchell, his former partner (Theis Rice), and several dozen investors sank $2.5 million into SportsBand before finding that, for 1990, no sponsor would bite. Still, Mitchell continues to pursue the idea on his own. He now works from his home and says he's talking with a broadcasting company, a radio manufacturer, and a possible sponsor about reviving the concept. If the partners are happy with the tests, maybe they'll sign on for 1992. Maybe.

It was a similar story in Albany, N.Y., where Todd W. LeRoy and Michael L. Atkinson started their Video's 1st chain of drive-through video stores in 1987. Dazzled by their idea, they boasted they would sell 5,000 franchises by the middle of 1990, and that each unit would rent 116 movies a day.

They figured wrong on both counts. By the middle of 1990 Video's 1st New Releases Inc., the parent company, had shut down. So, too, had the 10 Video's 1st kiosks that had dotted the country.

The founders had made grossly inaccurate projections because they hadn't investigated what was involved in setting up franchisees and because they failed to quantify how much customers really wanted the drive-through service; they started selling franchises before their corporate-owned units were even two months old. Franchisee Rick Taylor, who owned three Video's 1st kiosks, says he's learned something about due diligence: "I had an M.B.A., but this experience was my doctorate. If I did it again, I'd spend more time analyzing the market and the product, and I'd talk to competitors rather than rely on the information

366

provided by the franchisor. I was so enamored of the concept that I jumped, *then* looked."

How did the successful companies approach the market differently? Some, such as R. W. Frookies Inc., a cookie company, or Appliance Control Technology Inc. (ACT), a manufacturer of electronic controls for appliances, made sure their products were unique but not so different that customers didn't know what to make of them. Others, such as VideOvation, a purveyor of video yearbooks, took a year or more to test their programs and customer response, making sure they weren't misjudging demand or their ability to execute the concept.

"We've learned to pilot things," says Alan Khazei, who with cofounder Michael Brown runs City Year Inc., a nonprofit urban peace corps for 17- to 22-year-olds in greater Boston. The venture was originally approached as a nine-week summer pilot rather than a yearlong project. And changes in the program have been tried in small groups before being launched full-scale.

"We've really tried to build in time to evaluate what we've done," says Khazei. He and Brown hope to take their volunteer-for-a-year concept nationwide but don't plan to expand until they've honed the program a few more years in Boston.

• IF YOU DON'T HAVE EXPERIENCE, BUY IT

The strongest companies were led by people with experience in their industries. Companies started by people new to their fields didn't fare as well. It's all about respecting the marketplace—why waste time and money managing from ignorance? You have to know your business, and if you don't, you'd better find someone who does.

ACT, Rusmar, and The Plastic Lumber Co. have all carved out somewhat comfortable niches for themselves. ACT founder Wallace C. Leyshon says experience has made the difference. "Most of us here have been at this business a decade," notes Leyshon, who was business director of a division of Motorola Inc. before starting ACT. "We probably have a little higher probability of developing proper strategies than people who thought out their businesses over a shorter period of time."

Rusmar, the landfill-foam company, was founded by a scientist who was quick to bring in another chemist with experience in marketing and sales. Founder Paul A. Kittle also hired Arthur Andersen Co.'s emerging-business group as a resource. As a team, they brought revenues last year to a profitable $1.5 million. Similarly, the founder of Plastic Lumber (a manufacturer of "faux wood" lumber products) hired a key technical specialist in plastics manufacturing right at the start. Today Plastic Lumber is negotiating with some large companies that

A confession: When it came to grading the experts, we were easy. Why? Because any advice is better than none. (Even bad advice can help by forcing you to consider why one tactic may be smarter than another.) Better, we say, to pick every available brain than to skip a single critic.

VENTURE CAPITALISTS
Grade: A
Advantages: Evaluate businesses for a living; adept at spotting weaknesses and suggesting solutions; focus not on "Is it a good product?" but "Will it sell?"
Disadvantages: Usually return *Inc.'s* calls, but might not return yours

OPERATORS OF SIMILAR BUSINESSES
Grade: B+
Advantages: Know customer attitudes and margins necessary for profitable operation; have survived mistakes; know industry swings
Disadvantages: Experience can also mean entrenchment

DIRECT COMPETITORS
Grade: B+
Advantages: Know the industry
Disadvantages: Beware advice from the man whose lunch you are eating

CUSTOMERS
Grade: B
Advantages: Know what they want, what they'll pay, and criteria for buying again; their red flags are the ones to take most seriously
Disadvantages: Can't know what options they'll have or other issues they'll be facing when it actually comes to buying or not buying

OBSERVERS (trade association execs, academics, editors of trade journals, consultants)
Grade: B–
Advantages: Have watched lots of similar companies
Disadvantages: Less sensitive to internal operations issues

would, in return for processing, provide it with capital, long-term raw-material contracts, or technical assistance.

When expertise was needed, smart companies didn't just make educated guesses or even turn to consultants. They made seasoned people part of their crews. Those that didn't hire the necessary know-how—including Video's 1st, Sieben's River North Brewery, Oualie, and Landmark Legal Plans, all of which are now dormant—didn't fly.

• YOUR COMPETITORS AREN'T DUMB

Smart founders knew that starting out without the benefit of experience would hurt them. They also recognized that competitors are to be respected. Because even if you'll be pushing a product or service that represents an improvement on what's out there, your competitor still has one thing you don't: a viable business. When start-ups ignore that, they turn arrogance into red ink.

When our expert panel reviewed the plan for Sieben's River North Brewery Inc., for instance, one competitor cautioned that food at the Chicago restaurant should be kept simple. Another warned that unless one person took responsibility, details such as "making sure the salt-and-pepper shakers aren't greasy" would be missed.

Sieben's shut down this past September. Cofounder Bill Siebel concedes the main mistakes were underestimating the challenge of running a restaurant properly, and not having a restaurateur for a partner. "There were 180 people working on the restaurant side, and one on the brewery," he says. "That's how our headaches balanced out."

When we talked to our experts about the Queen Anne Inn Ltd.'s prediction of reaching 80% occupancy in its third year, four of them said it was unrealistic for the Denver operation to base its profit-and-loss projections on such high occupancy. Four years later the inn is finally profitable at nearly 70% occupancy—after raising its prices each year.

Richard N. Keener and Leif Blodee, founders of furniture manufacturer Keener-Blodee Inc., in Holland, Mich., thought they could sell $1.7 million worth of chairs their first year. But one analyst said, "For them to expect to be able to whack 7,100 units out of somebody else's hide is a gross miscalculation." This past December the bank auctioned off the company's equipment. "We overextended ourselves," says Blodee. "We tripled the size of the plant and then tried to build sales, and the sales didn't arrive."

The point is, all these companies should have learned more about what was coming down the pike by studying the competition—really studying what worked, what didn't work, what expectations other players had developed about the market. There rarely is a reason to think life is going to be easier for a new business just because it's new. "What would make companies smarter? Look at the examples of others, and don't assume those companies make mistakes," reflects Buddy Systems' Tom Manning.

• IT ISN'T THE SALES. IT'S THE SALES CYCLE

No founder has ever overestimated the amount of capital necessary to get started or the amount of time it will take to be legitimated by the marketplace. You know that; it's boring. But what a lot of companies repeatedly miscalculated was the sales cycle—the length of time between the first sales pitch to the customer and that customer's actual purchase.

Robert P. Bennett, founder of MicroFridge and a management novice when he started out, was caught off guard when sales to hotels didn't take off as he'd anticipated. Bennett proposed that they test the company's units in their lobbies and survey their patrons. Bennett found that 80% of those who tested the MicroFridge ordered within 45 days—faster than expected—but the test period still added an unplanned month and a half to his sales cycle.

Says Frederick A. Cardin, founder of the O! Deli Corp. chain of franchised delicatessens, "Our growth was substantially slower than I had hoped, because it can take a long time to get stores up and running in an office building." Landlord negotiations took longer; sites in new buildings had to wait until the facility was built and leased before opening; units replacing existing delis had to wait until leases either ran out or were bought out by the landlord.

"Those are timing issues, and over the long run those problems even out and go away," says Cardin. "But in the short run, we have a backlog of franchises waiting for sites"—and a cash-flow problem, since stores can't generate revenues if they're not open, and corporate overhead costs still mount. New investors not only bought out Cardin's share of the company last year but put additional money into operations. Miscalculating sales cycles led to similar cash-flow problems, from the mild to the ruinous, with other start-ups as well.

• DON'T UNDERESTIMATE HOW MUCH TIME SIMPLY BEING THE BOSS WILL EAT UP

Founders were thrown for a loop by the responsibilities of being CEO. Not only were they expected to be chief technologist or strategist or salesperson but interior decorator, human-resource director, and office manager, too. Those who delegated well didn't get overwhelmed by minutiae. Others got buried.

"Never having run my own business before, I didn't realize all there was to it," muses MicroFridge's Bennett. "I didn't have a concept of all the administrative aspects. They sound trivial when you try to list them—you know, expense reporting, supervision, sick days, holidays. But when you throw them all together, they're a huge chunk of management time. I had no idea."

More painful, though, is Daniel J. Dart's experience. In July 1987 Dart and his partner, Ann O. Hartman, opened Blackstone Bank & Trust Co., in Boston. Today Hartman is gone and Dart is a consultant to Blackstone, after resigning last fall in the wake of a crackdown by the Federal Deposit Insurance Corp. The bank's loan losses reached $2.2 million on its relatively small portfolio of $50 million; the bank is shrinking its asset base to maintain required minimum capital ratios.

What frustrates Dart is that this tenuous situation has stemmed in part from the distractions inherent in starting up. "You end up spending an incredible amount of time and management effort on things that other banks are taking for granted," he says. "Like designing our logo. Developing plans for our office space. Building facilities. Purchasing furniture. Installing computer systems. Training people. Developing personnel policies.

"At the same time," he continues, "you're hemorrhaging red ink, and you can't just sit back and say, `Gee, I'm kind of conservative.' " Result: The bank made loans, says Dart, before it had airtight procedures to oversee them. And it made mistakes.

Dart's main aim now? It remains, despite his troubles, similar to the one most start-up founders take to bed. "My number-one goal is to have the bank survive. Pure and simple. Basically, I'd do anything to ensure that happening."

An update on how each Anatomy subject has fared

Here are two oft-believed claims about start-ups: most fail, and many grow explosively. Neither is true, according to researchers who study loads of them. (See "Live Fast, Die Young," *Inc.*, August 1988, and "Late Bloomers," *Inc.*, September 1988.) You'll see for yourself in these updates of our Anatomy subjects. Growth comes slowly. The struggle to become viable more often takes 10 years than 2. If this were a sport, it would be played over a long, long season. That means fortunes can change; games lost are not the same as outcomes decided. Comebacks are possible, collapses conceivable. Our rankings, in short, are not final. That said, find your favorite start-ups. Here's how they stand:

COMPANIES WE'D BET ON

1. Wall Street Games Inc.
Four years old. Profitable with 1990 sales of $7.2 million. After initial attempt to market a simulated securities-trading game in retail stores and to college professors, WSG now puts on national "grow your portfolio" tournaments. Founder brought in new president and is exploring other business ventures such as fantasy sports challenge.

2. Appliance Control Technology Inc.
Four years old. Designer and manufacturer of electronic controls for appliance market. Aims to move its 145 employees to 80,000-square-foot factory later this year. Sales for 1990 topped previous year's $17 million, but because of slowing of economy and delays and difficulties in getting new products to market, fell short of $38.2 million projected; profits "marginal." Plans to establish base in Europe through acquisition of competitor there.

3. VideOvation
Five-year-old video-yearbook producer. Was sold last year to QSP Inc., the subsidiary of Reader's Digest that was its marketing partner. Revenues and losses in 1990 were almost exactly $577,000 and $882,000 as projected. Founder has two-year contract to stay on.

COMPANIES WE WOULDN'T BET AGAINST

4. Rusmar Inc.
Two and a half years old. Sells landfill-neutralizing foam to dumps and hazardous-waste sites. First-year sales: about $1.5 million (versus $2 million projected), but at a profit instead of break-even. Has license arrangement with Japanese chemical company to sell product in Japan. Twelve employees.

5. R.W. Frookies Inc.
In development since 1985. Makers of fruit-sweetened, "good-for-you" cookies had explosive first-year sales of $17.5 million; in 1990 company stabilized with break-even revenues "in the same range." Now has 14 cookie products. CEO Richard Worth became Avis pitchman last year.

6. City Year Inc.
Nonprofit "urban peace corps" began community work three years ago; this spring 70 young adults are participating. Corporate sponsorship totaled

$1.2 million, slightly better than projected. All but one of original sponsors signed on for 1990–1991 season.

7. The Plastic Lumber Co.

Exceeded projections by selling more than $500,000 worth of plastic parking stops, speed bumps, and picnic tables in 1990, its second year. Involved in ugly lawsuit with former technician over violation of noncompete clause. Negotiations now under way could lead to merger with producer of a complementary line.

8. Queen Anne Inn Ltd.

Family-run bed-and-breakfast has been open for four years. In 1990 enjoyed its second profitable year, at nearly 70% occupancy, with revenues of $210,000. Owners plan conversion of their adjacent home into high-end suites (name: the Queen Annex). Public relations savvy continues: Inn has received press from about 140 publications and broadcast stations.

9. MicroFridge Inc.

Two years old. Manufacturer of a combination microwave-refrigerator-freezer. Hoped for a profitable $15 million in sales in 1990 but instead reaped $4 million with losses. Still, recent infusion of $600,000 venture capital (for slightly below 20% equity) is helping to maintain cash flow, marketing, spirit.

10. The O! Deli Corp.

Founders spent some five years planning and operating this franchised chain of office-building delicatessens before they sold the bulk of their positions to investor group last year. In 1990, 21 O! Deli units were open nationwide. One founder now consulting to other franchisors and start-ups, and the other has started a venture firm.

STILL A CRAPSHOOT

11. Carousel Systems Inc.

Three years old. Franchised day-care-center operation. Grew more slowly than anticipated: 6 units open by end of 1990 versus 15 projected, for unprofitable revenues of $300,000 instead of profitable $1.65 million. Problems: finding the right real estate and having to reclaim center from first franchisee owing to breach of procedure.

12. Buddy Systems Inc.

Originally a manufacturer of machines that allow cardiac patients to monitor vital signs at home. After selling just three full systems in two years (for 1990, sales were far below the $5.7 million projected), shifted gears to become provider of clinical services, using system as competitive advantage. Investors added another $3 million.

13. Pizza Now! Inc.

Three years old. At end of 1990 had opened only original company-owned drive-through pizza unit. Recently signed master franchisor for Arizona to open three to four units by mid-1991. Effect of *Inc.* cover: 300 letters from women enticed by founder's smile, and $1.7-million personal investment in company.

14. Neurogen Inc.

Three years old. First sale in March 1990; revenues of handwriting-reading technology for all of 1990 were $350,000 at a loss (instead of $800,000 at break-even). Still looking for $2-million to $3-million financing; considers market a "horse race" between four other competitors. Eight employees.

15. Filmstar Inc.

Began raising capital about five years ago; in business for nearly three years. Public company; provides payroll services for independent filmmakers and acquires foreign-distribution rights. Revenues for 1990 were $6.5 million with a loss of $500,000. Stock plunged to 13¢ after underwriter went out of business. Has deal with 20th Century Fox Film Corp. to distribute five films starting this spring.

16. *The National*

National sports daily, now a little more than one year old. Had a year of adjustments: Expansion was slowed, local coverage cropped, Sunday edition canceled, prices raised, and staff trimmed. Has 30% fewer readers than projected; ad prices have been reduced.

17. American DreamCar Inc.

Two and a half years old. Total sales of remanufactured muscle cars for 1990: $490,397. Stock trading in February 1991 at less than a dime a share. Cash crunch last October forced layoff of 12 of 19 factory workers and trimmed salaries of remaining employees.

18. Animalens Inc.

The idea of outfitting egg-laying chickens with red contact lenses (to calm them so they eat less and fight less) was developed by Animalens's founder while a student at Harvard Business School in the 1970s. Three years ago company took shape. Sales for 1990 well below $2.5 million projected. Has five employees and continues to tinker with design and testing.

19. Blackstone Bank & Trust Co.

Boston-based bank, open since July 1987. Having tough time weathering current banking conditions. Last fall, following examination by FDIC, bank downsized to meet FDIC legal minimum capital rates. Loan losses hit $2.2 million on a $50-million portfolio; both founders resigned, although one remains as consultant. Faces rough haul raising additional money to boost capital as mandated.

DORMANT/FOUNDER PLANS RESURGENCE

20. WCCL-TV

In development six years; broadcast from March 1989 through May 1990. Shut down when leasing company seized equipment over conflict in payments due; lessor now trying to force company from Chapter 11 into liquidation. Year-one ad sales of $1.2 million, with losses of $2.2 million. Revival still planned, with new equipment and new investors—if all of this gets resolved.

21. SportsBand Network

In development for six years. The plan: Broadcast play-by-play commentary for spectators at golf tournaments. Operated at nine events in 1989, but none in 1990, when partnership "went inactive." Still, one of cofounders has formed new company to try to gather coalition of corporate partners and bring the beast back to life.

22. Oualie Ltd.

Founder never managed to land $1 million to bring her food products to market, nor did she nail down licensing deal. After spending three years' time and about $250,000 on prototypes and consultants, she put idea "on hold."

GONERS

23. Sieben's River North Brewery Inc.

Folded last fall. Large Chicago restaurant with on-site brewery. Struggled for three years, battling initial cost-overruns, poor control over food and personnel expenses, and investment team's lack of restaurant experience. Assets sold to another restaurateur.

24. Sanctuary Recording Inc.

A New York City recording studio. Shut down this past fall, two years after it opened. Reasons: the recession and increase in the home-studio business. Founder's other ventures, particularly rap label Tommy Boy Music Inc., saw intense growth, sapping his attention. He sank more than $500,000 of his own cash into Sanctuary.

25. Keener-Blodee Inc.

Furniture-manufacturing company. With bank loans and private investments, founders pumped in close to $1 million, but a new plant ballooned the company's overhead, and sales didn't follow. Business shut down and assets were liquidated this past December. Sales in 1990: about $200,000.

26. Video's 1st

Franchisor of drive-through video stores. Company shut down last year without having to declare bankruptcy, although its remaining cofounder filed for Chapter 7. Not one of its 10 kiosks is still open.

27. Landmark Legal Plans Inc.

Provider of prepaid legal services. Shut down at the end of 1988, a few months after our story was published.

SCORECARD

Would they do it again? Of the 26 founders asked, 19 said yes, 4 hedged, and 3 (the founders of Sanctuary Recording, Sieben's River North Brewery, and Video's 1st) said no.

■ The 19 companies still in operation at the end of 1990 employed 725 full-time and 239 part-time workers.

■ Top job creators: *The National* (290), ACT (145), Wall Street Games (135, of which 125 are part-time), City Year (90, of which 70 are student volunteers) and Carousel Systems (65).

■ Who spent the most? *The National* (between $50 million and $75 million), ACT ($10 million), Buddy Systems ($8 million), Blackstone Bank & Trust ($5 million), WCCL-TV ($4 million to $5 million).

Breakdown of companies by 1990 revenues:	
None	4
Less than $250,000	4
$250,000–$1 million	7
$1 million–$5 million	6
$5 million–$20 million	5
More than $20 million	1

■ Founders of five companies left or were asked by other partners to leave. Three ventures booted key managers who were part of the founding team.

Don't Bank On It

On March 15, 1991, Blackstone Bank & Trust Co. met the fate of five previous Anatomy of a Start-Up subjects: it folded.

The Boston bank was founded on some innovative ideas. Founders Daniel Dart and Ann Hartman, both of whom had big-bank experience, set up operations in a single facility. By keeping overhead costs low, they offered high interest rates to depositors, enticing even out-of-staters to bank by mail. They lent the money to commercial projects in communities that were generally overlooked by established lenders.

What went wrong? "The high rate of interest and the poor rate of return on their loans croaked them," said the Massachusetts banking commissioner, according to an article in *The Boston Globe* the day after the Federal Deposit Insurance Corp. packed up Blackstone's records. Dan Dart, who resigned as Blackstone's president last fall, adds that the bank received a fatal blow when the FDIC refused to allow it to raise additional capital through a form of subordinated debt securities back in the spring of 1989, then turned around and demanded it do so a year later. By then New England's banking situation had deteriorated so much that Blackstone hadn't a prayer of finding $2 million in new equity.

Blackstone's deposits were bought by BayBank Boston for the nominal sum of $1,000, and the FDIC assumed its loans.

—Leslie Brokaw

Sometimes, It **Is** Whether You Win or Lose

Can legions of loyal fans be created for a new daily paper that focuses on the already-saturated topic of sports? Less than a year and a half into the experiment that was *The National* the answer, suddenly, became no.

Launched in January 1990, with financing from Mexican media baron Emilio Azcarraga and expensive editorial talent plucked from the sports pages of top U.S. publications, *The National* ("A Whole New Game," page 303) printed its final issue on June 13, 1991. In the end, neither praise for its editorial product not Azcarraga's legendary deep pockets could save an operation that had already gone through as much as $100 million.

What went wrong? Except for the warm critical reception, almost everything. By June the paper was selling 200,000 copies a day (against a projected 1 million) and typically running just a handful of full-page, big-ticket color ads (the June 13, 1991 edition had only five). Its cover price had been raised 50%, to 75¢ a copy, and the publishing industry's brutal slump, which had begun almost concurrently with *The National*'s debut, was showing no signs of letup.

Unfortunately for *The National*, that wasn't all. As circulation and ad revenues stumbled along below target, the paper's overhead remained stubbornly high. Its editorial staff— nearly 200 strong—much of it hired at rates that inflated sports-journalism pay scales nationwide—couldn't be radically cut without wrecking the product.

And *The National* couldn't risk wrecking *its* product at a time when competitors were so aggressively improving their own. Local sports sections, general-interest newspapers such as *USA Today,* the national edition of *The New York Times,* and special-interest entries such as the new *USA Today Baseball Weekly* had all ramped up to counter the raid on market share. The ambitious, well-capitalized *National,* by its very presence, had raised the level of the game—only to find, ironically, that it wasn't a good enough business to play.

—*Leslie Brokaw*

"IF I KNEW THEN WHAT I KNOW NOW..."

The founders take a look back and testify about what they learned—about business and about themselves—as they launched their companies.

MICHAEL KUPERSTEIN
Founder and chairman
Neurogen Inc.

ON TEAMWORK:

It took me a while to settle into being a CEO. I remember the first meeting I had with three or four people. I was very nervous—what do they think of me? How can I tell them what to do? I was very conscious the first few months that I was asking these people to leave their comfy jobs, come work for me, for almost no salary.

I depend on them totally, and they know that. I tell them all the time that every person is a necessary component of the team, and without each person doing their job well, the whole team would suffer—me most, because as much as I've invested my energies and ego into this, I can't succeed without a team.

I've learned from *Inc.*'s articles about constantly communicating to your employees what you feel they're worth. Reminding them how important they are. And it shows on their faces. These people aren't getting paid very much. They're worth a lot more on the market than I'm paying them, but they're coming in whistling, they're having a good time.

The biggest pleasure I've ever had is not getting a sale, it's the process by which the team worked together to get that account. Something that was a twinkle in my eye a year ago is something that a group of people are working on now to be successful. That's a very satisfying feeling.

You know, I never understood sports until I started a business. It's like the stuff that Larry Bird talks about which I never understood before. He said the perfect game isn't whether you win or lose, it's that your opponent is playing his best, and you're playing your best, the game is at its best, and it's that magical quarter, when everyone's playing perfectly. It's the whole of you and your opponents. That's the feeling you get, not too often, but sometimes, and it makes all the frustrations and all the nightmares about cash flow go away.

ON MORAL SUPPORT:

It's very lonely. I have a great wife, and she's the source of my biggest support. You can't be successful in business unless you have the personal support of one person who says you're doing a good thing. Because there's so much stress, there's so much invalidation all the time: by lack of cash, lack of sales, lack of exposure, people telling you constantly you're going to fail. So if everyone's telling you you're going to fail, either you go insane, or you keep believing that you have a great idea that only needs time to happen. And the only way to judge sanity is to have another person validate you.

My wife has a difficult time, though. The business is so up and down—one day I come home and say, "We got this customer or that customer," and the next day I say, "Ah, the competition just won that one." Every day it's a different story. One day I'm flying high, and we're going to make a ton of money, and the next day, well, we didn't quite make it, or it's delayed. It's difficult for her to know how seriously to take me—to be supportive, she's got to take me seriously, but if she takes me too seriously, then she goes crazy. She wants to share her ego with me, but it's too upsetting if she's too close with it. So she has to have a little distance, and buffer it.

ON SUCCESS:

You can't run your business and not have your ego tied into it. If you don't have your ego in it, you won't succeed. Being an entrepreneur comes down to how comfortable you are with risk. That's the bottom line, and the second bottom line is self-image, who you think you really are.

I get asked to invest in other companies by people who don't realize that CEOs of start-ups don't have any money.

Here's a story: after we were in *Inc.*, we tried to negotiate a payment for an overdue bill with one of our vendors. And this woman said, "You're in *Inc.* magazine. How can you not afford this bill? I think you're lying to me." That's how people perceive it; they think that once you're in the magazine, you're *de facto* famous and rich.

My attitude, basically, is deal with whatever is in front of me. I try to find the right balance. I reevaluate everything every couple of weeks. I'll do that when I swim, or when I go cycling, in my off time.

RICHARD WORTH
Founder and CEO
R.W. Frookies Inc.

ON HELPING OTHER ENTREPRENEURS:

One of the problems with being so public is we have letters from every Tom, Dick, and Harry asking us to invest in their pie company, or pasta company, or whatever. I try to talk to them all, because it's the same distance from the outhouse to the castle as from the castle to the outhouse. I try to direct them to somebody else who can help them out, but it's a tough economy.

ON ENTREPRENEURIAL TERROR:

The *Inc.* article on entrepreneurial terror is my favorite. When it comes down to it, you have very few friends as an entrepreneur. The buck stops with you. People don't care. You get up in the morning and it's your house that's on the line, and it's your life that's on the line.

I was talking with another guy who won one of your Entrepreneur of the Year awards last year. He's sold his company and started again. And he says, "I don't know why I did it. Because I'm terrified all over again." It's like an addiction to terror. Sometimes it gets wearing, but it's also exciting. You get the good, the bad, and the ugly. You can win big, you can lose big, and nothing's safe. When you win, you win enormously. When you lose, you lose tremendously.

Some days you don't want to be in that position, and other days you love it. A lot of entrepreneurs are very ambiguous about the situation they're in. We love it, and we fear it. But when you're as unemployable as I am, you *have* to start your own company. That's no joke. Can you see me in a corporate boardroom? Pretty awesome. That would be like

Ben [Cohen, of Ben & Jerry's Homemade]; he's not employable. He'd be driving a taxi. I'm the same way.

ON PARTNERSHIP:

Working with your wife is a pain, but it's not a pain. It's a pain in the sense that you don't get a break from each other. On the other hand, she's the best friend I've got, and that makes up for everything. We try not to talk about the company at home, but inevitably it comes up. We're married to the company.

ON STARTING UP:

When you run a company, it controls you, but you still control it. If you control the company right, the company will control you well. But that's not always in your power.

Is this start-up easier than my last? They're all hard. There's no difference. The only thing that's easier, is that I used to manufacture the jams [at Sorrell Ridge], and that was one big pain in the butt. I'd be stirring the kettle and making the phone calls at the same time. But no, there is no business that's harder or easier, except that I've had more experience, and I know the players.

You understand a lot more of the grays of the business versus blacks and whites. But at the same time everybody pushes their companies as far as they can push them, so there's no lessening of the pressures in this business versus Sorrell Ridge. We just grew faster and sent it farther.

TIMOTHY DEMELLO
Founder
Wall Street Games Inc.

ON PARTNERSHIP:

When I started Wall Street Games out of my house, it was the loneliest period of my entire life. You're sitting there focusing on something no one can truly appreciate. Those two months I worked at home, I used to accost my wife in the driveway when she'd pull in because I needed some form of companionship. Plus, I came out of an environment with phones ringing a zillion times a day; for six years I was in that real active Wall Street mode. There's not a lot of people to talk to when you're in the planning stage, and I think it's one of the scariest things in the world to sit there and understand that nothing's going to happen unless I initiate it, so what in God's name do I do now?

I have a partner now, which I never imagined. Jeff Parker is 47 and I'm 31, and we play off each other very, very well. I don't know why it works so well. I never saw myself as a person who would have a partner, I guess because partnerships to me mean equality. Not that I don't see anyone as equal, but I go to work at six o'clock in the morning, and no partner is going to do that.

One day at a deli [Jeff] said, "How about I cut you a check and we become partners?" At first I was going to do it, then I wasn't. . . I saw my long term goal as developing a business that I owned [alone]—my name on the door, my business, here's the first day I started this company and so on. And then I realized that it really should be a two-step process: get the knowledge, get the reputation, get the experience—then liquidate your holdings and start fresh. So Jeff paid a million dollars cash to buy 40% of the company in January 1990.

The day Jeff made his first investment in the company, he put the check on my desk, looked at my assistant, Wendy, and said, "Oh, you can cash your paycheck now." I knew this was a priceless partner. Because right from the start there was no bullshit; the guy had gone through the loop before.

Jeff brings capital and experience, and he lets me be the freewheeling, entrepreneurial type I want to be. When I come up with an idea that I think is borderline ludicrous, he says, "Let's work with that." He encourages me; he says if you want to come up with something truly innovative, you have to start with something truly ludicrous.

ON GROWING A BUSINESS:

The most surprising thing, and one of the toughest I had to get through, was realizing I'm in the business of solving problems. And that problems are not a bad thing. When I started the company I was very guarded about the problems of the business. I would think, "Oh God, we don't have capital," or "Oh, jeez, we really screwed this up." And I would think I was really alone. Then I started thinking, how many of these problems are the result of our growth? And 50% or 60% were. If you want to sit around and run a little shop, you won't have any problems. But if you try to grow, you have personnel problems, capital problems, servicing problems. I realized that even money is just another thing that needed to be solved.

ON BEING AN ENTREPRENEUR:

This is a way of life; it's not a job, it's not a career, it's a way of life. You can't go into it to make money. I didn't leave the brokerage business at a good time; I went out to start a business to feel a sense of accomplishment, period. I was making $175,000 a year, and I was 27 years old. I wanted to create great wealth, there's no question, but you need a long-term focus. If you are interested in money, you should be interested in the creation of wealth, not income. If you want income, don't start your own company; income is the last thing you're going to get.

When I was in the brokerage business, people at Babson College used to have me speak about careers. I never really felt that great about making that presentation, because there were 30,000 or 40,000 other stock brokers around, and I was just somebody who was maybe in the top 25% of all those brokers, and who at a young age had done OK. However, when I moved out and started really taking my licks and facing the critics and developing a business, then I started feeling a lot better about myself.

When you do create a successful venture, or a venture that's just off the ground, the entrepreneur knows what you've gone through to get there, and all the criticism. You can really take pride in that. So now when I'm called to speak, I feel really good because putting a business together is not something the average guy can do. It's definitely one of the biggest thrills that I've ever had. I don't feel like just another stockbroker, I've done something that's not that simple to do.

WALLACE LEYSHON
Founder, president, and CEO
Appliance Control Technology (ACT)

ON LAUNCHING A COMPANY:

I f there's any lesson here to pass on to other entrepreneurs, it's that nothing happens in the time that you expect it to. Things take longer than you think, particularly during economic uncertainty. Fortunately, we've enjoyed broad product positioning, and we accomplished that a considerable time ago, so we're less affected [by the recession]. If ACT had started up this past year, we would have had a most difficult time.

If I were starting a business now, I would scale down my capital requirements accordingly, because the first thing that's going to be affected is the ability to raise money, simply because there are going to be reduced expectations. Reduced expectations means reduced revenues, which means reduced contribution, and accordingly, return.

We've enjoyed some advantages, despite the fact that consumer durables is down. It's analogous to air bags taking off with automotive sales. Although automotive sales are down, air bags sales are up, for obvious reasons. We're in a similar niche, and that may be true of someone else too, starting up.

ON SECURING FINANCING:

I thought getting people to understand my business and put money into it would be more difficult. It didn't take more than a few minutes to explain our technology, and I don't recall anyone we spoke to having a problem grasping it. The issue was how do we make money doing this. Therein, of course, lies our responsibility, and I hope we carried it off, given that we capitalized the company to the extent we have today.

ON BALANCE:

My life is heavily business oriented. If any entrepreneur
claims that he could enjoy the balance of his life from day
one, he either wasn't working hard enough or it was too easy.
Unquestionably, my family was compromised in the early
periods. Fortunately, we had a fabric there that was strong
enough to endure it. It could not have been done differently.
I have a responsibility not only to my family but to my
employees. Responsibility is key for me.

CHARLES HILLESTAD
Cofounder and co-owner, with wife Ann Hillestad
Queen Anne Inn Ltd.

ON MARKETING:

Marketing is basically common sense. It's so obvious that you sometimes wonder why the PR professionals are a separate profession: [you need] perseverance, a little creativity, friendliness, a thick skin, a sense of humor, courtesy, saying "thank you" now and then. . . common sense, all of it. It's just not that hard.

Unfortunately, most start-up businesses think of marketing and PR as something mysterious, a strange language handled only by professionals and experts. They have little confidence in themselves or their product. They also seem to think that PR promotions are something slightly sleazy, that upright places don't do that sort of thing. And they couldn't be more wrong! I think almost every successful business successfully does PR. That doesn't mean you have to lie or stretch the truth. In fact, a key rule of marketing and PR is you need to meet or exceed expectations, so you darn well better be truthful.

I didn't have enough money to hire somebody or to do an extensive advertising campaign. You know, it turned out to be one of the best things that ever happened to me; I had to learn how to do it myself. I expected to spend some money on advertising, but I was shocked when I realized how expensive it is.

I started thinking it would be a lot more credible to have other people say nice things about than me saying nice things about me. Fortunately I have some friends in marketing and PR, so I took them out to lunch, picked their brains, and watched them really closely to see what they were doing, and tried to emulate the professionals. I also went out and read everything I could. I didn't know what I wasn't supposed to be doing. I would try things [about which] a professional would have said, "Well, that's silly, don't do that," and some of them turned out to be remarkably successful.

Sometimes when I followed the rules, it turned out to be an utter waste of time and money and effort. One example is a set of radio ads we did a year or two ago. There's this classical music station whose market is upscale, romantic, well heeled, well educated, well traveled—perfect market demographics. So we started this series of radio promotions running from September to February, but we canceled at the end of December, because we track very closely where our clients come from, and we were getting nothing from it. We spent $1,000–$1,500 or so before we bailed out, which to a small bed and breakfast is a sizeable piece of change. The ads were heard, were recognized, were even complimented by professionals and people who should know, but they were an utter, absolute failure. We could only attribute a couple of room nights sold to that particular campaign.

Radio and TV are phenomenally expensive, and the ads weren't nearly as cost effective as some of the other stuff I was doing. The conclusion I came to is this: ads, whether oral, visual, classified, or display, don't work. They don't work in dailies, they don't work in weeklies, they don't work in monthlies, they don't work in local publications, they don't work in national publications, they just don't give any sort of return compared with some of the other things we were doing, for the same dollar, and the same time.

ROBERT BENNETT
Founder, president, and CEO
MicroFridge Inc.

ON LEARNING THE BUSINESS:

We've been making it up as we go along. We have talked with and studied some of the furniture manufacturers that sell to the same [customers], to see what works for them. But we've only been in the business 15 months, and it's taken that long to really learn what the business is about. I came from the computer industry, so the learning curve has been painful. But it's been valuable.

The most difficult aspect of the whole game has been maintaining enough cash to support the experimenting. We're constantly testing distribution channels and marketing channels—until we start selling to a hotel we don't understand all its objectives, and it's not until we hear the problems that we can start developing a program around that. With one hotel we developed a free trial system that, from the identification of the objective to the development of the program to the implementation, took nine months. It works, but it took us nine months to get there.

We're expanding our board to a five-person board, so there'll be three outsiders. Some of those contacts are coming from the venture capital firm that just funded us. I'm actually looking forward to having a skilled, experienced group that I will be, in essence, reporting to and bouncing our ideas off of—people who have made the thousand mistakes that I'm about to make.

We've been hunting for cash and trying to survive and getting sales and breathing from paycheck to paycheck, basically, since last spring. The money is a step up: it gives us breathing room so we can focus on the business and not on food on the table. It's not like I was out $20,000 on all my credit cards , or anything, but my wife and I had to sell properties. We owned a second home in Maine—that's history. And we owned a home in Burlington, [Mass.], and we sold that. But that's normal stuff.

Even though it's been a struggle, I've never had any doubt the product was viable. All I have to do is call customers to be reassured. Customers purchase, and check it out, and repurchase. The question was where I was going to get the money and when it was going to come in.

Running a business is more work than I imagined it would be. But you only go around once. I would have a hard time working for anyone else at this point. Starting a business wasn't really a lifestyle issue. Even when I was making decent money selling, I wasn't driving a fancy car. It's more basic competitive zest, or whatever. I like to succeed.

I thought I could do more on my own. Never having run a business before, I didn't realize all the administrative aspects. They sound trivial when you try to list them: expense reporting and reporting in general, supervision, sick days, holidays. But when you throw them all together, they're a huge chunk of management time. I'm an inexperienced manager, and I had no idea what I'd have to devote to the process.

I would caution anybody getting into business to forget about your estimates. Just throw them out the window—or at least triple them, or multiply them by 10. Unless they're sales projections—*divide* those by 10.

And the economy is really tough right now; it's just not cooperating at all. Budgets are tight. It's not like we've come out with a new air conditioner; hotels need air conditioners. We're creating a new market. If you're coming out with a product that's creating a new market, you've got to allow yourself a lot of time. It's a difficult process.

PAUL KITTLE
Founder and president
Rusmar Inc.

ON REACHING CUSTOMERS:

Reaching customers isn't particularly difficult for us. It's pretty easy to find out where all the potential customers are, because each of the states have lists of all the landfills, and you can just get the list.

But nobody wanted to be first [to take a risk on Rusmar's biodegradable landfill foam]. These guys have lots of things to think about and doing something that may not work is a distraction of funds and time, and so it's very comfortable if you can say, "Call up this guy, he's been using this stuff for a year."

Newness comes tough. Change is an anathema to regulated industry. But we knew that going in; we just didn't have it well enough quantified.

ON SELLING:

There's so much teaching that has to be done to sell. When you're working with something, or if you invented it, you know it intrinsically, like you know your birthday—you don't even think about it anymore. You take it for granted. But then you walk out on the street and grab the first guy you see by the collar and start to tell him all this stuff, and he says what about this and what about that and what if, and on and on.

ON HIS ROLE:

Some days I'm a lab person, some days I'm dealing with the banks and the investors, and I try to change those things around so that my attitude, mental image, and physical image meet what happens to be required. Much of the day-to-day business—dealing with the sales and the payables and the customers—is handled by [VP and general manager] Paul Russo.

We've divided the activity into two piles: the "ongoing" business pile, and the "to be" business pile. So I spend a fair amount of my time working on such things as new uses for the foam. The next step down is product development for current uses, then it's adjusting or modifying existing products to handle new tasks. The next below that is constantly making sure that we're making products cost effectively, so at this point we're down to the semi-day-to-day production issues. All the chemical responsibility is mine—upgrading the facilities, getting new reactors, mix tanks, dealing with the chemical vendors, things of that sort.

I deal with the investors and generating capital, because that, of course, is an ongoing issue of interest. These things never really get done, you just say, "All right, I'm going to stop here for now." And then you continue from there.

ON COMMITMENT:

If you decide you're going to do something like this, it's an all-or-nothing deal, and you have to do whatever is required. There are no other priorities. The idea that you're going to start a business and work five days a week is nuts, because a lot of this is just brute force. You get things done because you just have enough fortitude and muscle to pull it off. I'm sure—virtually positive—one of the reasons we're as competitive as we are with 3M is our attitude. The intellectual momentum and the commitment are extremely strong.

I'm only going to do this once. I wouldn't even consider doing it again. I'm driven to make the thing successful. A friend of mine said the thing that drives entrepreneurs is fear of failing. You would hate to wake up one morning and find yourself failing because you didn't work hard enough. So if you work all the time, you can erase that from your problems. If you put every ounce that you've got into it and you still can't make it go, then you can't say it's only because you didn't work hard enough.

ON LEADERSHIP:

One of the things that's surprised me is that you don't have employees that are friends. And that has been somewhat of a disappointment. That's not to say that they're hostile. But if you're working for a large company, you see your peers socially. It appears, in my one experience in this situation, there isn't any mingling. You're the boss and they're not, and that's the way it is. It's lonely. But you wouldn't do this if that was important.

The satisfaction and achievement are worth it all, as far as I'm concerned. It's a mind-over-matter contest. To a certain extent, the more people tell me I can't do it, the more pleased I am. When we were starting way back when, everyone would tell us all the reasons why we couldn't do it, and they would treat us like the plague, and now that we're up and running, everyone can tell us how to do it better than we do it.

FREDERICK CARDIN
Founder, and former chairman and CEO
O! Deli Corp.

ON SELLING THE COMPANY:

I'm interested in a company's concept, organizing it, drawing together the resources that are required to realize that potential, and getting the pieces in place and getting them going. Once I know this thing is headed down the track, then it's not as fascinating. I like to learn new industries and new things, and once you've been in something a while, you've learned it.

I had planned to be a shareholder of O! Deli indefinitely. But I hadn't planned to be in an operating capacity of any business much beyond five years. I don't really consider myself an operations executive by nature. I'm a director, or an entrepreneur, or a financial type. At O! Deli I had more operations responsibility as CEO than I would want to have on a permanent basis.

The CEO is responsible not only for developing the strategy but for making sure it's carried out. How many stores get opened, under what schedule, how profitable the company is, how the franchise sales are going, adjusting the company's long-term product mix. . . some of them sound fun, but after you've done them for a few years in one industry, they lose their excitement.

I'd contributed the part that I do the best, which is the strategy to get it going. Now I want to go on to something else. Over the last few years I've gotten more and more calls from people with good ideas who have seen something about O! Deli, or heard that I was interesting to talk to. But I wasn't in a position to do anything about it, because I was full-time with O! Deli. And now I am in a position to do something about it.

[Cofounder Joe Sanfellipo] felt the same way, that there were so many other opportunities that were passing us by, and we'd kind of, as they say in California, maxed out on our input to one thing. I was a consultant at the Cambridge Research Institute for seven years, and looking back on it, it was probably two years too long. Maybe five years is a good time for me to change around. I really believe that people should change careers in their lives. Certainly I'm a much happier person if I change and start learning something new.

When you're running any one company, it can be very lonely. Thank goodness I had Joe there as a friend and a soul mate. In a small company, you're dealing with a very limited set of people, and it's nice to have a chance to broaden your contacts, intellectually.

When I was younger, I didn't pay enough attention to thinking about whatever business things I did—who are the people you're going to talk to every day? Are they going to be interesting to you? Would you like to have them as friends? And now I'm talking to a wide range of very interesting, intelligent people that I hope will become friends, across a much broader range of issues than we dealt with at O! Deli.

ALAN ROBBINS
Founder and president
The Plastic Lumber Co.

ON BALANCE:

My wife, Mary, says I've got the "baby" now. When somebody calls me in the middle of the night with a processing problem, we kind of tongue-in-cheek say, "Well, the baby's got colic today." [A business's] growing pains are until two or three or five, and each age level has its own little problem. We're right in the infant stage. Fortunately, Mary gives me free rein to do that. I work a lot and I try to include her as best I can. I know it's difficult for her, but it's not the first goofy thing I've done in my life. We've allocated three years to make this thing work, and I think she understands that if we do a real good job here, we'll be rewarded.

It's difficult for me to balance, because the "baby" needs attention right now. You look to your left, and you look to your right, and there's no one there, especially when it comes to closing books, and financials, and analyzing potential business or sales relationships, pricing, and manufacturing problems. It's totally consuming, but I'm committed, and I'm truly enjoying all of it.

The kids—I have everything from a 13-year-old down to a 5-year-old—they're all in their own little worlds. I don't get to spend as much time with them as I'd like. But it's not like I'm a traveling salesman out on the road three or four days a week. That would be difficult for me—more so than running the business. I'm an early riser, and two of my kids have paper routes, so I get to visit with them a little bit. But the reality is they're playing basketball and soccer, and they have their own lives to live, too. We could use a bigger house, and we could use a vacation. And home maintenance and those kinds of deals have gone by the wayside. We just try to live within the scope of what's available to us right now. We're just maintaining the status quo. Not too many stresses. I think it's worked out all right.

But my social life is very low at this point. A professor of finance from Miami University told me the course he should be teaching for entrepreneurs would be called SSC—sex, sleep, and cash flow. If you get one out of the three, that's all you want when you're starting a company, if you get two out of the three you're doing pretty good, and if you get three out of the three, you're a mature company. Sometimes entrepreneurs get none of those things during the start-up phase, and that can be difficult, of course.

ON GETTING ADVICE:

It's lonely to stand alone with your decisions and make them work. I try to get input and information from people who would make good judgments on my behalf. More importantly, I want somebody to tell me this isn't a good idea, as opposed to somebody to agree with me. So when I look at advisers, I'm looking for people who will analyze from another point of view. I don't need another Al Robbins; I need somebody who thinks differently from me. I want somebody who's going to go through all the things that I can't think of, and challenge this as a better way of doing it. I'm not looking for yes people.

JOSEPH SCANDONE
Founder, President, and CEO
Carousel Systems Inc.

ON BANKS:

Banks have been holding us up. We got the financing for the franchisees, negotiated the lease with the developer, met our projections for all that. No problem. Then the developers go to the bank to get the funds to do the building, and the bank won't release the money. Nobody anticipated in January or February of 1990 the problems that bankers and real estate developers are having right now. The developers have lost control of the projects; the banks have taken over projects.

Now is that going to loosen up? Yeah, I think banks are running scared right now. We've made some adjustments. We're looking at bigger builders, bigger office park developers who have a stronger background and who already have the money for their project—in other words, when they go for a million-square-foot office park, they have enough money so that putting in a pad site for a child-care center is not going to be an issue for them. So we had to make adjustments in consideration of the economy and the real estate market.

ON ENTREPRENEURSHIP:

I don't think that I'm working that much harder than I did at General Electric, starting organizations both inside and outside the organization. I'm working differently. With a company like GE, you have a tremendous amount of financial support and staff support—you can draw on many many resources around the company. When I was starting my own business with the first two schools, we had zero support.

You start your own business, and you only move as quickly as your own finances can take you. When you're starting a franchise business, you're certainly going to move much faster than on your own, but you also are somewhat geared to the flow of the income from franchisees as you're selling and opening.

If a major company were doing this, and they were willing to put in millions of dollars to build it for the long run, we probably could have moved somewhat faster, because we probably would have opened a lot of these facilities with the idea of selling them to franchisees. From a very seasoned, experienced, franchisor, that was not the way he ever built his companies, and I'm certainly not about to challenge that with a guy who's been as successful as [partner] Tony Martino.

ON BEING LONELY:

I have a lot of autonomy in decision making and that part is lonely, but I know that in the same building, if I need to test ideas and strategies, that support is there. That is a level of support that most people starting a company don't have. Starting a business is a very lonely endeavor, because there isn't anyone you can go to. But I do have that additional support, so it's somewhat easier.

THOMAS MANNING
Founder and president
Buddy Systems Inc.

ON ADAPTATION:

In a small, new, business venture, one needs to be flexible, to be close to the market and understand the changes, the movements, the shifts, and so forth. You have to move fairly quickly and adapt. That adaptation, which is obviously essential to survival, is critical to the life of a new venture.

To spend too much time analyzing the original plan, the original goal, the exact nature of the response to the market is probably not wholly productive. What seems to come out of looking at a cross-section of these experiences is that certain companies adapt well and certain companies don't. And the ones that adapt well make adjustments, whatever those adjustments need to be, whether they're investor composition adjustment, or adjustments in strategy, or adjustments in organization, or product changes. It can [range] from the very simple to the very complex, but that adaptation spells survival and possibly success, or at least the chance for success. A failure to adapt gives quite the opposite, and shows what being a young, emerging venture is all about.

ON UNDERSTANDING THE MARKET:

The hardest thing is the estimation of market timing. Particularly with a brand-new technology, it is extremely difficult to be precise in terms of the emergence of a market, and the achievement of a critical mass in that market—not so much the emergence of some interest, but the emergence of substantial interest, substantial enough to fulfill goals of revenues or profitability or financing that several different enterprises in a market may have.

Timing is critical in this area and it's often something that's shortchanged as a legitimate variable to spend a lot of time on. In many ways, people who start businesses tend to evaluate the opening of the market, or the sales curve, but they do so in a fairly quick way, a few interviews, a few sales, and then the tendency is to reach for optimistic assumptions [predicated] on the growth curve moving from 2 to 8 to 16, and so forth. Or the implementation proceeding along a very predictable path, when in fact there's a certain amount of randomness to the introduction process, to the growth curve, to the sales development curve. And the randomness is driven in a lot of different ways, but it can be driven by things that the company controls to some extent, such as sales talent, sales incentives, product design, quality, and so on. It's also influenced by things that the company cannot control, like the attitude towards the adoption of a new technology or the perception that other existing alternatives compete, when in fact they may not compete at all.

So there are many variables involved in the proving of a new market, a new technology, and I think all of those come back to the issue of timing. That's typically a very underrecognized variable, and one that I would view as the most critical.

There are two ways to go at it. One is to be more rigorous in analyzing the market, and that could be accomplished through much more research at the front end, in terms of the likely adoption of a product or service through interviews, surveys, and so forth. Most ventures don't have the money necessary to spend on that sort of activity. Many have products or technologies that are hard to communicate in surveys, because they haven't been seen or heard of. Still, a number of people might benefit from further research and more rigorous analysis.

The second suggestion I have is looking at the example of other companies. Do not assume that those companies made mistakes—assume instead that the analogies simply happened in that fashion because of a whole variety of factors, some controllable, some uncontrollable. In that regard, a lot can be learned from other venture situations, other product introductions, other launches. Studying similar companies or other products which were introduced in somewhat similar ways can lend a whole lot of sobriety to the notion of market timing and planning a sales curve.

At the time, I thought we did quite a bit of that. Keep in mind an interesting factor here: the planning pays attention to—in fact, tries to capitalize on—the dynamic nature of a market or a business. It tries to sell its own change into that market—a new product, for instance. But most of the time, the assumptions are put together as if the market will eventually remain stagnant, and the only thing that will change will be the new product. The fact of the matter is the market keeps on evolving, and keeps on changing as well, and customers may find substitutes, or, as in our case, they continue finding growth in existing businesses. If that's the case, you're battling opportunity, you're always just battling problems. It makes it a challenge.

It's not an obvious thing. The nature of the beast is such that there's a certain amount of randomness that cannot be controlled. It simply needs to be dealt with as time goes on, and at times requires flexibility, and at other times requires great focus.

ON LEADERSHIP:

No one starts a business alone. There have been so many people involved in our business—not only investors and shareholders, but directors and staff and other managers and so on—so you get a lot of partners as this thing rolls along, and you find out you're not really doing much of it by yourself. I'm the most visible point, but the success or the failure of the business is based on what everyone is doing.

There's a certain amount of anxiety that must be borne by the founder or the CEO directly, and there's the question of whether he or she ought to share that anxiety, or not force it on other people. It's just not fair that others be asked to bear too many responsibilities that go beyond their normal roles. They obviously have responsibilities and concerns and anxieties within their own roles, so everyone is trying to juggle responsibility within functional roles as well as more managerial roles. Yet the general manager of the company, the CEO, is probably the only point where it all comes together, and that person has to shoulder a good amount of anxiety coming from all corners of the business. I don't view it as legitimate to disseminate or reflect back all that anxiety. An important role is to absorb some of that stress and do what's necessary to resolve it. Either make a decision that resolves it or defer a decision until more facts can be gained. That's an important aspect of the CEO's job.

There is, depending on the people involved, clearly a need for everybody in the company to feel a part of the company, and that, to some extent, takes some stress off the shoulders of the CEO. Everyone's fully informed, fully interested, well motivated, there's easy communication flowing throughout the company. That tends to make the team perform as a team, and really eases the responsibility of the coach so that he can be a player and a coach at the same time.

ALAN KHAZEI,
Cofounder, with Michael Brown
City Year Inc.

ON ADAPTATION:

We raise money from corporations, foundations, and individuals. We don't sell a product. One of the challenges we face is that we have three groups of customers: our kids, who are corps members, our project sponsors, and our funders. The funders are always the biggest challenge. If you have a successful product, people buy it and the money comes in, and you can use that money to expand, whereas with a nonprofit, the customers you serve are not necessarily directly funding you. So it's a kind of interesting challenge for us. A nonprofit is a little different from a for-profit, because we have to make the sale twice. If we were a start-up for-profit business with the success we've had, then sales would be driving growth. You can see that in the number of applicants we're getting, and the number of requests we're getting for projects.

We found that where we could get a chance to really explain the concept to people who were at a decision-making level, they would get excited about it. Getting to a person at that level is the hard part. There are a lot of people in the private sector looking for innovative answers to social issues, and the whole concept of social venture capital is increasing, because people are recognizing that everybody has a role to play.

A lot of getting to those decision makers was persistence, and you get back to lessons…going from one person to the next, people would refer you to people. We would meet with people who would say, "Well, I'm not sure what I can do, but I can introduce you to somebody else," and then eventually you meet with somebody who could make a decision or did have access to funds.

But also it takes thinking creatively—for example, going after the legal community as a group as opposed to as individual firms, as a way to bring a whole community together. We contacted the local bar, the Boston Lawyers Team, which organized a breakfast for us, and invited senior partners of all the major law firms in Boston, and we pitched them on doing a consortium contribution as a team.

We thought about approaching companies we thought could relate to our concept either because of their own interest in youth, or because of their own entrepreneurial style, for instance Reebok, which is a very entrepreneurial company. They've had tremendous growth; they also have a real interest in youth because of their market, so they could relate to both the entrepreneurial side and the youth side. Or a company like Bain—same thing, very entrepreneurial, a lot of significant growth, and also a real interest in youth, because a lot of their own employees are young people who have significant responsibility. So they could relate to young people like us trying to start something new and different.

ON GOALS:

We set a maxim for ourselves: "Establish what you think are achievable goals and meet them." Often what we think are achievable goals, other people who aren't as directly connected think are very difficult to achieve, or impossible to achieve. But every goal that we try to set internally we think realistically we can achieve.

ON WORKING HARD:

I work about 70 hours a week, and I think the only reason we can work so hard is that it's incredibly exhilarating.

ON SALARIES:

That's something we've had a lot of debates about here. When we first started, the spectrum for us was on one end what I would call the Ralph Nader model of public service. Ralph Nader is an incredible public servant. He's developed many public-service organizations in which the salary levels of the staff are roughly at subsistence levels. For us, the high end of the spectrum is what I'd call government-level public-service salaries, and that's high government level, or very prominent public service organization.

We've made a decision, at least in the beginning of City Year, to go more with the Ralph Nader model, or the subsistence model, primarily for programmatic and organizational integrity. When City Year started, nobody was paid a dime the entire first year. We didn't have any money, so in some ways we didn't have any choice. You don't have money, you don't spend any money. As a start-up organization, we wanted to make sure we did meet our programmatic goals, and that every dime possible could go into recruiting more kids for the program, so we made the sacrifice with the staff. But it was also important to us that we start the program at a level of integrity and commitment, and one way of demonstrating that was that everyone who got involved with the program made a significant sacrifice. We're still very close to that. The top salary here is $25,000. Nobody's suffering, but by comparison to what people could be making, it's very low, and in the spectrum of public-service salaries, it's very low.

How do we attract such talented people? Well, ironically, people have to be really committed to be here because they don't get the financial benefits. Nobody's here for the money, that's very clear. That gives the organization a bit of an edge.

Obviously, over time, salaries have to increase. We've got folks here now who have been doing this for more than three years. And as they start having families, I think our salary structure will go up. Nobody's ever going to get rich working for City Year. It's not part of the program. But our plan is to make it possible for people to stay here, and if not make this their career, at least make it a significant part of their career, and still be able to achieve other life goals. It's all balance.

HARLAN KLEIMAN
Founder, chairman, and CEO
Filmstar Inc.

ON GROWING THE COMPANY:

Things have happened almost as I anticipated: I knew the industry would consolidate, I knew that services businesses would be the most effective area for us to be in, and I knew that the global marketplace was the critical place to be. The thing that has happened a little faster than I anticipated is that the dependence of producers on distributors to help them finance their product has become much greater, much quicker. When I first started with the distribution business, there was a substantial supply of films to choose from to sell around the world. Now that supply is much smaller. That's the bad news. The good news is that there are a lot of companies that keep falling by the wayside because they can't compete as effectively as they need to—and that's a good thing, because there were too many companies in the business. The ones that are left will be the healthy ones, and will really have a first-class marketplace to deal with. And we will be one of those companies. We're healthy to the extent that we're growing, but as with any growing company, we need more capital to grow, and the problem is that capital formation right now in the traditional market—meaning the stock market—is difficult to accomplish. One of the problems with the stock trading as low as it is, is that the market cap, which everybody uses as a negotiating mechanism when they talk to you, is low enough so one has to find other ways of developing financing mechanisms.

Hindsight is your greatest feature. I would do this again, but a little bit differently. I have learned the horror, and I use the word advisedly, of being undercapitalized. Our initial plan was to raise $10 million, but the market crashed, so we ended up doing a plan for $2 million. If anything, being undercapitalized doesn't allow you to make the decisions as easily as you need to. It also means you have to go for third-party financing, or at minimum, credit enhancement, on many of the deals that you need to do. That limits your upside on the projects and also limits your flexibility to make a number of deals that would benefit the company in the short and medium run.

So from that point of view, I don't think we've made many bad decisions, as far as operators are concerned. I'm very pleased with the growth of the company, and I think that at the end of the day, we'll be just fine. We have eclipsed many companies that are our size and even larger, with less capital than they had. And our prestige, in our industry, is rather substantial at this time, which also pleases me a great deal. Where it has frustrated me is that in order to get the requisite capital to become a true industry leader, I'll have to end up giving away more of the company than I really want to. On the other hand, we have a company that's growing, and a company that I'm very proud to be chairman of.

PHILIP GOLDMAN
Founder, president, and CEO
Pizza Now! Inc.

ON GROWING A BUSINESS IN A SLOW ECONOMY:

I s this business more difficult than others I've started? No. I think this one is kind of easy. The times are more difficult. Everybody in the business community and also in the public sector at large is scared to death. Nobody knows what's going to happen to the economy, and being on the fence and not knowing is an uncomfortable place to be. So, almost every economic adviser and financial services person in the country is saying, "Stay liquid. Don't invest. Get out of equities, be in the money market." There's a tremendous trickle-down effect in that kind of thing to building businesses. Go try and sell a franchise to somebody.

The potential franchisee, in our case, is a fairly sophisticated guy or woman who has been in another company. The financial services end of business has laid off a lot of very qualified businesspeople who are now looking for something to do. That's created an opportunity and a market that a franchise really fits into well. And I think those people are aware of the success rate of franchises versus the success rate of independent start-ups. For that reason, it's a matter of time. We're in a valley of the cycle.

ON FLEXIBILITY:

It's stimulating—and always gratifying—to come up with something that more or less solves the problems created by whatever the extenuating circumstances may be. I think that's part of being in business—flexibility and creativity. If you're chipped in granite as to what your program is, and you've got an inability to change and to function under *today's* circumstances, I don't think you're going to be here.

ON WORKING WITH HIS SON:

Scott's great. He has a lot of tenacity and perseverance. It's been very rewarding to me personally to be able to work with him. He has been an inspiration even though he's my junior. He's tremendously optimistic and has an ability to see the good things at the end of the tunnel, and he has a lot of drive. Obviously, because of our personal relationship, it probably has been more enjoyable than had it been somebody I wasn't as close with.

Of course, there are pluses and minuses. The minuses are that you're running a business, and your expectations of somebody who's related to you tend to be greater. So, you expect more. And if that's not delivered on a consistent basis, it can be pretty disappointing. Fortunately that hasn't been the case with me, although there have been incidents where I, maybe unjustly, expected more. He bears the brunt of that, but he's resilient. He's willing to accept the fact that he's able to make mistakes that need to be corrected. I'm glad that I did it. He's a rather pleasurable character.

ON BALANCE:

Starting a new business is a very lonely endeavor. I guess that's another reason why it's nice that my son has been around. There aren't a lot of people to bounce ideas off, and you're also generally writing the check. You're left to your own resources mentally, physically, and financially. That's very difficult. It taxes you. If you have financial problems, it affects you mentally, and if you're affected mentally, it can affect you physically.

When people do what I do, they generally have an outlet to help them maintain their sanity. In my case I go to a gym and work out every night. Some guys play golf. They do something that lets them concentrate on an area that is detached from the day-to-day thing.

When you're in a start-up situation, and you're really the single individual that's responsible, it's a 24-hour-a-day thing. If you don't find something to take your mind off it some of the time, it can be pretty devastating. Six years ago, with another business, I lost a lot of sleep. I probably didn't sleep for a year. Insomnia, only worse. It's called anxiety. You do nothing but think about the problems you're going to face the next morning, and you don't sleep.

People take the responsibilities of business far more seriously than the general public would imagine. There are people involved, people who are reliant on your ability to sustain and grow. You can close the building down, or you can run it over with a bulldozer, and it doesn't really hurt anybody. But there are people with families who depend on the success of the business. Those people are directly or indirectly the responsibility of the people running the business and making the decisions. You can lose a lot of sleep over that kind of thing.

So, you give yourself a break. Do something for two hours that gives you a break. I guess some people go to a bar and have four martinis. I don't recommend it, but the results, maybe, are the same. It gives you that break. You're much more prepared to deal with it—at least I am. Some people go out and jog five miles. I've heard about people who can take a nap for an hour. Taking a break makes me much more capable of dealing with the stress and the responsibility of the business.

FRANK MITCHELL
Founder, president, and CEO
SportsBand Network

ON LESSONS LEARNED:

I'm a brighter guy than I was five years ago, when this thing started. It's hard to think back on what I knew at the time and what I know now.

Everybody that I'm affiliated with now turned me down at the beginning. Nobody would really take this seriously. You had to go up and knock them over the head with it, and let them see it and hear it firsthand. I'd love to have done all kinds of research, market studies, and tried to [convince] somebody that this could be done the way I was describing it. But I found that no one was willing to make that assumption.

I'm not going to say I didn't make any mistakes. I did things that I felt at the time were half right and half mistakes, but a lot of times you have to do that to advance the cause. You just have to do it. Could I do it more efficiently if I had it to do over again? Yes, I could certainly do it more efficiently. But I probably could have done it more efficiently *this* time if I had not had to overcome the hurdle of showing that the actual product could be delivered—not only that I could do it, but it would have the sound, and the impact, and the appeal that I said it would.

ON REGROUPING:

I stayed at my offices until January 1990. Since then, I've pretty much run this business out of my home. I have a pretty nice little office. I've got a separate three-room little house. I've got all my equipment out there. There wasn't a whole lot of reasons to maintain expensive office space.

SportsBand is now a new company. I purchased the trade names, trademarks, the equipment, all the assets of the old company. The new company is named Spectator Communications Network. I may still use the SportsBand name—I can use both.

ON TENACITY:

It seems like an eternity to me. I've kept a low profile, because I didn't want to jump the gun on anything. There are many things I've had to wait out.

Sometimes I feel like quitting. Who wouldn't? I'm human. There's a lot of uncertainty, a lot of anxiety that goes along with it. And it's not something that you can do part-time. You've either got to say, "This is what I'm going to do" and do it, or not, but you can't do it part-time.

I probably don't do as much as I should to get inspiration when I'm down. A friend of mine called the other day and he said, "You're carrying all this around, and you're doing all this. Do you ever seek inspiration from a higher source?" I said, "No, not really. I don't." Anybody who's an entrepreneur will take heart in the trials and tribulations and success stories of other people who have done the same thing. Any one of them. Henry Ford was bankrupt four times. You read so many stories. It's the old thing about once you make it with something, everybody thinks it's an overnight success. They don't know about the 5 or 10 years it took to get there. I take heart in that kind of stuff. And I couldn't do this without a lot of support from my family and friends.

PAUL GRUENBERG
Founder, president, and CEO
VideOvation

ON SELLING THE COMPANY:

Prior to the acquisition [by Reader's Digest] I had administrative authority and control, I had P&L responsibility and control, I was the ultimate decision maker in the company. When an entrepreneur gets used to making decisions, that becomes a way of life, and I liked it. I liked it a lot. At the same time, I also felt like I was spread thin, because I was trying to wear too many hats. And I never had enough time to do the creative production stuff that I wanted to do because I was torn away from that to do administrative and financial stuff.

The good news is that I have the time to do the creative production function now—working on the evolution of the product, redesigning the program formats, upgrading the music and the graphics, defining what we're selling in conjunction with what marketing wants, the whole structure and look of the program—because I'm spared the interruptions from the other functional areas. The flip side is that it's hard to let go of all that power. Having accepted it, having lived with it, having been predisposed to use it, to be cut back from that is difficult.

There are times when I disagree with how Reader's Digest is spending money, personnel they're hiring, the timing of decisions. Now that we're part of a much larger company, it takes a lot longer to get a decision made than it used to, because there are all these layers of signing off on a specific decision. The more cooks there are in the kitchen, and the more decisions you have to evaluate, the longer it takes. Obviously that's anathema to anybody who's been used to making decisions and acting on a situation quickly. I'm sure that's every founder's lament, when they get to be part of a much larger organization.

I was very excited that we could sell to such a well-known name that was so enthralled with what we were doing. It was a huge endorsement to get Reader's Digest to buy this company. Given that they had just gone public, that they had raised $500 million in the market, that they were looking to really grow, become a communications company as opposed to a publishing company, and that they already had a fairly sizable home-video component to their business, I thought that this was a good fit, a very good fit.

I went back to my shareholders, who were very sophisticated, high-net-worth people, whom I had worked with before starting the company, and said, "Look at the investor climate, look at the environment, look at how deals are going [all over the world], and we have a chance to sell to a household name that's really going to get behind this. They've got deep pockets, and they're really going to be able to support this, not only from a money side, but also from their position in schools." I thought that was a real coup! I still think it is. I see so many small companies unable to take a joint venture and turn it into something that's positive, make an idea happen from a financial standpoint. I think we have a very good chance of making this thing grow into a major industry. With their support, both financial and human, that will mean a lot of money for people who got into this thing early. Everybody's building companies today and looking for exit strategies that are going to be financially rewarding, and this typifies that scenario.

ON BALANCE:

I've balanced out my life a lot more. I'm exercising consistently now every day. I feel 100% better than I did a year ago at this time. I was so totally steeped in the business, there was no time for anything else. Now I feel a lot more even.

Starting anything up from scratch is a very steep, difficult proposition. I don't care what anybody says. Your life becomes unbalanced, and that's just the way it's going to be when you're starting something from square one. You can delude yourself into thinking that you're going to have the requisite time to do other things, but you don't.

If I were to do something new now, I'd be inclined not to start something from scratch, simply because I know the price you pay to do that. It would have to be incredibly compelling for me to do it, and I'd have to do it with a couple of partners, so I could spread the risk as well as the most valuable currency of all, which is time. I would have to have more time to live a more balanced existence, and I would gladly give up some of the equity to people I really trusted, who I thought were going to work as hard as me, to have more balance in my life.

ON FAST GROWTH:

There's pain with growth. The production side, for which I'm primarily responsible, has as its mission continuing the level of quality that we had when we were at 40 schools, and being able to deliver on time, so that we don't lose any credibility with our customers and or the sales force. To be able to adhere to those two goals is very, very difficult when you're moving this fast, so it makes me anxious. I don't want to sound pejorative, but when you move quickly, there's an inevitable added sense of concern that you be able to keep up with the growth.